3604 738913

KT-583-177

FOR
REFERENCE ONLY

WITHDRAWN
FROM
UNIVERSITIES
AT
MEDWAY
LIBRARY

FOR USE IN THE
LIBRARY ONLY

Social trends 30

2000 edition

UNIVERSITIES AT MEDWAY
-3 JUL 2013
DRILL HALL LIBRARY

Editors: Jil Matheson
  Carol Summerfield

Authors: Nicola Amaranayake
  Jenny Church
  Catherine Hill
  Jackie Jackson
  Victoria Jackson
  Craig Myers
  Zobia Saeed
  Conor Shipsey
  Tony Symmonds

Production team: Betty Ankamah
  Max Bonini
  Rebecca Deacon
  Suzanne Dunn
  Jan Kiernan
  Christine Lillistone
  Anne-Marie Manners
  Alistair Price
  Tahir Raja
  David Sharp
  Keith Tyrrell
  Katie White
  Steve Whyman

Design & Artwork: Andy Leach
  Bob Arkell
  Dave Pike
  Chris Watts

Maps: Alistair Dent

Reference
314·
2
SOC

London: The Stationery Office

Contents

CANTERBURY CHRIST
CHURCH COLLEGE

3604739913

Cypher Group	23.2.00
314.2SOC(OS)	£39.50

Page

3: Education and Training

Contents

Social Trends 30, © Crown copyright 2000

Page

5: Income and Wealth

Contents

Page

Contents

Contents

Page

11: Environment

Contents

Social Trends 30, © Crown copyright 2000

Foreword

My mind inevitably goes back to that day in November 1970 when *Social Trends* was born. Surely there has never been a launch of a Government publication like it. Not only was it clearly an unusual and remarkable publication, but this was a launch celebrated at 10 Downing Street with chamber music played by the Amadeus Quartet. That is what came of having Muriel Nissel, wife of the Quartet's second violin, as our first Editor.

For me, and indeed for all of us in the Central Statistical Office, it was special in many ways. I had been charged, on appointment as Head of the CSO in 1967, to try to develop social statistics. This made sense because social statistics had long tended to drag behind economic statistics in priority and quality (an ever-present danger to be avoided). So we aimed to strengthen social statistics generally and to launch, amongst other things, the General Household Survey, an improved Family Expenditure Survey and – the jewel in our statistical crown – *Social Trends*.

What we had in mind was in a sense straightforward. We planned an annual picture of social conditions and changes. Nothing very novel in that. What *was* novel was the proposed approach. We wanted this publication to be exciting, non-technical and accessible to the general public well beyond Westminster and Whitehall. It had to be authoritative with the statistical material beyond criticism. But above all it was to be written and produced by us statisticians without political interference. What we included in any issue was up to us to decide, even if the material touched sensitive political nerves, and even if our comments were not popular with our political masters.

It was a daring operation but it succeeded. *Social Trends* was a success, widely reported in the media and widely read. Once it was even the *Observer's* choice of reading for Christmas. It was soon copied internationally, and such has been its strength that ONS can now celebrate its 30th birthday. I hope that the original aims will remain sacrosanct, and in that spirit I congratulate all those who have kept it so successfully alive.

Sir Claus Moser
December 1999

Introduction

Social Trends draws together statistics from a wide range of government departments and other organisations to paint a broad picture of British society today, and how it has been changing. The 13 chapters each focus on a different social policy area, described in tables, charts and explanatory text. In addition, this 2000 edition includes comparisons spanning the last 100 years to mark the end of the twentieth century. This year *Social Trends* also features an article on 'A Hundred Years of Social Change'. It describes the changes which took place in British society during the twentieth century from a sociologist's perspective.

Social Trends is aimed at a very wide audience: policy makers in the public and private sectors; service providers; people in local government; journalists and other commentators; academics and students; schools; and the general public.

The editorial team always welcomes readers' views on how *Social Trends* could be improved. Please write to the Editors at the address shown below with any comments or suggestions you have.

New material and sources
To preserve topicality, over half of the 326 tables and charts in the chapters of *Social Trends 30* are new compared with the previous edition, and draw on the most up-to-date available data.

In all chapters the source of the data is given below each table and chart and where this is a major survey, the name of the survey is also given. At the end of each chapter a list of references directing readers to other published sources of data (both government and non government) and a list of contact telephone numbers are given, including the contact number of the chapter author. Those using *Social Trends* as a first point of reference should find this particularly useful. Regional and other sub-national breakdowns of some of the information in *Social Trends* may be found in the ONS's publication *Regional Trends* published by The Stationery Office.

Appendix
The Appendix gives definitions and general background information, particularly on administrative and legal structures and frameworks. Anyone seeking to understand the tables and charts in detail will find it helpful to read the corresponding entries in the Appendix in addition to the footnotes relevant to each table and chart. A full index to this edition can be found starting on page 239.

Availability on electronic media
The data contained in the tables and charts in *Social Trends 30* are available on diskette for £15 (plus VAT). Please contact ONSDirect on 01633 812078 for more details.

The first 25 editions of *Social Trends* are available on CD-ROM and an update is being considered. Please contact ONSDirect for details.

Details of the electronic availability of *Social Trends* can also be found on the ONS internet site at **http://www.ons.gov.uk**

Contributors
The Editors wish to thank all their colleagues in the Government Statistical Service and contributors in other organisations without whose help this publication would not be possible. Thanks also go to onsdesign.

Social and Regional Division
Office for National Statistics
B4/10
1 Drummond Gate
London
SW1V 2QQ

Social Trends 30, © Crown copyright 2000

A Hundred Years of Social Change

A H Halsey

Emeritus Fellow, Nuffield College, Oxford

The convenience of the annual *Social Trends* is that it provides an invaluable resource for those concerned with the study of social change. It reveals on the whole a progressive story of advances in social statistics. Official statistics have undoubtedly improved in the twentieth century. For example the General Household Survey is now an important data source for academic research as are the other official surveys outlined in the book.

This article summarises a hundred years of change in four institutional systems which can be categorised as: production, population, power and communication. The rest of this volume of *Social Trends* describes in more detail some of the major changes in each of these, in chapters on the labour market and income and wealth, population and households and families, lifestyles and social participation, and transport.

A.1

Gross domestic product per head at factor cost[1]

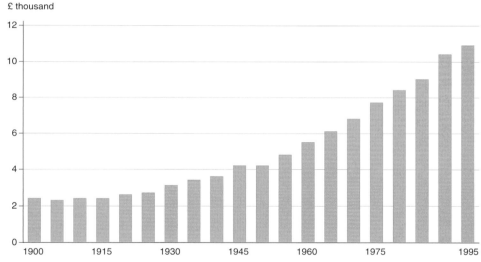

United Kingdom

£ thousand

1 At 1997 prices and on the old ESA 79. Figures up to 1965 are from Feinstein (1976).
Source: Feinstein; Office for National Statistics

Social Trends began life in 1970. In the 1960s the author had planned a beginner's guide to the triumphs and traps of official statistics on social trends since 1900. Macmillans published it in 1972. Now the ONS celebrates 30 years of *Social Trends* and in February 2000 the author, with Josephine Webb, has a third edition of his book covering the whole of the twentieth century.[1]

Production

Though twentieth-century Britain can be characterised as a contracting society because of its transition from the position of a dominant imperial power, it is nonetheless important to note the expansion of its productive system. After inflation and population increase are taken into account, gross domestic product (GDP) per head in 1995 was four and a half times that in 1900 at constant prices (Chart A.1). More recent information on growth in GDP is shown in Chart 5.28 on page 98.

GDP as a measure of economic activity follows an agreed international framework and definition, but cannot be wholly satisfactory to the sociologist because it includes only those activities which are capable of formal measurement. Thus it excludes a wide range of activities (for example in the home and between friends) which are not defined as economic activity. It also focuses on outputs rather than outcomes. For example a larger prison population generates extra economic activity through the employment of more warders, but is a symptom of a social problem. Similarly, but in the opposite direction, the successful elimination of tuberculosis (TB) in the twentieth century brings with it a fall in the economic activity involved with caring for TB patients. Nonetheless, the amelioration of material conditions must be taken as a central fact of this century and especially of the period since the Second World War.

Trends in the distribution of national income and wealth give an indication of changes in the structure of classes, gender and ethnic minority groups. Inequality remains the outstanding feature of both income and, especially, wealth distributions, even given the likelihood that tax avoidance is positively correlated with income and therefore inequality may be underestimated. There has been a marked fall in the share of wealth held by the richest 5 per cent of the population since 1922 when it was over 80 per cent. Taking occupational and state pension rights into account reduces the inequality in wealth distribution: in 1994 the richest 5 per cent held a quarter of wealth. On the other hand as A B Atkinson writes, 'we are ending the century just as we began with a widespread concern about poverty'[2]. Wealth is analysed in more detail in the Wealth section of the Income and Wealth chapter that begins on page 96.

The changing occupational structure can be traced through the development of the division of labour[3]. More people, both absolutely and proportionately, are now engaged in education or training or work than ever before. More too are self-employed or in part-time jobs. White-collar workers are now in a majority, and within their ranks the growing number of managers and professionals, especially in the most recent decades, reflects the development of an increasingly complex division of labour on the basis of an increasingly scientific and capital-intensive technology (see also Chart 4.1 on page 65).

As a proportion of those in employment, manual workers fell from three-quarters to under a half between 1911 and 1981 and further to just over a third by 1991 (Chart A.2). The productive life of the employed has been gradually transformed in the process. Hours of work have been reduced and paid holidays dramatically increased. However, the numbers (though not rate) of unemployed in the late 1970s and 1980s returned to, or exceeded, the levels of the 1930s, though they were reduced in the late 1990s (see Chart 4.20 on page 75). Men also figure less prominently on the work scene for the reasons of their extended education and increased longevity, as well as the rise in female participation in the labour market (see Chart 4.4 on page 67).

At the beginning of the twentieth century T H C Stevenson, the then Registrar-General, accepted the use of a division of the British population into five classes in analysing the 1911 Census. As the century advanced the old rough and visible class categories, popularly and properly thought of as an unequal hierarchy of ways of life tied to virtually hereditary occupations, became more blurred, more challenged as to their legitimacy and more blessed with opportunities to enter new occupations through secondary and even higher

A.2

Percentage of manual workers[1]

Great Britain
Percentages

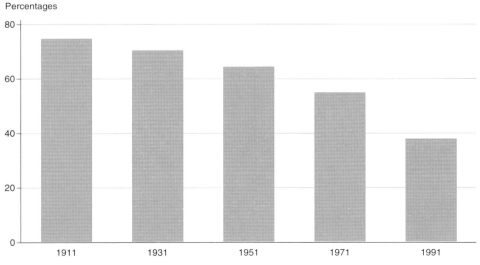

1 As a percentage of people in employment.
Source: Gallie[3] from Census

education and changes in the structure of the economy. By the end of the century millions of children of manual workers had risen into non-manual jobs and many thousands had become the graduate grandchildren of butchers, bakers and candlestick-makers, following professional careers. The occupational and therefore the class structure had shifted. In 1900 the vast majority of Britons were elementary schooled proletarians: by 1970 Stevenson's classification divided the employed half-and-half between white and blue-collar jobs. By 2000 the balance has been tipped decisively to form a white-collar majority. These changes are reflected in the new social classification, the National Statistics Socio-economic Classification (NS-SEC) which will be introduced in Autumn 2000 when re-based on the revised occupational classification, Standard Occupational Classification 2000.

Population

Changes in the population and their family lives have been no less spectacular. Britain diversified ethnically, aged, and moved from a net exporter to a net importer of people. The country began in 1900 as a leading example of the Western European system of kinship based on the nuclear family with high fertility and also high mortality, characterised by delayed marriage, relatively high bachelordom and spinsterhood, and virtually non-existent (though harshly punished) divorce and illegitimate births. Government largely left all this to the severe customs of 'civil society' and the moral surveillance of religion. Britain moved finally into the first demographic transition, between the two world wars, a period of falling fertility (Chart A.3) without any sign of weakening kinship; indeed the popularity of marriage increased with ever higher proportions marrying at earlier ages. Only after the Second World War did divorce, separation, cohabitation and lone motherhood

begin to rise against the background of a net reproduction rate of less than population replacement. Thus Britain ended the century as a European leader of extramarital and teenage births (see Chart 2.15 on page 43), divorce and rising cohabitation – the hallmarks of the second demographic transition phase (ageing population with low mortality and still lower fertility).

In the second half of the century huge strides have been made towards transforming the life of women. Feminism has taken advantage of changes in the economy to narrow gender gaps in welfare and educational opportunity. The upward trends in women's participation in paid employment are the opposite of those of men. There was, as Duncan Gallie makes plain[3], and Chapter 4 of this volume of *Social Trends* illustrates, a post-war surge in paid employment for women. By 1981 women formed 39 per cent of the total occupied population and, by 1998, over 46 per cent. Women have contributed heavily to the growth of white-collar, especially clerical and

A.3

Total period fertility rate[1]

England & Wales

Children per woman

1 The average number of children who would be born per woman if women experienced the age-specific fertility rates of the reference years throughout their child-bearing lifespan.

Source: Office for National Statistics

sales, employment. This is all the more remarkable in the light of developments in the institution of marriage. In the first half of the century, domesticity was the norm for women after marriage. But especially since the early 1950s, the increasing participation of married women has been the most outstanding factor in the changing balance between employment and non-employment – a fact which raises many questions about the changing character of family life, and the relation between marriage, kinship and economy in an advanced industrial society.

Apart from the increasing presence of old people and the reduction in the proportion of children, there has been another noteable demographic change: the pattern of imperial migration inherited from the nineteenth century and continuing into the twentieth to give a net outflow of migrants numbering over a million, was reversed in the second half of the century. As David Coleman concludes[4], 'immigration from the indigenous populations of former colonies … comprises half the century's growth and has permanently transformed major cities into racially mixed populations unimaginable in 1950, let alone the 1900s'. People from ethnic minority groups comprised one in 15 of Britain's population in the late 1990s (see Table 1.8 on page 25).

The experiences of immigrant groups have varied. Though disadvantage persists over the generations, even among the Irish and Western Europeans, Ceri Peach's measures of segregation show that ethnic ghettos are much less marked than in the cities of the United States and there is evidence of Black British and British Asian identity and of mixed households[5]. On the other hand there are pockets of high unemployment and still widespread racist attitudes. Bangladeshis are the most deprived of ethnic minorities, and there is increasing analysis of the circumstances for different minority ethnic groups. At all events, the Britain of the twenty-first century will be multi-ethnic.

Power

Power and authority were democratized early in the century and bureaucratized thereafter. The two principles of authority – democracy and bureaucracy – were in complicated interaction at the end of the twentieth century, with involvement with the European Parliament, and its bureaucracy in Brussels, at one end and devolving power to Scotland, Wales and Northern Ireland at the other. The effects of these developments for the United Kingdom will continue into the twenty-first century.

It can be argued that all forms of traditional authoritative power faltered in the second half of the century – parents, politicians, priests and police as well as scoutmasters and schoolteachers all became less trusted and less popularly admired as the century wore on. In party terms the rise of the Labour Party dominated the House of Commons after the First World War, mostly at the expense of the Liberals but leaving the Conservative Party in office for 58 of the 82 years from 1918 to 2000 (see Chart 13.21 on page 220). The general net thrust of government over the century, aided by the two world wars, can be seen as being towards centralisation.

Communication

The system of communication was dramatically elaborated with growing wealth, the private motor car, enlarging labour markets, radio, television and a range of inventions in information technology. The period 1940-1975 was when 'motorisation' happened: cars became commonplace, motorways were built, bringing in their wake the huge changes, pleasures, opportunities and horrors which we know about, and the consequences of which are still unfolding.

Railway development was, of course, a feature of the nineteenth century but in the first half of the twentieth century it further opened opportunities for travel, loosening traditional forms of communities through cheap commuting, moving troops in both wars and thousands of evacuee children in the second war. After the war and in the closing decades of the century, communication was accelerated by television, telephones and finally the computer and the World Wide Web.

Economic growth, the increase of leisure and technological advances have together scattered population, and air travel, telephone and the internet have accelerated communication globally. In 1900 the majority of people existed at subsistence level. Britain now spends more on leisure activities than on either food, housing or clothing. Overseas holidays were then enjoyed by a small proportion of the upper classes; they are now commonplace as illustrated in Chart 13.1 on page 209. Tourism has become a major industry.

Conclusion

At the beginning of the century, Britain was still an Imperial nation. At the end of the century all that is left territorially, quite apart from the subtraction of Eire, are a few small islands and promontories like St Helena and Gibraltar which once guarded the passages of world-wide British shipping. At the beginning the Union Flag flew over a fifth of the world's people and territory. At the end its fluttering was confined to one hundredth of the world's population.

Accordingly, the story might be interpreted as one of rapid decline, especially if nothing else had changed to offset our nineteenth century notions and means of empire. In fact the whole structure of human life the world over has been transformed. Mr Blair presided at the end of the century over a country totally different from that over which the third Marquis of Salisbury was prime minister in 1900. Economies have grown, communications have accelerated, and kinship, friendship, power and authority have changed fundamentally. Some economic, political and social institutions are no longer British or national but international and global. Britain has thus, in some ways, become less distinctive. George Orwell, writing as late as 1940, could still observe that 'when you come back to England from any foreign country, you have immediately the sensation of breathing a different air…. The crowds in the big towns, with their mild knobby faces, their bad teeth and gentle manners, are different from a European crowd'[6].

It is doubtful whether he would say so in 1999. What would strike him perhaps would be the rapidity of change from his death in 1950 and the degree of assimilation of life in Britain to that of the other advanced industrial countries in Europe and North America. He would certainly notice the upward shift of life expectancy since 1900, life expectancy at birth of women rising from 50 to 80 during those 100 years. (See also Table 7.4 on page 117.) Looking more closely, the period after the Second World War probably brought the most rapid improvements in wealth, the elongation of individual life, and the advance of women towards freedom in occupation, in sex, and in politics.

Detailed study of the assembled statistics will convince readers that no simple story of better or worse will suffice. For example, despite many advances, the life of women has not become unequivocally more leisured. As Gershuny and Fisher show[7], hours of paid employment have been shortened and domestic chores eased by affluence; but sharing of domestic labour has moved glacially and at the end of the century remained in favour of men; women did 260 minutes a day of unpaid work, men 172. Nor is the record of an elongation of life a simple gain. There remain debates about how far the longer average life is marred by elderly infirmity.

So, at least for some observers, the story of decline nevertheless predominates. For example, divorce, birth outside marriage, crime, traffic congestion and atmospheric pollution all rose while, as Peter Brierley's[9] figures demonstrate, attendances at church services fell. Others point to such advances as the occupational liberation of women, rising educational attainment, possibly greater tolerance of homosexuals and ethnic minorities, greater leisure, better housing, and more freedom of movement. Again, debate rages over the distribution of chances in life between traditionally privileged and deprived groups. Is society more open in 2000 than it was in 1900? In absolute terms mobility chances have carried several million Britons from working-class origins to white-collar careers, especially in the second half of the century. And Anthony Heath and Clive Payne produce evidence[8] of an equalisation of relative chances in the same period. On the other hand, the distribution of income and wealth,

having shown a tendency towards less inequality for the first three-quarters of the century is now shown by A B Atkinson[2] to have widened again in the final decades.

It has been an exciting century of progress and barbarism throughout the world, with paradoxical movements towards both a longer and fuller life and towards unprecedented genocide and slaughter, towards democracy and towards dictatorship. For the aristocrat perhaps a century of dispossession, culminating in the last days of the century in the removal of the right of hereditary peers to vote in the House of Lords. For the old and the ill, perhaps a rather more comfortable hundred years. For the homeless and dispossessed, a time of persistent degradation accentuated by surrounding opulence. For women, the young and the fit and ordinary citizens, perhaps the greatest century in the whole history of humankind.

References

1. A H Halsey with Josephine Webb, eds. (2000) *Twentieth Century British Social Trends*, Macmillan

2. A B Atkinson, *Distribution of Income and Wealth* in A H Halsey with Josephine Webb, eds. (2000) *Twentieth Century British Social Trends*, Macmillan

3. Duncan Gallie, The Labour Force in A H Halsey with Josephine Webb, eds. (2000) *Twentieth Century British Social Trends*, Macmillan

4. David Coleman, *Population and Family* in A H Halsey with Josephine Webb, eds. (2000) *Twentieth Century British Social Trends*, Macmillan

5. C Peach et al, *Immigration and Ethnicity* in A H Halsey with Josephine Webb, eds. (2000) *Twentieth Century British Social Trends*, Macmillan

6. Orwell, G. (1941) *The Lion and the Unicorn: Socialism and the English Genius*, Secker and Warburg, London

7. Jonathan Gershuny and Kimberly Fisher, *Leisure* in A H Halsey with Josephine Webb, eds. (2000) *Twentieth Century British Social Trends*, Macmillan

8. Anthony Heath and Clive Payne, *Social Mobility* in A H Halsey with Josephine Webb, eds. (2000) *Twentieth Century British Social Trends*, Macmillan

9. Peter Brierley, *Religion* in A H Halsey with Josephine Webb, eds. (2000) *Twentieth Century British Social Trends*, Macmillan

The inclusion of this article does not imply any endorsement by the ONS or any other government department of the views or opinions expressed.

Chapter 1 Population

Population change

In 1998 the population of the United Kingdom was estimated to be 59.2 million, the 18th largest in the world. In 1901 it was 38.2 million. (Table 1.2)

The fastest population growth of the twentieth century in the United Kingdom occurred in the first decade, when the population increased by an average of 385 thousand each year; this compares with 204 thousand a year between 1991 and 1998. (Table 1.3)

The number of births in the United Kingdom peaked in 1920 at just over 1.1 million, the highest number in any year of the twentieth century. (Chart 1.1)

Population profile

The United Kingdom has an ageing population – in 1901 about one person in 20 was aged 65 and over; by 1998 this had increased to just over one in six. (Page 24)

The number of centenarians in England and Wales increased from fewer than 300 in 1951 to about 5,500 in 1996. (Chart 1.7)

About one person in 15 in Great Britain is from an ethnic minority group. (Table 1.8)

International perspective

Since 1750 the world's population has increased more than sevenfold, and much of this increase occurred in the twentieth century. (Table 1.18)

In October 1999 the world's population exceeded 6 billion people, an increase of a billion in only 12 years. Almost half of the population is aged under 25. (Page 31)

1.1

Births and deaths

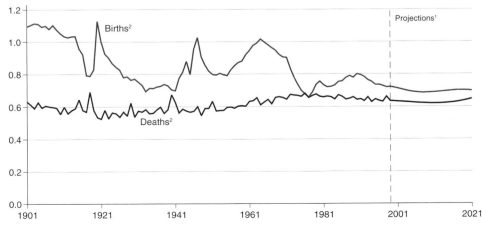

United Kingdom

Millions

1 1998-based.
2 Data for 1901 to 1921 exclude the Irish Republic which was constitutionally a part of the United Kingdom during this period.
Source: Office for National Statistics; Government Actuary's Department; General Register Office for Scotland; Northern Ireland Statistics and Research Agency

1.2

Population[1] of the United Kingdom

	1901	1931	1961	1991	1998	Thousands 2021
England	30,515	37,359	43,561	48,208	49,495	53,715
Wales	2,013	2,593	2,635	2,891	2,933	3,047
Scotland	4,472	4,843	5,184	5,107	5,120	5,058
Northern Ireland[2]	1,237	1,243	1,427	1,601	1,689	1,821
United Kingdom	38,237	46,038	52,807	57,808	59,237	63,642

1 Data are Census enumerated for 1901 and 1931, mid-year estimates for 1961 to 1998 and 1998-based projections for 2021. See Appendix, Part 1: Population estimates and projections.
2 1931 figures for Northern Ireland relate to the 1937 Census.

Source: Office for National Statistics; Government Actuary's Department; General Register Office for Scotland; Northern Ireland Statistics and Research Agency

1.3

Population change[1]

United Kingdom   Thousands

	Population at start of period	Live births	Deaths	Annual averages Net natural change	Net migration and other	Overall change
Census enumerated						
1901-1911	38,237	1,091	624	467	-82	385
1911-1921	42,082	975	689	286	-92	194
1921-1931	44,027	824	555	268	-67	201
1931-1951	46,038	785	598	188	25	213
Mid-year estimates						
1951-1961	50,287	839	593	246	6	252
1961-1971	52,807	963	639	324	-12	312
1971-1981	55,928	736	666	69	-27	42
1981-1991	56,352	757	655	103	43	146
1991-1998	57,808	748	637	112	93	204
Mid-year projections[2]						
1998-2001	59,237	714	630	84	155	239
2001-2011	59,954	701	614	87	95	182
2011-2021	61,773	712	620	92	95	187

1 See Appendix, Part 1: Population estimates and projections.
2 1998-based projections.

Source: Office for National Statistics; Government Actuary's Department; General Register Office for Scotland; Northern Ireland Statistics and Research Agency

Information on the size and structure of the population is important for understanding many aspects of society such as the labour market and household composition. Changes in demographic patterns not only affect social structures but they also have implications for public policy decisions, including those on housing and the provision of health, education and social services.

Population change

There are now more people living in the United Kingdom than at any time in the past. In 1998 the population was estimated to be 59.2 million (Table 1.2), the 18th largest in the world. The population of the United Kingdom has increased by just over half since the beginning of the twentieth century, although there have been variations in the rate of increase between the constituent countries. England experienced the greatest percentage increase in population between 1901 and 1998 at 62 per cent, while Scotland experienced the smallest increase at 14 per cent.

Projections suggest that growth in the population of the United Kingdom will continue until it peaks at nearly 64.9 million people in 2036. It is then anticipated that the population will gradually decline. Different rates of growth are expected in the four constituent countries. Scotland is projected to have a smaller population in 2021 than it currently has, while estimates suggest that England will continue to have the fastest rate of increase.

The rate of population change depends upon the net natural change – the difference between the number of births and deaths – and the net effect of people migrating to and from the country. Most of the population growth of the United Kingdom in the twentieth century can be attributed to net natural change. However, in recent years net inward migration has become an increasingly important determinant of population growth (Table 1.3). Migration is examined in greater detail later in this chapter.

The fastest population growth of the twentieth century occurred in the first decade, when the population increased by an average of 385 thousand each year. This rapid growth at the start of the century, and again during the 1960s, was due to the high number of births during these decades. The considerable fall in the number of births following the 1960s' 'baby boom' helps to explain the very slow population growth of the 1970s.

The two World Wars had a major impact on the number of births and, to a lesser extent, deaths in the United Kingdom (Chart 1.1). There was a noticeable fall in births during the First World War, followed by a post-war 'baby boom' when the number of births peaked at just over 1.1 million in 1920 – the highest number in any year of the twentieth century. The number of births then decreased and remained low during the 1930s' depression and the Second World War. This was followed by a 'baby boom' shortly after the Second World War and another in the 1960s.

One factor influencing trends in the number of births is the number of women of reproductive age. For example, the number of births rose during the 1980s as the large number of women born in the 1960s entered their peak reproductive years. As these women have got older the number of births each year has fallen. Fertility is discussed in more detail in the Family formation section of Chapter 2: Households and Families (page 41).

Babies' most popular first names

England & Wales

	1904	1934	1964	1994	1998
Males					
1st	William	John	David	Thomas	Jack
2nd	John	Peter	Paul	James	Thomas
3rd	George	William	Andrew	Jack	James
4th	Thomas	Brian	Mark	Daniel	Daniel
5th	Arthur	David	John	Matthew	Joshua
Females					
1st	Mary	Margaret	Susan	Rebecca	Chloe
2nd	Florence	Jean	Julie	Lauren	Emily
3rd	Doris	Mary	Karen	Jessica	Megan
4th	Edith	Joan	Jacqueline	Charlotte	Jessica
5th	Dorothy	Patricia	Deborah	Hannah	Sophie

Source: Office for National Statistics

Babies' names are constantly changing in popularity. Jack and Chloe were the most common names given to boys and girls born in England and Wales in 1998 (Table 1.4). However, neither of these names featured in the top 50 most popular names in 1984, and they were not even in the top 100 names ten years before that. By contrast, John was a very popular boy's name in the first half of the twentieth century, but was in fifth place in 1964 and by 1998 was outside the top 50. Similarly, Margaret was a popular girl's name earlier this century, but by 1964 it was the 39th most popular name and was also outside the top 50 in 1998.

Despite the considerable population growth since 1901, the annual number of deaths has remained relatively constant this century. There were 661 thousand deaths in the United Kingdom in 1998 compared with 632 thousand in 1901. However, this masks large declines in mortality rates. Early in the twentieth century, infant and childhood mortality declined considerably, while in more recent years the death rates among older people have also fallen. Rising standards of living and new developments in medical technology help to explain these declines in mortality rates.

1.5

Deaths: by gender and age

United Kingdom									Rates
	Death rates per 1,000 in each age group								All deaths (thousands)
	Under 1[1]	1-15	16-34	35-54	55-64	65-74	75 and over	All ages	
Males									
1961	26.3	0.6	1.1	5.0	22.4	54.8	142.5	12.6	322
1971	20.2	0.5	1.0	4.8	20.4	51.1	131.4	12.1	329
1981	12.7	0.4	0.0	4.0	18.1	46.4	122.2	12.0	329
1991	8.3	0.3	0.9	3.1	14.2	38.7	110.6	11.1	314
1998	6.4	0.2	1.0	3.0	12.5	34.8	110.1	10.9	316
2011[2]	3.7	0.2	0.9	2.4	9.5	24.6	88.1	9.7	298
2021[2]	3.1	0.2	0.9	2.3	8.1	23.0	80.7	10.3	329
Females									
1961	18.2	0.4	0.6	3.2	11.0	31.6	110.4	11.4	310
1971	15.5	0.4	0.5	3.1	10.3	26.6	96.6	11.0	317
1981	9.5	0.3	0.4	2.5	9.8	24.7	90.2	11.4	329
1991	6.3	0.2	0.4	1.9	8.4	22.3	83.9	11.2	332
1998	5.2	0.2	0.4	1.9	7.5	21.1	88.7	11.5	346
2011[2]	3.1	0.1	0.3	1.8	6.2	15.7	78.7	10.0	311
2021[2]	2.4	0.1	0.3	1.7	5.5	14.9	69.0	9.8	315

1 Rate per 1,000 live births.
2 1998-based projections.

Source: Office for National Statistics; Government Actuary's Department; General Register Office for Scotland; Northern Ireland Statistics and Research Agency

1.6

Population: by gender and age

United Kingdom									Percentages
	Under 16	16-24	25-34	35-44	45-54	55-64	65-74	75 and over	All ages (=100%) (millions)
Males									
1901[1]	33.6	19.7	15.7	12.2	8.8	5.8	3.1	1.2	18.5
1931[1,2]	25.6	17.8	15.9	13.0	11.9	9.2	5.0	1.7	22.1
1961[1]	24.8	13.9	13.1	13.9	13.9	11.2	6.3	3.1	25.5
1991	21.4	13.7	16.3	14.1	11.6	10.0	8.0	4.8	28.2
1998	21.3	11.4	16.2	14.7	13.3	9.9	7.9	5.3	29.1
Females									
1901[1]	31.4	19.6	16.4	12.2	9.0	6.2	3.6	1.6	19.7
1931[1,2]	23.0	17.0	16.0	14.0	12.5	9.3	5.7	2.4	24.0
1961[1]	22.1	12.9	12.1	13.2	13.7	12.0	8.7	5.3	27.3
1991	19.3	12.5	15.1	13.4	11.1	10.0	9.5	9.0	29.6
1998	19.6	10.5	15.0	14.0	12.9	9.9	8.9	9.3	30.1

1 Figures for 1901, 1931 and 1961 relate to age bands under 15 and 15 to 24. Figures for 1901 and 1931 are Census enumerated; figures for later years are mid-year estimates.
2 1931 figures for Northern Ireland relate to the 1937 Census.

Source: Office for National Statistics; General Register Office for Scotland; Northern Ireland Statistics and Research Agency

Death rates are higher for males than for females in all age groups (Table 1.5), resulting in the life expectancy of women being higher than that for men. Death rates among men and women in Scotland were higher at most ages in 1998 than among those in the other constituent countries of the United Kingdom. The fact that the overall crude death rate has been higher for women than for men in the United Kingdom since 1991 can be explained by the differing age structures of the male and female populations. Information on causes of death is contained in Chapter 7: Health.

Population profile

Although more boys are born each year than girls, lower survival rates among males help to explain the fact that there are more females than males living in the United Kingdom (Table 1.6). The ratio of females to males increases with age. Women currently begin to outnumber men from around the age of 50, and by the age of 89 there are about three women to every man.

In common with the rest of the European Union (EU), the United Kingdom has an ageing population. In 1901 about one person in 20 was aged 65 or over, and just over one person in 100 was aged 75 or over. This increased to just over one in six and about one in fourteen respectively by 1998. Conversely, the proportion of the population under the age of 16 fell from a third to just over a fifth over the same period. Projections suggest these trends will continue so that by 2016 it is expected that, for the first time, the number of people aged 65 and over will exceed those aged under 16.

Historically the ageing of the population was largely a result of the fall in fertility that began towards the end of the nineteenth century. Early in the twentieth century lower mortality helped to increase the number of people surviving into old age, but the effects of improved survival were even greater among younger people which

1.7

operated as a counterbalance to the trend towards population ageing. More recently, with lower fertility and mortality rates, improvements in mortality rates for older people are now contributing to the ageing of the population.

Falls in death rates have contributed to a considerable increase in the number of people living to the age of 100 or over during the second half of the twentieth century. In 1951 there were fewer than 300 centenarians alive in England and Wales; by 1996 this had risen to about 5,500 people (Chart 1.7). This increase has been largest among women. In 1911 women centenarians outnumbered men by about three to one, but by 1996 there were more than eight women centenarians to every man. While the numbers of centenarians are still fairly small, the rate of increase has been very large at about 7 per cent per year, roughly doubling every decade. This trend is similar to those in other industrialised countries for which reliable data are available. Projections suggest that the numbers eligible to receive their 100th birthday congratulations from the Queen will continue to rise into the next century. By 2036 there could be over 40 thousand centenarians alive in England and Wales.

An increase in the numbers of births in the second half of the nineteenth century helps to explain only part of the recent growth in the number of centenarians. The increase in survival from birth to age 80 is another contributory factor, and for people born between 1871 and 1901 this increase has been greater for females than for males. Part of the explanation for this difference between the genders is that these cohorts include men who served in the First World War when many service personnel began smoking. Those men who survived the war are likely to have died of smoking-related disease before reaching the age of 80. In addition, the reduction in maternal death associated with childbirth may also be an explanation. More recently, there have been large increases in the rates of survival from age 80 to 100, again greater for women than for men.

The age profile of the population varies between ethnic groups. Members of ethnic minority groups were present in Great Britain in small numbers throughout the period of the Empire. However, their numbers increased dramatically after the Second World War. This growth was initiated by large scale immigration from the countries of the New Commonwealth following the passing of the *1948 British Nationality Act*. This trend was subsequently curtailed by legislation passed in the 1960s and 1970s.

In general, ethnic minority groups in Great Britain have a younger age structure than the White population, reflecting past immigration and fertility patterns. The Bangladeshi group has the youngest age structure: 43 per cent of Bangladeshis were under the age of 16 in 1998-99, compared with 20 per cent of White people (Table 1.8).

Population aged 100 and over[1]

England & Wales

Thousands

1 Estimated as at 1 January each year.

Source: Max Planck Institute for Demographic Research

1.8

Population: by ethnic group and age, 1998-99[1]

Great Britain Percentages

	Under 16	16-34	35-64	65 and over	All ages (=100%) (millions)
White	20	26	38	16	53.1
Black					
Black Caribbean	23	29	38	9	0.5
Black African	32	37	29	2	0.4
Other Black group	43	37	18	..	0.1
All Black groups	29	33	33	6	0.9
Indian	24	32	38	7	0.9
Pakistani/Bangladeshi					
Pakistani	35	36	25	3	0.6
Bangladeshi	43	32	22	3	0.2
All Pakistani/Bangladeshi	37	35	24	3	1.0
Other groups					
Chinese	15	40	39	6	0.2
None of the above	43	30	24	2	0.8
All other groups[2]	38	32	27	3	1.0
All ethnic groups[3]	21	26	38	15	56.8

1 Population living in private households. Combined quarters: Spring 1998 to Winter 1998-99.
2 Includes those of mixed origin.
3 Includes those who did not state their ethnic group.
Source: Labour Force Survey, Office for National Statistics

1.9

Population of working age[1]: by gender and social class, Spring 1999

United Kingdom
Percentages

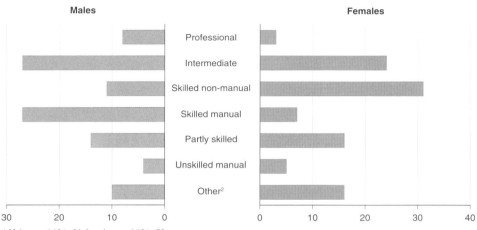

1 Males aged 16 to 64, females aged 16 to 59.
2 Includes members of the armed forces, those who did not state their current or last occupation, and those who had not worked in the last eight years.
Source: Labour Force Survey, Office for National Statistics

1.10

Population density: by area[1], 1891 and 1991

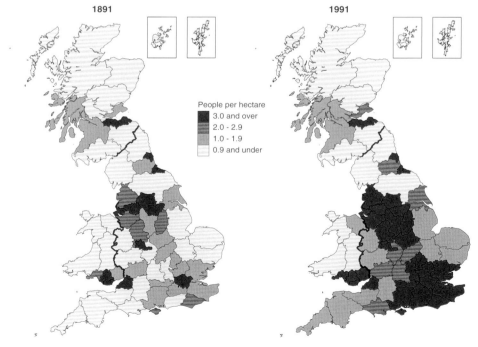

1 Counties of England and Wales; regions of Scotland and islands areas.
Source: Census, Office for National Statistics

In contrast, 16 per cent of the White population were aged 65 and over compared with 3 per cent of Pakistani and Bangladeshis. Progressive ageing of ethnic minority populations is anticipated in the future, but changes will be dependent upon fertility levels, mortality rates and the degree of future net immigration.

About one person in 15 in Great Britain is from an ethnic minority group. For each ethnic minority group, children are more likely than older people to have been born in the United Kingdom. This is particularly the case among Indians: over nine in ten Indian children under the age of 16 were born in the United Kingdom compared with only one in 50 adults aged 35 and over.

The occupational composition of the population has also changed this century. Among the male labour force there has been a strong upward trend in the share of professional, managerial and supervisory grades. There have also been increases in the proportion of women in higher socio-economic occupations, albeit more slowly than for men, along with rises in clerical and unskilled manual groups. However, these trends are accompanied by other factors such as the increasing participation rate of women in the workforce. Further information on economic activity rates is contained in Chart 4.4 in the Labour Market chapter. In Spring 1999 men were nearly three times more likely than women to be in the professional group (Chart 1.9). Conversely, women were about three times more likely than men to be in the skilled non-manual group. This reflects the predominance of women in certain occupations such as clerical and secretarial jobs.

1.11

Geographical distribution

In 1998 the majority of the population of the United Kingdom (about 84 per cent) lived in England, with Northern Ireland having the smallest population of the four constituent countries at 1.7 million (3 per cent). The population density of the four countries varies considerably: in 1998 England had about 379 people per square kilometre compared with only 66 people per square kilometre in Scotland.

There are difficulties in tracing population distribution and density over time, not least due to boundary and classification changes. However, using historical Census tables, Chart 1.10 shows estimates of population densities for 1891 and 1991 respectively for Great Britain, based on 1991 boundaries. Greater London had by far the greatest concentration of people in both 1891 and 1991, while the Highland region of Scotland had the lowest population density in both years. The maps also reveal the relatively high population density of the south and east of England compared with more northern areas.

The population of Great Britain has been highly urbanised for much of the twentieth century. However, there has been a trend for people to move away from more densely populated urban centres into the suburbs during this period, and in recent years from metropolitan areas to smaller settlements and rural districts. During the 1980s urban decentralisation was particularly clear in London, Birmingham and Manchester.

Population of metropolitan counties[1]

Great Britain						Millions
	1891	1911	1931	1951	1971	1991
Greater London	5.6	7.2	8.1	8.2	7.5	6.4
West Midlands	1.4	1.8	2.1	2.5	2.8	2.5
Greater Manchester	2.2	2.6	2.7	2.7	2.7	2.5
West Yorkshire	1.6	1.9	1.9	2.0	2.1	2.0
Merseyside	1.1	1.4	1.6	1.7	1.7	1.4
South Yorkshire	0.7	1.0	1.2	1.3	1.3	1.3
Tyne & Wear	0.8	1.1	1.2	1.2	1.2	1.1
All metropolitan counties	13.2	16.9	18.9	19.6	19.2	17.1
Great Britain	33.0	40.8	44.8	48.9	54.0	54.2

1 Areas as constituted at 21 April 1991. Data for 1991 differ from mid-year estimates due to under-enumeration in the Census.
Source: Census, Office for National Statistics

Almost 90 per cent of the population of Great Britain were living in urban areas in 1991. Slightly over half of people were resident in the 66 urban areas with populations of 100 thousand or more, although urban areas occupied just 6 per cent of total land area. The largest of these urban areas is Greater London which had about two and a half times the population of the next largest areas, the West Midlands Metropolitan County and Greater Manchester (Table 1.11).

The proportion of the population living in the seven major metropolitan counties of England has declined over the last 100 years. In 1891 about four people in ten in Great Britain were resident in these areas compared with three in ten in 1991. In 1891 about 17 per cent of people were living in Greater London, but by 1991 this had fallen to about 12 per cent.

1.12

Percentage of people over state pension age[1]: by area[2], 1998

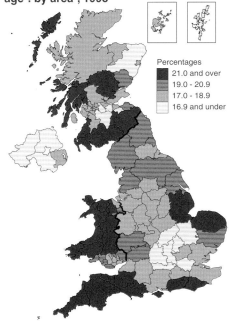

Percentages
- 21.0 and over
- 19.0 - 20.9
- 17.0 - 18.9
- 16.9 and under

1 Men aged 65 and over, women aged 60 and over.
2 Counties for England, unitary authorities for Wales, council areas for Scotland and boards for Northern Ireland.

Source: Office for National Statistics; General Register Office for Scotland; Northern Ireland Statistics and Research Agency

In 1998 the county, unitary authority, council or board with the highest proportion of people of state pension age or over was the seaside area of Conwy in Wales, where over one in four people were over state pension age (Chart 1.12). This compares with an average of just under one person in five for the United Kingdom as a whole. In England there are also high proportions of older people in some of the counties along the south coast, including the Isle of Wight, Dorset and Sussex. Of the four countries of the United Kingdom, Northern Ireland has the youngest population with the highest proportion of children and the lowest proportion of older people.

Migration

Migration flows influence the size, growth and profile of the population. Regional populations are affected by people relocating within the country, supplemented by international migration. During much of the twentieth century there has been a movement of population from the old coal, shipbuilding and steel industries in the north and Wales to the light industries and services of the south and the midlands. Population gains and losses due to internal migration have important implications for local land use and housing planning, as well as for the provision of welfare services.

During 1998 England and Wales both gained people due to inter-regional migration, while Scotland and Northern Ireland experienced net outward migration (Table 1.13). At a regional level within England, the greatest fall occurred in London where 228 thousand people moved from there to other regions in the United Kingdom, and 180 thousand moved into that region, yielding a net loss of 48 thousand for London due to internal migration. However, this was more than offset by the net inflow of international migrants settling in the capital. Almost 40 per cent of people leaving London for elsewhere in the United Kingdom moved into the neighbouring South East region. The South West experienced the highest net gain of all the regions due to internal migration, of 27 thousand people.

Young adults are the most mobile age group, reflecting in part the move most young people make from their parental home either to study, to seek employment or to set up their own home.

1.13

Net internal migration[1]: by age of migrants and region, 1998

Thousands

	North East	North West	Yorkshire and the Humber	East Mid- lands	West Mid- lands	East	London	South East	South West	England	Wales	Scot- land	North- ern Ireland
Age													
Under 15	-0.7	-0.9	0.2	3.6	0.1	5.4	-21.5	5.4	7.1	-1.4	1.3	-0.2	0.4
15-24	0.1	-4.1	-0.7	-0.9	-3.1	-3.0	22.7	-1.2	-3.9	5.9	-0.8	-1.8	-3.5
25-34	-2.2	-3.2	-3.0	1.9	-2.2	6.4	-6.2	7.5	4.1	3.2	-1.1	-2.6	0.5
35-44	-0.6	-1.0	-0.3	2.4	-0.1	3.4	-15.2	4.8	5.5	-1.1	0.9	-0.2	0.4
45-54	-0.3	-1.4	-0.1	1.3	-0.4	1.6	-8.6	0.5	5.5	-1.8	1.3	0.2	0.3
55-64	-	-1.1	-	1.5	-0.7	1.9	-8.3	-0.3	5.1	-1.9	1.3	0.4	0.2
65-74	-0.1	-0.6	-0.1	0.7	-0.4	1.5	-5.2	1.2	2.4	-0.6	0.3	0.2	0.1
75 and over	-0.1	-0.6	-0.4	0.8	0.2	2.0	-5.3	2.1	1.4	-	-0.1	-	-
All ages	-4.0	-12.9	-4.4	11.4	-6.6	19.3	-47.7	20.0	27.0	2.2	3.2	-3.8	-1.6

1 Data are based on patient movements recorded by the National Health Service Central Registers at Southport and Edinburgh and the Central Services Agency in Belfast. A negative figure implies a net outflow of people from the region.

Source: Office for National Statistics; General Register Office for Scotland; Northern Ireland Statistics and Research Agency

1.14

In 1998 London experienced the largest net increase of people aged 15 to 24 due to migration within the United Kingdom, while the North West experienced the biggest net loss of people in this age group. Information about the reasons why people move home can be found in Table 10.14 in the Housing chapter.

The pattern of people entering and leaving the United Kingdom changed over the twentieth century. There was a net loss due to international migration during the first three decades of the twentieth century and again during the 1960s and 1970s. However, since 1983 there has been net migration into the United Kingdom, and in 1998 there was a net inflow of 178 thousand migrants into the country. (See Appendix: Part 1 for international migration methodology.) People offer various reasons for moving into and out of the country. Over the period 1991 to 1998 the International Passenger Survey found that the most common reason given for inward migration was to accompany or join a partner already in the United Kingdom, while the most common reason given for outward migration was work related. These figures should be treated with some caution, however, as not all migrants give a reason for their movement.

In 1997 there were over 440 thousand Irish nationals living in the United Kingdom, more than the total of all the other European Union (EU) nationals living here (Table 1.14). Of those UK nationals living in other EU countries, about a third were living in Germany, with the Irish Republic being the next most common country.

Nationals of the European Economic Area (EU plus Norway, Iceland and Liechtenstein) have the right to reside in the United Kingdom provided they are working or able to support themselves

financially. Nearly all other overseas nationals wishing to live permanently in the United Kingdom require Home Office acceptance for settlement. The number of people accepted for settlement in the United Kingdom was 70 thousand in 1998, the highest number of the decade, although lower than in some of the years in the 1970s (Table 1.15). There was a particularly large proportionate rise in acceptances from the Americas in 1998 compared with 1997, mainly due to evacuees from Montserrat.

The United Kingdom has a tradition of granting protection to those in need, and has certain obligations under the 1951 United Nations Convention, and the 1967 Protocol, relating to the Status of Refugees. These provide that refugees lawfully resident should enjoy treatment at least as favourable as that accorded to the indigenous population. The number of people seeking asylum

UK nationals living in other EU states, and nationals of other EU states living in the United Kingdom, 1997

Thousands

	UK nationals living in other EU states	EU nationals living in the United Kingdom
Germany	117	62
Irish Republic	64	443
France[1]	50	59
Netherlands	39	29
Belgium	26	5
Italy	23	82
Greece	14	21
Denmark	13	13
Portugal	12	26
Sweden	12	18
Spain	7	34
Luxembourg	4	..
Austria[2]	3	9
Finland	2	4
All	386	..

1 Data relate to 1990.
2 Data relate to 1991.
Source: Eurostat

1.15

Acceptances for settlement: by region of origin

United Kingdom								Thousands
	1974	1976	1981	1986	1991	1996	1997	1998
Asia	18.3	34.6	30.0	22.8	25.2	27.9	25.6	30.1
Africa	7.9	8.6	4.1	4.1	9.6	13.0	13.2	16.1
Americas	9.0	7.7	6.3	6.4	7.2	8.5	7.8	10.8
Europe[1]	12.8	9.5	6.6	5.2	5.6	7.5	7.7	7.6
Oceania	3.0	5.0	4.5	5.4	2.4	3.5	3.1	3.7
Other[2]	17.9	15.4	7.5	3.8	3.9	1.4	1.3	1.5
All regions	68.9	80.7	59.1	47.8	53.9	61.7	58.7	69.8

1 Includes all European Economic Area (EEA) countries throughout the period covered. EEA nationals are not obliged to seek settlement and the figures relate only to those who chose to do so.
2 Mainly British Overseas citizens and those whose nationality was unknown and, up to 1991, acceptances where the nationality was not separately identified; from 1996 these nationalities have been included in the relevant geographical areas.
Source: Home Office

1.16

Asylum applications[1]: by region of origin

United Kingdom					Thousands
	1986	1991	1996	1997	1998
Europe	0.2	3.7	6.5	9.1	17.7
Africa	1.1	27.5	11.3	9.5	12.4
Asia	1.8	10.5	7.9	8.6	11.9
Middle East	1.2	2.5	2.1	2.3	2.8
Americas	-	0.2	1.8	2.8	1.0
Nationality not known	-	0.4	0.1	0.1	0.2
All regions	4.3	44.8	29.6	32.5	46.0

1 Excluding dependants.
Source: Home Office

1.17

Components of EU population change

European Union						Thousands
				Annual averages		
	Population at start of period	Live births	Deaths	Net natural change	Net migration	Overall change
1960-1964	314,826	6,001	3,445	2,556	208	2,764
1965-1969	328,648	5,913	3,619	2,295	-29	2,265
1970-1974	339,975	5,254	3,715	1,539	194	1,734
1975-1979	348,644	4,648	3,740	908	278	1,185
1980-1984	354,572	4,449	3,723	727	54	781
1985-1989	358,475	4,304	3,705	600	458	1,058
1990-1994	363,763	4,222	3,713	509	1,056	1,565
1995-1997	371,589	4,028	3,714	314	684	998

Source: Eurostat

varies considerably from year to year, although there has been an overall increase from about 4 thousand during 1985 to 1988 to almost 45 thousand in 1991 and 46 thousand in 1998 (Table 1.16). This can be attributed to a combination of factors, including world events, economic pressures and easier access to travel. The greatest number of applicants in 1998 was from the Federal Republic of Yugoslavia.

The *Immigration and Asylum Act*, which received Royal Assent in November 1999, will implement key elements of the July 1998 *Fairer, Faster and Firmer* White Paper. Its provisions include introducing measures which aim to speed up immigration and asylum appeals, tackle clandestine entry, and create a coherent, national system of support for asylum seekers in genuine need.

International perspective

Most of the countries of the EU have growing and ageing populations. However, EU population growth has slowed significantly over the last 35 years. In the 1960s annual growth occurred at an average rate of over 2 million per year (Table 1.17). In comparison, this growth rate slowed to about 1 million people per year in the period 1995 to 1997.

During the 1960s, and to a lesser extent the 1970s and early 1980s, most of the population growth was a result of a high number of births. However by the 1990s, with fewer babies being born, average annual net inward migration accounted for more of the population growth than did net natural change. In 1997 net migration was the sole contributor to population growth in Germany, Italy and Sweden, counterbalancing natural population decline in these countries.

1.18

Population growth in Europe has been considerably slower than the average growth rate for the world in recent years. Since 1750 the world's population has increased more than sevenfold (Table 1.18). Much of this increase occurred in the twentieth century: in 1999 the population was three and a half times bigger than it was in 1900. The world's population is growing at 78 million per year, almost equivalent to the total population of Germany. In October 1999 the world's population exceeded 6 billion people, an increase of a billion in only 12 years. Almost half of the population is aged under 25, with one person in six aged between 15 and 24.

Over 95 per cent of world population growth is occurring in developing countries where there is high fertility and where death rates have declined substantially since 1950. Conversely 61 countries, including much of Europe and North America, have fertility rates of less than 2.1 births per woman, below the long-term replacement rate. Projections suggest that the world's population will reach almost 9 billion by 2050, when one in five people will live in Africa compared with just over one person in eight in 1999.

The Greenwich Meridian line of zero degrees longitude marked the start of the year 2000, and runs through several countries whose populations and societies are very diverse (Table 1.19). Less than half of people in Mali, Burkina Faso, Togo and Ghana lived in urban areas in 1995 compared with over seven in ten people in each of the European countries on the Meridian line. In 1996 less than half of women in Mali knew about a contraceptive method whether medical, barrier, natural or traditional. Over one in ten babies born in Mali die before their first birthday, compared with less than one in 100 born in the United Kingdom. Those Malian babies that do survive childhood can expect to live only about two-thirds as long as their contemporaries born in the United Kingdom.

World population

| | | | | | | Millions |
	1750	1800	1850	1900	1950	1999
Asia	502	635	809	947	1,402	3,634
Africa	106	107	111	133	224	767
Europe	163	203	276	408	547	729
Latin America and Caribbean	16	24	38	74	166	511
North America	2	7	26	82	172	307
Oceania	2	2	2	6	13	30
World	791	978	1,262	1,650	2,524	5,978

Source: United Nations

1.19

Demographic indicators of countries on the Greenwich Meridian Line

	Population (millions) 1999	Average annual growth rate 1995-2000[1] (percentage)	Percentage in urban areas 1995	Infant mortality rate[2]	Life expectancy at birth (years) Males	Females
United Kingdom[3]	59.5	0.2	89	7	74.5	79.8
France	58.9	0.4	73	6	74.2	82.0
Spain	39.6	-	76	7	74.5	81.5
Algeria	30.8	2.3	56	44	67.5	70.3
Mali	11.0	2.4	27	118	52.0	54.6
Burkina Faso	11.6	2.7	27	99	43.6	45.2
Togo	4.5	2.6	31	84	47.6	50.1
Ghana	19.7	2.7	36	66	58.3	61.8

1 Medium variant.
2 Per 1,000 live births.
3 Population figure for 1999 is the 1998-based projection from the Government Actuary's Department.
Source: United Nations

References and further reading

The following list contains selected publications relevant to **Chapter 1: Population**. Those published by The Stationery Office are available from the addresses shown on the inside back cover of *Social Trends*.

1991 Census Historical Tables: Great Britain, The Stationery Office

A Statistical Focus on Wales: Women, Welsh Office

Annual Report of the Registrar General for Northern Ireland, The Stationery Office

Annual Report of the Registrar General for Scotland, General Register Office for Scotland

Asylum Statistics - United Kingdom, Home Office

Birth statistics (Series FM1), The Stationery Office

British Social Trends Since 1900, MacMillan Press

Control of Immigration: Statistics, United Kingdom, The Stationery Office

Demographic Statistics, Eurostat

Demographic Yearbook, United Nations

International Migration Statistics (Series MN), The Stationery Office

Key Population and Vital Statistics (Series VS/PP1), The Stationery Office

Mid-year Population Estimates (Series PP1), The Stationery Office

Mid-year Population Estimates, Scotland, General Register Office for Scotland

Mortality Statistics for England and Wales (Series DH1, 2, 3, 4), The Stationery Office

National Population Projections (Series PP2), The Stationery Office

Persons Granted British Citizenship - United Kingdom, Home Office

Population Projections for the Counties and District Health Authorities of Wales, Welsh Office

Population Projections, Scotland (for Administrative Areas), General Register Office for Scotland

Population Trends, The Stationery Office

Regional Trends, The Stationery Office

Social Focus on Ethnic Minorities, The Stationery Office

Social Focus on Older People, The Stationery Office

Social Focus on Women and Men, The Stationery Office

The State of World Population, UNFPA

Contacts

Telephone contact points for further information relating to
Chapter 1: Population

Office for National Statistics	
Chapter author	020 7533 5782
Internal migration	01329 813889
International migration	01329 813255
Labour market enquires helpline	020 7533 6094
Population estimates general enquiries	01329 813318
General Register Office (Northern Ireland)	028 9025 2031
General Register Office for Scotland	0131 314 4254
Government Actuary's Department	020 7211 2622
Home Office	020 8760 8280
National Assembly for Wales	029 2082 5085
Eurostat	00 352 4231 13727
United Nations	020 7630 1981

Chapter 2 Households and Families

Households and families

The average household size in Great Britain had been about 4.6 people for many years until the early twentieth century. Since then it has almost halved to 2.4 people per household in 1998-99. (Page 34)

The population of Great Britain increased by a half between 1901 and 1996 while the number of households almost tripled. (Chart 2.1)

In 1901 about one in 20 households in Great Britain comprised one person living alone; this increased to just under one in three in 1998-99. (Page 34)

Partnerships

In 1997 there were 310 thousand marriages in the United Kingdom, among the lowest annual figures recorded during the twentieth century. (Page 37)

The proportion of all non-married women aged 18 to 49 who were cohabiting in Great Britain more than doubled between 1979 and 1998-99, from 11 per cent to 29 per cent. (Page 40)

Family formation

The fertility rate for women aged 35 to 39 nearly doubled between 1981 and 1998 to 40 live births per 1,000 women aged 35 to 39, although it still remains lower than in 1961. (Table 2.13)

In 1997 the rate of conceptions for teenagers under 18 was 46 per 1,000 women aged 13 to 17 years in England and Wales. (Chart 2.14)

Almost four in ten live births in Great Britain in 1998 occurred outside marriage, more than four times the proportion in 1974. (Chart 2.16)

2.1

Population and private households[1]

Great Britain

Millions

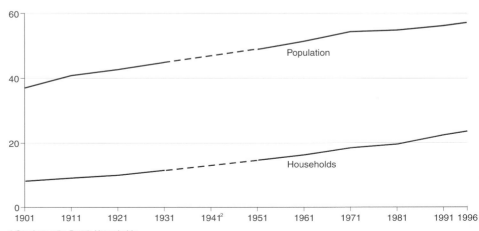

1 See Appendix, Part 2: Households.
2 No Census was taken in 1941.

Source: Census and population estimates, Office for National Statistics; Department of the Environment, Transport and the Regions; National Assembly for Wales; Scottish Executive

Home life, partnering and social relationships are important influences on people's self-development and well being. Most people share their living arrangements with others in the same household, and families can provide a source of support and care for people. Trends in household and family formation are therefore of particular interest to policy makers, for example in determining housing needs, and to the caring professions.

Households and families

The average household size in Great Britain had been about 4.6 people for many years until the early twentieth century. Since then it has almost halved to 2.4 people per household in 1998-99, as the number of households has grown at a faster rate than the population. The population of Great Britain increased by a half between 1901 and 1996, while the number of households almost tripled (Chart 2.1). Trends towards smaller families, and more people living alone, help to explain this increase in the number of households.

One person households increased particularly rapidly during the twentieth century. In 1901 about one in 20 households in Great Britain comprised one person living alone; this had increased to just under one in three by 1998-99. In 1971, two-thirds of one-person households comprised people over pensionable age (Table 2.2). However, by 1998-99 this proportion had fallen to around a half. The increasing proportion of one-person households who are under pensionable age reflects the decline in marriage, an increase in the average age at marriage, and the rise in separation and divorce. Increases in longevity and the number of widows living by themselves help to explain the rise in the proportion of one-person households among those over pensionable age.

Since the early 1960s there has also been a decline in the proportion of 'traditional' households consisting of a couple family with dependent children. In 1961, 38 per cent of households in Great Britain were of this type but by 1998-99 this had decreased to 23 per cent. There has also

2.2

Households[1]: by type of household and family

Great Britain					Percentages
	1961	1971	1981	1991	1998-99
One person					
Under pensionable age	4	6	8	11	14
Over pensionable age	7	12	14	16	15
Two or more unrelated adults	5	4	5	3	2
One family households[2]					
Couple					
No children	26	27	26	28	30
1-2 dependent children[3]	30	26	25	20	19
3 or more dependent children[3]	8	9	6	5	4
Non-dependent children only	10	8	8	8	6
Lone parent					
Dependent children[3]	2	3	5	6	7
Non-dependent children only	4	4	4	4	3
Multi-family households	3	1	1	1	1
All households					
(=100%)(millions)	16.3	18.6	20.2	22.4	..

1 See Appendix, Part 2: Households and Families.
2 Other individuals who were not family members may also be included.
3 May also include non-dependent children.
Source: Census and General Household Survey, Office for National Statistics; Department of the Environment, Transport and the Regions; National Assembly for Wales; Scottish Executive

2.3

been a decline in the proportion of multi-family households – from 3 per cent of all households in 1961 to only 1 per cent in 1998-99. The proportion of lone parent households with dependent children, however, more than trebled over the period to 7 per cent of all households in 1998-99. These trends reflect changes in family and partnership formation (which are discussed later in this chapter) as well as increases in housing provision. An analysis by the Office for National Statistics suggests that lone parent families, who were historically more likely than other families to live in multi-family households, have increasingly become lone parent households during this period.

Whereas Table 2.2 shows that about three-fifths of the households in Great Britain in 1998-99 were headed by a couple, Table 2.3 is based on people; it shows that about three-quarters of people living in private households were in a couple family household. More people lived in the so-called 'traditional' family household than in any other type of family, while just over one in 10 people lived alone and a similar proportion lived in a lone parent household.

There is a strong link between ethnic group and household type. In Spring 1999, 29 per cent of White households in Great Britain were single person households (see Table 2.4 overleaf). This compares with 30 per cent of Black households but only 7 per cent of Pakistani/Bangladeshi households. Households headed by a Pakistani/ Bangladeshi, on the other hand, were most likely to contain dependent children. This is at least partly explained by the young age structure of the

People in private households: by type of household and family in which they live[1]

Great Britain					Percentages
	1961	1971	1981	1991	1998-99
One family households					
Living alone	4	6	8	11	12
Couple					
No children	18	19	20	23	26
Dependent children[2]	52	52	47	41	39
Non-dependent children only	12	10	10	11	8
Lone parent	3	4	6	10	11
Other households	12	9	9	4	4
All people in private households					
(=100%)(millions)	..	53.4	53.9	55.4	..
People not in private					
households (millions)	..	0.9	0.8	0.8	..
Total population (millions)	51.4	54.4	54.8	56.2	57.5

1 See Appendix, Part 2: Households and Families.
2 May also include non-dependent children.
Source: Census and General Household Survey, Office for National Statistics

For many decades censuses did not distinguish adequately between households and families, and a definitive distinction was not made until 1961. A household is defined as one person living alone, or a group of people at the same address who share living arrangements. Families are defined as a married or cohabiting couple with or without their never-married children who have no children of their own, or a lone parent with such children. Most household surveys do not consider a person living alone to form a family. A household can contain one or more families and also members other than those belonging to a nuclear family (see Appendix: Part 2: Households and Families).

South Asian groups. South Asian families also tend to be larger and are more likely than those from other ethnic groups to live in households of two or more families. These South Asian households may contain three generations, with grandparents living with a married couple and their children. In contrast, a relatively high proportion of households headed by a member of the Black ethnic group are lone parent families.

Not all people live in a private household; some people are in accommodation that provides common catering facilities to inhabitants. The Census is currently the only comprehensive source of information on people living in this sort of communal establishment, which includes hospitals, prisons and accommodation for students and elderly people. In 1991 there were higher proportions of single and widowed people in communal establishments, and far lower

proportions of married people, than in the rest of the population. There were also greater proportions of people in the age groups 16 to 29 and 65 and over. This reflects the need to cater for students, young people, the ill and the infirm elderly.

The stage at which people are in their life-cycle influences the type of family in which they live. Children usually live with either both or one of their parents. As they become young adults they may move on either to live alone or with other unrelated young adults, or form a couple household with, or without, children. When the youngest child moves out of their parental home this household often becomes a couple household with no children and may eventually become a one person household if one of the partners dies. Couple households may also be changed by divorce or separation.

2.4

Ethnic group of head of household[1]: by type of household, Spring 1999

Great Britain   Percentages

	White	Black	Indian	Pakistani/ Bangladeshi	Other groups[2]	All[3]
One person	29	30	14	7	25	28
Two or more unrelated	3	6	..	..	8	3
One family households[4]						
Couple						
No children	29	10	18	9	13	28
Dependent children[5]	23	21	42	56	33	24
Non-dependent children only	7	3	8	7	..	7
Lone parent						
Dependent children[5]	6	24	5	8	13	7
Non-dependent children only	3	5	4	..	..	3
Multi-family households	-	..	7	10	..	1
All households[6]						
(=100%)(millions)	22.2	0.4	0.3	0.2	0.2	23.7

1 Percentages of heads of household in each ethnic group living in each household type.
2 Includes those of mixed origin.
3 Includes ethnic group not stated.
4 Other individuals who were not family members may also be included.
5 May also include non-dependent children.
6 Includes same sex couples, but percentages are based on totals which exclude this group.
Source: Labour Force Survey, Office for National Statistics

2.5

One noticeable change in the last couple of decades has been the increase in lone mother families. In 1971, 7 per cent of families with dependent children were lone mother families; by 1998-99 this had trebled to 22 per cent (Table 2.5). Before the mid-1980s much of the rise in lone parenthood was due to divorce, while since then single lone motherhood (never-married, non-cohabiting women with children) grew at a faster rate. Lone parenthood is not just a recent phenomenon. There is some evidence that lone parent families were just as frequent in the sixteenth and seventeenth centuries as they are now although they declined in the nineteenth and early twentieth century. However, widowhood was usually the cause for these families then, whereas today there are relatively few widowed lone parents.

Families headed by lone parents as a percentage[1] of all families with dependent children: by marital status

Great Britain							Percentages
	1971	1976	1981	1986	1991-92	1996-97	1998-99
Lone mother							
Single	1	2	2	3	6	7	9
Widowed	2	2	2	1	1	1	1
Divorced	2	3	4	6	6	6	8
Separated	2	2	2	3	4	5	5
All lone mothers	7	9	11	13	18	20	22
Lone father	1	2	2	1	1	2	2
Married/cohabiting couple[2]	92	89	87	86	81	79	75
All families with dependent children	100	100	100	100	100	100	100

1 Dependent children are persons under 16, or aged 16 to 18 and in full-time education, in the family unit, and living in the household.
2 Includes married women whose husbands are not defined as resident in the household.
Source: General Household Survey, Office for National Statistics

Partnerships

Changes in household and family patterns reflect changes in the partnering and marital status of the population over time. Marriage is still the usual form of partnership between men and women. However, the total number of marriages in the United Kingdom has fallen from a peak in 1972 (Chart 2.6). In 1997 there were 310 thousand marriages, among the lowest figures recorded during the twentieth century.

The number of first marriages has decreased substantially since its peak in 1970. In 1997 there were 181 thousand first marriages for both partners, less than half the number in 1970. Slightly over two-fifths of marriages in 1997 were remarriages for either or both partners. Early in the twentieth century remarriage was relatively uncommon, but since the 1960s the number of

2.6

Marriages and divorces

United Kingdom

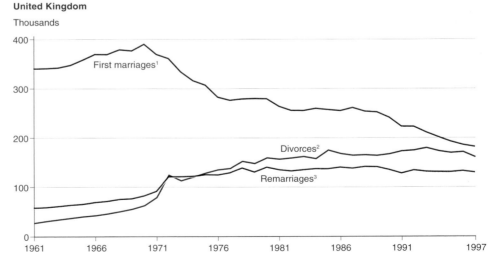

1 For both partners.
2 Includes annulments.
3 For one or both partners.
Source: Office for National Statistics; General Register Office for Scotland; Northern Ireland Statistics and Research Agency

remarriages has increased. While most of the few remarriages at the turn of the century in England and Wales involved a widow or widower, more recently at least one partner remarrying has usually been divorced. These trends were notably accentuated following the implementation of the *Divorce Reform Act 1969* in 1971.

Following falls in the average age at first marriage between 1919 and 1970, there has been a tendency for people to marry for the first time slightly later in life in recent years. Between 1971 and 1997 the mean age at first marriage in England and Wales rose from 24 years to 29 years for men, and from 22 years to 27 years for women. Rises in pre-marital cohabitation help to explain the recent trend towards later marriage,

but other factors such as the increased and longer participation in further and higher education, particularly among women, have also contributed.

The types of marriage ceremonies people have been able to choose have changed over time. Civil wedding ceremonies were first permitted in England and Wales under the *Marriage Act 1836* that was implemented the following year. This Act also allowed Catholics and Non-conformists to marry in their own place of worship. In 1995 the *Marriage Act 1994* came into force in England and Wales. The first part of the act allowed couples to marry by civil ceremony outside their district of residence, and the second part introduced the ability to marry in 'approved premises'. For venues to be registered as approved premises, the local authority must be satisfied that they are readily identifiable wedding venues that will support the dignity of marriage, and have no recent or continuing connection with any religion. There were just over 2 thousand approved premises in May 1998, about half of which were hotels.

Since the introduction of civil wedding ceremonies in 1837 there has been a shift away from religious to civil marriages. In 1993 the number of civil ceremonies started to outnumber religious ones, and by 1997 three in five weddings in Great Britain were conducted with civil ceremonies (Table 2.7). Differences exist between the types of ceremonies for first and subsequent marriages. In 1997 more first marriages had a religious than a civil ceremony but, for second and subsequent marriages, civil ceremonies outnumbered religious ones by four to one.

Over the past few decades there has been a trend for first marriages to last successively shorter periods of time. Analysis of the General Household Survey also suggests that women who were aged under 20 when they married for the first time were generally more likely to separate

2.7

Marriages: by type of ceremony

Great Britain			Percentages
	Religious ceremonies	Civil ceremonies	All marriages (=100%)(thousands)
First marriages[1]			
1971	..	..	380
1981	69	31	255
1991	67	33	215
1997	56	44	175
Remarriages[2]			
1971	..	..	67
1981	19	81	134
1991	25	75	126
1997	20	80	128
All marriages			
1971	60	40	447
1981	52	48	388
1991	51	49	341
1997	41	59	302

1 For both partners.
2 For one or both partners.

Source: Office for National Statistics; General Register Office for Scotland

within five years than women who married at older ages. About one in ten marriages entered into by teenage women in Great Britain during the late 1960s ended in separation within five years compared with one in four similar marriages that took place between 1985 and 1989 (Table 2.8).

Before 1857 a divorce could only be obtained by a private Act of Parliament and therefore was only available to a very wealthy few. The *Matrimonial Causes Act 1857* first introduced the possibility of being granted a divorce in a civil court in England and Wales. Until 1922 adultery was effectively the only ground for divorce, and a woman could only petition against her husband if his adultery was accompanied by one or more other specified matrimonial offences. The annual number of divorces remained relatively low and steady until the First World War. The additional conditions for petitioning wives were abolished in 1924, and the grounds for divorce were widened in 1938. In 1971 the *Divorce Reform Act 1969* was implemented, introducing 'the irretrievable breakdown of marriage' as the sole ground for divorce, removing the concepts of 'guilty party' and 'matrimonial offence'. The number of divorces increased dramatically in 1971 and 1972. The *Matrimonial and Family Proceedings Act 1984* reduced the effective minimum period after marriage that a petition for divorce could be filed from three years to one year. Recent data suggest the trend towards increasing numbers of divorces could have levelled out.

Legislative changes also help to explain trends that have occurred in the party petitioning for divorce and on which fact proven decrees are awarded. In the first two decades of the twentieth century the number of men filing for divorce in England and Wales outnumbered the number of women, with the exception of the war period. However, in 1925, following divorce law reform, over 60 per cent of all divorces were granted to

wives. This was the first time that the number of decrees awarded to wives decisively outnumbered those awarded to husbands; this did not happen again for another 50 years. There was a substantial increase in the proportion of decrees granted on petition of the husband in the 1940s and 1950s. However, in the 1970s and early 1980s the proportion of decrees granted to wives increased considerably and, in 1997, seven in ten decrees were awarded to women.

The most common reason overall for women to be granted divorce in 1997 was the unreasonable behaviour of their husbands, while for men it was the adultery of their wives (Chart 2.9). However, for men in their fifties, separation was the most common fact proven for divorce.

2.8

Women separated within five years of first marriage: by year of, and age at, marriage, 1998-99

Great Britain			Percentages
	Age at marriage		
	Under 20	20-24	25-29
Year of marriage			
1965-1969	*11*	*6*	*3*
1970-1974	*13*	*9*	*7*
1975-1979	*18*	*10*	*14*
1980-1984	*14*	*13*	*16*
1985-1989	*24*	*16*	*8*

Source: General Household Survey, Office for National Statistics

2.9

Decrees awarded: by fact proven, 1997

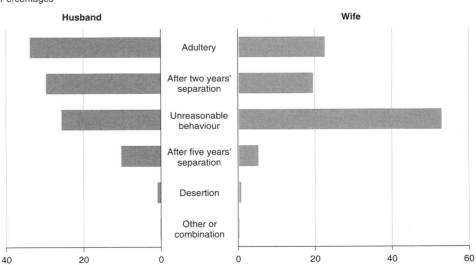

England & Wales
Percentages

Source: Office for National Statistics

2.10

Percentage of non-married[1] people cohabiting: by age and gender, 1998-99

Great Britain		Percentages
	Males	Females
16-19	1	8
20-24	18	27
25-29	39	39
30-34	44	35
35-39	36	29
40-44	31	26
45-49	28	16
50-54	17	16
55-59	18	12
All non-married aged 16 to 59	26	25

1 Includes separated, but legally married, people.

Source: General Household Survey, Office for National Statistics

One of the major changes in family patterns in recent decades, and a contributory factor towards the trend for later first marriage, has been the growth in cohabitation before marriage. Cohabitation prior to marriage was rare in the 1950s and early 1960s. Findings from the General Household Survey suggest that only a very small proportion of women in Great Britain, 2 per cent, whose first marriage was in the late 1960s had lived with their future spouse before marriage. By the early 1990s more first marriages were preceded with pre-marital cohabitation than not. In addition to the growing proportion of couples living together before marriage there has been an increase in the proportion of people cohabiting, irrespective of whether or not the cohabitation led to marriage. The proportion of all non-married women aged 18 to 49 who were cohabiting in Great Britain more than doubled between 1979 and 1998-99, from 11 per cent to 29 per cent. It is estimated by the Office for National Statistics that there were about 1.6 million cohabiting couples in England and Wales in 1996, and 1996-based projections suggest that the trend towards increasing cohabitation will continue in the future, although the total proportion of people living in couples is expected to fall.

While the social stigma associated with people living together without marrying has diminished in recent years, findings from the British Household Panel Survey in 1996 suggest that older people were more likely than people in younger age groups to think that 'living together outside marriage is always wrong'. These attitudes reflect people's experiences, as young people are generally more likely to cohabit than older people. Women also tend to cohabit at younger ages than men (Table 2.10). The peak age group for cohabitation among unmarried women in Great Britain in 1998-99 was 25 to 29, with 39 per cent of women cohabiting, while for men it was the 30 to 34 year age group, with 44 per cent of men cohabiting.

Findings from the Omnibus Survey indicate that the younger people are upon entering their first cohabiting union the less likely they are to marry their partner. As with marriage, cohabiting unions among younger people are more likely to end in relationship breakdown than those among older people.

2.11

Number of sexual partners in the previous year: by gender and age, 1998

England						Percentages
	16-19	20-24	25-34	35-44	45-54	All aged 16-54
Males						
None	48	14	7	8	11	13
One	24	49	78	80	82	71
Two or more	28	38	16	13	8	16
All males	100	100	100	100	100	100
Females						
None	30	17	9	10	13	13
One	37	53	81	86	85	76
Two or more	33	30	10	4	2	11
All females	100	100	100	100	100	100

Source: Health Education Monitoring Survey, Office for National Statistics and Health Education Authority

Results from the Health Education Monitoring Survey in 1998 suggest that only a relatively small proportion of people aged 16 to 54 in England had had more than one sexual partner in the previous year, and the proportion was lower for women than for men (Table 2.11). People aged 44 to 54 were less likely to have had two or more sexual partners in the last 12 months than younger people. Among men in their early twenties, 38 per cent said that they had had more than one sexual partner in the last year compared with 8 per cent of men in the 45 to 54 year age group.

In 1997 the Omnibus Survey found that 3 per cent of men under the age of 70 in Great Britain in had had sex at least once with another man, and about 2 per cent had only ever had same sex intercourse. However, these findings do not represent estimates of homosexual orientation as the survey was only investigating sexual behaviour.

Older people are less likely than younger people to have tolerant attitudes towards same sex sexual relations. In 1998 the British Social Attitudes Survey found that almost two-thirds of people aged 65 and over thought sexual relations between two adults of the same sex were 'always wrong' compared with less than a fifth of people aged 18 to 24. Overall almost two in five people thought such relationships were 'always wrong', with about one in five thinking they were 'not wrong at all' (Table 2.12). Four in five people thought it 'always' or 'mostly' wrong for a married person to have sexual relations with someone other than their spouse, and a similar proportion thought that sex between a boy and a girl aged under 16 was 'always' or 'mostly' wrong.

Family formation

Changes in fertility patterns influence the size of households and families, and also affect the age structure of the population. At the start of the twentieth century there were about 115 live births per 1,000 women aged 15 to 44 in the United Kingdom. The fertility rate has fluctuated since then, falling until the 1930s, rising up to the 1960s and then falling again. Since the early 1980s the fertility rate has been relatively stable. In 1998 there were less than 60 births per 1,000 women of childbearing age.

Women born around 1937 had the largest families of all women born in England and Wales since the 1920s, with an average of 2.4 children per woman. In the early 1970s fertility fell below the level needed for natural population change to keep the population at a stable size, and has remained below that level since.

2.12

Attitudes towards sexual relations[1], 1998

Great Britain Percentages

	Always wrong	Mostly wrong	Some-times wrong	Rarely wrong	Not wrong at all	Other[2]	All
A man and a woman having sexual relations before marriage	8	8	12	10	58	5	100
A married person having sexual relations with someone other than their spouse	52	29	13	1	2	4	100
A boy and a girl having sexual relations aged under 16	56	24	11	3	3	3	100
Sexual relations between two adults of the same sex	39	12	11	8	23	8	100

1 People aged 18 and over were asked whether they thought different types of sexual relations were wrong, on a five-point scale ranging from 'Always wrong' to 'Not wrong at all'.
2 Includes those who did not reply, those who replied 'don't know' and those responding 'depends' or 'varies'.
Source: British Social Attitudes Survey, National Centre for Social Research

2.13

Fertility rates: by age of mother at childbirth

United Kingdom						Live births per 1,000 women
	1961	1971	1981	1991	1997	1998
Under 20[1]	37	50	28	33	30	31
20-24	173	154	107	89	75	74
25-29	178	155	130	120	105	102
30-34	106	79	70	87	89	90
35-39	51	34	22	32	39	40
40 and over[2]	16	9	5	5	7	8
All ages[3]	91	84	62	64	60	59

1 Live births to women aged under 20 per 1,000 women aged 15 to 19 at last birthday.
2 Live births to women aged 40 and over per 1,000 women aged 40 to 44.
3 Total live births per 1,000 women aged 15 to 44.

Source: Office for National Statistics; General Register Office for Scotland; Northern Ireland Statistics and Research Agency

2.14

Conception rates of young women

England & Wales
Rates per 1,000 women[1]

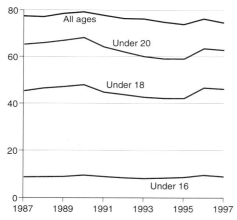

1 Rates for girls aged under 16, under 18 and under 20 are based on the population of girls aged 13 to 15, 13 to 17 and 13 to 19 respectively. Rates for all ages are based on the population of women aged 15 to 44.

Source: Office for National Statistics

Fertility patterns have also varied by age. In Victorian times women frequently continued to produce large families into their 30s and early 40s. Reductions in the age at marriage from the late 1930s reduced the average age at first birth so that it reached a minimum of just under 24 years from 1967 to 1970. In general fertility rates for older women have increased since the early 1980s while those for younger women have declined. The fertility rate for women aged 35 to 39 has risen fastest, nearly doubling between 1981 and 1998, although it still remains lower than in 1961 (Table 2.13). Women aged 25 to 29 are still the most likely to give birth, but since 1992 those in the 30 to 34 age group have been more likely to give birth than those aged 20 to 24. Later marriage, increased female participation in higher education and the labour market, and the greater choice and effectiveness of contraception have encouraged the trend towards the increased average age of mother at birth and the decline in the fertility rate.

Despite the overall trend towards later childbearing, the proportion of teenage girls becoming pregnant rose in the 1980s, following falls in the 1970s. By 1990 there were 68 conceptions per 1,000 women aged 13 to 19 in England and Wales; in 1997 the rate was slightly lower at 63 (Chart 2.14). In June 1999 the Social Exclusion Unit produced a report on teenage pregnancy and parenthood. One of the action points in the report was to halve the rate of conceptions among women aged under 18 by 2010. In 1997 the rate of conceptions to teenagers under 18 was 46 per 1,000 women aged 13 to 17 years. This rate has remained within the range of 42 to 48 conceptions for the last ten years. Slightly under two-thirds of conceptions to women aged under 20 in England and Wales in 1997 led to a maternity. For women of all ages about three-quarters of conceptions led to a maternity.

The total number of live births to teenage girls in England and Wales peaked at almost 87 thousand in 1966. By 1997 the number of births to teenagers had fallen to 46 thousand, representing a fall of 47 per cent from their peak compared with a decline of only 24 per cent in the total number of live births over the same period. Despite this fall, in 1995 the United Kingdom had the highest rate of live births to teenage women in the European Union – it was over twice the EU average (Chart 2.15). The Netherlands was the country with the lowest rate of births to teenagers, at 4.2 per 1,000 women aged 15 to 19, which was under half the EU average.

Births to teenage mothers are particularly likely to take place outside marriage. In 1998 almost nine in ten live births to women aged under 20 in England and Wales occurred outside marriage. Mothers in this age group are also the most likely to have a birth outside marriage that was registered without the father's details: 29 per cent of births to teenage mothers were solely registered by the mother.

With the exception of the periods immediately after the world wars, few births occurred outside marriage during the first 60 years of the twentieth century. From the 1960s and 1970s this proportion rose and the increase became more rapid from the late 1970s onwards. Almost four in ten live births in Great Britain in 1998 occurred outside marriage, more than four times the proportion in 1974 (Chart 2.16). Most of the increase in the number of births outside marriage since the late 1980s has been to cohabiting couples, that is parents living at the same address. In 1998 about four-fifths of births outside marriage were jointly registered by both parents; three-quarters of these births were to parents living at the same address.

The *1967 Abortion Act*, introduced in 1968, permitted termination of pregnancy by a registered practitioner subject to certain conditions. Following its introduction the number of abortions for women of all ages resident in England and Wales rose rapidly to 111 thousand in 1973. This fell to 102 thousand in 1976 but was followed by an upward trend through to 1990, after which numbers fell again each year to 1995. In October that year the Committee on Safety of Medicines issued a health warning that there was evidence that seven brands of the contraceptive pill carried an increased risk of thrombosis. The subsequent pill scare may have contributed to an increase in the number of abortions in 1996. By 1998 the number of abortions had continued to increase to 178 thousand. This continuing rise in the number of abortions may be due to longer term effects of the pill scare, or other unknown factors.

Live births to teenage women[1]: EU comparison, 1995

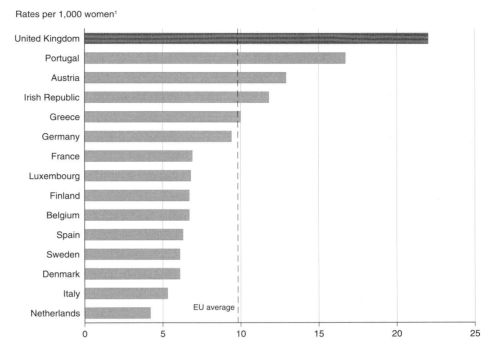

Rates per 1,000 women[1]

1 Rates per 1,000 women aged 15 to 19 at 31 December 1995.
Source: Eurostat; Office for National Statistics

Births outside marriage as a percentage of all live births

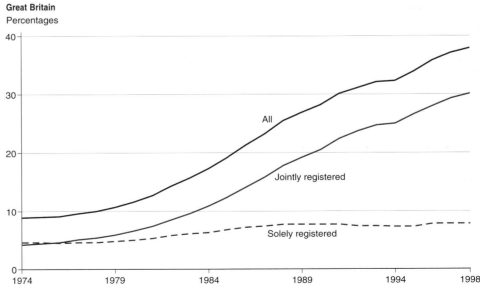

Great Britain
Percentages

Source: Office for National Statistics; General Register Office for Scotland

2.17

Abortion rates[1]: by age

England & Wales

Rates per 1,000 women

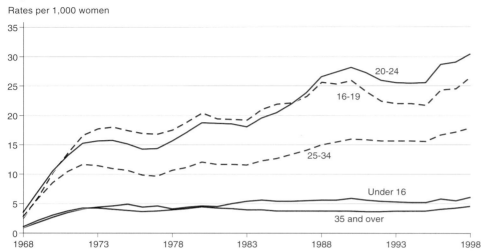

1 The rates for women aged under 16 are based on the population of women aged 14 and 15. The rates for women aged 35 and over are based on the population of women aged 35 to 49.

Source: Office for National Statistics

2.18

Percentage of women childless at age 25, 35 and 45[1]: by year of birth

England & Wales

Percentages

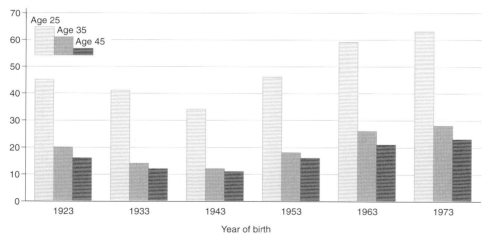

1 Data for women aged 35 born in 1973, and those aged 45 born since 1963, are projections. All other percentages are based on actual data up to the end of 1998.

Source: Office for National Statistics

Trends in abortion rates vary by age of the woman. Since 1968, abortion rates have risen particularly rapidly for women aged 16 to 19 and 20 to 24 (Chart 2.17). For women in these age groups the rates were about ten times higher in 1998 than those in 1968; increasing from 2.5 abortions per thousand women aged 16 to 19 in 1968 to 26.5 per thousand in 1998, and from 3.4 to 30.4 abortions per thousand women aged 20 to 24. For those under the age of 16 the number of abortions remains at a much lower level, although the rate has increased sixfold since 1968.

In 1998 the British Social Attitudes Survey asked adults in Great Britain about their attitudes to abortion. Around nine in ten people agreed that abortion should be allowed by law for women whose health is seriously endangered by pregnancy, or who become pregnant by rape. However, only just over half of people agreed that abortion should be allowed where the woman decides on her own that she does not wish to have the child, where the woman is not married and does not want to marry, or where the couples cannot afford any more children.

Part of the decline in fertility in recent years may be attributed to an increasing number of childless women. About 16 per cent of women born in 1923 were childless by the age of 45 (Chart 2.18). This proportion fell to only 11 per cent for women born in 1943, but then increased to 16 per cent for those born in 1953. Projections suggest that this will continue to increase so that about 23 per cent of women born in 1973 will be childless when they reach the age of 45.

Not all women may be childless through choice. In Vitro Fertilisation (IVF), where the egg is removed from the woman for fertilisation before being returned to the womb, became available for use in the United Kingdom in 1978. Since its introduction the total number of treatment cycles, and the success rate, have increased dramatically. In 1997-98, 34,638 cycles were carried out, nearly

Social Trends 30, © Crown copyright 2000

five times as many as in 1986. Over this period the number of live births as a percentage of the total number of treatment cycles has almost doubled from 8.6 per cent in 1986 to 16.4 per cent in 1997-98.

The availability and use of contraception allows people greater control over when to start a family and how many children to have. Most British middle-class families practised contraception by the 1900s, although it was still condemned by some professional bodies for its supposed spiritual and physical adverse effects. Contraception was not taught in medical schools until 1928. In 1998-99, 72 per cent of 16 to 49 year old women in Great Britain used some form of contraception (Table 2.19). In Northern Ireland the proportion of women of the same age using contraception was slightly lower at 63 per cent. In Great Britain the proportion of women who had been sterilised, or had a partner who had been sterilised, almost doubled between 1976 and 1986, although there has been little change since. The pill continues to be the most popular method of contraception overall.

Differences exist in the types of contraception used by women of different ages. In 1998-99, use of the pill was highest among women in their twenties in Great Britain, with 45 per cent of women saying they used this method. Sterilisation was most often used as a form of contraception among older people; 24 per cent of women in their forties had been sterilised, or had a partner who had been sterilised.

Adoption was placed on a legal footing in England and Wales by the *1926 Adoption Act*. The annual number of adoptions increased following the Act's introduction and further increased after the Second World War (Chart 2.20). Numbers remained fairly stable during the 1950s, at about 13 thousand adoptions per year. There was an increase in adoptions in the 1960s and numbers peaked in 1968. This rise is related to the increase

Contraception[1]: by method used

Great Britain				Percentages
	1976	1986	1995-96	1998-99
Non-surgical				
Pill	29	23	25	24
Male condom	14	13	18	18
IUD	6	7	4	5
Withdrawal	5	4	3	3
Injection	..	..	1	2
Cap	2	2	1	1
Safe period	1	1	1	1
Spermicides	..	1	-	-
Surgical				
Female sterilisation	7	12	12	11
Male sterilisation	6	11	11	12
At least one method	68	71	73	72

1 By women aged 16 to 49, except for 1976 which is for women aged 18 to 44.
Source: Family Formation Survey and General Household Survey, Office for National Statistics

2.20

Children adopted

England & Wales
Thousands

Source: Office for National Statistics

2.21

Percentage of dependent children[1] living in different family types

Great Britain				Percentages
	1972	1981	1991-92	1998-99
Couple families				
1 child	16	18	17	15
2 children	35	41	37	36
3 or more children	41	29	28	26
Lone mother families				
1 child	2	3	5	6
2 children	2	4	7	8
3 or more children	2	3	6	7
Lone father families				
1 child	-	1	-	1
2 or more children	1	1	1	1
All dependent children	100	100	100	100

1 See Appendix, Part 2: Families.

Source: General Household Survey, Office for National Statistics

2.22

Children in families of couples divorced: by age of child

England & Wales				Thousands
	1971	1981	1991	1998
Under 5	21	40	53	40
Aged 5-10	41	68	68	68
Aged 11-15	21	52	40	43
All aged under 16	82	159	161	150
All couples divorcing	74	146	159	145

Source: Office for National Statistics

in the number of births outside marriage. Since the late 1960s numbers have fallen so that the total of just over 4 thousand adoptions in 1998 was less than a fifth of the number in 1968. In particular, the number of children available for adoption has fallen since the introduction of legal abortion. Other factors include the use of contraception and changes in attitudes towards lone parents. There were also large falls in adoption in 1976 and 1977 just after the implementation of the *1975 Children Act*.

Family relationships

One consequence of the changes in family patterns in the last couple of decades has been the increasing diversity of home settings which children experience as they pass through childhood and adolescence. Since the 1970s there has been a growth in the proportion of children living in lone parent families. In 1972, 7 per cent of dependent children in Great Britain were living in such a family; by 1998-99 this proportion had increased to 23 per cent (Table 2.21). There has also been a decline in the proportion of children living in couple families with three or more children, from 41 per cent in 1972 to 26 per cent in 1998-99. In Northern Ireland a higher proportion of children live in these larger families – 37 per cent of children did so in 1998-99. However, despite these changes most children still live in couple families.

The number of divorces in England and Wales involving couples with children under the age of 16 peaked in 1993 at 95 thousand. In 1998 just over 150 thousand children experienced divorce in their family compared with 176 thousand in the peak year of 1993 and only 82 thousand in 1971 (Table 2.22). In 1998 around one in four children affected by divorce were under five years old, and about seven in ten were aged under ten years old. An analysis by the Office for National Statistics suggests that almost one in four children born in 1979 was likely to have been affected by divorce before reaching the age of 16.

Analyses of the National Child Development Study suggests people who experienced parental divorce during childhood are more likely to form partnerships at a younger age than those whose parents did not divorce. For example, 48 per cent of women born in 1958 who had experienced parental divorce during childhood had entered their first co-residential partnership as a teenager, compared with 29 per cent of women brought up with both parents. Furthermore, by the age of 33, men and women born in 1958 who had experienced parental divorce were also more likely to have experienced partnership and marriage dissolution themselves, although unobserved differences between those whose parents had divorced and those whose parents remained together could account for these findings.

Stepfamilies may be created when lone parents – whether single, separated or widowed – form new partnerships. These new families can be either married or cohabiting couples, with dependent children living in their family, one or more of whom are not the birth children of both the man and the woman. Information on stepfamilies is available from the General Household Survey. In 1996-97, stepfamilies with dependent children accounted for about 8 per cent of all families with dependent children in Great Britain where the head of family was aged under 60. In 84 per cent of stepfamilies at least one child was from a previous relationship of the woman, while in 12 per cent of families there was at least one child from the man's previous relationship. In 4 per cent of stepfamilies there were children from both partners' previous relationships.

Whether through choice or economic necessity a large proportion of young adults in England still live in their parental home into their mid-twenties, particularly men. In 1998-99 over half of men aged 20 to 24 lived with their parents, compared with just over a third of women (Table 2.23). In Northern Ireland the proportion of adults living with their parents is higher than in England: three-

quarters of men and over two-fifths of women aged 20 to 24 lived with their parents in 1998-99. Some young people may be delaying leaving home because of difficulties in entering the housing market. The later age at marriage may also be a factor despite the increasing tendency for people to leave home before marriage.

Findings from a special Omnibus Survey module in 1999 suggests that nearly all people in Great Britain have either a living parent or child, and many have both. With the exception of those in their fifties, close to three-quarters of people are members of three-generational families. Intergenerational exchanges of help are also fairly common. Most mothers with children aged under 18 years receive some help from their mothers, and half of mothers aged 50 and over receive help from their eldest child.

In 1995 the British Social Attitudes Survey asked people how often they saw relatives. Nearly half of adults in Great Britain with a mother living elsewhere saw her at least once a week while two-fifths saw their father as frequently (Table 2.24). Furthermore, 9 per cent of people reported never seeing their father compared with only 3 per cent never seeing their mother. Women were more likely than men to keep in contact with relatives.

Changes in relationship formation have meant living arrangements and family structures have become more diverse. Despite these changes, families continue to play a very important role in people's lives, with family contact and support being common.

2.23

Adults living with their parents: by gender and age

England			Percentages
	1977-78	1991	1998-99
Males			
20-24	52	50	56
25-29	19	19	24
30-34	9	9	11
Females			
20-24	31	32	38
25-29	9	9	11
30-34	3	5	4

Source: National Dwelling and Household Survey and Survey of English Housing, Department of the Environment, Transport and the Regions; Labour Force Survey, Office for National Statistics

2.24

Contact with relatives and friends[1], 1986 and 1995

Great Britain		Percentages
	1986	1995
Mother	59	49
Father	51	40
Sibling	33	29
Adult child	66	58
Other relative	42	35
'Best friend'[2]	65	59

1 Percentage of adult respondents seeing relative or friend at least once a week excluding those without the relative in question, as well as those living with this relative.
2 Best friend is the respondent's own definition.

Source: British Social Attitudes Survey, National Centre for Social Research

References and further reading

The following list contains selected publications relevant to **Chapter 2: Households and Families**. Those published by The Stationery Office are available from the addresses shown on the inside back cover of *Social Trends*.

Abortion Statistics (Series AB), The Stationery Office

Annual Report of the Registrar General for Northern Ireland, The Stationery Office

Annual Report of the Registrar General for Scotland, General Register Office for Scotland

Birth statistics (Series FM1), The Stationery Office

Birth statistics: historical series, 1837-1983 (Series FM1), The Stationery Office

British Social Attitudes, Ashgate Publishing

Human Fertilisation and Embryology Authority Annual Report, Human Fertilisation and Embryology Authority

Key Population and Vital Statistics (Series VS/PP1), The Stationery Office

Living in Britain: Results from the General Household Survey, The Stationery Office

Marriage, divorce and adoption statistics (Series FM2), The Stationery Office

Marriage and divorce statistics 1837-1983 (Series FM2), The Stationery Office

Population Trends, The Stationery Office

Social Focus on Children, The Stationery Office

Social Focus on Ethnic Minorities, The Stationery Office

Social Focus on Families, The Stationery Office

Social Focus on Older People, The Stationery Office

Social Focus on Women and Men, The Stationery Office

Teenage Pregnancy, Report by the Social Exclusion Unit, The Stationery Office

The British Population, Oxford University Press

The Fragmenting Family: Does it matter?, The Institute for Economic Affairs

The Legacy of Parental Divorce, ESRC Research Centre for Analysis of Social Exclusion

Contacts

Telephone contact points for further information relating to
Chapter 2: Households and Families

Office for National Statistics	
Chapter author	020 7533 5782
General Household Survey	020 7533 5444
Health Education Monitoring Survey	020 7533 5329
Labour market enquiries helpline	020 7533 6094
Marriages and divorces	01329 813772
Department of the Environment,	
Transport and the Regions	020 7944 3303
General Register Office for Scotland	0131 314 4243
General Register Office (Northern Ireland)	028 9025 2031
Human Fertilisation and Embryology Authority	020 7377 5077
Institute for Social and Economic Research	01206 872957
National Centre for Social Research	020 7250 1866 extn 347

Chapter 3 Education and Training

Schools, pupils and staffing

The number of pupils at school in England rose from 4.7 million in 1946/47 to 8.4 million in 1975/76. Declining birth rates led to a decline in pupils in the 1980s and since then numbers have increased but are still below the peak of the 1970s. (Chart 3.1)

In January 1999, 98 per cent of all four year olds in England were in early years provision. (Page 51)

In 1998/99, 93 per cent of secondary schools and 62 per cent of primary schools in England were connected to the internet. (Table 3.7)

Post-compulsory education

The proportion of 16 to 18 year olds in full-time education increased from 35 per cent in 1988 to 55 per cent in 1998. (Page 55)

In 1997/98, there were around 350 thousand students enrolled on postgraduate courses in the United Kingdom, nearly six times as many as in 1970/71. (Table 3.12)

Educational attainment

In 1998, 54 per cent of Indian pupils and 61 per cent of 'Other Asian' pupils in England and Wales achieved five or more GCSE grades A* to C, compared with 47 per cent of White pupils. (Page 57)

The proportion of young women in the United Kingdom achieving two or more A levels or equivalent has doubled since the mid-1970s, to 25 per cent. For young men there has been an increase of just under a half. (Chart 3.17)

Resources

Nearly three in ten eligible students in the United Kingdom had student loans in 1990/91; this increased to more than six in ten in 1997/98. (Table 3.27)

3.1

Pupils[1] in primary and secondary schools

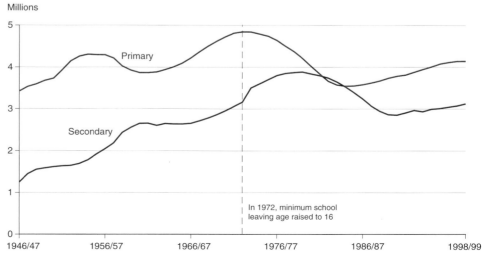

England

Millions

In 1972, minimum school leaving age raised to 16

1 Full-time pupils only.

Source: Department for Education and Employment

Education and training are no longer confined to early life as a precursor to work but are part and parcel of later life, of ongoing development and of job change. The emphasis now is on lifelong learning. Education starts earlier and continues longer.

Schools, pupils and staffing

The number of children of school age in the United Kingdom has fluctuated considerably since 1901. This is due to changes in the school-leaving age, in the birth rate and in infant mortality. At the beginning of the century, full-time attendance at school often stopped at the age of 12 when children were permitted to work part time, then the compulsory school-leaving age was raised to 14 in

1921 and to 15 in 1947. Between 1946/47 and 1980/81, the total number of pupils at school in England increased (Chart 3.1), firstly following the two 'baby booms' of 1946 and 1961, and then with the further raising of the school-leaving age, to 16 in 1972/73. (Information on births is shown in Chart 1.1 in the Population chapter.) The number of pupils at school in England rose from 4.7 million in 1946/47 to 8.4 million in 1975/76. Then declining birth rates during the late 1970s led to a decline in pupil numbers in the 1980s. Since then, pupil numbers have increased but are still below their peak level of the 1970s. By 1998/99, there were 7.3 million pupils in primary and secondary schools in England.

As well as the fluctuation in student numbers, there have been changes to the structure of secondary education. After the *1902 Education Act* established a national system of secondary schools, grammar schools received grants of public money and many new maintained secondary schools were built. Fees were charged for these schools. In 1907, grants to secondary schools were made dependent on the establishment of 25 per cent of free places for pupils recruited from public elementary schools. After the *1944 Education Act*, which fixed 11 as the age when children in state-run schools moved from primary to secondary education, the elementary schools were abolished. Primary school pupils aged 11 were required to take a test (the 11-plus) which determined the type of secondary school they attended. The top 20 per cent of pupils who passed the test proceeded to grammar schools; the rest went to secondary modern or technical schools.

In the 1960s, following the abolition of the 11 plus examination in many areas, comprehensive schools progressively replaced secondary modern and grammar schools. By 1998/99, 85 per cent of pupils in state secondary schools in the United Kingdom attended comprehensive schools

3.2

School pupils[1]: by type of school[2]

United Kingdom					Thousands
	1970/71	1980/81	1990/91	1994/95	1998/99[3]
Public sector schools[4]					
Nursery[5]	50	89	105	111	109
Primary[5]	5,902	5,171	4,955	5,230	5,376
Secondary					
Modern	1,164	233	94	90	92
Grammar	673	149	156	184	203
Comprehensive[6]	1,313	3,730	2,843	3,093	3,205
Other	403	434	300	289	291
All public sector schools	9,507	9,806	8,453	8,996	9,276
Non-maintained schools[4]	621	619	613	600	616
Special schools[7]	103	148	114	117	115
Pupil referral units	.	.	.	.	9
All schools	10,230	10,572	9,180	9,714	10,016

1 Head counts.
2 See Appendix, Part 3: Main categories of educational establishments and stages of education.
3 All data for Wales and data for nursery schools in Scotland are for 1997/98.
4 Excludes special schools.
5 Nursery classes within primary schools are included in primary schools except for Scotland from 1990/91 when they are included in nursery schools.
6 Excludes sixth form colleges from 1980/81.
7 Includes maintained and non-maintained sectors.

Source: Department for Education and Employment; National Assembly for Wales; Scottish Executive; Department of Education (Northern Ireland)

compared with 37 per cent in 1970/71, with much of this increase occurring during the 1970s (Table 3.2). The number of pupils attending special schools increased by 44 per cent between 1970/71 and 1980/81. Since then, the number attending this type of school has decreased, although the current level of 115 thousand is still higher than the 1970/71 level.

The number of pupils attending non-maintained schools has changed very little since 1970 at just over 600 thousand. Non-maintained schools are run by voluntary bodies, and include independent schools and non-maintained special schools. In 1998/99, 6 per cent of all full-time pupils attended independent schools in the United Kingdom. Since 1988, the number of full-time pupils aged under five attending independent schools has increased by 45 per cent, from 39 thousand, to 57 thousand in 1997. Over the same period, there was a 32 per cent increase in the overall number of under fives attending school.

This expansion of education for children under the age of five is one of the more striking changes in education. In 1970/71, around 20 per cent of three and four year olds in the United Kingdom attended schools and by 1998/99 this had risen to 62 per cent (Chart 3.3). Attendance for under fives in maintained nursery schools and primary schools in England varies widely between the government office regions: the percentage ranged from 84 per cent in the North East to under 50 per cent in the East of England, the South East and South West.

In January 1999, 98 per cent of all four year olds in England were in early years provision: 78 per cent were in maintained nursery and primary schools, 15 per cent in the private and voluntary sector and 5 per cent in independent schools. (Information on day care places is shown in Table 8.24 in the Social Protection chapter). The Government pledged it would provide a free early education place to all four year olds whose

parents want it by September 1998, with a place being defined as a two and a half hour session up to five times a week for 33 weeks of the year.

The Government has also pledged to reduce class sizes for five, six and seven year olds to a maximum of 30 in England and Wales by September 2001. In 1998/99, 18 per cent of classes at key stage 1 (ages 5 to 7) in England had more than 30 pupils, compared with 23 per cent in 1995/96 (Table 3.4). Between 1995/96 and 1998/99, the percentage of classes with more than 30 pupils fell in all the regions of England, with the exception of the East of England where it remained at 18 per cent. In contrast, the percentage in Scotland increased from 13 per cent in 1995/96 to 16 per cent over the three years, although average class sizes in Scotland

Children under five[1] in schools as a percentage of all children aged three and four

United Kingdom

Percentages

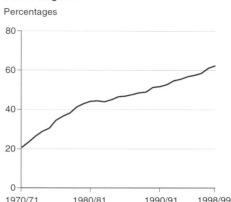

1 Pupils aged 3 and 4 at 31 December each year. Data for 1998/99 for Wales and Scotland relate to 1997/98.

Source: Department for Education and Employment; National Assembly for Wales; Scottish Executive; Department of Education (Northern Ireland)

Class sizes in primary schools[1] at key stage 1: by region, 1995/96 and 1998/99

	1995/96		1998/99	
	Average number in class	Percentage of classes of more than 30 pupils	Average number in class	Percentage of classes of more than 30 pupils
North East	26.5	18	25.8	13
North West	27.3	28	26.6	21
Yorkshire and the Humber	26.8	23	26.3	17
East Midlands	26.6	20	25.9	15
West Midlands	27.1	26	26.1	16
East	25.8	18	26.2	18
London	27.1	19	27.1	15
South East	26.7	23	26.9	22
South West	26.5	23	26.4	19
England	26.8	23	26.5	18
Wales	..	..	25.1	11
Scotland[2]	24.9	13	25.9	16

1 In England includes classes taught by one teacher only while figures for Wales and Scotland include classes where more than one teacher may be present.
2 In Scotland primary P1-P3 is equivalent to key stage 1. See Appendix, Part 3: Stages of education.
Source: Department for Education and Employment; National Assembly for Wales; Scottish Executive

3.5

Permanent exclusion rates[1]: by ethnic group, January 1998

England	Percentages
	January 1998
White	0.17
Black Caribbean	0.76
Black African	0.29
Black Other	0.57
Indian	0.06
Pakistani	0.13
Bangladeshi	0.09
Chinese	0.05
All	0.18

1 Number of permanent exclusions as a percentage of the number of full and part-time pupils of all ages.

Source: Department for Education and Employment

3.6

Students with a special educational need[1] statement in maintained schools: by type of school, January 1999

England

Percentages

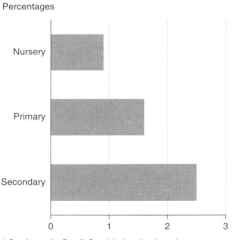

1 See Appendix, Part 3: Special educational needs.

Source: Department for Education and Employment

(at its equivalent of key stage 1) continued to be smaller than those in most of the regions of England. Wales has the lowest average class size at key stage 1 and the lowest proportion of classes with more than 30 pupils. More up-to-date information on class size data for England was published in October 1999.

Although the majority of pupils attend school regularly, there are some who truant or are permanently excluded. In December 1997, the Government set up the Social Exclusion Unit (SEU) to examine the economic, social and educational causes of alienation and disaffection. The SEU's first report looked at exclusions from school which reflected growing concerns about the perceived link between truancy or exclusion from school and welfare dependency, joblessness and crime.

Rates of exclusion from school have been mounting in recent years. However, the numbers permanently excluded from all schools in England fell by 3 per cent from 12,668 in 1996/97 to 12,298 in 1997/98. Boys accounted for 84 per cent of permanently excluded pupils in 1997/98. Ethnicity is also an important factor. While the overall exclusion rate was 0.18 per cent, the rate for Black Caribbean pupils was highest at 0.76 per cent, and lowest for Chinese pupils at 0.05 per cent (Table 3.5). Poor parental supervision and lack of commitment to education are crucial factors behind truancy. Children who are looked after by local authorities are ten times more likely to be excluded from school than other children. In addition, in 1997/98 the exclusion rate for children with special education needs (SEN) statements was 0.96 per cent, which was almost seven times the rate for pupils without statements. This represents a decrease from 1996/97 where the exclusion rate was almost eight times higher.

Almost 250 thousand pupils in schools in England had a SEN statement in January 1999. The percentage of pupils with statements has continued to climb from 2.6 per cent in 1995 and

2.9 per cent in 1998 to 3.0 per cent in 1999. The proportion with a statement varied by type of school, from 2.5 per cent in maintained secondary schools to 0.9 per cent in maintained nursery schools (Chart 3.6). The proportion of pupils in special schools and pupil referral units with a statement of SEN was 94 per cent and 23 per cent respectively.

The *Education Act 1981* and the *Education Act 1993* placed a qualified duty on local education authorities in England and Wales to ensure that children with a SEN should have their needs met wherever possible in mainstream schools. In Scotland, education authorities are also encouraged to integrate children with a SEN into mainstream schools wherever possible. In January 1999, 60 per cent of all pupils in England with statements of SEN were in maintained mainstream schools (nursery, primary and secondary), compared with 54 per cent in 1995. The percentage of all pupils with SEN statements who were placed in special schools (maintained and non-maintained) or pupil referral units (PRUs) fell to 38 per cent in 1999 from 44 per cent in 1995.

As technology has changed, so have the subjects that pupils study at school. Traditional subjects such as metalwork and woodwork have been replaced with information and computer technology (ICT). Increasing importance is placed on the use of technology in schools. In November 1998, the National Grid for Learning was set up. The grid involves the collection of data from schools and local education authorities and the sharing of these data with them and other government department and agencies. It will be used to help with learning in all subjects. The aim is to have all schools, colleges, universities and libraries connected to the Grid by 2002. In both 1997/98 and 1998/99 there was an average of 101 computers per secondary school in England, while the average in primary schools increased by around 20 per cent, to 16 per school in 1998/99

3.7

(Table 3.7). In addition, 93 per cent of secondary schools and 62 per cent of primary schools were connected to the Internet in 1998-99.

In the last decade or so, there have been changes in the number of primary and secondary school teachers. Between 1985 and 1998, the number of full-time secondary school teachers in England and Wales decreased by 21 per cent, from 237 thousand to 188 thousand. In contrast, the number of full-time teachers in primary schools increased over the same period from 172 thousand to 181 thousand, although the increase has fluctuated in intervening years. There have also been changes in the composition of the teaching profession. Between 1985 and 1998 the number of full-time female primary school teachers in England and Wales increased by 13 per cent, from 134 thousand to 151 thousand while the number of male teachers declined by 21 per cent (Chart 3.8). In 1998, females represented 83 per cent of all full-time primary school teachers compared with 78 per cent in 1985. In secondary schools, the gender split between full-time teachers is more balanced. However, the number of male full-time secondary school teachers fell by 31 per cent between 1985 and 1998, to 88 thousand, while the number of female teachers at this level has declined by 9 per cent, with most of the decline occurring in the 1980s.

In 1998, women made up 53 per cent of full-time secondary school teachers, compared with 46 per cent in 1985. Since 1986, the age structure of both primary and secondary school teachers has gradually become older. The proportion of full-time teachers aged under 40 has fallen from 58 per cent, to 40 per cent in 1998. There has been a corresponding rise in the proportion of teachers in the 40 to 49 age group, from 27 per cent to 41 per cent over the same period.

These changes in the age structure reflect a large cohort of teachers recruited in the 1970s, with smaller numbers of teachers recruited since then.

Computers in schools: by type of school, 1997/98 and 1998/99

England   Numbers

	Primary		Secondary		Special	
	1997/98	1998/99	1997/98	1998/99	1997/98	1998/99
Average computers per school	13	16	101	101	19	..
Average pupils per computer	18	13	9	8	4	..
Percentage of schools connected to the internet	17	62	83	93	31	..

Source: Department for Education and Employment

3.8

Full-time primary and secondary school teachers[1]: by gender

England & Wales

Thousands

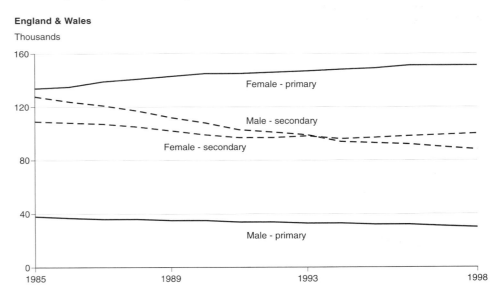

1 Qualified teachers only. As at 31 March of each year.

Source: Department for Education and Employment; National Assembly for Wales

3.9

Enrolments[1] on teacher training courses: by type of subject and course, 1998/99

England & Wales			Numbers
	PGCE[2]	Undergraduate	All
Primary	5,640	7,434	13,074
Secondary			
Science	2,193	221	2,414
English[3]	2,070	179	2,249
Languages	1,719	68	1,787
Physical education	779	801	1,580
Mathematics	981	210	1,191
History	983	0	983
Art	946	7	953
Design and technology	536	365	901
Geography	779	13	792
Religious education	642	17	659
Music	490	43	533
Other technology	380	128	508
Information technology	283	147	430
Other[4]	359	0	359
All secondary subjects	13,140	2,199	15,339
All enrolments	18,780	9,633	28,413

1 Head counts.
2 Post Graduate Certificate in Education.
3 Includes drama.
4 Includes classics, economics, other social sciences and other subjects.
Source: Department for Education and Employment; National Assembly for Wales

3.10

Young people in education and training[1]: by gender and age

England									Percentages
	1986	1988	1991	1993	1994	1995	1996	1997	1998
Males									
16	80	81	85	87	87	85	84	82	83
17	58	70	78	79	79	78	78	76	78
18	41	46	54	60	62	61	61	61	61
All aged 16-18	60	66	72	75	76	75	75	73	74
Females									
16	81	81	88	90	89	88	87	86	89
17	53	63	73	80	80	79	80	79	79
18	33	35	45	56	56	60	60	59	59
All aged 16-18	55	59	68	75	75	76	76	75	75

1 Data are at end of each year. All in full-time education and government-supported training plus employer-funded training and other education and training. There is a slight discontinuity in the data series in 1994 due to changes in the data sources. See Appendix, Part 3: Discontinuity in further and higher education statistics.
Source: Department for Education and Employment

In the autumn of 1997, the Teacher Training Agency launched a new, five year teacher recruitment strategy, with the slogan, 'No-one forgets a good teacher'. The aim is to attract more and better qualified candidates into the teaching profession, particularly graduates, to subject areas where labour market competition makes the recruitment of secondary school teachers difficult, such as mathematics, science, modern foreign languages and technology. It also aims to make teaching more representative of society as a whole by encouraging more applications from members of minority ethnic groups, men (especially into primary teaching) and people with disabilities, and to address regional differences in the pattern of supply and demand. In addition to this, the Government introduced, from September 1999, 'golden hello' incentives for those studying for secondary Post Graduate Certificate in Education (PGCE) in mathematics or science. Students receive £2,500 while they are training and a further £2,500 on taking up a relevant post in a maintained secondary school. The incentives will be extended to modern foreign languages from September 2000.

In 1998/99, around 15 thousand students were enrolled on secondary teacher training courses in England and Wales, 13 thousand of whom were taking PGCE courses (Table 3.9). Compared with the previous year, the number enrolled on a mathematics PGCE course in England and Wales decreased by 20 per cent and the number on a science PGCE decreased by 15 per cent. In 1998/99, the greatest percentage shortfall in the recruitment for teachers against the targets the Government set was for mathematics, followed by technology, and then modern languages.

Post-compulsory education

A number of factors, including an increased risk of unemployment and other forms of exclusion for young people with insufficient education, influence the decision to continue with education beyond the end of compulsory schooling. Over the last ten years, young people have become more likely to continue with their education. At the end of 1998, 74 per cent of those aged between 16 and 18 in England were in education or training compared with 62 per cent ten years previously. The proportion of 16 to 18 year olds in full-time education increased from 35 per cent in 1988 to 55 per cent in 1998, while the total proportion on government-supported education and training rose from 57 per cent to 67 per over the same period. The proportion of 17 year olds in education or training increased markedly between 1986 and the early 1990s, after which it remained fairly stable (Table 3.10). The increase in participation of 18 year olds has been most noticeable, particularly for women. In 1998, six in ten 18 year olds were in education or training compared with just over three in ten in 1986.

Although young people in the United Kingdom are increasingly likely to continue with their education, compared with the rest of Europe the United Kingdom has one of the lowest full-time participation rates of 16, 17 and 18 year olds in secondary and tertiary education. This can partly be explained by the compulsory school leaving age varying from country to country and the United Kingdom being one of the few countries to have a nationally recognised and labour market relevant qualification at age 16. The school leaving age in Europe varies between 14 (Italy and Portugal) and 18 (Belgium, Germany and the Netherlands) with the most common ages being 15 or 16. In 1996, full-time participation rates of 18 year olds in secondary education varied between 17 per cent in Greece and 93 per cent in Sweden (Chart 3.11).

During the twentieth century, there has been a substantial increase in the number of students in higher education in Great Britain. The number of students in full-time higher education has risen from 25 thousand at the beginning of the century, to more than twice as many between the wars, and then to 216 thousand in 1962/63. Between 1963/64 and 1972/73, the numbers of full-time home domiciled students doubled again to 453 thousand. Since then the numbers in higher education in the United Kingdom have continued to increase and by 1997/98 there were 1.2 million students enrolled on full-time higher education courses.

The number of enrolments by men on undergraduate courses in higher education institutions increased by around 83 per cent between 1970/71 and 1997/98. For women the increase has been even more dramatic, with more than four times as many enrolments as in the early 1970s. Whereas the number of students participating in all the categories of higher

3.11

Full-time participation rates by 18 year olds in secondary education: EU comparison[1], 1996

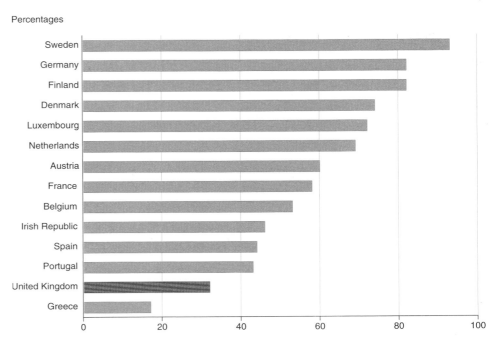

Percentages

1 Data for Italy are not available.

Source: OECD

3.12

Students[1] in further and higher education: by type of course and gender

United Kingdom   Thousands

	Males				Females			
	1970/71	1980/81	1990/91	1997/98[2]	1970/71	1980/81	1990/91	1997/98[2]
Further education[3]								
Full time	116	154	219	416	95	196	261	448
Part time	891	697	768	654	630	624	986	962
All further education	1,007	851	987	1,070	725	820	1,247	1,410
Higher education[4]								
Undergraduate								
Full time	241	277	345	498	173	196	319	554
Part time	127	176	193	174	19	71	148	235
Postgraduate								
Full time	33	41	50	75	10	21	34	66
Part time	15	32	50	105	3	13	36	102
All higher education[5]	416	526	638	918	205	301	537	1,021

1 Home and overseas students.
2 1997/98 figures are not quite comparable with other years since those refer to enrolments rather than headcounts. Further education institution data for England and Wales relate to 1996/97.
3 Dates differ by country, but are snapshots taken at around November each year. Excludes adult education centres.
4 At December each year. Includes Open University.
5 Data for 1997/98 include students whose level of study is unknown.

Source: Department for Education and Employment; National Assembly for Wales; Scottish Executive; Department of Education (Northern Ireland)

3.13

Participation rates[1] in higher education: by social class

Great Britain   Percentages

	1991/92	1992/93	1993/94	1994/95	1995/96	1996/97	1997/98	1998/99
Professional	55	71	73	78	79	82	79	72
Intermediate	36	39	42	45	45	47	48	45
Skilled non-manual	22	27	29	31	31	32	31	29
Skilled manual	11	15	17	18	18	18	19	18
Partly skilled	12	14	16	17	17	17	18	17
Unskilled	6	9	11	11	12	13	14	13
All social classes	23	28	30	32	32	33	33	31

1 The number of home domiciled initial entrants aged under 21 to full-time and sandwich undergraduate courses of higher education in further education and higher education institutions expressed as a proportion of the average 18 to 19 year old population. The 1991 Census provided the population distribution by social class for all years.

Source: Department for Education and Employment; Office for National Statistics; Universities and Colleges Admission Service

education has expanded, the number studying for postgraduate courses has grown the fastest. In 1997/98, there were nearly six times as many students enrolled on postgraduate courses as in 1970/71 (Table 3.12).

There are differences in participation in higher education across the ethnic and socio-economic groups. Students from ethnic minorities are more than proportionately represented in higher education compared with the general population. In 1998, ethnic minorities accounted for 13 per cent of young (under the age of 20) higher education students in the United Kingdom compared with 9 per cent of the total population of the same age. Students from the Indian and Chinese groups are more likely to continue with their education than other ethnic minority groups. However, young Bangladeshi and Pakistani women and young Black-Caribbean men and women are still under-represented in higher education. Between 1994 and 1998, the growth in participation by Bangladeshi women was particularly strong, increasing at four times the rate for White young women.

Young people (aged 21 and under) from the partly skilled and unskilled socio-economic groups are particularly under-represented in higher education in Great Britain. The participation rate for the unskilled group more than doubled, from 6 per cent in 1991/92 to 13 per cent in 1998/99 (Table 3.13). However, their participation rate is still only a fraction of that for the children of professional families. This, in part, reflects lower achievements at A level and equivalent for these groups.

Many adults continue their education, either for enjoyment or to develop new skills. Among the many general courses that are available are subjects as diverse as languages, physical education/sport/fitness and practical craft/skills. Nearly seven out of ten of all enrolments on adult education courses in England in November 1998 were for courses that do not lead to a formal qualification, for example, painting, basic languages and writers' workshops. In total, there were 1.1 million adults in England and Wales enrolled on adult education courses, and enrolment rates are higher for women than for men (Table 3.14).

Educational attainment

Schools pupils in England and Wales are formally assessed at three key stages before GCSE level – at the ages of 7 (key stage 1), 11 (key stage 2) and 14 (key stage 3). The assessments at all three key stages cover the core subjects of English, mathematics and science (and Welsh in Welsh speaking schools in Wales). The purpose of these tests is to help inform teachers and parents about the progress of individual pupils and to give a measure of the performance of schools. There are two forms of assessment: tests and teacher assessment. Pupils' attainment is shown as a level on the national curriculum scale. A typical 7 year old is expected to achieve level two, a typical 11 year old level four, and a typical 14 year old between levels five and six.

In 1999, girls again outperformed boys at all key stages in all subjects in teacher assessments (Table 3.15). However, similar proportions of boys as girls reached the expected level in tests for mathematics at key stages 2 and 3. The proportion of pupils achieving the expected level generally falls with age for both genders, with the biggest fall between key stages 1 and 2.

The Youth Cohort Study, which is conducted by the Department for Education and Employment, shows that the proportion of final year pupils in England and Wales achieving five or more GCSE grades A* to C has increased over the last decade, and at a faster rate for girls than boys. The performance of Indian and Other Asian pupils outstrips that of other ethnic groups. In 1998, 54 per cent of Indian pupils and 61 per cent of Other Asian pupils achieved five or more GCSE grades A* to C, compared with 47 per cent of

Enrolments on adult education courses: by age, type of course and gender, November 1998

England & Wales							Thousands
	Academic		Vocational		Other[1]		All enrol-ments[2]
	Males	Females	Males	Females	Males	Females	
16-18	4.8	7.7	4.5	7.0	14.7	21.6	60.3
19 and over	15.5	39.9	52.9	153.3	205.9	616.9	1,084.5
All aged 16 and over	20.3	47.6	57.3	160.3	220.6	638.6	1,173.6

1 Includes those on basic education and general courses (that is, languages, physical education/sport/fitness, practical craft/skills, other adult education).
2 The all aged 16 and over figure for Wales includes contracted out and assisted numbers, which are not available by age or qualification.

Source: Department for Education and Employment; National Assembly for Wales

Pupils reaching or exceeding expected standards[1]: by key stage and gender, 1999

England				Percentages
	Teacher assessments		Tests	
	Boys	Girls	Boys	Girls
Key stage 1[2]				
English	78	87	..	..
Mathematics	84	88	85	88
Science	85	88	..	..
Key stage 2[3]				
English	61	73	64	75
Mathematics	68	69	68	68
Science	74	75	78	78
Key stage 3[4]				
English	55	73	54	72
Mathematics	63	65	62	62
Science	59	62	55	55

1 See Appendix, Part 3: The National Curriculum: assessments and tests.
2 Percentage of pupils achieving level 2 or above at key stage 1.
3 Percentage of pupils achieving level 4 or above at key stage 2.
4 Percentage of pupils achieving level 5 or above at key stage 3.

Source: Department for Education and Employment

3.16

Examination achievements[1] of pupils[2] in schools: by gender and ethnic origin, 1998

England & Wales   Percentages

	5 or more GCSEs grades A* to C	1-4 GCSEs grades A* to C	No graded GCSEs
Males			
White	43	25	7
Black	23	24	7
Indian	52	23	2
Pakistani/Bangladeshi	29	29	6
Other groups[3]	37	28	11
All males	42	25	7
Females			
White	51	25	6
Black	35	42	7
Indian	55	28	3
Pakistani/Bangladeshi	32	45	6
Other groups[3]	52	31	3
All females	51	26	6

1 See Appendix, Part 3: Qualifications.
2 Pupils aged 16.
3 Includes those who did not state their ethnic group.
Source: Youth Cohort Study, Department for Education and Employment

3.17

Achievement at GCE A level or equivalent[1]: by gender

United Kingdom
Percentages

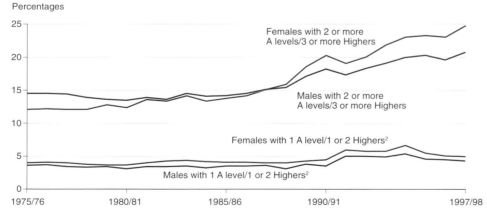

1 Based on population aged 17 at the start of the academic year. Data to 1990/91 (1991/92 in Northern Ireland) relate to school leavers. From 1991/92 data relate to pupils of any age for Great Britain while school performance data are used for Northern Ireland from 1992/93. Figures exclude sixth form colleges in England and Wales which were reclassified as FE colleges from 1 April 1993. Excludes GNVQ Advanced Qualifications throughout.
2 From 1996/97, figures only include two SCE Highers.
Source: Department for Education and Employment; National Assembly for Wales; Scottish Executive; Department of Education (Northern Ireland)

White pupils. The proportion achieving this is lowest among Black and Pakistani pupils at 29 per cent in 1998.

In all ethnic groups, girls do as well as, or outperform, boys at GCSE level (Table 3.16). In England and Wales, the greatest difference in performance between boys and girls in 1998 (excluding 'Other groups') was for pupils from the Black group. Twenty-four per cent of Black boys achieved one to four GCSE grades A* to C compared with 42 per cent of Black girls, while 23 per cent of Black boys achieved five or more GCSE grades A* to C compared with 35 per cent of Black girls. A greater proportion of Indian boys and girls achieved five or more GCSE grades A* to C than those in any other group. The performance of Indian pupils also outstripped that of other pupils at A level. In 1998, 36 per cent of Indian pupils achieved two or more A levels compared with 29 per cent of White pupils.

Overall, there has been an increase in the proportion of young men and women in the United Kingdom achieving two or more A levels or equivalent. The proportion of young women achieving this has doubled since the mid-1970s, to 25 per cent (Chart 3.17). The increase in the proportion of young men achieving this has been more modest, with a rise of just under a half over the same period. In 1987/88, an equal proportion of young men and women achieved two or more A levels or equivalent (15 per cent) but since 1988/89 women have outperformed men at this level. These figures exclude Advanced GNVQs; an advanced GNVQ is equivalent to two GCE A levels or AS equivalents.

Although the proportion of young people with GCSEs and GCE A levels has increased considerably over time, distinct geographical differences still exist. The proportion of Scottish pupils receiving their Certificate of Education is very striking (particularly for girls with 'Highers') (Table 3.18), but it should be noted that the

3.18

education system and examination structures are different in Scotland which means the results are not strictly comparable with those in England and Wales. To some extent, a north-south divide in achievement exists within England, with the North East, North West and Yorkshire and the Humber having lower proportions achieving five or more GCSEs and two or more A levels than the South East, South West and the East of England. Across all regions girls perform markedly better than boys.

While many people have enjoyed the benefits of education, there are some who have problems with basic literacy and numeracy. Research for the Basic Skills Unit by the Centre for Longitudinal Studies at the Institute of Education used data from the 1958 and 1970 birth cohort studies to investigate this. It found that adults with the lowest literacy or numeracy scores had long histories of low achievement starting at school and continuing into employment, where they were often the most marginalised participants in the labour market with women typically leaving it early, often to have children.

For the first time in 1996, Great Britain participated in the International Adult Literacy Survey which examined the levels of literacy of people aged 16 to 65 and some of the results are shown in Table 3.19. Literacy was measured on three scales: prose, document and quantitative. Prose literacy is the ability to understand such things as newspaper articles and passages of fiction; document literacy involves the ability to locate and use information in graphs, timetables and charts; and quantitative literacy is the ability to apply arithmetic operations, such as calculating the interest on your bank account. Performance was grouped into five literacy levels with level 1 being the lowest and level 5 being the highest. The Organisation for Economic Co-operation and Development considers level 3 to be the minimum level required to cope with modern life and work. See also the Appendix, Part 3: Literacy levels.

Examination achievements[1] of pupils in schools: by region and gender, 1997/98

Percentages

	2 or more GCE A levels[2]		5 or more GCSEs grades A*-C[3]		No graded GCSEs[3]	
	Males	Females	Males	Females	Males	Females
Great Britain	26	33	42	52	8	5
North East	19	25	35	43	10	7
North West	25	31	39	49	9	6
Yorkshire and the Humber	22	27	36	46	10	7
East Midlands	26	32	40	51	7	5
West Midlands	25	31	38	48	8	6
East	31	36	46	56	6	4
London	26	33	40	51	8	5
South East	32	39	47	58	7	5
South West	28	37	46	57	6	4
England	27	33	41	52	8	5
Wales	23	30	40	51	11	8
Scotland	25	33	50	61	5	4

1 See Appendix, Part 3: Qualifications.
2 Pupils aged 17 to 19 at the end of the school year in England and Wales as a percentage of the 18 year old population. For Scotland the figures relate to pupils in years S5/S6 gaining three or more SCE Higher passes as a percentage of the 17 year old population.
3 Pupils aged 16 at the end of the school year as a percentage of the 15 year old population at start of school year. Scotland pupils are in year S4.

Source: Department for Education and Employment; National Assembly for Wales; Scottish Executive

3.19

Document literacy level of adults[1]: by gender and age, 1996

Great Britain

Percentages

	Males			Females		
	16-49	50-65	All aged 16-65	16-49	50-65	All aged 16-65
Level 1	15	31	20	22	40	27
Level 2	24	29	25	30	30	29
Level 3	33	28	31	31	24	30
Level 4/5	28	12	24	17	6	15
All	100	100	100	100	100	100

1 Level 1 is the lowest level of literacy; level 4/5 is the highest. See Appendix, Part 3: Literacy levels.
Source: Adult Literacy Survey, Office for National Statistics

3.20

Economically active adults qualified to at least NVQ level 3 or above[1], Spring 1999

United Kingdom
Percentages

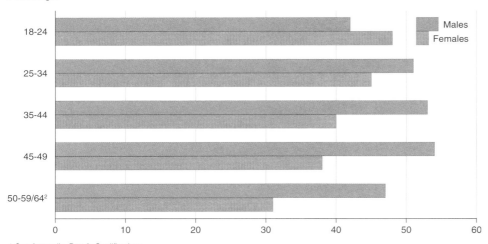

1 See Appendix, Part 3: Qualifications.
2 Men aged 50 to 64; women aged 50 to 59.
Source: Department for Education and Employment from Labour Force Survey

3.21

National Learning Targets[1]

England   Percentages

	Males			Females			All		
	1997	1998	1999	1997	1998	1999	1997	1998	1999
Young people									
85 per cent of 19 year olds with an NVQ level 2 qualification	69	70	74	72	74	75	71	72	75
60 per cent of 21 year olds with an NVQ level 3 qualification	51	51	55	46	49	52	48	50	54
Adults[2]									
50 per cent of adults with an NVQ level 3 qualification	46	48	49	36	38	40	41	42	45
28 per cent of adults with an NVQ level 4 qualification	24	25	26	24	25	26	24	25	26

1 At Spring each year. Targets relate to objectives for the year 2002. See also Appendix, Part 3: National Learning Targets.
2 Males aged 18 to 64 and females aged 18 to 59, who are in employment or actively seeking employment.
Source: Department for Education and Employment from Labour Force Survey

In general, a greater proportion of women than men in Great Britain had lower levels for both document and quantitative literacy, although there was little gender difference on the prose scale. In addition, a greater proportion of those aged 50 to 65 than those aged under 50 had lower levels on all three types of literacy scales. On the document scale, 70 per cent of older women and 60 per cent of older men scored at the lower levels of 1 and 2 compared with around 52 per cent of women and 39 per cent of men in the 16 to 49 age group.

Literacy is strongly associated with education, the proportion of people performing at the higher literacy levels increasing with their level of education. In addition, for those aged over 25, men were better qualified than women and the difference in attainment increased with age. Fifty-one per cent of men aged 25 to 34 were educated to at least NVQ level 3 compared with 45 per cent of women in this age group. Among those aged 50 and over, 47 per cent of men were educated at this level compared with 31 per cent of women. In Spring 1999, there was little difference between the qualification levels of men and women aged 18 to 24, reflecting women's greater recent participation in further and higher education (Chart 3.20).

In recent years, much emphasis has been placed on the concept of 'lifetime learning'. The Government has set National Learning Targets for England which are that by 2002, 85 per cent of 19 year olds will be qualified to NVQ level 2 or its equivalent and 60 per cent of 21 year olds will be qualified to NVQ level 3 or its equivalent. In England, steady progress has been made towards the targets. In 1999, 75 per cent of 19 year olds and 54 per cent of 21 year olds met these standards (Table 3.21).

In addition to these targets for young people, a set of targets also exists for adults of working age. The first states that by the year 2002, 50 per cent of the workforce is to be qualified to NVQ level 3 or its equivalent, while the second states that

3.22

28 per cent of the workforce will have a professional, vocational, management or academic qualification at NVQ level 4 or above. By 1999, 45 per cent and 26 per cent of adults had achieved levels 3 and 4 qualifications respectively.

Training

In England and Wales the Government supports a number of training initiatives. Work-based training for Young People is a government initiative that ensures that young people are in education or in training. It consists of National Traineeships (NTr), Modern Apprenticeships (MA) and 'Other Training', which replaced Youth Training from April 1998. These programmes aim to provide participants with training leading to vocational qualifications for NTr and MA at NVQ levels 2 and 3 or above. Between 1990-91 and 1998-99, the number of young people in work-based training increased by more than a third (Table 3.22). In 1998-99, there were around five times as many young people on the Modern Apprenticeship scheme than in 1995-96, when they were first introduced. In contrast, the number on Other Training (formerly Youth Training) has decreased by over 40 per cent during the same period. In addition, there were 38 thousand young people in work-based training in Scotland in 1997-98.

As well as supporting work-based training for young people, the Government also supports work-based learning for adults. In March 1999, Work-based Learning for Adults replaced Work-based Training for Adults in England and Wales which had been in existence since April 1998; prior to that it was known as Training for Work and Employment Training. This scheme is designed to help unemployed and disadvantaged adults find jobs through training and work experience, and is open to those age 18 to 63 who have been unemployed for six months or longer.

Work based training for young people[1]: by type of training

England & Wales   Thousands

	Modern Apprenticeships[2]	National Traineeships[3]	Other Training[4]	Total
1990-91	.	.	209.5	209.5
1991-92	.	.	249.6	249.6
1992-93	.	.	246.9	246.9
1993-94	.	.	250.2	250.2
1994-95	.	.	239.5	239.5
1995-96	27.8	.	224.2	252.0
1996-97	81.9	.	203.9	285.8
1997-98	117.7	0.8	168.7	287.2
1998-99	134.6	30.4	120.5	285.6

1 Numbers in training at the end of the period.
2 Modern Apprenticeships was launched as an initiative in September 1994 and was fully operational from September 1995.
3 National Traineeships were introduced nationally in September 1997. Figures for Wales are not available for 1997-98.
4 Formerly Youth Training.
Source: Department for Education and Employment; National Assembly for Wales

The proportion of adult leavers who were in a job within six months of leaving the scheme increased between 1991-92 and 1996-97 and then levelled off in 1997-98. In 1997-98, 44 per cent of adults were in a job within six months of leaving compared with 33 per cent in 1991-92 (Chart 3.23). A greater proportion of women than men were in a job following this type of training. Although the primary aim of work-based training for adults is to get people into jobs, working towards a recognised qualification is also an important feature of the programme. In both 1996-97 and 1997-98, the proportion of men in England and Wales gaining a qualification was slightly higher than the proportion of women.

Training and development in the workplace are increasingly important aspects of working life for employees. The proportion of men and women of working age in the United Kingdom who had received job-related training in the four weeks prior to interview has increased since 1995, with a slightly greater proportion of women than men

3.23

Leavers from work-based training that were in a job within six months[1] of leaving training

England & Wales

Percentages

1 Those who had completed the agreed training when they left the training programme: Employment Training in 1991/92; Employment Training and Employment Action in 1992/93; Training for Work from April 1993 onwards.
Source: Department for Education and Employment; National Assembly for Wales

3.24

Employees[1] receiving job-related training[2]: by occupation and method of training, Spring 1999

United Kingdom   Percentages

	On-the-job training only	Off-the-job training only	Both on and off-the-job training	All methods of training
Professional	7	15	6	28
Associate professional and technical	5	14	6	25
Managers and administrators	4	9	2	15
Personal and protective services	5	9	3	18
Sales	4	9	2	15
Clerical and secretarial	5	8	2	15
Craft and related	3	5	3	12
Plant and machine operatives	3	3	1	7
Other occupations/no answer	2	4	1	7
All occupations	4	9	3	16

1 Excludes unpaid family workers and those on government schemes.
2 Data are for people of working age (males aged 16 to 64 and females aged 16 to 59) receiving job-related training in the four weeks prior to the interview.

Source: Department for Education and Employment, from Labour Force Survey

3.25

Government expenditure on education in real terms[1]: by type

United Kingdom   £ million at 1997-98 prices[1]

	1995-96[2]	1996-97[2]	1997-98
Schools			
Nursery and primary	10,449	10,462	10,951
Secondary	9,894	9,979	9,924
Special	1,638	1,675	1,699
Higher, further and continuing education[2]	11,969	11,744	11,460
Other education expenditure	1,032	1,336	1,384
Total	34,983	35,197	35,418
Related education expenditure	3,275	2,987	2,841
VAT incurred on above expenditure	793	823	818
Total expenditure	39,050	39,007	39,077
Total expenditure as a percentage of GDP	5.1	5.0	4.8

1 Adjusted to 1997-98 prices using the GDP market prices deflator.
2 Figures include expenditure on training programmes in England (such as Work Based Training for Young People) reclassified as education.

Source: Department for Education and Employment; National Assembly for Wales; Scottish Executive; Department of Education (Northern Ireland)

having done so. The amount and type of job-related training varies in different occupations. Professionals, associate professionals and those in technical occupations were the most likely to receive training, with over one in four in each of these groups having doing so in the four weeks prior to being interviewed (Table 3.24). Plant and machine operatives were the least likely of the occupations shown to receive any form of training.

Resources

Total government expenditure on education was some £39.1 billion in 1997-98 (Table 3.25) – expenditure on nursery and primary education accounting for £11 billion. Total expenditure on education as a percentage of GDP was 4.8 per cent.

In 1998 the British Social Attitudes Survey asked people aged 18 and over in Great Britain about their highest priority for extra government spending on education. The response varied according to the family circumstances of the respondent. Respondents who had children aged 16 or under felt that the highest priority for extra spending on education should be primary school children (Chart 3.26). Respondents who did not have any children aged 16 or under in the household felt the greatest priority should be given to secondary school children. Very few people, 9 per cent in total, felt that students at colleges and universities should be given the highest priority for extra government spending on education.

3.26

In recent years, funding higher education has become a pressing concern. In 1997 a report of the National Committee of Inquiry into Higher Education recognised that further improvement and expansion of higher education cannot be afforded on the basis of current funding arrangements. As a result, new student support arrangements for those in higher education in the United Kingdom came into effect on 12 August 1998. From 1998/99, new entrants to full-time higher education courses have, with certain specified exceptions, been expected to contribute towards the cost of their tuition (up to £1,000 in 1998/99), the amount depending on their own, and if appropriate their parent's or spouse's income.

In 1990/91 student loans were introduced as part of the student support package and have gradually replaced grants. The proportion of students taking out student loans has increased rapidly since 1990/91 (Table 3.27). Nearly three in ten eligible students in the United Kingdom had student loans in 1990/91 and by 1997/98 this had increased to more than six in ten. New entrants to higher education from 1998/99 receive support for living costs solely through loans that are partly income-assessed. Grants for living costs are no longer available except in special circumstances.

Attitudes[1] towards highest priority for extra government spending on education, 1998

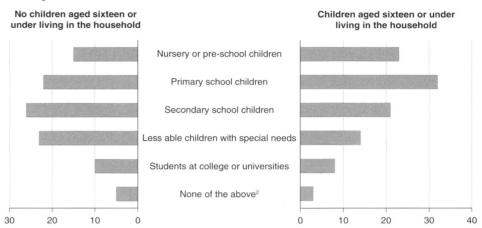

Great Britain

Percentages

| No children aged sixteen or under living in the household | | Children aged sixteen or under living in the household |

Nursery or pre-school children

Primary school children

Secondary school children

Less able children with special needs

Students at college or universities

None of the above[2]

1 People aged 18 or over were asked to give one of the above responses to the question 'Which group would be your highest priority for extra government spending on education?'.
2 Includes those who replied 'don't know' or refused to answer.

Source: British Social Attitudes Survey, National Centre for Social Research

3.27

Students taking out student loans[1]

United Kingdom	Percentages
	Students
1990-91	28
1991-92	36
1992-93	41
1993-94	47
1994-95	55
1995-96	59
1996-97	62
1997-98	64

1 Loans as a percentage of eligible students. See Appendix, Part 3: Student support.

Source: Department for Education and Employment

References and further reading

The following list contains selected publications relevant to **Chapter 3: Education and Training**. Those published by The Stationery Office are available from the addresses shown on the inside back cover of *Social Trends*.

Achievement for All, HM Inspectors of Schools, Scotland

Adult literacy in Britain, The Stationery Office

Annual Survey of Trends in Education, National Foundation for Educational Research

Basic Skills of Young Adults, Basic Skills Agency

Bridging the gap: new opportunities for 16-18 year olds not in education, employment or training, Social Exclusion Unit

British Social Trends Since 1900, MacMillan

Difficulties with Basic Skills, Basic Skills Agency

Education and Training Statistics for the United Kingdom, The Stationery Office

Education at a Glance, OECD

Examination Results in Scottish Schools, HM Inspectors of Schools, Scotland

Higher Education in the Learning Society, The Stationery Office

Higher Education Statistics for the United Kingdom, The Stationery Office

It Doesn't Get Any Better, Basic Skills Agency

Raising Behaviour 2, Nil Exclusion?, Policy and Practice, NFER

Scottish Education Statistics, The Stationery Office

Social Focus on Children, The Stationery Office

Social Focus on Ethnic Minorities, The Stationery Office

Social Focus on Women, The Stationery Office

Statistical Bulletins, from: Department for Education and Employment, Scottish Executive; Department of Education (Northern Ireland)

Statistics of Education, The Stationery Office

Statistics of Education and Training in Wales, Welsh Office

Truancy and Social Exclusion, Social Exclusion Unit

Vocational Qualifications in Northern Ireland, Department of Higher and Further Education, Training and Employment (Northern Ireland)

Contacts

Telephone contact points for further information relating to
Chapter 3: Education and Training

Office for National Statistics	
Chapter author	020 7533 5807
Labour market statistics helpline	020 7533 6094
Department for Education and Employment	01325 392658
Department of Education (Northern Ireland)	01247 279472
Department of Higher and Further Education, Training and Employment (Northern Ireland)	028 9025 7625
National Assembly for Wales	029 2082 3507
Scottish Executive	0131 2447927
Centre for Longitudinal Studies, Institute of Education	020 7612 6900
National Centre for Social Research	020 7250 1866

Chapter 4 Labour Market

Overview

The 1901 Census notes that around 10 per cent of 10 to 14 year old boys in Great Britain were already 'engaged in occupations' and nearly 40 per cent of men aged 75 or over were still in work. (Page 67)

Economic activity

Between Spring 1971 and Spring 1999, the proportion of economically active women in the United Kingdom increased from 56 per cent to 72 per cent. (Chart 4.4)

In 1996-97, over three-fifths of couples with dependent children had both partners in employment; this compares with around half in 1979-80. (Chart 4.6)

Type of employment

Between 1901 and 1991 the proportion of employees working in agriculture fell from 12 per cent to 2 per cent. In contrast, the proportion working in office jobs more than doubled from 18 per cent to 40 per cent over the same period. (Chart 4.1)

In Spring 1999, around 24 per cent of female, and 15 per cent of male full-time employees in the United Kingdom worked some form of flexible working patterns. (Table 4.17)

Time at work

Compared with the rest of Europe, full-time employees in the United Kingdom worked on average the longest hours in 1998, at 45.7 hours a week for men and 40.7 hours for women. (Table 4.18)

Unemployment

In Spring 1999, 22 per cent of unemployed men in the United Kingdom had been unemployed for two years or more compared with 11 per cent of unemployed women. (Chart 4.22)

The working environment

The Labour Force Survey shows that trade union membership in Great Britain fell by 1.9 million (21 per cent) between 1989 and 1998, although there was little change in the latest year. (Page 78)

4.1

Workforce: by selected industry

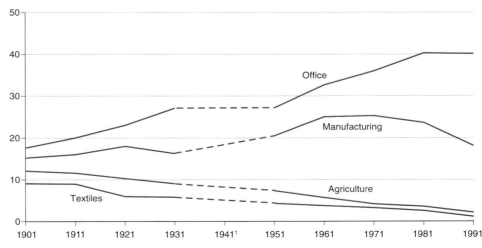

Great Britain

Percentages

1 There was no Census in 1941.

Source: Census, Office for National Statistics

4.2

Population of working age[1]: by employment status and gender, Spring 1999

United Kingdom			Millions
	Males	Females	All
Economically active			
In employment			
Full-time employees	11.4	6.2	17.7
Part-time employees	0.9	4.6	5.6
Self-employed	2.2	0.7	3.0
Others in employment[2]	0.1	0.1	0.2
All in employment	14.7	11.7	26.4
Unemployed[3]	1.1	0.6	1.7
All economically active	15.8	12.3	28.2
Economically inactive	3.0	4.8	7.8
Population of working age	18.8	17.1	35.9

1 Males aged 16 to 64, females aged 16 to 59.
2 Those on government employment and training schemes and unpaid family workers.
3 Based on the ILO definition. See Appendix, Part 4: ILO unemployment.
Source: Labour Force Survey, Office for National Statistics

After completing their initial education, most people join the labour force for a good deal of the rest of their lives. Over the years, the structure of the labour force has changed considerably. For example, more and more women have entered paid employment, particularly part-time work, and returned to work after having their children.

Overview

In Spring 1999 there were 35.9 million people of working age in the United Kingdom; 26.4 million of whom were in employment (Table 4.2), which is the highest level since the current records began in 1959. Conversely, the employment rate was below the 1990 level due to growth in the population - nearly three-quarters of the population of working age were employed in Spring 1999. ILO unemployment is at its lowest level since the current series began in 1984.

Glossary of terms

Employees (Labour Force Survey measure) - a measure, obtained from household surveys, of people aged 16 and over who regard themselves as paid employees. People with two or more jobs are counted only once.

Self-employed - a measure, obtained from household surveys, of people aged 16 and over who regard themselves as self-employed, ie who in their main employment work on their own account, whether or not they have employees.

In employment - a measure, obtained from household surveys and censuses, of employees, self-employed people, participants in government employment and training programmes, and people doing unpaid family work.

Government employment and training programmes - a measure, obtained from household surveys, of those who said they were participants on Youth Training, Employment Training, Employment Action or Community Industry or a programme organised by a TEC/LEC.

ILO unemployed - an International Labour Organisation (ILO) recommended measure, used in household surveys such as the Labour Force Survey, which counts as unemployed those aged 16 and over who are without a job, are available to start work in the next two weeks, who have been seeking a job in the last four weeks or are waiting to start a job already obtained.

Economically active (labour force) - those **in employment** plus those **ILO unemployed.**

ILO unemployment rate - the percentage of the **economically active** who are **ILO unemployed.**

The economically inactive - people who are neither in employment nor ILO unemployed. For example, all people under 16, those looking after a home or retired, or those permanently unable to work.

Economic activity rate - the percentage of the population in a given age group which is economically active.

Social Trends 30, © Crown copyright 2000

4.3

Changes which have taken place over the course of the century have been influenced, among other things, by demographic factors, such as changes in the birth and death rates (see Chapter 1: Population), differences in attitudes and in pension provision, and the raising of compulsory school-leaving age. At the beginning of the twentieth century, the absence of a formal, state-supported benefit system meant that most people had to engage in some form of paid employment as the only means they had of supporting themselves. Consequently, males tended to enter the labour market at an early age and leave it fairly late. The 1901 Census identified around 10 per cent (140 thousand) of 10 to 14 year old boys in Great Britain who were already 'engaged in occupations' and nearly 40 per cent (around 110 thousand) of men aged 75 or over were still working. Nowadays, children have to stay in education until they are 16 and due to the increase in pension provision (both public and private), very few men (less than one in ten) are in employment after they reach the state pension age of 65.

Labour force[1]: by gender and age

United Kingdom   Millions

	16-24	25-44	45-54	55-59	60-64	65 and over	All aged 16 and over
Males							
1971	3.0	6.5	3.2	1.5	1.3	0.6	16.0*
1981	3.2	7.1	3.0	1.4	1.0	0.3	16.0
1991	3.1	8.1	3.0	1.1	0.8	0.3	16.4
1997	2.4	8.1	3.4	1.1	0.7	0.3	16.0
2001[2]	2.4	8.2	3.4	1.3	0.7	0.3	16.3
2011[2]	2.8	7.3	3.9	1.3	0.9	0.3	16.5
Females							
1971	2.3	3.5	2.1	0.9	0.5	0.3	10.0
1981	2.7	4.6	2.1	0.9	0.4	0.2	10.9
1991	2.6	6.1	2.4	0.8	0.3	0.2	12.4
1997	2.0	6.4	2.9	0.8	0.4	0.2	12.7
2001[2]	2.1	6.4	3.0	0.9	0.4	0.2	13.1
2011[2]	2.3	6.2	3.6	1.0	0.7	0.2	14.1

1 The former civilian labour force definition of unemployment has been used to produce the estimates for 1971 and 1981; in later years the ILO definition has been used and members of the armed forces excluded.
2 Data for 2001 and 2011 are based on Spring 1996 Labour Force Survey and mid-1996 based population projections.
Source: Census and Labour Force Survey, Office for National Statistics

4.4

Economic activity

The number of young people aged 16 to 24 either in work or available for work in the United Kingdom fell by nearly a million between 1971 and 1997 (Table 4.3). One of the reasons for this is that there are fewer young people than there were 30 years ago, since the birth rate was low in the second half of the 1970s (see Chart 1.1 in the Population chapter). In addition, a much higher proportion of those of compulsory school-leaving age continue in full-time education than previously (see Table 3.10 in the Education and Training chapter). At the other end of our working life, fewer men are in the labour force than in the past. The number of men aged 60 to 64 in the labour force has declined by nearly half since 1971.

Economic activity rates[1]: by gender

United Kingdom

Percentages

1 Males aged 16 to 64, females aged 16 to 59. The percentage of the population that is in the labour force. The definition of the labour force changed in 1984 when the former Great Britain civilian labour force definition was replaced by the ILO definition which excludes members of the armed forces.
Source: Labour Force Survey, Office for National Statistics

4.5

Economic activity status of women[1]: by marital status and age of youngest dependent child, Spring 1999

United Kingdom
Percentages

	Age of youngest dependent child				No dependent children	All[1]
	Under 5	5-10	11-15	16-18[2]		
Not married/cohabiting[3]						
Working full time	11	19	32	48	47	40
Working part time	20	30	32	25	20	22
Unemployed[4]	7	11	6	..	5	6
Economically inactive	62	39	31	21	28	32
All (=100%)(millions)	0.7	0.6	0.4	0.1	4.5	6.2
Married/cohabiting						
Working full time	21	25	37	41	50	38
Working part time	38	50	42	38	25	34
Unemployed[4]	3	3	2	..	2	2
Economically inactive	38	22	19	20	23	25
All (=100%)(millions)	2.3	1.7	1.2	0.5	5.2	10.9

1 All women aged 16 to 59
2 Those in full-time education.
3 Includes single, widowed, separated or divorced.
4 Based on the ILO definition. See Appendix, Part 4: ILO unemployment.
Source: Labour Force Survey, Office for National Statistics

4.6

Couples[1] with dependent children: by number of earners

Great Britain
Percentages

1 Married and cohabiting couples with males aged 16 to 64 and females aged 16 to 59. See also Appendix, Part 4: Labour market analyses.
2 Calendar years up to 1987.
Source: General Household Survey, Office for National Statistics

One of the most striking overall features of the labour market is that women are taking an increasingly important role. In 1971, 56 per cent of women in the United Kingdom were economically active (that is, either in work or seeking work); this had risen to 72 per cent by Spring 1999 (see Chart 4.4 on the previous page). While the proportion of economically active women has increased, the proportion of economically active men has declined. In 1971, 91 per cent of men were economically active compared with 84 per cent in Spring 1999. Projections, which are only available for Great Britain, indicate a further narrowing of the gender gap.

The increase in the female labour force during the twentieth century has come mainly from a strong rise in the participation rates of married women. A major change took place during and immediately following the Second World War. By Spring 1999, 75 per cent of married or cohabiting women of working age in the United Kingdom were economically active (Table 4.5).

Among women with dependent children, those who are married or cohabiting are more likely to be economically active than lone mothers. The differences in economic activity rates between the two groups of women are most pronounced when their children are younger. In Spring 1999, just over six in ten married or cohabiting women with pre-school age children were economically active, compared with nearly four in ten lone mothers. The availability of suitable childcare provision is one of the determining factors in whether a mother works full time, part time, or not at all. The 1995 British Social Attitudes Survey found that the most common form of childcare for working mothers in Great Britain was provided by either a relative or their partner. Just over three in five working mothers with children under 12 said that their partner or a relative looked after their children.

Social Trends 30, © Crown copyright 2000

4.7

The proportion of working age households which are workless (that is, those with no one in employment) has roughly doubled over the last 20 years. This is partly related to the change in structure of households (see Chapter 2: Households and Families). Nevertheless, the proportion of households which were workless increased from 14 per cent in Spring 1990 to 19 per cent in Spring 1996; since then it has decreased to 17 per cent in Spring 1999.

The increasing participation of women in the labour force has led to an increase in the proportion of couples in Great Britain with dependent children where both partners are in employment, and a decrease in the proportion of households where only the man is working (Chart 4.6). According to the General Household Survey, in around 50 per cent of couples with dependent children both adults were in employment in the early 1980s. By 1994-95 this had increased to 62 per cent and stayed at this level until 1996-97. In contrast, the proportion of couple families with only the man in employment has decreased from around 40 per in the early 1980s to 26 per cent in 1996-97. The proportion of couple families with no earners has fluctuated between 6 and 11 per cent since the beginning of the 1980s.

Disability has long been recognised as a barrier to employment. In order for valid comparisons to be made between men and women with disabilities, the analysis in Table 4.7 is limited to those aged 16 to 59, as the likelihood of having a long-term health problem or disability increases with age. In Spring 1999, the economic activity rate for disabled people aged 16 to 59 in the United Kingdom was 54 per cent compared with 85 per cent for non-disabled people of the same age. (See Appendix, Part 4: Disabled people for the definition used.) In addition, unemployment rates

for disabled people tend to be higher than for non-disabled people; the ILO unemployment rate for disabled people was 11 per cent compared with 5 per cent for non-disabled people in Spring 1999.

Economic activity rates vary widely between people from the different ethnic groups in Great Britain (Table 4.8). The variation between the ethnic groups is greatest among women. In 1998-99, the economic activity rate among women of working age in the White, Black Caribbean and 'Other Black' groups was between 72 and 77 per cent. This compared with far lower rates of 19 per cent and 30 per cent for Bangladeshi and Pakistani women, partly reflecting cultural tendencies within these two ethnic groups. Among men of working age there was less variation: the activity rates were highest for White men (85 per

Economic activity status of disabled[1] people: by gender, Spring 1999

United Kingdom			Percentages
	Males	Fe-males	All
In employment			
Working full time	47	23	34
Working part time	6	21	14
All in employment	52	44	48
Unemployed[2]	7	4	6
Economically inactive	40	52	46
All disabled (=100%)			
(millions)	2.8	3.1	5.9

1 People aged 16 to 59 with current long-term or work-limiting disability. See Appendix, Part 4: Disabled people.
2 Based on the ILO definition. See Appendix, Part 4: ILO unemployment.
Source: Labour Force Survey, Office for National Statistics

4.8

Economic activity rates[1]: by ethnic group, gender and age, 1998-99[2]

Great Britain								Percentages
	Males				Females			
	16-24	25-44	45-64	All aged 16-64	16-24	25-44	45-59	All aged 16-59
White	79	94	78	85	71	77	71	74
Black Caribbean	74	88	72	81	53	78	68	72
Black African	53	84	81	77	34	67	55	59
Other Black groups	..	85	..	80	..	79	..	77
Indian	60	94	71	80	52	70	51	62
Pakistani	54	88	55	71	37	29	21	30
Bangladeshi	52	85	..	68	31	..	..	19
Chinese	31	83	70	62	..	65	66	62
None of the above[3]	54	82	82	75	55	59	69	60
All ethnic groups[4]	77	93	77	85	69	75	70	73

1 The percentage of the population that is in the labour force.
2 Combined quarters: Spring 1998 to Winter 1998-99.
3 Includes those of mixed origin.
4 Includes those who did not state their ethnic group.
Source: Labour Force Survey, Office for National Statistics

4.9

Reasons for economic inactivity[1]: by gender, Spring 1999

United Kingdom   Percentages

	Males	Females	All of working age
Does not want a job	68	71	70
Wants a job but not seeking in last four weeks			
Long-term sick or disabled	15	6	10
Looking after family or home	2	13	9
Student	5	3	3
Discouraged worker[2]	1	1	1
Other	5	4	4
All	28	26	27
Wants a job and seeking work but not available to start[3]	4	3	3
All reasons (=100%)(millions)	3.0	4.8	7.8

1 At Spring each year. Males aged 16 to 64, females aged 16 to 59.
2 People who believed no jobs were available.
3 Not available for work in the next two weeks. Includes those who did not state whether or not they were available.
Source: Labour Force Survey, Office for National Statistics

4.10

Full and part-time employment[1]: by gender

United Kingdom
Millions

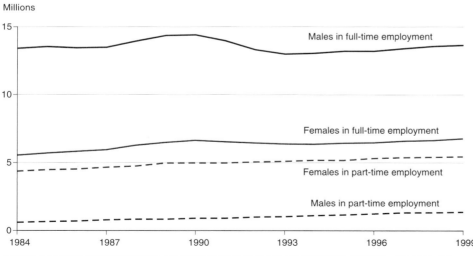

1 At Spring each year. Includes employees, self-employed, those on government employment and training schemes and, from 1992, unpaid family workers. Full/part-time is based on respondents' self-assessment.
Source: Labour Force Survey, Office for National Statistics

cent) and Black Caribbean, Other Black and Indian men, all at around 80 per cent. The rates for Chinese, Pakistani and Bangladeshi men were lower – around 60 to 70 per cent.

People who do not have a job and either do not want one, or who are not both seeking and available to start a job, are termed economically inactive. This includes people who have retired, long-term sick or disabled, discouraged workers and students. In Spring 1999 there were 7.8 million people in the United Kingdom who were economically inactive (Table 4.9). The most common reason for economic inactivity among men of working age who wanted a job but had not sought one in the four weeks before interview was long-term sickness or disability. For women the most common reason was looking after the family and home.

Type of employment

More and more people are working part time, although women are more likely than men to do so. Since 1984 (the earliest date for which figures are available on a consistent basis) the rate of increase in part-time working has been higher among men. The number of men working part time in the United Kingdom has more than doubled while the number of women in part-time work has increased by only a quarter (Chart 4.10). Reasons for working part time differ between men and women. In Spring 1999, around 80 per cent of women said they worked part time because they did not want a full-time job, compared with about 40 per cent of men. Most of these women did not want a full-time job because they wanted to spend more time with their family, or had other domestic commitments. Men were far more likely than women to be working part time because they could not find a full-time job – 21 per cent of men compared with 8 per cent of women.

Despite the increase in part-time working, about three times as many people are employed full time as are employed part time. In Spring 1999, 13.6 million men were in full-time employment, a similar number as in 1984. However, the number of women in full-time paid employment has increased by a fifth over the period.

In 1993 the British Household Panel Survey gathered information from women of all ages on their working life histories. It is possible from this analysis to find out how the working patterns of 30 year old women with and without children have changed during the twentieth century. For women with children, 30 per cent of those born in the 1900s had a job at some point during the year in which they were 30 (Table 4.11). For women born in the 1940s this proportion increased to nearly 50 per cent and for those who turned 30 in the early 1990s, the proportion in paid work was just over 50 per cent.

Employment rates for women without children have been consistently higher than for those with children. Just over 70 per cent of those who were born in the 1900s and were childless at the age of 30, had a job; over 90 per cent of such women in the early 1990s were in employment. It should be noted that this analysis gives higher numbers of women in employment than if a count had been

taken at a single point in the year, but it does indicate that women with or without children are more likely to be working now than in the past.

Employment rates vary between different areas of the United Kingdom, with inner city areas and former industrial areas having particularly low rates in recent years. Chart 4.12 looks at employment rates for the former counties in England and Wales and regions in Scotland. In Spring 1999, Glasgow had the lowest employment rate of these types of areas in the United Kingdom, with 53 per cent of its working age population in employment. However, there are often wide differences within these areas. For example, parts of Inner London, such as Tower Hamlets, have lower employment rates than Glasgow.

The pattern of industrial employment in Great Britain has changed considerably since 1901. Most notable has been the growth of the service sector and the decline in the agriculture and textiles sectors (see Chart 4.1 at the beginning of the chapter). In 1901, 12 per cent of the workforce were employed in agriculture; by 1991 this had declined to 2 per cent. The proportion working in the mining and transport industries also halved during this time. In contrast, the proportion working in office jobs more than doubled from 18 per cent to 40 per cent over the same period.

In June 1999, 23 per cent of male employee jobs were in the manufacturing industries, while 40 per cent of female employee jobs were in 'other services', an umbrella heading including health, education and public administration services.

4.11

Women aged 30 in employment[1]: by birth cohort, 1993

Great Britain			Percentages
	With children	Without children	All
Year of birth			
1900-1909	30	71	47
1910-1919	22	74	42
1920-1929	34	78	50
1930-1939	36	85	48
1940-1949	48	86	56
1950-1959	52	94	65
1960-1963	54	92	67

1 In employment at any time at age 30.

Source: British Household Panel Survey, Institute for Social and Economic Research

4.12

Employment rates[1]: by area[2], Spring 1999

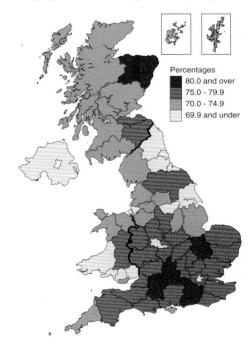

Percentages
- 80.0 and over
- 75.0 - 79.9
- 70.0 - 74.9
- 69.9 and under

1 Total employed as a percentage of all people of working age.
2 Counties and former counties, except for Northern Ireland.

Source: Labour Force Survey, Office for National Statistics

4.13

Employees[1]: by gender and occupation, 1991 and 1999

United Kingdom	Males		Females	Percentages
	1991	1999	1991	1999
Managers and administrators	16	19	8	11
Professional	10	11	8	10
Associate professional and technical	8	9	10	11
Clerical and secretarial	8	8	29	26
Craft and related	21	17	4	2
Personal and protective services	7	8	14	17
Selling	6	6	12	12
Plant and machine operatives	15	15	5	4
Other occupations	8	8	10	8
All employees[2] (=100%)(millions)	11.8	12.4	10.1	10.8

1 At Spring each year. Males aged 16 to 64, females aged 16 to 59.
2 Includes a few people who did not state their occupation. Percentages are based on totals which exclude this group.
Source: Labour Force Survey, Office for National Statistics

4.14

Self-employment: by gender and industry, Spring 1999

United Kingdom	Males	Females	Percentages All persons
Construction	27	2	21
Distribution, hotels and restaurants	18	23	19
Banking, finance and insurance	19	18	19
Public administration, education and health	5	24	10
Manufacturing	7	7	7
Agriculture and fishing	7	4	6
Transport and communication	8	3	6
Other services	8	19	11
All industries[1] (=100%)(millions)	2.4	0.8	3.2

1 Includes those in energy and water supply industries for which figures are not shown separately because of the small sample sizes. Also includes those who did not state industry and those whose workplace was outside the United Kingdom, but percentages are based on totals which exclude these groups.
Source: Labour Force Survey, Office for National Statistics

Women employees outnumbered men in the clerical and secretarial occupations in the United Kingdom by nearly three to one in Spring 1999, while there were nearly twice as many men as women managers and administrators (Table 4.13). However, in recent years, there has been some breakdown in traditional gender differences. For example, the proportion of managers and administrators who were women increased from 30 per cent in Spring 1991 to 33 per cent in Spring 1999.

In Spring 1999, 16 per cent of men in employment and 7 per cent of women in employment were self-employed. Over a quarter of self-employed men worked in the construction industry compared with around one in 50 women. Conversely, around one in 20 self-employed men worked in the public administration, education and health industries compared with one in four self-employed women (Table 4.14). Wanting to be independent was the most common reason given by both men and women for becoming self-employed, more so among men (33 per cent) than women (26 per cent).

Self-employment is particularly high among some ethnic groups. In 1998-99, employed Pakistani and Bangladeshi people were more likely than any other group in Great Britain to be self-employed (Chart 4.15). Those from the Black group were least likely to be so. A greater proportion of self-employed people from the Indian, Pakistani/Bangladeshi and Chinese groups worked in the distribution, hotels and restaurant industries than in any other industry group. Self-employed people from the White group were more likely than those

4.15

from ethnic minority groups to work in the construction industry while those from the Black group were spread more evenly across the different industries.

During the first half of the 1990s an increasing number of employers used temporary workers to help meet their changing requirements. Temporary workers include people on fixed-term contracts, agency temps, casual workers and seasonal workers. The proportion of men working in temporary jobs increased rapidly between Spring 1991 and Spring 1995 from 3.9 per cent to 6.3 per cent (Chart 4.16). Since then, it has fluctuated and in Spring 1999, 6.3 per cent of men were in temporary employment. However, this is still low compared with the level of temporary employment in most EU countries.

Women are more likely than men to work in temporary jobs. For women there was an increase between 1992, when 6.8 per cent of women were in temporary employment, and 1997, when 8.5 per cent of women were in this type of employment. The last two years have seen a slight decline in the proportion of women in temporary employment and by Spring 1999, the proportion doing so was 7.6 per cent. In Spring 1999, there were 1.6 million temporary employees in the United Kingdom accounting for around 7 per cent of all employees. Gender differences are apparent when employees give reasons for taking on temporary work. A higher proportion of women than men state that they do not want a permanent job, whereas a higher proportion of men than women state that they cannot find a permanent job.

Self-employment[1]: by ethnic group, 1998-99[2]

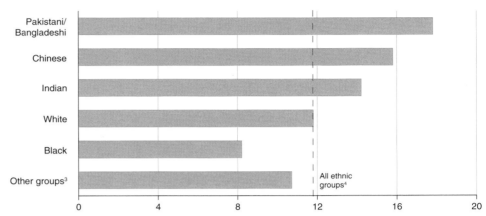

Great Britain
Percentages

1 Percentage of all in employment who were self-employed.
2 Combined quarters: Spring 1998 to Winter 1998-99.
3 Includes those of mixed origin.
4 Includes those who did not state their ethnic group.
Source: Labour Force Survey, Office for National Statistics

4.16

Temporary employees[1]: by gender

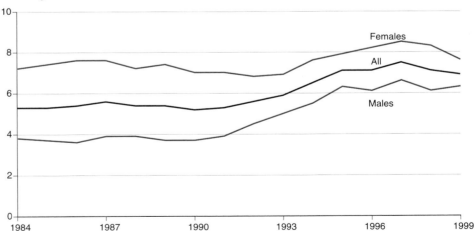

United Kingdom
Percentages

1 As a percentage of all employees. Temporary employees are those who assess themselves to have either a seasonal or casual job, a job done under contract or for a fixed period, or were temporary for some other reason. At Spring each year.
Source: Labour Force Survey, Office for National Statistics

4.17

Employees with flexible working patterns[1]: by gender, Spring 1999

United Kingdom			Percentages
	Males	Females	All employees
Full-time employees			
Flexible working hours	8.4	13.3	10.2
Annualised working hours	2.9	3.0	2.9
Four and a half day week	2.5	1.9	2.3
Term-time working	1.0	4.6	2.3
Nine day fortnight	0.4	0.2	0.3
Any flexible working pattern[2]	15.5	23.5	18.3
Part-time employees			
Flexible working hours	5.9	8.1	7.7
Annualised working hours	1.4	2.3	2.1
Term-time working	4.8	10.1	9.2
Job sharing	-	2.7	2.3
Any flexible working pattern[2]	15.1	24.2	22.6

1 Percentages are based on totals which exclude people who did not state whether or not they worked a flexible working arrangement.
2 Includes other categories of flexible working not separately identified.

Source: Labour Force Survey, Office for National Statistics

4.18

Average hours usually worked[1] per week by full-time employees: by gender, EU comparison, 1998

	Hours	
	Males	Females
United Kingdom	45.7	40.7
Portugal	42.1	39.6
Greece	41.7	39.3
Spain	41.2	39.6
Germany	40.4	39.3
Luxembourg	40.3	37.4
France	40.3	38.7
Austria	40.2	39.8
Sweden	40.2	40.0
Finland	40.1	38.2
Italy	39.7	36.3
Denmark	39.3	37.7
Netherlands	39.2	38.5
Belgium	39.1	37.5
EU average[2]	41.3	39.0

1 Excludes meal breaks but includes regularly worked paid and unpaid overtime.
2 Average calculated with 1997 data for Irish Republic.

Source: Labour Force Surveys, Eurostat.

In general, women are more likely than men to have flexible working patterns. In Spring 1999, around 24 per cent of women full-time employees in the United Kingdom had flexible working patterns compared with around 15 per cent of men (Table 4.17). The most common form of flexible working for full-time employees was flexible working hours (flexi-time). This was also the most common option for men working part time. For women part-timers, however, the most common form of flexible working was term-time working. In Spring 1999 around half a million women in the United Kingdom worked during term-time. However, it should be noted that this includes teachers. Home working was also more prevalent among women than men. Around 3.6

per cent (441 thousand) of women in employment in the United Kingdom mainly worked from home compared with 1.4 per cent (202 thousand) of men.

Time at work

On 1 October 1998 the Working Time Regulations became law in the United Kingdom. The main provision of the regulations requires employers to ensure that workers do not work, against their will, more than an average of 48 hours a week. (This is usually averaged over a period of 17 weeks, although it can be up to a year.) In addition, it gives workers an entitlement to four weeks' paid annual leave. In Autumn 1998, full-time employees in the United Kingdom received an average of 24 days annual leave. The Working Time Regulations do not apply to the genuinely self-employed. Nor do they apply to transport, sea fishing and other work at sea and junior hospital doctors because of the differing needs of the work performed.

In Spring 1999, 22 per cent of full-time employees in the United Kingdom usually worked in excess of 48 hours per week, with men more likely to work these longer hours than women. Compared with the rest of the European Union (EU), full-time employees in the United Kingdom work on average the longest hours per week (Table 4.18). In 1998 male full-time employees in the United Kingdom usually worked on average 45.7 hours a week in their main job, while female full-time employees worked on average 40.7 hours a week. For the rest of the EU, average hours usually worked by male full-time employees varied from 39.1 in Belgium to 42.1 in Portugal. For female

4.19

full-time employees, the hours varied from 36.3 in Italy to 40.0 in Sweden. Research for the Institute for Employment Studies identified work pressure and a long hours culture as two of the main reasons that employees in the United Kingdom work long hours. In addition, it was identified that working long hours can have an adverse impact on personal relationships and, in some instances, could lead to ill health.

In the United Kingdom, sickness absence rates follow a seasonal trend, with the rates being highest during the winter months. The proportions of men and women who have been absent from work owing to sickness in the United Kingdom have remained fairly steady over the years, with women slightly more likely to be absent than men. In Spring 1999, 5.0 per cent of women and 3.8 per cent of men had been absent from work for at least one day in the week preceding interview. For both men and women, the proportion having at least one day off sick in the reference week was highest for those in the pre-retirement age groups (Table 4.19).

(Chart 4.20). In Spring 1999 the ILO unemployment rate was 6.8 per cent for men and 5.1 per cent for women. These are the lowest rates since the ILO measure became available in 1984.

The claimant count (the number of people claiming unemployment related benefits and national insurance credits) has also been falling since the early 1990s, and both the level and rate are now at their lowest since 1980. However, the rate is still higher than that which prevailed from the end of the Second World War until the mid-1970s.

Employees absent from work owing to sickness or injury[1]: by gender and age

United Kingdom			Percentages
	1984	1991	1999
Males			
16-24	3.3	4.2	4.8
25-44	3.3	3.7	3.4
45-54	3.5	3.6	3.7
55-59	4.5	5.5	4.6
60-64	6.1	5.9	5.2
65 and over	..	..	..
All aged 16 and over	3.6	4.0	3.8
Females			
16-24	4.3	5.8	5.0
25-44	4.0	5.4	5.0
45-54	4.7	5.7	4.9
55-59	5.0	7.1	5.8
60 and over	3.0	4.7	4.1
All aged 16 and over	4.3	5.6	5.0

1 At Spring each year. Absent from work for at least a day during the reference week due to sickness or injury.

Source: Labour Force Survey, Office for National Statistics

4.20

Unemployment

The number of unemployed people is linked to the economic cycle, albeit with a time lag. Broadly speaking, as the country experiences economic growth so unemployment falls. Conversely, as the economy slows and goes into recession so unemployment tends to rise. The latest peak in unemployment occurred in 1993. Between Spring 1993 and Spring 1999 the number of people unemployed under the International Labour Organisation (ILO) definition (See glossary of terms on page 66) fell by 1.2 million to 1.7 million

Unemployment[1]: by gender

United Kingdom

Millions

1 At Spring each year. Unemployment based on the ILO definition. See Appendix, Part 4: ILO unemployment.

Source: Labour Force Survey, Office for National Statistics

4.21

Unemployment rates[1]: by gender and age

United Kingdom									Percentages
	1991	1992	1993	1994	1995	1996	1997	1998	1999
Males									
16-17	15.4	17.7	18.5	18.8	18.9	21.2	19.3	18.0	21.6
18-24	15.7	19.0	21.1	19.2	17.7	17.1	14.8	13.0	12.5
25-44	8.0	10.5	10.9	10.2	9.0	8.7	7.0	5.8	5.6
45-54	6.3	8.4	9.4	8.6	7.4	6.4	6.1	4.8	4.9
55-59	8.4	11.2	12.3	11.6	10.2	9.9	8.0	6.7	6.4
60-64	9.9	10.2	14.2	11.6	9.9	8.9	7.6	7.0	6.4
65 and over	5.9	4.9	4.6	3.7	..	4.1	4.0	..	..
All aged 16 and over	9.2	11.5	12.4	11.4	10.1	9.7	8.1	6.8	6.8
Females									
16-17	14.3	14.0	15.1	17.0	15.6	15.1	16.0	15.2	14.0
18-24	10.5	11.0	12.9	11.8	11.5	10.2	9.7	9.3	9.3
25-44	7.1	7.3	7.3	7.0	6.7	6.3	5.4	5.2	4.8
45-54	4.6	5.0	5.0	5.0	4.5	4.1	3.8	3.1	3.2
55-59	5.5	4.5	6.0	6.5	4.7	4.2	4.8	3.5	3.6
60 and over	4.4	3.1	3.9	2.9	..	..	2.0	2.0	1.9
All aged 16 and over	7.2	7.3	7.6	7.3	6.8	6.3	5.8	5.3	5.1

1 At Spring each year. Unemployment based on the ILO definition as a percentage of all economically active. See Appendix, Part 4: ILO unemployment.

Source: Labour Force Survey, Office for National Statistics

4.22

People unemployed[1] for two years or more: by gender

United Kingdom

Percentages

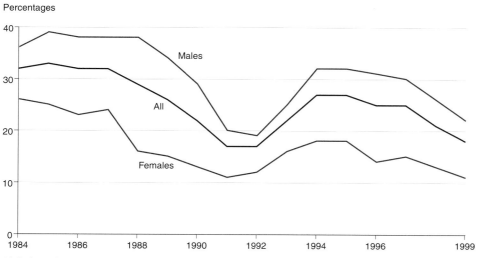

1 At Spring each year. Percentage of ILO unemployed who had been unemployed for two years or more. See Appendix, Part 4: ILO unemployment.

Source: Labour Force Survey, Office for National Statistics

Young people are much more likely than older people to be unemployed. In Spring 1999, 21.6 per cent of 16 to 17 year old men, and 14.0 per cent of women of the same age, were ILO unemployed (Table 4.21). The rates for 18 to 24 year olds were lower at 12.5 per cent and 9.3 per cent respectively, but these were still almost double the rates for all people of working age. Youth unemployment can be due to a number of factors, but is often associated with relative lack of skills, qualifications and experience.

In April 1998 the Government introduced the New Deal for Young Unemployed people as part of its Welfare to Work strategy. The aim of the scheme is to help young people who have been unemployed and claiming jobseeker's allowance for six months or more, to find work and to improve their longer-term employability.

Men are more likely to experience long-term unemployment than women. In Spring 1999, 22 per cent of unemployed men in the United Kingdom had been unemployed for two years or more, compared with 11 per cent per cent of unemployed women (Chart 4.22). As part of its Welfare to Work scheme, the Government also set up the New Deal for Long-Term Unemployed aged 25 and over in June 1998. In addition to this, the Chancellor announced in the March 1999 budget that personalised advice would be given to people aged 50 and over who had been on benefits for more than six months, to help them return to work. These people would also be given a new employment credit, which would guarantee a minimum income of £9,000 a year, for their first year back in full-time work, the equivalent of at least £170 a week.

4.23

Registering as an unemployed claimant is a recurrent experience for many people. The extent to which the same people move in to and out of unemployment can be examined using a cohort of the Joint Unemployment and Vacancies Operating System (JUVOS). This is a longitudinal dataset which records those who claim unemployment related benefit at any one period of time, and traces their successive periods of unemployment based on their national insurance number. The database contains a historical record of 5 per cent of all claimants along with a variety of personal characteristics, such as gender, date of birth and occupation, as well as geographical information. At present, the JUVOS cohort is the only source of information on exact duration of completed spells of claimant unemployment, length of time between spells and the number of times a person becomes unemployed.

Men in the JUVOS cohort are more likely than women to have made a previous claim and are more likely to have had a larger number of previous claims (Chart 4.23). Of those people who began claiming unemployment-related benefit between 1 April and 8 July 1999, 44 per cent of men and 23 per cent of women had claimed on four or more occasions in the previous ten years; 18 per cent of men and 32 per cent of women had not made a claim in the same period.

Most people leave the unemployment count because they find work, although older people are less likely than younger people to leave for this reason (Table 4.24). The second most common reason for leaving the count for young people aged 16 to 24 was transferring to a government supported training scheme or some other form of

New claims for unemployment benefit: by number of previous claims[1] and gender, 1999[2]

Great Britain

Thousands

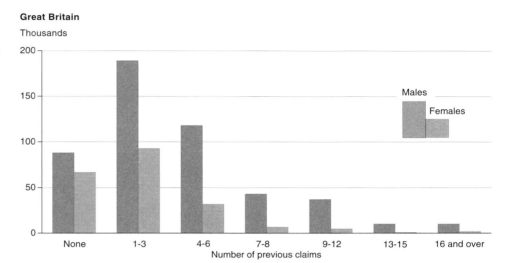

1 Previous claims started after 13 April 1989.
2 Males aged 16 to 64 and females aged 16 to 59 who started claiming between 1 April and 8 July inclusive.
Source: Office for National Statistics

4.24

Destination of leavers[1] from the claimant count: by gender and age, 1998-1999[2]

United Kingdom

Percentages

	Males			Females		
	16-24	25-54	55-64	16-24	25-54	55-59
Found full-time work	68.3	70.9	51.5	62.5	64.9	46.7
Found part-time work[3]	1.7	2.5	3.0	3.0	5.1	6.1
Full-time education	2.4	0.7	0.1	3.3	0.8	0.1
Transferred to government supported training/other training	14.1	7.2	3.8	10.1	5.2	3.6
Claimed incapacity benefit	4.0	6.9	11.1	4.2	6.8	13.6
Claimed other benefit	2.0	3.6	10.7	8.2	5.5	6.4
Gone abroad	3.5	4.8	8.3	5.0	7.3	12.1
Automatic credits	0.1	0.0	4.7	0.0	0.0	0.0
Main claim withdrawal[4]	3.1	2.7	4.8	3.7	4.2	6.5
Other[5]	1.0	0.7	2.0	0.1	0.1	4.8
All leavers[1] (=100%)(thousands)	528	1,039	130	278	408	41

1 Excludes claimants who failed to sign and leavers whose destination is not known.
2 People who left the claimant count between 9 July 1998 and 7 July 1999 inclusive.
3 Work which exceeds 16 hours per week averaged over a period of 5 weeks or longer.
4 Includes defective claims and new claim reviews.
5 Includes those deceased, reached state pension age, were attending court, or gone to prison.
Source: Office for National Statistics

4.25

Unemployment rates[1]: by area[2], Spring 1999

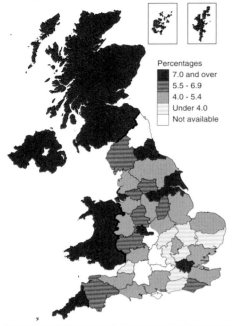

Percentages
- 7.0 and over
- 5.5 - 6.9
- 4.0 - 5.4
- Under 4.0
- Not available

1 Unemployment based on the ILO definition as a percentage of all economically active.
2 Counties for England.
Source: Labour Force Survey, Office for National Statistics

training, with men being more likely than women to do so. Older people are much more likely than younger people to switch to claiming incapacity benefit. Of all those who left the count between 9 July 1998 and 7 July 1999, 11 per cent of men aged 55 to 64 and 14 per cent of women aged 55 to 59 went on to claim incapacity benefit. In addition, 11 per cent of men in this age group went on to claim some other benefit.

Unemployment rates vary across the country (Chart 4.25). In Spring 1999, the counties of England with the highest unemployment rates included the former county of Cleveland at 12.9 per cent and Tyne and Wear at 10.9 per cent. Surrey had the lowest level of unemployment at 1.8 per cent.

The working environment

Work-related issues such as union membership and employee satisfaction levels provide further insight into the state of the labour market. The largest number of working days lost through stoppages in one year in the United Kingdom was during the General Strike in 1926 when just over 160 million working days were lost – the coal industry alone accounted for 146 million of these days (Chart 4.26). Further periods of high industrial dispute occurred in 1972, 1979 and 1984. In 1972, a miners' strike accounted for 45 per cent of the 24 million days lost and a strike by the engineering workers in 1979 resulted in just over half of the 29 million days lost; another miners' strike in 1984 was responsible for over 80 per cent of the 27 million days lost in that year. The number of working days lost through stoppages of work has fallen to historically low levels in the 1990s. The number of stoppages taking place is also very low – in 1998 there were only 166 stoppages, the lowest calendar year total since records began in 1891. The reasons for working days lost have changed with the economic cycle. During the economic slowdown of the early 1990s, redundancy was one of the main causes of working days lost. Then, as the economy recovered the main cause was disputes over pay.

In Autumn 1998, fewer than one in three employees in Great Britain were members of trade unions or staff associations. Since 1989 when the Labour Force Survey began collecting information on union membership, membership has fallen by 1.9 million or 21 per cent, although it only fell by ten thousand in the latest year. In fact, union membership has fallen each year since it peaked

4.26

Labour disputes[1]: working days lost

United Kingdom
Millions

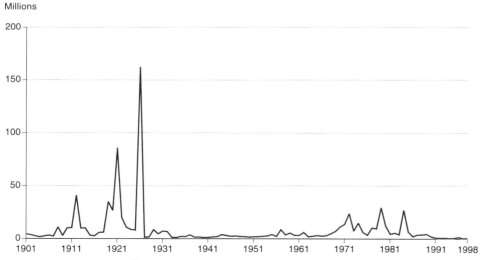

1 See Appendix, Part 4: Labour disputes.
Source: Office for National Statistics

4.27

in 1979. The largest fall in union membership occurred in 1992, a period of substantial job losses, and unions have failed to recover membership loss as employment growth has recovered. Trade union membership varies between occupations. In Autumn 1998, over six in ten women employed in professional occupations were trade union members (Table 4.27). For men, around four in ten of those employed as professional, personal and protective and plant and machine operatives were trade union members.

Trade union membership[1] of employees: by occupation and gender, 1992 and 1998

Great Britain   Percentages

	1992		1998	
	Males	Females	Males	Females
Managers and administrators	24	24	18	21
Professional	44	62	39	62
Associate professional and technical	40	59	34	54
Clerical and secretarial	41	27	30	22
Craft and related	45	34	33	28
Personal and protective	47	26	40	22
Selling	16	13	8	12
Plant and machine operatives	51	37	40	31
Other occupations	41	26	32	21
All occupations[2]	40	32	31	28

1 At Autumn each year. Includes staff associations. Percentages are based on totals that exclude the armed forces and those who did not state whether or not they were a member of a trade union.
2 Includes those who did not state their occupation.

Source: Labour Force Survey, Office for National Statistics

References and further reading

The following list contains selected publications relevant to **Chapter 4: Labour Market**. Those published by The Stationery Office are available from the addresses shown on the inside back cover of *Social Trends*.

Breaking the Long Hours Culture, Institute of Employment Studies

British Social Attitudes, Ashgate Publishing

British Social Trends Since 1900, MacMillan

How Exactly is Unemployment Measured?, Office for National Statistics

Labour Force Survey Historical Supplement, Office for National Statistics

Labour Force Survey Quarterly Bulletin, Office for National Statistics

Labour Market Quarterly Report, Office for National Statistics

Labour Market Trends, The Stationery Office

Living in Britain, The Stationery Office

Northern Ireland Labour Force Survey, Department of Enterprise, Trade and Investment, Northern Ireland

Northern Ireland Labour Force Survey Historical Supplement, Department of Enterprise, Trade and Investment, Northern Ireland

Social Focus on Ethnic Minorities, The Stationery Office

Social Focus on Families, The Stationery Office

Social Focus on Older People, The Stationery Office

Social Focus on the Unemployed, The Stationery Office

Social Focus on Women and Men, The Stationery Office

Statistics in Focus, Population and Social Indicators, Eurostat

Contacts

Telephone contact points for further information relating to
Chapter 4: Labour Market

Office for National Statistics

Chapter author	020 7533 5807
General Household Survey	020 7533 5444
Labour market enquiry helpline	020 7533 6094
Department of Enterprise, Trade and Investment, Northern Ireland	028 902 9585
Institute for Employment Studies	01273 686 751
National Centre for Social Research	020 7250 1866 extn 369
Eurostat	00 352 4301 33209

Chapter 5 Income and Wealth

Household income

Men's incomes outstripped those of women at all ages in 1996-97, with the peak average income, attained for both genders in their late forties, being nearly twice as high for men as for women. (Chart 5.6)

Earnings

During most of the 1990s, the growth in average earnings has outpaced the growth in retail prices. (Chart 5.7)

Around seven in ten employees in agriculture and fishing earned less than £6 per hour in Spring 1999, compared with less than three in ten of those in the finance and business sector. (Table 5.11)

Income distribution

During the 1980s, there was an increase in inequality in the distribution of household disposable income, but this has slowed down in the 1990s. (Chart 5.1)

Low income

The proportion of people living in households with income below 60 per cent of median equivalised household disposable income rose from 13 per cent in 1961 to 21 per cent in 1992, and has since fallen to around 18 per cent in 1997-98. (Chart 5.19)

Nearly two-thirds of Pakistani/Bangladeshi people were living in low income households (that is, those with incomes below 60 per cent of median equivalised household disposable income) in 1996-1998. (Table 5.20)

Wealth

Half the population shared between them only 7 per cent of total marketable wealth in 1996, a proportion which barely changed over the previous 20 years. (Table 5.25)

Around 30 per cent of households reported having no savings at all in 1997-98. (Table 5.26)

5.1

Distribution of real[1] household disposable income[2]

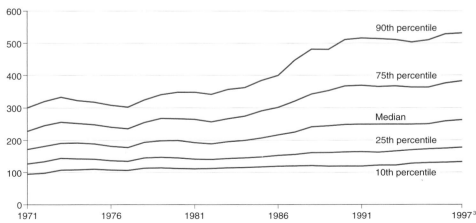

United Kingdom
£ per week

1 Before housing costs adjusted to April 1999 prices using the retail prices index less local taxes.
2 Equivalised disposable household income has been used for ranking the individuals. See Appendix, Part 5: Equivalisation scales.
3 Data from 1993 onwards are for financial years; data for 1994-95 onwards exclude Northern Ireland.
Source: Institute for Fiscal Studies

5.2

Real[1] household disposable income per head and gross domestic product per head

United Kingdom

Index (1971=100)

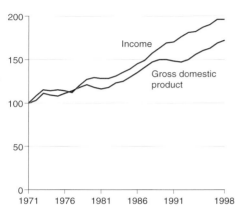

1 Adjusted to real terms using the expenditure deflator for the household sector. See also Appendix, Part 5: Household sector.
Source: Office for National Statistics

The level of income which individuals and households receive has a major influence on their standard of living. Income levels are determined by the level of activity within the economy as a whole – the national income – and by the way in which national income is distributed. Wealth, on the other hand, represents the ownership of assets valued at a point in time.

Household income

The amount of income available for distribution to households depends on the overall level of economic activity. The most commonly used measure of economic activity is gross domestic product (GDP), sometimes also referred to as the amount of 'value added' generated within the economy of a country. The total income generated is divided between individuals, companies and other organisations (for example in the form of profits retained for investment), and government (in the form of taxes on production). Analysis of the trends in GDP may be found in the final section of this chapter.

Household income is derived not only directly from economic activity in the form of wages and salaries and self-employment income but also through transfers such as social security benefits. It is then subject to a number of deductions such as income tax, local taxes, and contributions towards pensions and national insurance. The amount of income remaining is referred to as household disposable income – the amount people have available to spend – and it is this measure which is commonly used to analyse living standards. Household disposable income per head, adjusted for inflation, almost doubled between 1971 and 1998 (Chart 5.2). During the 1970s and early 1980s growth was somewhat erratic, and in some years there were small year-on-year falls, such as in 1977 and 1981. However, since then there has been annual growth, even in years when GDP per head was static or fell, for example 1991 and 1992. Over the period since 1971, a comparison of the patterns of growth of household disposable income and GDP per head shows that there has been a small shift between the shares of households and organisations in GDP in favour of households.

Table 5.3 illustrates how the shares of the various components of household income have changed since 1987. This shows a fall in the proportion derived from wages and salaries (including employers' social contributions for pensions and national insurance) from 60 per cent to 56 per cent in 1998, and small rises in most other components, particularly social benefits. More information about social benefits and the characteristics of their recipients may be found in Table 8.5 in the Social Protection chapter.

5.3

Composition of household income[1]

United Kingdom   Percentages

	1987	1991	1996	1997	1998
Source of income					
Wages and salaries[2]	60	58	54	55	56
Operating income[3]	11	10	11	11	11
Net property income	7	8	9	9	8
Social benefits[4]	19	19	21	21	21
Other current transfers[5]	3	4	5	4	4
Total household income					
(=100%)(£ billion at 1998 prices[6])	616	706	784	805	825
Taxes etc as a percentage of					
total household income					
Taxes on income	11	12	10	10	11
Social contributions	17	15	15	16	16
Other current taxes	2	2	2	2	2
Other current transfers	3	3	3	2	2
Total household disposable income					
(£ billion at 1998 prices[6])	416	481	546	566	566

1 See Appendix, Part 5: Household sector.
2 Includes employers' social contributions.
3 Includes self-employment income for sole-traders and rental income. See Appendix, Part 5: Household sector.
4 Comprises pensions and benefits.
5 Mostly other government grants, but including transfers from abroad and non-profit making bodies.
6 Adjusted to 1998 prices using the expenditure deflator for the household sector.

Source: Office for National Statistics

5.4

Sources of gross household income: by household type, 1997-98

Great Britain   Percentages

	Wages and salaries	Self-employment income	Investment income	Social security benefits[1]	Private pensions	Other income	Gross household income (=100%) (£ per week)
One adult above pensionable age, no children	3	1	7	63	24	2	150
Two adults one or both above pensionable age, no children	18	5	8	38	29	2	310
Two adults below pensionable age							
No children	76	10	3	4	5	2	560
One or more children	75	13	2	8	1	1	580
One adult below pensionable age							
No children	71	9	3	11	3	3	290
One or more children	31	5	-	52	1	11	230
Other households	72	10	2	9	4	3	680
All households	64	9	3	15	7	2	430

1 Includes state pensions.
Source: Family Resources Survey, Department of Social Security

Changes in the overall proportion of household income taken in deductions such as income tax have been relatively minor over this period. The third section of this chapter analyses the payment of taxes in more depth.

The data in Chart 5.2 and Table 5.3 are derived from the UK national accounts (see Appendix, Part 5: Household sector). In the national accounts the household sector is defined as including a variety of non-profit making institutions such as universities, charities and clubs, and people living in institutions such as nursing homes, as well as people living in private households.

In most of the remainder of this chapter, the tables and charts are derived directly from surveys of households (such as the Family Resources Survey, the Family Expenditure Survey, the Labour Force Survey and the British Household Panel Survey) and surveys of businesses (such as the New Earnings Survey). Data from these surveys cover the population living in private households and some cover certain parts of the population living in institutions, but all exclude non-profit making institutions.

The main income sources identified in Table 5.3 differ considerably in their importance between different types of households, particularly according to their family and employment circumstances. Not surprisingly, social security benefits and private pensions form the main sources of income for households where one or both members are above pensionable age (Table 5.4). Pensioner households also derive higher proportions of income than other households from investments, reflecting their ability to have built up savings through their working lives. About half the income of lone parent households is derived from social security benefits, and 'other income' also forms a significant proportion of their income – including child support payments from the absent parent. For other types of households, 80 per cent or more of their income is derived from their participation in the labour market, as either employees or self-employed.

5.5

Sources of disposable income: EU comparison[1], 1994

Percentages

	Wages and salaries	Self-employment	Social benefits[2]	Other income	Total income
Belgium	52	5	35	7	100
Denmark	60	7	29	4	100
Germany	61	5	29	5	100
Greece	42	27	22	9	100
Spain	56	11	28	5	100
Irish Republic	53	16	29	2	100
Italy	54	13	29	4	100
Luxembourg	61	7	27	6	100
Netherlands	62	5	30	3	100
Austria	59	7	31	4	100
Portugal	63	11	23	3	100
United Kingdom	62	8	26	5	100

1 Data are not available for Finland, France and Sweden.
2 Includes private pensions.

Source: European Community Household Panel, Eurostat

5.6

Mean individual income[1]: by gender and age, 1996-97

Great Britain

£ per week

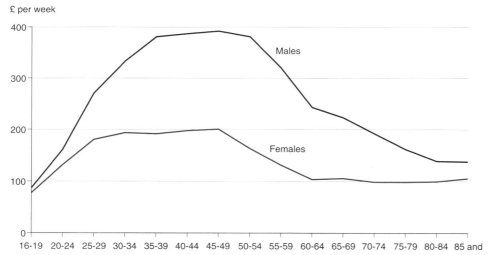

1 See Appendix, Part 5: Individual income.

Source: Family Resources Survey, Department of Social Security

The European Community Household Panel Survey is a recent attempt by the Statistical Office of the European Communities (Eurostat) to introduce a longitudinal household income and resources survey using the same concepts and definitions in each member state, though the fieldwork is undertaken by a different organisation in each country. The objective of comparability across countries means that the results will not necessarily be consistent with national sources, and the relatively small sample sizes in each country also mean that some estimates should be treated with caution. However, for the United Kingdom the proportions of income derived from different sources compare well with national sources.

Employment is the most important source of household income in each of the member states for which data are available (Table 5.5). Self-employment plays an important role in those countries where small-scale agriculture is an important part of the economy – particularly Greece, but also the Irish Republic, Italy, Spain and Portugal. Social benefits (including private pensions) are of least importance in Greece and Portugal where social protection expenditure overall is the lowest in the European Union (EU) and of most importance in Belgium.

The information presented in this section so far has been in terms of household income, since the household is generally considered to be the unit across which resources are shared (see Appendix Part 2: Households for definition of a household). Thus total household income can be taken as representing the potential standard of living of each of its members. The assumption of equal sharing of resources between each member of the household is very difficult to test. Using certain assumptions it is possible to use household survey data to derive estimates of the income accruing to individuals, but it is not possible to infer their living standards from these.

The results of such an exercise are shown in Chart 5.6 which compares the gross personal income of men and women by age group (see Appendix Part 5: Individual incomes for details of how these estimates were derived). The chart shows men's incomes outstripping those of women at all ages in 1996-97. For the youngest and the oldest age groups the gap is quite narrow, but the peak average income, attained for both genders in their late forties, is nearly twice as high for men as for women (£392 compared with £201 per week). Men's incomes rise steeply through their twenties and thirties, then level off through their forties, before falling as occupational pensions and social security benefits take over from labour market participation as the main sources of income. Women, on the other hand, tend to reach an income plateau at a much earlier age, as childbearing and childcare limit their participation in the labour market.

The data in Chart 5.6 are derived from the Family Resources Survey and therefore represent a 'snap-shot' of the various age groups in 1996-97 rather than a longitudinal perspective on lifetime incomes. The decline in incomes across the years of retirement is partly a result of the increased likelihood of the more recently retired to have income from occupational pensions compared with those in their eighties who had less opportunity to contribute to such a pension during their working lives (see Table 8.20 in the Social Protection chapter). It is also partly because those with occupational pensions tend to live longer than those without.

Earnings

Income from employment is the most important component of household income. The average earnings index (AEI), a monthly measure of the pay of a representative sample of all employees across all sectors of the economy, is one of the indicators used to judge the state of the UK economy. If the index rises rapidly, this may

Average earnings index[1] and retail prices index[2]

Percentage change over 12 months

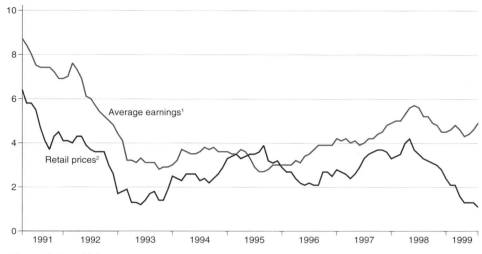

1 Data are for Great Britain.
2 Data are for United Kingdom.
Source: Office for National Statistics

indicate that the labour market is under-supplied with employees in the right numbers and with the right skills to meet the level of demand within the economy. In addition, a rapid rise may indicate that wage settlements are higher than the rate of economic growth can sustain and thus create inflationary pressures. A fall in the index may be a reflection of reduced demand within the economy and may presage a fall in GDP and an increase in unemployment. The relationship between the AEI and the retail prices index (RPI) is also of importance. If the AEI rises faster than the RPI, this means that employees' pay is increasing faster than the prices they have to pay for goods and services and that therefore, all things being equal, their purchasing power will rise and they will feel 'better off'.

During most of the 1990s, the AEI outpaced the RPI (Chart 5.7). This was made possible mainly through increases in productivity, enabling employers to pay higher wages whilst not increasing their prices to the same extent to finance their wage bill. The periods during which prices have risen faster than earnings – for example in the latter half of 1995 – have been times of economic downturn when a fall in demand for labour depressed earnings growth.

5.8

Employees'[1] expectations regarding their own pay in the year ahead

Great Britain					Percentages
	1983	1986	1991	1996	1998
Wages will rise by:					
More than the cost of living	15	20	19	18	17
Same as cost of living	46	45	47	43	44
Less than the cost of living	27	22	24	24	25
Will not rise at all	9	10	7	12	11
Other[2]	3	3	3	3	3
All	100	100	100	100	100

1 Employees working ten or more hours per week.
2 Will not be in same job, do not know or did not answer.
Source: British Social Attitudes, National Centre for Social Research

5.9

Average gross weekly earnings[1]: by area[2], April 1999

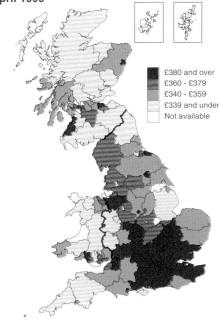

£380 and over
£360 - £379
£340 - £359
£339 and under
Not available

1 Earnings including overtime for full-time employees on adult rates whose pay was not affected for the survey period by absence.
2 Areas refer to normal place of work, rather than normal place of residence.
Source: New Earnings Survey, Office for National Statistics

Average gross earnings for full-time employees in Great Britain in 1999 were highest in a central band of England running roughly from Warwickshire in the south midlands to Hampshire and West Sussex (Chart 5.9). Within this geographic band, earnings in Bracknell Forest Unitary Authority were the highest at £540 per week, followed by London at £520 per week. A number of isolated pockets of high earnings also exist elsewhere: for example, in the City of Aberdeen where the North Sea industries have a substantial influence, earnings averaged £420 per week. The lowest earnings were to be found in parts of Wales such as Conwy, in Devon and Cornwall, and in parts of Scotland.

However, employees' expectations regarding their pay are considerably more pessimistic than the picture painted in Chart 5.7. Only around a fifth of those interviewed in the British Social Attitudes Survey since the question was first asked in 1983 thought that their wages would rise by more than the cost of living, while about a third thought that they would rise by less than the cost of living or not at all (Table 5.8).

A wide variety of factors influence the level of earnings which an employee receives such as their skills and experience, their occupation, the economic sector in which they work, the hours they work, and so on. The area of the country in which they work and their gender may also have an impact. The remainder of this section explores some of these factors. However, it should be borne in mind that these are all very much interlinked, and it is not possible here to disentangle the effect that any single factor may have.

For many employees, overtime and other additions can supplement basic weekly pay. Overtime is particularly important to men in manual occupations, accounting on average for 14 per cent of total weekly earnings in the United Kingdom in 1998 compared with only 3 per cent of earnings for men in non-manual occupations (Table 5.10). Overtime was a much smaller component of the total pay of women in manual work, but nevertheless of greater importance than for those in non-manual occupations. Payments for shift work were less important but showed a similar pattern. However, profit-related pay was only a minor element of earnings for all employees, irrespective of gender or occupation.

For some workers, the value of income 'in kind' forms an important part of their overall remuneration package. Such benefits may include a company car, free fuel, or private medical insurance. Information is available from the Inland Revenue on those benefits whose value to the recipient is liable to taxation. In 1997-98, 3.7 million people received such benefits (including 540 thousand company directors) and the amount received increased with the level of income. The average value of taxable benefits was £3,200 per recipient.

5.10

Wage rates can vary considerably between industrial sectors. Agriculture and fishing have traditionally been relatively low-paid sectors and this is still the case, with 70 per cent of employees on wage rates of less than £6 per hour in Spring 1999 (Table 5.11). The distribution, hotel and restaurant sector is also relatively low paid, with 61 per cent earning less than £6 per hour and 23 per cent earning less than £4 per hour. At the other end of the scale, around 30 per cent of those in the finance and business sector and energy and water industries earned more than £12 per hour. Averaged over all industries, one in ten employees earned less than £4 per hour.

In the past, government legislation has had an effect on wages. For example the *Equal Pay Act 1970* and subsequent revisions, together with the *Sex Discrimination Act*, established the principle of equal pay for work which the employee considers to be of equal value to that done by a member of the opposite sex, employed by the same employer, under common terms and

Composition of weekly pay of employees[1]: by gender and type of work, April 1998

United Kingdom					Percentages
	Overtime	Profit related	Payment-by-results	Shift premia	Average gross weekly earnings (£)
Males					
Manual	14.1	1.1	3.7	3.4	327
Non-manual	2.8	1.0	3.7	0.6	505
Females					
Manual	6.7	0.9	2.9	2.8	210
Non-manual	1.8	1.0	1.6	0.8	329
All employees	5.4	1.0	3.1	1.4	383

1 As a percentage of average gross weekly earnings.
Source: New Earnings Survey, Office for National Statistics

5.11

Distribution of hourly earnings[1]: by industry, Spring 1999

United Kingdom						Percentages
	Less than £4	£4 but less than £6	£6 but less than £8	£8 but less than £10	£10 but less than £12	£12 and over
Agriculture and fishing	16	54	15	5	3	7
Energy and water	1	10	18	25	16	30
Manufacturing	5	23	24	18	11	19
Construction	5	23	29	17	10	15
Distribution, hotels and restaurants	23	38	15	8	4	12
Transport and communication	5	22	29	17	9	18
Finance and business sector	7	20	19	13	9	31
Public administration, education and health	8	24	19	12	10	26
Other services	19	29	18	11	6	17
All industries[2]	10	26	20	13	9	21

1 Both full and part-time employees, including overtime payments, whose gross hourly earnings were less than £100. See also Appendix, Part 5: Combining NES and LFS data.
2 Includes those whose workplace is abroad and those who did not state their industry.
Source: Labour Force Survey and New Earnings Survey, Office for National Statistics

5.12

Weekly earnings gender differential[1]

Great Britain
Ratio

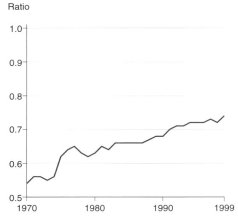

1 The ratio of women's to men's gross weekly earnings for full-time employees at April each year. Until 1982, women aged 18 and over, men aged 21 and over. From 1983 onwards for employees on adult rates whose pay for the survey period was not affected by absence.

Source: New Earnings Survey, Office for National Statistics

5.13

Income tax payable: by annual income[1], 1999-00[2]

United Kingdom

	Number of taxpayers (millions)	Total tax payable (£ million)	Average rate of tax payable (percentages)	Average amount of tax payable (£)
£4,335-£4,999	0.7	20	1	30
£5,000-£7,499	3.3	650	3	200
£7,500-£9,999	3.5	2,200	7	630
£10,000-£14,999	6.3	8,810	11	1,400
£15,000-£19,999	4.4	10,900	14	2,480
£20,000-£29,999	4.8	19,100	16	3,960
£30,000-£49,999	2.3	16,100	19	7,100
£50,000-£99,999	0.7	12,500	27	17,700
£100,000 and over	0.2	15,300	33	69,700
All incomes	26.2	85,600	17	3,260

1 Total income of the individual for income tax purposes including earned and investment income. Figures relate to taxpayers only.
2 Based on projections from 1997-98 data.

Source: Inland Revenue

conditions of employment. The impact of this legislation, together with other important factors such as the opening up of higher paid work to women, has been to narrow the differential between the weekly earnings of men and women (Chart 5.12). There was a sharp narrowing of the differential in the mid-1970s, followed by a more gradual erosion in the ensuing 20 years. In 1999 women's weekly earnings were 74 per cent of those of men, compared with only 54 per cent in 1970. Because even those women working full time tend not to work as many hours as men, the gap for hourly earnings is narrower. In 1999 women earned 82 per cent of the hourly earnings of men.

The national minimum wage (NMW), which came into effect on 1 April 1999, is £3.00 per hour for 18 to 21 year olds and £3.60 for those aged 22 or over. However, there are a number of exemptions and special rates set out in the legislation. The NMW has had an impact on the earnings distribution. The New Earnings Survey (NES) shows a considerable upward shift between 1998 and 1999, with a large peak evident at £3.60 per hour. However, the NES does not provide a comprehensive picture of earnings at the lower end of the distribution.

Taxes

Taxation is as old as the organisation of society and government. In 1086 one of the main purposes of the Domesday Book was to register the country's landed wealth and thus determine the revenues due to the king. Governments needed to raise taxes primarily to finance wars, and over the centuries tax liabilities were based on a variety of proxies for the value of property, for example the number of hearths or the number of windows which a property possessed. Taxes on income were first raised by the government of Pitt in the 1790s to finance the Napoleonic Wars.

Table 5.3 showed that in 1998, 29 per cent of household income was paid out in taxes and social contributions. Since every taxpayer is entitled to a personal allowance, which in 1999-00 is £4,335, those with income below this do not pay any tax. If they are married, widowed, a lone parent, or aged over 65 they may be entitled to further allowances. The income tax regime for 1999-00 includes three different rates of tax. Taxable income of up to £1,500 (ie after the deduction of allowances and any other tax relief to which the individual may be entitled) is charged at 10 per cent. Taxable income above £1,500 but less than £28,000 is charged at 23 per cent, whilst income above this level is charged at 40 per cent. Special rates apply to savings income.

5.14

The Inland Revenue estimates that in 1999-00 there will be around 26.2 million taxpayers in the United Kingdom, just over half the adult population (Table 5.13). Of these, 2.3 million pay tax only at the lowest rate and the same number are higher rate taxpayers. Because of the progressive nature of the income tax system, the amount of tax payable increases both in cash terms and as a proportion of income as income increases, averaging £30 per year for those with taxable incomes under £5,000 and £69,700 for those with incomes of £100,000 and above.

National insurance (NI) contributions are paid according to an individual's earnings rather than their total income, and for employees payments are made both by the individual and by their employer. Employees' contributions tend to be slightly smaller as a proportion of earnings for those on higher weekly earnings compared with those on lower earnings because there is a ceiling on contributions: in 1999-00 contributions were levied only on the first £500 of weekly earnings. Table 5.14 uses modelled data to show the impact of income tax and NI contributions on the earnings of individuals at different earnings levels and with different family circumstances. This illustrates how both income tax liabilities and NI contributions increase as a proportion of earnings as earnings increase. It also shows that the effect of the married allowance in reducing tax liability is of particular significance to those on lower earnings.

In addition to income tax and NI contributions, households also pay local taxes, as well as indirect taxes through their expenditure. Indirect taxes include value added tax (VAT), customs duties and excise duties and are included in the prices of consumer goods and services. These taxes are specific to particular commodities: for example, in 1999-00 VAT was payable on most consumer goods at 17.5 per cent of their value, though not on most foods nor on books and newspapers and at a reduced rate on heating fuel.

Percentage of earnings paid in income tax and national insurance contributions[1]: by marital status and level of earnings[2]

United Kingdom					Percentages
	1971-72	1981-82	1991-92	1996-97	1999-00[3]
Single man					
Half average earnings					
Tax	16	19	15	14	13
NIC	7	8	7	7	7
Average earnings					
Tax	23	25	20	19	18
NIC	6	7	8	8	9
Twice average earnings					
Tax	27	29	26	26	25
NIC	3	5	5	5	5
Married man[4]					
Half average earnings					
Tax	10	13	10	11	11
NIC	7	8	7	7	7
Average earnings					
Tax	20	22	18	18	17
NIC	6	7	8	8	9
Twice average earnings					
Tax	25	27	24	26	25
NIC	3	5	5	5	5

1 Employee's contributions. Assumes contributions at Class 1, contracted in, standard rate.
2 Average earnings for full-time male employees in all occupations working a full week on adult rates.
3 Based on projections from the 1997-98 Survey of Personal Incomes.
4 Assuming wife not in paid employment.
Source: Inland Revenue

Customs and excise duties on the other hand tend to vary by the volume rather than the value of goods purchased. Because high income households are more likely to devote some of their income to investments or repaying loans, and low income households may be funding their expenditure through taking out loans or drawing down savings, the proportion of income paid in indirect taxes tends to be higher for those on low incomes than for those on high incomes.

Local taxes paid by households in 1997-98 comprised council tax in Great Britain and domestic rates in Northern Ireland. These taxes are raised by local authorities to part-fund the services they provide. For both council tax and domestic rates, the amount payable by a

5.15

Local taxes[1]: by region, 1997-98

	Net local taxes (£ per year)	Net local taxes as a percentage of gross income
United Kingdom	660	2.9
North East	610	3.4
North West	680	3.2
Yorkshire & the Humber	620	3.2
East Midlands	690	3.0
West Midlands	650	2.9
East	700	3.0
London	660	2.3
South East	750	2.8
South West	720	3.2
England	680	2.9
Wales	590	3.2
Scotland	590	2.9
Northern Ireland	290	1.5

1 Council tax net of council tax benefit in Great Britain; domestic rates net of rates rebate in Northern Ireland.

Source: Office for National Statistics

household depends on the value of the property they occupy. However, for those on low incomes assistance is available in the form of council tax benefits (rates rebates in Northern Ireland). In 1997-98 the average council tax/rates payable was £660 per household, after taking into account the relevant benefit payments (Table 5.15). Net council tax varied from £750 in the South East to £590 in Wales and Scotland. Net domestic rates in Northern Ireland, which are based on a quite different valuation system, averaged £290. Net local taxes as a percentage of gross income were also lower in Northern Ireland than elsewhere in the United Kingdom. Within Great Britain, the proportions varied within a fairly narrow band, with London the lowest (2.3 per cent) and the North East the highest (3.4 per cent).

Income distribution

We have already seen how the various components of income differ in importance for different household types and how the levels of earnings vary between individuals. The result is an uneven distribution of total income between households, though this inequality is reduced to some extent by the deduction of taxes and social contributions and their redistribution to households in the form of social security benefits and other payments from government.

During the 1970s, there was relatively little change in the distribution of disposable income amongst households (see Chart 5.1 at the beginning of this chapter). However, between 1981 and 1997, whereas average (median) income rose by 36 per cent when adjusted for inflation, income at the ninetieth percentile rose by 53 per cent and that at the tenth percentile rose by only 19 per cent. This increase in inequality of the income distribution slowed down considerably in the 1990s and a degree of stability appears to have been reached, albeit at a higher level of inequality than was the case in the 1970s.

People in single and couple households where all are in full-time work were nearly twice as likely as the average individual to be in the top quintile group of disposable income in 1997-98 (Table 5.16). Also over-represented in this group are the self-employed and, to a smaller extent, those in couple households where one is in full-time and one in part-time work. At the other end of the distribution, individuals in households where the head or spouse is unemployed are over three times more likely than average to be in the bottom quintile group. The section below on low incomes examines the characteristics of those at the lower end of the income distribution in more depth.

The Department of Social Security's Households Below Average Income analysis from which Table 5.16 is derived, provides an annual cross-sectional snapshot of the distribution of income

5.16

Distribution of equivalised disposable income[1]: by economic status of family, 1997-98

Great Britain — Percentages

	Bottom fifth	Next fifth	Middle fifth	Next fifth	Top fifth	All (=100%) (millions)
Self-employed[2]	23	15	18	16	29	5.4
Single/couple all in full-time work	3	7	19	32	39	13.1
Couple, one in full-time work, one in part-time work	4	16	29	28	22	8.5
Couple, one in full-time work, one not working	16	23	24	20	16	6.8
One or more in part-time work	26	27	19	16	12	4.5
Head or spouse aged 60 or over	28	32	21	12	8	9.8
Head or spouse unemployed	66	19	9	4	2	2.5
Other[3]	47	31	12	6	4	5.9
All individuals	20	20	20	20	20	56.4

1 Equivalised household disposable income, before housing costs, has been used for ranking the individuals into quintile groups. See Appendix, Part 5: Equivalisation scales.
2 Those in benefit units which contain one or more adults who are normally self-employed for 30 or more hours a week.
3 Includes long-term sick and disabled people and non-working single-parents.

Source: Family Resources Survey, Department of Social Security

5.17

based on the Family Resources Survey. The British Household Panel Survey (BHPS) complements this by providing longitudinal information about how the incomes of a fixed sample of individuals change from year to year. This enables us to track how people move through the income distribution over time, and to identify the factors associated with changes in their position in the distribution.

Just under three-fifths of those adults in the top quintile group of gross income in 1991 were in the same group in 1997, though they did not necessarily remain in that group throughout the period (Table 5.17). There is more movement in and out of the three middle quintile groups, partly because it is possible to move out of these groups through either an increase or a decrease in income. Movement out of the top group generally only occurs if income falls – an individual will remain in the group however great an increase in income is experienced. The converse is true at the bottom of the distribution. Nevertheless, the table shows that there is a considerable degree of turnover within each income group. Whereas half those in the bottom quintile group in 1991 were also in the same group in 1997, further analysis of the BHPS shows that only 4 per cent of individuals remained in the bottom quintile group throughout the seven year period.

A person's household income can change either because the contributions to household income from different sources change (income events), or because of a change in the composition of the household (demographic events). Further evidence from the BHPS indicates that for the majority of households, the greatest contribution to variability over time in household income appears to be the earnings from employment or self-employment of the household head. However, the incidence of demographic events is also substantial: between 1991 and 1996, a fifth of all people had experienced a change in household head.

Adults moving within the income distribution[1] between 1991 and 1997

Great Britain						Percentages
	1997 income grouping					
	Bottom fifth	Next fifth	Middle fifth	Next fifth	Top fifth	All adults
1991 income grouping						
Bottom fifth	50	27	13	7	4	100
Next fifth	23	37	21	13	6	100
Middle fifth	13	21	30	24	13	100
Next fifth	6	13	21	35	26	100
Top fifth	4	6	12	22	57	100

1 Equivalised household gross income has been used for ranking the adults. See Appendix, Part 5: Equivalisation scales.

Source: British Household Panel Survey, Institute for Social and Economic Research

As discussed earlier in this chapter, households initially receive income from various sources such as employment, occupational pensions, investments, and transfers from other households. The state then intervenes to raise taxes and national insurance contributions from individuals. The revenue thus raised is then redistributed in the form of cash benefits to households and in the provision of services which are free or subsidised at the point of use. Some households will pay more in tax than they receive in benefits, while

Equivalisation – in analysing the distribution of income, household disposable income is usually adjusted to take account of the size and composition of the household. This is in recognition of the fact that, for example, to achieve the same standard of living a household of five would require a higher income than would a single person. This process is known as equivalisation (see Appendix, Part 5: Equivalisation scales). Adjustments may also be made to deduct housing costs, but these have not been made in the estimates in this chapter.

Decile or quintile groups – the main method of analysing income distribution used in this chapter is to rank units (households, individuals or adults) by a given income measure, and then to divide the ranked units into groups of equal size. Groups containing 20 per cent of units are referred to as 'quintile groups' or 'fifths'. Thus the 'bottom quintile group' is the 20 per cent of units with the lowest incomes.

Percentiles – an alternative method also used in the chapter is to present the income level above or below which a certain proportion of units fall. Thus the ninetieth percentile is the income level above which only 10 per cent of units fall when ranked by a given income measure. The median is then the mid-point of the distribution above and below which 50 per cent of units fall.

others will benefit more than they are taxed. Overall, this process results in a redistribution of income from households with higher incomes to those on lower incomes.

The average taxes paid and benefits received by each quintile group in 1997-98 are set out in Table 5.18. The distribution of 'original' income – before any state intervention – is highly unequal, with the average income of the top quintile group nearly 19 times greater than that of the bottom quintile group. Payment of cash benefits reduces this disparity so that the ratio of gross income in the top group compared with the bottom is 7:1, and deduction of direct taxes reduces the ratio further to around 6:1. Based on people's expenditure patterns it is then possible to calculate an estimated payment of indirect taxes such as VAT and excise duties, which are deducted to produce a measure of post-tax income. Finally, an estimate is made for the value of the benefit they receive from government expenditure on services such as education and health. Addition of these estimates gives a household's final income. The ratio of average final income in the top quintile group to that in the bottom quintile group is 4:1. It is not possible to estimate the benefit to households of some items of government expenditure, for example defence and road-building. Taken together with cash benefits, around 56 per cent of general government expenditure is allocated to households in this analysis.

5.18

Redistribution of income through taxes and benefits[1], 1997-98

United Kingdom						£ per year
	Quintile group of households[2]					All
	Bottom fifth	Next fifth	Middle fifth	Next fifth	Top fifth	house-holds
Average per household						
Wages and salaries	1,510	4,680	12,090	20,780	35,110	14,830
Imputed income from benefits in kind	10	30	90	320	1,010	290
Self-employment income	320	570	1,070	1,700	5,580	1,850
Occupational pensions, annuities	300	940	1,500	2,060	2,770	1,520
Investment income	220	340	610	920	2,980	1,020
Other income	160	210	170	180	160	170
Total original income	2,520	6,780	15,530	25,960	47,610	19,680
plus Benefits in cash						
Contributory	2,010	2,510	1,910	1,150	760	1,670
Non-contributory	2,770	2,490	1,680	900	360	1,640
Gross income	7,300	11,780	19,120	28,000	48,720	22,980
less Income tax[3] and NIC[4]	320	960	2,710	5,090	10,530	3,920
less Local taxes[5] (net)	430	540	660	770	910	660
Disposable income	6,550	10,280	15,760	22,140	37,280	18,400
less Indirect taxes	2,010	2,550	3,570	4,680	5,770	3,720
Post-tax income	4,540	7,730	12,180	17,460	31,520	14,690
plus Benefits in kind						
Education	1,750	1,280	1,190	1,040	640	1,180
National Health Service	1,910	1,870	1,850	1,530	1,320	1,700
Housing subsidy	90	80	40	20	10	50
Travel subsidies	50	60	60	70	110	70
School meals and welfare milk	80	20	10	-	-	20
Final income	8,430	11,030	15,330	20,120	33,590	17,700

1 See Appendix, Part 5: Redistribution of income.
2 Equivalised disposable income has been used for ranking the households. See Appendix, Part 5: Equivalisation scales.
3 After tax relief at source on mortgage interest and life assurance premiums.
4 Employees' national insurance contributions.
5 Council tax net of council tax benefits, rates and water charges. Rates net of rebates in Northern Ireland.

Source: Office for National Statistics

Low incomes

The incidence of low incomes, the factors contributing to low income and the ways of mitigating their effects have been an enduring focus of attention of governments from the introduction of the first poor laws in the sixteenth century up to the present day. The concerns of investigators such as Charles Booth in the latter part of the nineteenth century were taken up by governments in the twentieth century, from the introduction of the first old age pensions in 1909 to the welfare state of Beveridge some forty years later.

Being disadvantaged, and thus 'excluded' from many of the opportunities available to the average citizen, has often been seen as synonymous with having a low income. Whilst low income is clearly central to poverty and social exclusion, it is now widely accepted that there is a wide range of other factors which are important. People can experience poverty of education, of training, of health, and of environment, as well as poverty in purely cash terms. Nevertheless, the prevalence of low income remains an important indicator of social exclusion and is the focus of this section. Information on many of the other aspects may be found in other chapters of *Social Trends*.

The definition of 'low' income has always been a source of debate and to some extent has to be arbitrary. Only in countries at a very low level of economic development is it sensible to take an absolutist, 'basic needs' approach, which costs the bare essentials to maintain human life and uses this as the yardstick against which incomes are measured. All other approaches are to a greater or lesser extent relative: 'low' income is defined in terms of what is generally considered adequate to maintain an acceptable standard of living given the norms of a particular society at a particular time. With such approaches, it is possible and indeed perfectly acceptable for 'low' income to differ both temporally and spatially. So for example, whilst in one country the possession of sufficient income to pay for central heating might be considered a necessity, this might not have been the case in the same country a generation ago and nor might it be so for a different country today.

In this section, the threshold adopted to define low income is 60 per cent of median equivalised household disposable income. This is one of the definitions used in the Department of Social Security's anti-poverty strategy. In 1997-98, 18 per cent of the population lived in households with income below this level (Chart 5.19). This proportion was fairly static during the 1960s, 1970s and early 1980s, fluctuating between 10 and 15 per cent. It then rose steeply from 1985 to reach a peak of 21 per cent in 1992. Since then there has been a slight drop. This pattern is also

Percentage of people whose income is below various fractions of median income[1]

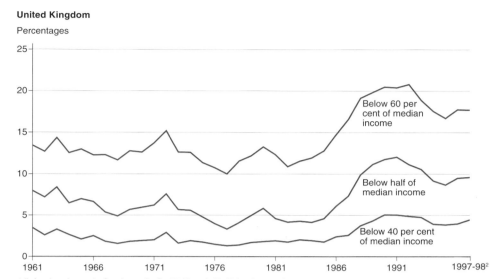

United Kingdom

Percentages

1 Before housing costs. See Appendix, Part 5: Households Below Average Income.
2 Data from 1993 onwards are for financial years; data for 1994-95 onwards exclude Northern Ireland.
Source: Institute for Fiscal Studies

reflected in the proportions of people with incomes less than 50 per cent and 40 per cent of the median.

Children are disproportionately present in low income households: in 1997-98 there were 3.2 million children living in such households in Great Britain. Two out of five of these children were living with one parent only, and more than half were living in households where no one was in paid work. The government has set a target to end child poverty in 20 years through improved education, increased financial support for families and supporting vulnerable young people in the transition to adulthood. Initiatives include Sure Start in England and Wales (Family Centres in Scotland) which brings together a variety of services to support disadvantaged families with children under the age of four.

People from the ethnic minority communities are also over-represented amongst low income households. Nearly two-thirds of Pakistani and Bangladeshi people live in low income households, compared with over a quarter of Black, Indian and people from other ethnic

5.20

People in households below 60 per cent median income: by economic status and ethnic group, 1996-1998[1]

Great Britain
Percentages

	White	Black	Indian	Pakistani/ Bangla- deshi	Other	All
All above pensionable age	24	..	..	..	..	24
Other households						
No members in work	47	52	55	75	40	49
At least one member in work	9	..	20	56	23	10
All households	17	28	27	64	29	18

1 Combined financial years: 1996-97 and 1997-98.

Source: Family Resources Survey, Department of Social Security

5.21

Events associated with the beginning of a spell on low income[1]: by household type in first year of the spell, 1991-1996[2]

Great Britain
Percentages

	Head aged 60 or over Single	Head aged 60 or over Couple	Head aged under 60 Single	Head aged under 60 Couple, no children	Head aged under 60 Couple, with children	Lone parent	Other	All persons
Fall in household head's earnings	..	30	27	45	40	16	..	31
Fall in earnings of other household members	..	19	..	..	20	13	24	16
Fall in non-labour income	66	42	..	..	..	17	..	15
Demographic event	19	9	58	37	34	53	58	38
All	100	100	100	100	100	100	100	100

1 Low income defined as equivalised household disposable income less than half the wave 1 (ie 1991) average.
2 Analysis based on all persons entering a period of low income in waves 1 to 6 of the survey.

Source: British Household Panel Survey, Institute for Social and Economic Research

minority groups and only 17 per cent of White people (Table 5.20). The contrasts are even more marked amongst low income households where at least one member was working. Only 10 per cent of working households on average have low household incomes, but 56 per cent of Pakistani/ Bangladeshi working households fall into this category. Indeed, the likelihood of low income amongst Pakistani/Bangladeshi working households was greater than the likelihood amongst non-working White households.

In the previous section, changes in income from employment were identified as a major factor in determining whether a household's position in the income distribution changed over time, with demographic changes also playing a major role. In Table 5.21 the British Household Panel Survey (BHPS) is used to analyse the main events associated with the beginning of a spell of low household income. Note that in this table, low income is defined as an income below 50 per cent of 1991 average disposable income, and that it is based on an analysis of all spells of low income beginning during the first six waves of the survey (ie between 1991 and 1996).

The BHPS also shows that about three-fifths of transitions into low income were income events of some kind. A person's income can change because they get a different amount of earnings whilst staying in the same job, or because they get or lose a job altogether. Among those for whom a fall in the household head's earnings was the main event associated with the transition, the household head moved from working to not working in 56 per cent of cases. Among those living in lone parent households or single adult households, demographic rather than income events accounted for the majority of transitions into low income. For those living in lone parent households, the most common demographic event associated with the transition to low income was the birth of a child. For single adults, most of these changes refer to children leaving their parents' household.

5.22

Demographic events are of less importance in movements out of poverty, accounting for less than a fifth of such transitions. However, changes in the earnings of household members other than the head are almost as important as changes for the head.

The European Community Household Panel Survey allows us to compare the proportions of people with incomes below 60 per cent of the national median equivalised disposable income throughout the European Union (EU) (Chart 5 22). Across those countries for which data are available, 18 per cent of households had low incomes on this definition in 1994. Most member states clustered fairly closely around this average. However, Denmark and Netherlands stand out as having substantially lower proportions of low income households – only about 10 per cent in each case. Note that in order to achieve comparability across the EU there are differences in income concepts used and in methods of measurement compared with national sources, and the relatively small sample sizes in each country may mean that the margin of error around the estimates is of the same order of magnitude as the differences between them.

Table 5.16 showed that workless households are substantially over-represented in the bottom quintile group. Table 5.23 takes this analysis further by examining the numbers of individuals receiving the main social security benefits available to those without work. In February 1999 there were 2.6 million people in Great Britain who had been receiving income support for more than two years, and 56 per cent of these were under pension age. In addition, there were 195 thousand people who had been receiving jobseeker's allowance for two years or more. The number receiving this allowance or its predecessor has more than halved since February 1995, but the number receiving income support has remained fairly static. Further information on social security benefits and their recipients may be found in Table 8.5 in the Social Protection chapter.

Percentage of people with incomes[1] below 60 per cent of the median: EU comparison, 1994

Percentages

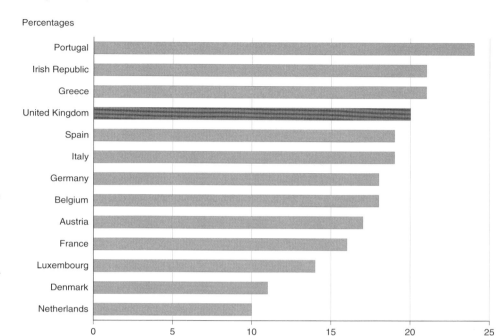

1 Equivalised disposable income in each country. Data are not available for Finland and Sweden.

Source: European Community Household Panel, Eurostat

5.23

Long term[1] recipients of income support and jobseeker's allowance[2]

Great Britain   Thousands

	1994	1995	1996	1997	1998	1999
Income support recipients						
Working age	1,277	1,430	1,523	1,565	1,518	1,464
Pensioners	1,073	1,203	1,221	1,225	1,207	1,166
Jobseeker's allowance recipients	..	474	418	342	233	195
All	..	3,107	3,162	3,132	2,958	2,825

1 Recipients for two years and over.
2 At February of each year.
Source: Department of Social Security

However, the existence of income from employment is not always sufficient to lift a household out of low income. For people in some occupations and industries, wage rates may be so low that their household income may still be insufficient for them to support a family adequately. The aim of working family tax credit, which replaced family credit from October 1999, is to guarantee a minimum income of £200 per week to working families with children.

Wealth

Although the terms 'wealthy' and 'high income' are often used interchangeably, in fact they relate to quite distinct concepts. 'Income' represents a flow of resources over a period, received either in cash or in kind. 'Wealth' on the other hand describes the ownership of assets valued at a particular point in time. These assets may provide the owner with a flow of income, for example interest payments on a building society account, or they may not, for example the ownership of works of art – unless of course the asset is sold. However, not all assets can be sold and their value realised. In particular, an individual's stake in an occupational pension scheme often cannot be 'cashed in'. The distinction is therefore usually made between 'marketable wealth' which the owner can sell if they so desire, and 'non-marketable wealth'. Wealth may be accumulated either by the purchase of new assets, or by the increase in value of existing assets.

The wealth of the household sector, net of any loans outstanding on the purchase of assets such as housing, has shown strong growth in recent years, averaging 4 per cent annually between 1987 and 1998 adjusted for inflation (Table 5.24). Holdings in life assurance and pension funds formed the most important component of the net wealth of the household sector in 1998, followed by the value of residential buildings net of mortgage and loan debt on them. This is a reversal of the position ten years ago, a result partly of strong growth in the take-up of private pensions and partly the fall in value of owner-occupied housing during the early 1990s.

Wealth is considerably less evenly distributed than income. It is estimated that the most wealthy 1 per cent of individuals owned nearly a fifth of the total marketable wealth of the household sector in 1996 (Table 5.25). In contrast, half the population shared between them only 7 per cent of total wealth. This distribution has changed very little over the past 20 years. If the value of housing is omitted from the wealth estimates, the resulting distribution is even more skewed indicating that this form of wealth is rather more evenly distributed than the remainder.

5.24

Composition of the net wealth[1] of the household sector

United Kingdom					Percentages
	1987	1991	1996	1997	1998
Life assurance and pension funds	25	27	36	38	38
Residential buildings net of loans	35	33	24	23	25
Securities and shares	10	11	15	16	15
Notes, coins and deposits	16	17	16	15	15
Non-marketable tenancy rights	9	8	5	5	5
Other fixed assets	4	3	3	3	3
Other financial assets net of liabilities	1	1	1	1	1
Total (=100%)(£ billion at 1998 prices[2])	2,511	2,808	3,164	3,565	3,892

1 See Appendix, Part 5: Net wealth of the household sector.
2 Adjusted to 1998 prices using the expenditure deflator for the household sector.
Source: Office for National Statistics

5.25

This analysis of the aggregate data available on the distribution of wealth is borne out by information available from the Family Resources Survey based on individuals' own estimates of their savings. In 1997-98, over 50 per cent of households reported having less than £1,500 in savings, with 30 per cent reporting no savings at all (Table 5.26). In particular, 71 per cent of single parent households and 41 per cent of single adult households had no savings. Couples where at least one partner was over state pension age were the most likely to have substantial savings: 30 per cent of such households had more than £20,000. These patterns partly reflect the income levels of the various household types which may or may not allow them to save, and partly the stage reached in their life cycle.

The most popular savings instrument amongst adults is an interest bearing building society account, and over a quarter of children also have such an account (see Table 5.27 overleaf). Premium bonds continue to be popular, but ownership is now on a par with that of stocks and shares. Most people of working age have a bank or building society current account which may also be used to accumulate savings, though a substantial minority do not (18 per cent of men and 21 per cent of women aged 16 to 65).

The term 'financial exclusion' has been coined to describe those people who do not use financial services at all. Qualitative research has suggested that the largest group of those who have never made use of financial services are householders who have never had a secure job. Other groups affected are people over 70 who are part of a cash-only generation, women who became single mothers at an early age, and some ethnic minority groups, particularly Pakistani and Bangladeshi households.

Distribution of wealth[1]

United Kingdom Percentages

	1976	1981	1986	1991	1995	1996
Marketable wealth						
Percentage of wealth owned by[2]:						
Most wealthy 1%	21	18	18	17	19	19
Most wealthy 5%	38	36	36	35	38	39
Most wealthy 10%	50	50	50	47	50	52
Most wealthy 25%	71	73	73	71	72	74
Most wealthy 50%	92	92	90	92	92	93
Total marketable wealth (£ billion)	280	565	955	1,711	1,965	2,042
Marketable wealth less value of dwellings						
Percentage of wealth owned by[2]:						
Most wealthy 1%	29	26	25	29	28	27
Most wealthy 5%	47	45	46	51	51	50
Most wealthy 10%	57	56	58	64	64	63
Most wealthy 25%	73	74	75	80	81	82
Most wealthy 50%	88	87	89	93	93	94

1 See Appendix, Part 5: Distribution of personal wealth.
2 Adults aged 18 and over.
Source: Inland Revenue

5.26

Household savings: by household type and amount, 1997-98

Great Britain Percentages

	No savings	Less than £1,500	£1,500 but less than £10,000	£10,000 but less than £20,000	£20,000 or more	All households
One adult above pensionable age, no children	30	17	28	9	16	100
Two adults one or both above pensionable age, no children	17	15	25	13	30	100
Two adults below pensionable age						
No children	21	22	30	11	16	100
One or more children	31	27	26	8	8	100
One adult below pensionable age						
No children	41	23	22	7	8	100
One or more children	71	20	8	..	..	100
Other households	22	24	28	11	16	100
All households	30	22	25	9	14	100

Source: Family Resources Survey, Department of Social Security

5.27

Adults holding selected forms of wealth: by gender and age, 1997-98

Great Britain Percentages

	Males				Females				All individuals
	Under 16	16-65	65 and over	All ages	Under 16	16-65	65 and over	All ages	
Current account	0	82	77	64	0	79	68	62	63
Building society account[1]	27	49	58	46	28	54	57	49	48
Stocks and shares	1	23	27	19	1	18	20	15	17
Premium bonds	7	18	25	16	6	18	23	16	16
TESSA	..	9	13	8	..	10	12	8	8
PEPs	..	10	11	8	..	9	7	7	8
Post Office account	8	5	8	6	9	6	11	8	7
National Savings bonds	8	3	10	5	8	3	12	6	5
Unit trusts	-	4	6	4	-	3	5	3	3
Save as you earn	..	1	1	1	..	1	-	1	1
Gilts	-	-	2	-	-	-	2	1	1
Any	40	89	90	79	40	88	87	78	79

1 Excluding current accounts and TESSAs.
Source: Family Resources Survey, Department of Social Security

5.28

Annual growth in gross domestic product

United Kingdom
Percentages

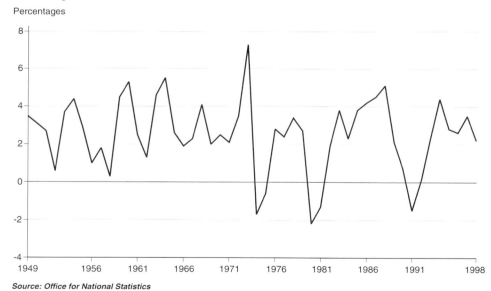

Source: Office for National Statistics

National income and expenditure

Gross domestic product (GDP) measures the level of income generated by economic activity in the United Kingdom in accordance with international conventions. Chart 5.2 at the beginning of this chapter showed that when adjusted for inflation, the trend in GDP per head since 1971 has generally been one of steady growth. However, within this long-term trend the United Kingdom is nevertheless subject to cycles of weaker and stronger growth usually referred to as the business cycle.

The year on year growth rates for GDP shown in Chart 5.28 suggest that the UK economy contracted in the mid-1970s, at the time of the OPEC oil crisis, and again in the early 1980s and early 1990s. However, growth has exceeded

Social Trends 30, © Crown copyright 2000

5.29

Gross domestic product per head at factor cost[1]: by region

Indices (UK[2]=100)

	1991	1992	1993	1994	1995	1996	1997
North East	83	85	85	83	82	82	83
North West	91	91	91	91	90	90	91
Yorkshire & the Humber	90	89	89	88	89	90	89
East Midlands	96	96	95	95	95	96	96
West Midlands	92	93	92	93	93	93	93
East	103	102	102	102	102	102	102
London	131	131	131	131	129	127	125
South East	115	115	115	116	116	118	118
South West	95	95	94	94	95	96	98
England	102	102	102	102	102	102	102
Wales	83	82	82	82	83	82	82
Scotland	96	97	97	98	99	97	96
Northern Ireland	80	80	81	81	81	80	80

1 This measure of GDP excludes taxes on expenditure and subsidies.
2 United Kingdom less that part of GDP that cannot be allocated to a specific region.
Source: Office for National Statistics

4 per cent per year a number of times in the post-war period, most recently in 1994. The long-term average annual growth rate was 2.5 per cent between 1948 and 1998.

GDP per head shows marked variations between the regions of the United Kingdom. During the 1990s, GDP per head in Northern Ireland has been the lowest, at around a fifth lower than the UK average, followed by Wales and the North East (Table 5.29). GDP per head in London has remained considerably higher than the UK average, though the differential has eroded slightly in the latter part of the 1990s. The South East and the East of England have also maintained above average levels of GDP per head.

A comparison of GDP per head across the countries of the European Union (EU) in 1997 shows Luxembourg with the highest level of economic activity (Table 5.30). This is because of the importance of the financial sector in the Luxembourg economy. At the other end of the scale, Portugal and Greece have GDP per head a third below the EU average, though in both countries it has grown relative to the EU average in the 1990s. Other countries are clustered more closely around the EU average, with the United Kingdom and Sweden at the average. During the 1990s, the countries with GDP per head above the average in 1991 have in general further improved their position, with the exception of France. However, the most dramatic increase has been in GDP per head for the Irish Republic, rising from 75 per cent of the EU average in 1991 to just above average in 1997. These estimates have been converted to a comparable basis making adjustments for the relative purchasing power of national currencies.

Government receives income primarily through transfers from individuals, companies and other organisations in the form of taxes, national insurance contributions and other payments, though they may also engage in economic activity from which income is derived. This revenue is then spent in the provision of goods and services such as health care and education, on servicing government debt, and on transfer payments such as social security benefits. The sum of all such expenditure and transfer payments net of requited receipts is known as general government expenditure (GGE) and it is this measure which until recently has been used to analyse trends in public expenditure. The present government's main measure of public expenditure is however Total Managed Expenditure: one of the main differences between this aggregate and GGE is that it excludes privatisation proceeds.

5.30

Gross domestic product[1] per head: EU comparison, 1991 and 1997

Index (EU=100)

	1991	1997
Luxembourg	156	172
Denmark	107	118
Belgium	107	114
Austria	107	113
Netherlands	101	108
Germany	104	107
France	111	104
Irish Republic	75	102
Italy	103	102
Sweden	103	100
United Kingdom	95	100
Finland	92	98
Spain	80	80
Portugal	64	72
Greece	60	69

1 Gross domestic product at current market prices using current purchasing power standard.
Source: Eurostat

5.31

General government expenditure[1] as a percentage of gross domestic product

United Kingdom
Percentages

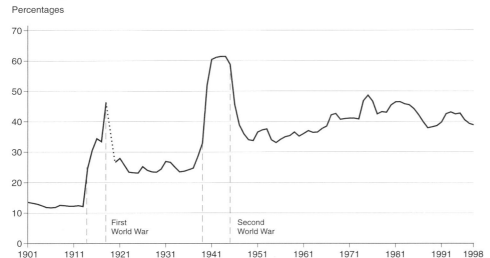

1 See Appendix, Part 5: General government expenditure. Data for 1919 are not available.
Source: Office for National Statistics

5.32

Expenditure of general government[1] in real terms[2]: by function

United Kingdom					£ billion at 1998 prices[2]
	1987	1991	1996	1997	1998
Social protection	99	112	136	136	133
Health	34	38	45	45	46
Education	32	34	37	38	38
Defence	31	31	24	24	24
Public order and safety	12	16	17	17	18
General public services	9	13	16	15	17
Housing and community amenities	11	11	7	6	6
Recreation, culture and religion	4	5	4	4	4
Other economic affairs and environmental protection[3]	25	26	28	24	23
Gross debt interest	31	23	30	31	31
All expenditure	288	309	345	340	340

1 See Appendix, Part 5: General government expenditure.
2 Adjusted to 1998 prices using the GDP market prices deflator.
3 Includes expenditure on transport and communication, agriculture, forestry and fishing, mining, manufacture, construction, fuel and energy and services.
Source: Office for National Statistics

During the twentieth century the long-term trend in GGE as a proportion of GDP has been upward (Chart 5.31). During the two World Wars, the proportion of income from economic activity devoted to government expenditure not surprisingly showed sudden increases, to reach a peak of 46 per cent in 1918 and 61 per cent in 1942 to 1944. However, although the proportion fell back after each war, in each case it never regained its pre-war level. Throughout the 1980s and early 1990s, an aim of government policy was to reduce the share of public expenditure of GDP and the proportion fell from 46 per cent in 1981 and 1982 to 38 per cent in 1988. There was a slight rise in the early 1990s during the period of economic downturn, but in 1998 the proportion had fallen back again to 39 per cent.

Although the way in which public expenditure is allocated to different purposes depends on government policy priorities, significant shifts in expenditure patterns tend only to be discernible over a relatively long time period. Over the last ten years by far the most important category of expenditure both in cash terms and as a percentage of total expenditure has been social protection – for example, social security payments (Table 5.32). Expenditure on social protection rose by a third between 1987 and 1998, and accounted for 39 per cent of expenditure in 1998 compared with 34 per cent in 1987. Expenditure on defence and on housing and community amenities fell in real terms during the 1990s.

As well as expenditure for purely domestic purposes, GGE also includes the contributions made to the EU budget. In 1997 the United Kingdom contributed 12 per cent of the EU's total receipts and received 9 per cent of total expenditure. The other net contributors to the EU budget in 1997 were Germany, the Netherlands, Sweden, Belgium, France, Austria, Italy and Luxembourg.

5.33

Of total EU expenditure of £55 billion in 1997, just over half was spent in support of agriculture in the form of Agricultural Guarantee (Table 5.33). Although still substantial, this proportion has fallen over the last ten years and expenditure through structural funds has increased in importance. Structural funds aim to reduce regional disparities and thus to achieve a more even economic and social balance across the EU. Within the United Kingdom, Northern Ireland, most of Scotland and Wales, and large parts of the North of England, the Midlands and the West Country were eligible for structural funds during the period 1994 to 1999.

The United Kingdom, in common with most other developed economies, also allocates part of its public expenditure each year to the support of poorer countries and the elimination of world poverty. Concepts and definitions for the measurement of aid flows are agreed by the Development Assistance Committee (DAC) of the Organisation for Economic Cooperation and Development. Most donor countries are committed to a target set by the United Nations in 1970 of allocating 0.7 per cent of their gross national product (GNP) to official development assistance. (GNP comprises GDP plus income received from other countries (notably interest and dividends), less similar payments made to other countries.)

In 1998, none of the G7 countries met the United Nations target and even France, which was the closest, still fell substantially short at 0.41 per cent (Chart 5.34). Scandinavian countries perform considerably better than the G7 in meeting the target: Denmark, Norway and Sweden all met it in 1998, as did the Netherlands. The best performance by the United Kingdom took place in 1979 when official development assistance reached 0.51 per cent of GNP. In 1998, the UK proportion was 0.27 per cent compared with the DAC average of 0.23 per cent: the UK proportion has remained above the DAC average since 1993.

European Union expenditure[1]: by sector

					Percentages
	1981	1986	1991	1996	1997
Agricultural Guarantee	62	64	58	51	51
Structural funds					
Agricultural guidance	3	2	4	4	4
Regional policy	14	7	12	14	14
Social policy	3	7	8	8	8
Other	.	.	3	6	6
All structural funds	20	16	26	32	33
Research	2	2	3	4	4
External action	4	3	4	5	5
Administration	5	4	5	5	5
Other	6	10	4	3	3
All expenditure (=100%)(£ billion)	9.8	23.3	37.5	61.8	55.0

1 At current prices. See also Appendix, Part 5: European Union expenditure.
Source: European Commission

5.34

For a number of years virtually all official development assistance from the United Kingdom has been in the form of grants rather than loans, and most loans from earlier years have now either been repaid or written off. Nevertheless, a number of the poorest developing countries have built up unsustainable levels of debt. Agreement was reached in 1996 on an International Monetary Fund/World Bank initiative to help these countries achieve a permanent exit from these burdens. In response to concerns that debt relief was getting through fast enough, the G7 countries agreed to an enhanced Heavily Indebted Poor Countries (HIPC) Initiative at their Cologne Summit in June 1999. This supports faster, deeper and broader debt relief for the poorest countries that demonstrate a commitment to reform and poverty alleviation. At the IMF/World Bank Annual Meetings in September 1999 the enhanced HIPC Initiative was agreed by all member countries.

Official development assistance to developing countries as a percentage of donor country gross national product: G7 comparison, 1998

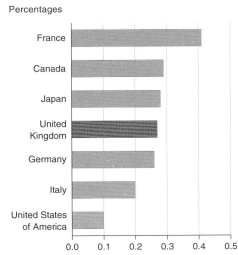

Percentages

Source: Department for International Development

References and further reading

The following list contains selected publications relevant to **Chapter 5: Income and Wealth**. Those published by The Stationery Office are available from the addresses shown on the inside back cover of *Social Trends*.

British Social Attitudes, Ashgate Publishing

Changing Households: The British Household Panel Survey, Institute for Social and Economic Research

Economic Trends, The Stationery Office

Eurostat National Accounts ESA, Eurostat

Family Resources Survey, Corporate Document Services

Fiscal Studies, Institute for Fiscal Studies

For Richer, For Poorer, Institute for Fiscal Studies

Households Below Average Income, A Statistical Analysis, Corporate Document Services

Income and Wealth. The latest evidence, Joseph Rowntree Foundation

Inland Revenue Statistics, The Stationery Office

Labour Market Trends (incorporating Employment Gazette), The Stationery Office

Monitoring Poverty and Social Exclusion, Joseph Rowntree Foundation

National Accounts, Main Aggregates, OECD

New Earnings Survey, The Stationery Office

Regional Trends, The Stationery Office

Social Security, Departmental Report, The Stationery Office

Social Security Statistics, The Stationery Office

Tax/Benefit Model Tables, Department of Social Security

The Distribution of Wealth in the UK, Institute for Fiscal Studies

The Income of Ethnic Minorities, Institute for Social and Economic Research

The Pensioners' Income Series, Department of Social Security

United Kingdom National Accounts (The ONS Blue Book), The Stationery Office

Women's Individual Income, Department of Social Security

Contacts

Telephone contact points for further information relating to
Chapter 5: Income and Wealth

Office for National Statistics	
Chapter author	020 7533 5783
Effects of taxes and benefits	020 7533 5770
Labour market enquiry helpline	020 7533 6094
National accounts	020 7533 6003
New Earnings Survey	01928 792077/8
Regional accounts	020 7533 5790
Department for International Development	01355 843329
Department of Social Security	
Family Resources Survey	020 7962 8236
Households Below Average Income	020 7962 8232
Individual Income	020 7712 2258
Inland Revenue	020 7438 7370
Institute for Social and Economic Research	01206 873374
Institute for Fiscal Studies	020 7291 4800
National Centre for Social Research	020 7250 1866 extn 347
Eurostat	00 352 4335 2251

Chapter 6 Expenditure

Household and personal expenditure

Total household expenditure more than tripled in real terms between 1951 and 1998. (Chart 6.1)

After falling between 1963 and 1978, total expenditure on domestic services at constant prices increased steadily every year up to 1997, to over £4 billion. (Table 6.4)

Over the past 40 years there have been marked shifts in our expenditure patterns – the proportion of household expenditure spent on services has increased from 28 per cent in 1963 to 48 per cent in 1998. (Page 105)

Average household expenditure on television, video and audio equipment quadrupled in real terms between the late 1960s and 1998-99, from £2 to nearly £8 per household per week. (Chart 6.5)

In 1998 around £5 per person per week was spent on food eaten outside the home in Great Britain. (Chart 6.6)

In 1998-99 the average weekly expenditure of a household headed by a professional, employer or manager, at £580, was over twice the average for households with a head from an unskilled manual occupation. (Page 107)

Prices

In 1997 Portugal and Spain would have seemed cheaper to a UK resident, while the Northern European EU member states would have appeared more expensive. (Chart 6.13)

Transactions and credit

The number of plastic card transactions in the United Kingdom increased by more than 10 per cent each year in the 1990s, from 2.0 billion in 1991 to 4.8 billion in 1998. (Table 6.14)

6.1

Household expenditure at constant prices[1]

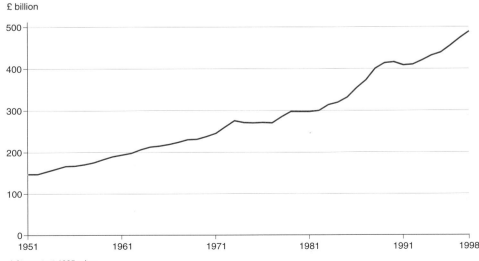

United Kingdom

£ billion

1 At constant 1995 prices.

Source: Office for National Statistics

How and where people choose to spend their income, and what they spend money on, influences, as well as reflects, the way that society is organised and how its members behave.

Household and personal expenditure

In real terms, that is, after allowing for inflation, household expenditure has increased most years over the past 45 years or so. Years when household expenditure showed less than buoyant growth are linked to periods of recession and downturns in the economic cycle. Despite the occasional blip, long-term growth has been remarkably steady: total household expenditure in real terms in 1998, was just over three times the equivalent figure in 1951 (Chart 6.1).

Not only are we spending more as a society, we are also able to afford to spend more. One useful way of measuring increasing relative prosperity can be found by comparing the increase in prices as measured by the retail prices index (RPI) with the increase in wages as measured by the average earnings index (AEI) (see Chart 5.7 in the previous chapter). Generally, earnings increase at a faster rate than prices, although during 1995 prices rose more quickly than earnings. Since then, wages have again risen at a consistently higher rate than prices, giving a strong indication that the 'spending power' of those in work has also increased. The income of those primarily dependent on state benefits is linked to RPI increases and has therefore not kept pace with the AEI. However, the other income sources of some economically inactive groups (particularly retired households holding private pension arrangements) has increased in recent years, indicating that the higher 'spending power' of particular groups in society has not been confined to those in work.

The volume of retail sales reflects the trends in overall consumers' expenditure and, to a certain extent, the level of consumer confidence at any time. The volume of retail sales increased by around 44 per cent between January 1991 and January 1999 (Chart 6.2). Retail sales follow a strong seasonal pattern, peaking in December each year. For example, the weekly average in December 1998 was about a third higher than the average for the year as a whole.

Individuals and households are faced with a range of decisions about what to do with their money. Expenditure on some items is particularly seasonal. Expenditure on alcohol peaks towards the end of the year, when Christmas and New

6.2

Volume of retail sales

Great Britain
Index (1995=100)

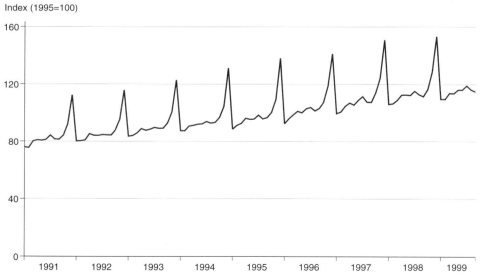

Source: Office for National Statistics

6.3

Year celebrations are in full swing (Chart 6.3). More fuel and power is used during cold spells, so expenditure on this is highest in the winter months. Spending on air travel peaks in the summer months, when people are more likely to go on holiday.

Long-term comparisons of expenditure patterns over the course of the twentieth century are made difficult by two factors: scarcity of reliable information collected at the start of the century; and the major disruption to the economy caused by the Second World War. *Britain, An Official Handbook*, noted in 1952 that 'changes in relative prices, in the quality and character of goods and services supplied and in the relative importance of different types of expenditure, make any precise statistical comparisons of the volume of consumption before and after the Second World War unrealistic, especially as it is clear that at least a part of the change in spending habits has been caused by controls (rationing) which restrict consumers' choice and therefore lessen their satisfaction.' Official collection of a wider range of economic statistics started in the immediate post-war years.

Over the past 40 years, there have been marked shifts in expenditure patterns. The proportion of household expenditure spent on services increased from 28 per cent in 1963 to 48 per cent in 1998. Conversely, the proportion spent on goods such as food, clothing and power fell from 63 per cent to 42 per cent over the same period.

The availability of free time and disposable income levels may also influence decisions people make about how to carry out their household chores, an area where spending patterns have seen a reversal in trends over the course of the

century. The 1901 Census recorded that around 40 per cent of all women in employment were engaged in some sort of domestic service. Accurate records of household expenditure on domestic service date back to 1963. The amount spent in real terms, that is after allowing for inflation, declined steadily until 1978, when it reached a figure of just under £1 billion. Expenditure on domestic services then increased steadily every year from 1978 until 1997, when it stood at over £4 billion (Table 6.4). This category includes domestic help, childcare payments and nursery, creche and playschool payments. The type of domestic service we are likely to spend money on has, of course, changed over the years.

Consumers' expenditure on air travel, alcohol and fuel and power at constant prices[1]

United Kingdom

£ billion

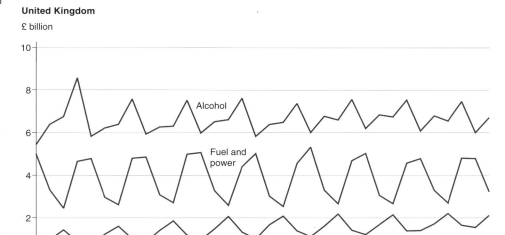

1 Expenditure each quarter at constant 1995 prices.
Source: Office for National Statistics

6.4

Expenditure on domestic services at constant prices[1]

United Kingdom	£ million
	Domestic services
1963	2,080
1966	2,033
1969	1,777
1972	1,519
1975	1,364
1978	993
1981	1,134
1984	1,433
1987	2,163
1990	2,805
1993	3,501
1996	4,000
1997	4,088
1998	3,992

1 At constant 1995 prices.
Source: Office for National Statistics

The expansion of certain service sector industries reflects in more detail how household and personal expenditure patterns are changing. For example, better transport links (such as the Channel Tunnel) and cheaper air fares have contributed to the growth in the tourist industry. In 1998-99, the Family Expenditure Survey recorded that households in the United Kingdom spent an average of over £18 a week on holiday expenses; this was almost four and a half times the amount in real terms spent 30 years previously (Chart 6.5). (Further information on holidays is given in Chapter 13: Lifestyles and Social Participation.)

The emergence of new products and services on the market means that consumers are also given a wider choice of what to spend money on. The expansion of cable, satellite and digital television has contributed to the continuing longer-term increase in expenditure on home entertainment equipment. Average household expenditure on television, video and audio equipment rose in real terms from £2 per household per week in the late 1960s to nearly £8 per household per week in 1998-99.

As well as spending proportionately more on services and less on goods than we did a generation ago, we also spend proportionately more on non-essential items (such as leisure goods and services) and less on essential items (such as fuel, light and power). For the first time in 1998-99, average weekly expenditure on leisure goods and services was the largest element of household expenditure. Our higher levels of disposable income have enabled us to spend more on non-essential items.

The increasing popularity of eating out is reflected in the fact that there were over two thousand more restaurants and takeaways operating in the United Kingdom in 1999 than there were in 1996. According to the National Food Survey, British people spent, on average, £5.20 per person per week on food eaten outside the home (excluding alcohol) in 1998.

There are also important regional variations in how much is spent on eating out. People in London spent more on eating out than people in any other region – almost £7.20 per person per week (Chart 6.6). Inhabitants of the North East

6.5

Household expenditure on holidays and home entertainment equipment in real terms[1]

United Kingdom

£ per week at 1998-99 prices

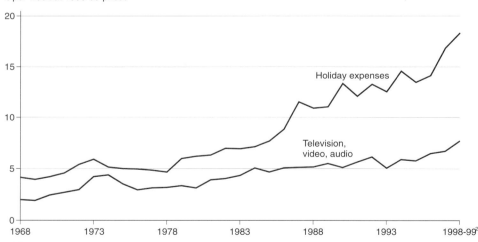

1 Adjusted to 1998-99 prices using RPI deflator series.
2 From 1994 onwards, data are for financial years.

Source: Family Expenditure Survey, Office for National Statistics

Social Trends 30, © Crown copyright 2000

6.6

Expenditure on food eaten out[1]: by region, 1998

£ per person per week

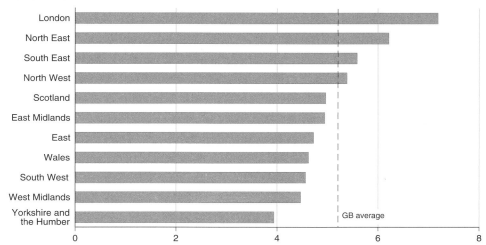

1 Individual expenditure on all food and drink (excluding alcohol) consumed outside the home and not obtained from household stocks, whether consumed by the purchaser or others or both. Expenditure which is to be reclaimed as business expenses is not included.

Source: National Food Survey, Ministry of Agriculture, Fisheries and Food

region spent the next highest figure, an average of just over £6.20 per person per week. The region with the lowest amount spent on eating out was Yorkshire and the Humber, at just under £4.00 per person per week.

Different groups in society spend their money in different ways. There are, for instance, some notable differences in expenditure patterns associated with different levels of equivalised household income (that is, income after the size and composition of the household has been taken into account in order to recognise differing demands on resources – see page 91 in the Income and Wealth chapter for a fuller definition). In 1997-98 the households in the bottom fifth of the equivalised income distribution spent around 30 per cent of their expenditure on the essentials of food, fuel, light and power – almost double the proportion for those households with the top fifth of incomes (17 per cent) (Table 6.7). Conversely, those in the highest income groups spent a higher proportion of their income than those on low incomes on less essential items, such as leisure goods and services.

Households where the head is aged between 30 and 50 tend to have higher than average expenditure: £429 per household per week in 1998-99 compared with an average of £352 per household per week for all households. When classified by occupational group, households where the head is either a professional, employer or manager had the highest average weekly expenditure. This was, at £583, over twice the average expenditure of households where the head belonged to an unskilled manual occupational group.

6.7

Household expenditure[1]: by income grouping, 1997-98

United Kingdom   Percentages

	Quintile groups of households[2]					All house-holds
	Bottom fifth	Next fifth	Middle fifth	Next fifth	Top fifth	
Food	23	20	19	16	14	17
Leisure goods and services	13	15	16	17	20	17
Motoring and fares	11	15	16	19	18	17
Housing	16	16	15	15	16	16
Household goods and services	13	13	14	13	14	13
Clothing and footwear	6	5	5	6	6	6
Fuel, light and power	6	5	4	3	3	4
Alcohol	4	4	4	5	4	4
Tobacco	3	3	2	2	1	2
Other goods and services	4	4	5	4	4	4
All household expenditure (=100%)(£ per week)	171	218	305	407	556	331

1 See Appendix, Part 6: Household expenditure.
2 Equivalised disposable income has been used for ranking the households into quintile groups. See Appendix, Part 5: Equivalisation scales.

Source: Family Expenditure Survey, Office for National Statistics

6: Expenditure

6.8

Household expenditure[1]: by economic activity status[2] of head of household, 1998-99

United Kingdom	In employment	Self-employed[3]	Un-employed	Retired	Un-occupied	All
Motoring and fares	18	19	17	13	15	17
Leisure goods and services	17	17	14	19	17	17
Food	16	17	20	19	20	17
Housing	18	15	12	14	12	16
Household goods and services	14	14	12	15	14	14
Clothing and footwear	6	7	7	5	7	6
Alcohol	4	4	5	3	4	4
Fuel, light and power	3	3	4	5	5	3
Tobacco	1	1	4	1	3	2
Other goods and services	4	4	4	5	4	4
All household expenditure (=100%)(£ per week)	450	485	239	194	244	352
Expenditure per person (£ per week)	169	164	91	125	101	149

1 See Appendix, Part 6: Household expenditure.
2 See Chapter 4: Labour market glossary on page 66 for fuller definition of economic activity status.
3 Includes other economically active.

Source: Family Expenditure Survey, Office for National Statistics

6.9

Expenditure of working age couple households[1] with children and without children: by type of household, 1998-99

United Kingdom	Without children	With children
Housing	17	18
Food	14	18
Leisure goods and services	17	17
Motoring and fares	19	16
Household goods and services	14	14
Clothing and footwear	6	6
Alcohol	4	3
Fuel, light and power	3	3
Tobacco	1	2
Other goods and services	4	4
All household expenditure (=100%)(£ per week)	441	465

1 See Appendix, Part 6: Household expenditure.
Source: Family Expenditure Survey, Office for National Statistics

The average expenditure of households will also vary according to the economic activity status of the household head. Households where the head is self-employed tend to have higher than average expenditure: £485 per week in 1998-99, nearly 40 per cent higher than the average for all groups (Table 6.8). The average amount spent on housing by households where the head was unemployed was roughly half the average of £57 per week for all households. This is partly because the housing costs measured in the table are net of any benefits received, and unemployed people are more likely than those in work to receive housing benefit.

The size of each household helps to determine expenditure patterns within the household and presence or absence of children is an important factor in determining household size. In 1998-99, households comprising two adults of working age with children had an average weekly expenditure of £465 (Table 6.9). Working age couple households without children spent, on average, 5 per cent less than this (£441). They also spent less on food as a household than did their counterparts with children (£64 compared with £82). But the smaller average size of the childless household group means they spent much more on food per person than households with children (£32 compared with £21). Larger households comprising three or more adults with or without children, perhaps unsurprisingly, had the highest expenditure of any household group, at £552 per week.

Household size is also an important factor in the expenditure levels of different ethnic groups. For example, Indian households tend to be larger than White households. Consequently, household expenditure of Indian households was the highest of all ethnic groups at £404 per week, but expenditure per person of this group, at £117 per week, was well below that in the White group, at £147 (Table 6.10). Pakistani/ Bangladeshi households spent, in the years 1997 to 1999, proportionately more on food than households from other ethnic groups (25 per cent compared with 17 per cent for all groups).

Prices

In the immediate post-war years, rationing was still in operation, and prices were subject to strict government control. Prices of other goods could be controlled by voluntary agreement between the responsible department and the trade concerned. Rationing did not formally end until 1954, and after that price controls still existed on basic foodstuffs such as bread and milk.

The rate of inflation in the United Kingdom is measured through the retail prices index (RPI). The index monitors the cost of a representative 'shopping basket' of goods and services of the sort bought by a typical household. Around 135 thousand different prices are collected each month, at various locations across the country, making a total of over 1.6 million prices collected each year. As the RPI is often used to uprate certain payments in line with inflation, such as wages, rents, pensions and other social security benefits, it affects the lives of millions of people. Inflation rates have ranged from a 12 month rise of 26.9 per cent in August 1975 to 1.1 per cent in August 1999, which was the lowest inflation rate for over 30 years (Chart 6.11). The rate has remained below 5 per cent since August 1991. In the 1999 Budget the government confirmed its target of 2.5 per cent for the underlying rate of inflation (RPI excluding mortgage interest payments – RPIX). Between April and October 1999, RPIX stayed within government targets, averaging just over 2 per cent.

There are measures of inflation other than the RPI. A different measure, the harmonised index of consumer prices (HICP), started in 1996 and enables direct comparisons to be made in inflation rates across all European Union (EU) member states. The HICP is particularly important because it is used to construct the inflation index for the European Monetary Union area. The UK HICP tends to be lower than RPIX. The main reasons are the different formulae used to construct the two measures and the housing component included in the RPI, which is not part of the HICP. An explanation of HICP methodology is contained in the Appendix, Part 6.

Annual changes in some of the component price indicators of the RPI can be seen in Table 6.12 overleaf. Between 1997 and 1998 the all items

Household expenditure: by ethnic group of head of household, 1997-1999[1]

United Kingdom   Percentages

	White	Black	Indian	Pakistani/ Bangladeshi	All[2]
Motoring and fares	17	15	20	17	17
Leisure goods and services	17	15	14	9	17
Food	17	17	16	25	17
Housing	16	19	18	15	16
Household goods and services	14	15	15	13	14
Clothing and footwear	6	7	7	11	6
Fuel, light and power	6	3	3	1	6
Alcohol and tobacco	4	4	3	4	4
Other goods and services	4	4	3	4	4
All household expenditure (=100%)(£ per week)	344	263	404	289	343
Expenditure per person (£ per week)	147	114	117	64	145

1 Combined years: 1997-98 and 1998-99.
2 Includes those of other ethnic origins and those of mixed origin.
Source: Family Expenditure Survey, Office for National Statistics

6.11

Retail prices index[1]

United Kingdom

Percentage change over 12 months

1 See Appendix, Part 6: Retail prices index.
Source: Office for National Statistics

RPI increased by 3.4 per cent. However, over the same period the housing index increased by more than twice this rate, while the food index showed little increase. Housing has shown the greatest fluctuation, due at least partly to changes in mortgage interest rates. The composition of the 'basket,' that is the relative importance or weight attached to each of the various goods and services it contains, is revised every year to reflect the changes in household expenditure patterns. For example, out of a total weight of 1,000, food accounted for 250 in 1971 but only 130 in 1998.

The purchasing power of the pound abroad is measured by way of Purchasing Power Parities (PPPs). A PPP between the United Kingdom and another country is the exchange rate that would be required to purchase the same quantity of goods or services costing £1 in the United Kingdom. PPPs represent the purchasing power

of currencies better than official exchange rates as exchange rates do not always fully reflect the price level differences which exist between countries. When the ratio of a PPP to the official exchange rate is expressed as an index, countries with an index above 100 would seem more expensive to a UK resident, while those below 100 would seem less expensive. In 1997, Portugal and Spain would have seemed cheaper to a UK resident, and France, Germany and Austria's price levels would have appeared similar to that of the United Kingdom (Chart 6.13). Other EU member states, particularly those of Northern Europe, would have appeared more expensive. Countries that do appear cheaper to UK residents are also among those popular destinations for UK residents taking their holidays abroad. (See Table 13.15 in the Lifestyles and Social Participation chapter.)

Transactions and credit

The services available to households and individuals wishing to save and spend their money have altered dramatically since the turn of the century. A well-established banking system and flourishing overseas trade in the nineteenth century contributed to Britain's industrial and commercial success. During the First World War, National Savings Certificates were issued by the Government through the existing structure of Trustee and Post Office Savings banks. The certificates (which were guaranteed tax free with interest) were successful in encouraging more people, especially those on lower incomes, to save.

By 1951 the Post Office Savings Bank had grown to become the largest organisation of its kind in the world, with 23 million depositors (around half the adult population) and total balances averaging out at around £100 per depositor. This network of 20 thousand post office branches gave customers some flexibility in terms of where they withdrew or deposited their money.

6.12

Retail prices index: rates of change[1]

United Kingdom							Percentages
	1993	1994	1995	1996	1997	1998	1998 (weights)
Housing	-5.4	3.3	6.7	1.3	6.5	8.8	197
Motoring expenditure	4.3	3.5	1.8	3.0	5.3	3.1	136
Food	1.8	1.0	3.9	3.2	0.1	1.3	130
Household goods	1.2	0.3	3.7	3.3	1.2	1.2	72
Alcoholic drink	4.5	2.5	3.8	2.9	2.8	3.4	71
Leisure services	4.5	3.7	3.2	3.6	4.9	4.4	61
Clothing and footwear	0.8	0.5	0.2	-0.7	0.8	-0.6	55
Household services	3.6	0.1	-0.3	0.1	1.8	2.6	54
Catering	5.2	4.2	4.3	4.0	3.8	3.8	48
Leisure goods	1.4	-0.6	-0.1	1.6	0.2	-2.3	46
Personal goods and services	4.0	3.7	3.2	3.7	3.6	4.7	40
Fuel and light	-1.3	4.4	2.1	0.2	-3.1	-4.3	36
Tobacco	8.5	7.5	6.7	6.7	7.4	8.6	34
Fares and other travel costs	5.2	2.6	2.5	3.0	3.4	2.2	20
All items	1.6	2.4	3.5	2.4	3.1	3.4	1,000
All items except housing	3.1	2.3	2.7	2.7	2.4	2.2	803
All items except mortgage interest payments	3.0	2.3	2.9	3.0	2.8	2.6	955

1 Annual average percentage changes on the previous year. See also Appendix, Part 6: Retail prices index.
Source: Office for National Statistics

Social Trends 30, © Crown copyright 2000

6.13

In the past 20 years, plastic cards have become an increasingly popular means of acquiring cash and making purchases. The number of plastic card transactions (including their use to obtain cash) increased by more than 10 per cent each year in the 1990s, from 2 billion in 1991 to 4.8 billion in 1998 (Table 6.14). Debit cards are used more than twice as often as credit cards: in 1998, there were 2.9 billion debit card transactions compared with 1.2 billion by credit card. The value of plastic card transactions has increased at a similar rate to the number of transactions, rising from £85 billion in 1991 to £228 billion in 1998. The average value of a plastic card transaction in 1998 was £47. Although the use of plastic cards has increased dramatically in the last decade, all the indications are that we are a long way from a cashless society.

Plastic cards are also an increasingly popular means of acquiring cash. Plastic card cash acquisition in the United Kingdom in 1991 stood at £44 billion; by 1998, this figure has more than doubled to over £100 billion. One factor helping to explain the increasing use of these cards to obtain cash is that cash dispensing facilities have become much more widespread and readily available. In 1975 there were only 568 automated teller machines (ATMs) in Great Britain. ATMs were introduced to building societies in 1982, and by 1998 there were over 24 thousand ATMs in operation in the United Kingdom, offering cash and other banking facilities to customers on a 24 hour basis.

Many purchases are paid for over a period of time using one of the many forms of credit available. New borrowing by consumers, net of repayments, provides the best measure of current growth in consumer credit in the United Kingdom and its movements clearly mirror the effects of the economic cycle. People will tend to borrow more to make large purchases when their confidence is high and economic prospects are good. A rise in interest rates, making borrowing comparatively

Relative price levels[1]: EU comparison, 1997

Indices (UK=100)

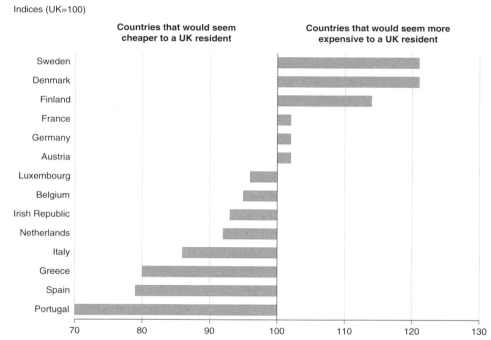

1 Price level indices for private consumption - the ratio of purchasing power parities to the official exchange rates.
Source: Eurostat

6.14

Plastic card transactions[1]

United Kingdom

	1991	1992	1993	1994	1995	1996	1997	1998
Number of transactions								
(millions)								
Debit cards	720	933	1,215	1,432	1,727	2,248	2,539	2,918
Credit cards	659	681	704	772	869	976	1,089	1,184
ATM (standalone)[2]	536	571	582	593	663	564	589	568
Charge cards	96	105	108	116	125	149	163	177
All cards	2,011	2,291	2,609	2,914	3,384	3,938	4,380	4,847
Value of transactions								
(£ billion)								
Debit cards	25	33	43	53	65	85	99	119
Credit cards	27	29	30	35	40	46	54	60
ATM (standalone)[2]	26	29	31	31	36	32	34	33
Charge cards	6	7	8	9	10	12	14	15
All cards	85	98	112	128	150	175	201	228

1 Includes cash acquisition and purchases in the United Kingdom and abroad.
2 ATM transactions using plastic cards that cannot be used for any other purpose.
Source: Association of Payment Clearing Services

6.15

Net borrowing by consumers in real terms[1]

United Kingdom

£ billion at 1998 prices[1]

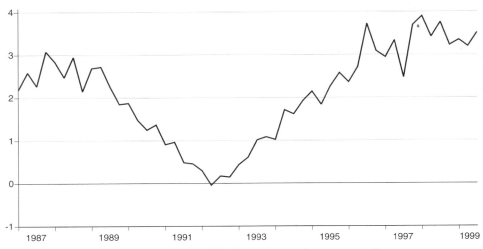

1 Seasonally adjusted. Adjusted to 1998 prices using the RPI deflator; excludes lending secured on dwellings.

Source: Bank of England

6.16

Composition of consumer credit[1] in real terms[2]

United Kingdom   Percentages

	1987	1989	1991	1993	1996	1997	1998
Bank loans	80	81	81	78	72	74	72
Retailers	6	5	4	5	3	3	3
Insurance companies	3	2	2	3	2	1	1
Building society loans[3]	-	1	1	2	2	-	-
Other specialist lenders[4]	12	11	11	13	21	21	24
Credit outstanding at end of year (=100%)(£ billion at 1998 prices[2])	58.0	68.7	65.9	61.3	82.0	90.4	101.4

1 Excludes mortgage borrowing. See also Appendix, Part 6: Consumer credit.
2 Adjusted to 1998 prices using the retail prices index.
3 Building society unsecured loans to individuals or companies (ie Class 3 loans as defined in the Building Societies Act 1986).
4 Includes new non-bank credit granters from 1995.

Source: Bank of England; Office for National Statistics

more expensive, and the decreasing job security which can be associated with a downturn in the economic cycle, may result in a decrease in borrowing levels. Net borrowing by consumers fell in real terms from around £2 billion in the second quarter of 1989 to a small net repayment in the second quarter of 1992 (Chart 6.15). Since 1992, borrowing has risen each year to £14 billion in 1998. More details on how households save, rather than spend their money, are given in the Wealth section of Chapter 5: Income and Wealth.

Table 6.16 shows the total indebtedness of consumers after allowing for inflation. This definition of consumer credit excludes mortgage borrowing. The amount of consumer credit outstanding in the United Kingdom increased rapidly in real terms between 1987 and 1989, mirroring the movements in net lending shown above, before decreasing through to 1993. Since then it has increased again to £101 billion in 1998, an increase of nearly three-quarters in real terms on the 1987 level. Bank loans, while still accounting for the majority of consumer credit, represented a smaller share of outstanding credit in 1998 (72 per cent) compared with 1987 (80 per cent).

Some people will borrow and spend more than they can afford. If this pattern persists, they may end up as declared bankrupts. The amount of declared individual cases of bankruptcy in England and Wales in 1998 was comparatively low, at around 9 thousand. Certainly, attitudes towards bankrupts have relaxed since the 'debtors prisons' of Victorian times. The number of declared bankrupts mirrors, quite closely, fluctuations in the economic cycle. Table 6.17 gives details of bankruptcies among individuals who are not self-employed. The number of bankruptcies are fairly evenly split between

Social Trends 30, © Crown copyright 2000

employees and the unemployed, with a large proportion of declared bankrupts classified as 'occupation unknown'. The number of total individual bankrupts over the past 30 years first peaked at just over 2 thousand in the recession of the mid-1970s, and then again in the recession of the early 1990s – a total of around 12.5 thousand individuals were declared bankrupt in 1993. It then declined, and has stayed at a roughly similar level between 1996 and 1998.

A detailed analysis of retail trade figures in the United Kingdom gives a clearer picture of where households and individuals choose to spend their money. In 1998 total turnover for all VAT-based enterprises in the United Kingdom in the retail industry amounted to £4 thousand billion. Less than 1 per cent of all enterprises had a turnover of £10 million or more and yet these (predominantly multi-outlet) enterprises accounted for 86 per cent of the value of all retail trade in the United Kingdom (Table 6.18). The number of small retail businesses (having a turnover of less than £100 thousand) was 74 thousand– over a third of the total number of businesses, yet only accounting for around 1 per cent of the total turnover of retail trade. These figures suggest, perhaps unsurprisingly, that by far the most popular places for us to spend money as consumers are supermarkets, large department stores and high street chains.

The dominance of self-service shopping has been comparatively recent. In 1957 it accounted for only 15 per cent of retail sales in the grocery and provisions trades. Over half of all retail trade was still carried out by independent retail businesses (small shops excluding co-ops, multiple traders and department stores).

The way we spend our money has altered radically through much of the course of the twentieth century driven, among other things, by increasing incomes, technological innovations and changing fashions. Shopping on the internet has become increasingly popular as more and more households acquire a personal computer. Electronic commerce (or e-commerce), defined in a wider sense as 'the exchange of information across electronic networks, at any stage in the supply chain,' has become a rapid growth area in the United Kingdom. Initial research by IDC puts the estimated value of e-commerce (excluding telephone-based services) at around £2.8 billion in 1999. The very recent establishment of the first internet bank is a strong indication that growth in this area is set to continue and new trends will emerge.

6.17

Individual bankruptcies: by occupation

England & Wales Numbers

	Employees	Unemployed	Company directors	Occupation unknown	All individual bankruptcies
1969		930	220	..	1,150
1971		594	255	33	882
1975		1,511	405	115	2,031
1981		555	486	91	1,132
1986	504	492	524	229	1,749
1991	1,639	2,811	667	2,906	8,023
1993	2,507	4,816	862	4,270	12,455
1996	2,471	3,294	368	3,003	9,136
1997	2,625	3,051	310	2,637	8,623
1998	3,141	3,384	272	2,430	9,227

Source: Department of Trade and Industry

6.18

Retail businesses: by size of turnover, 1998

United Kingdom Percentages

	Percentage of businesses	Share of total value of retail trade
Turnover		
Below £100,000	36	1
£100,000-£999,000	59	5
£1 million to £10 million	4	8
£10 million and over	-	86
Total	100	100

Source: Office for National Statistics

References and further reading

The following list contains selected publications relevant to **Chapter 6: Expenditure**. Those published by The Stationery Office are available from the addresses shown on the inside back cover of *Social Trends*.

British Social Attitudes, Ashgate Publishing

Business Monitor MM23 (Consumer Price Indices), The Stationery Office

Consumer Trends, The Stationery Office

Court of Auditors - Annual report, European Community

Economic Situation Report, Confederation of British Industry

Economic Trends, The Stationery Office

Family Spending, The Stationery Office

Financial Statistics, The Stationery Office

Social Focus on Families, The Stationery Office

Statistical Yearbook, Credit Card Research Group

United Kingdom National Accounts (The ONS Blue Book), The Stationery Office

e-commerce@its.best.uk, A Performance and Innovation Unit Report, Cabinet Office

Contacts

Telephone contact points for further information relating to
Chapter 6: Expenditure

Office for National Statistics

Chapter author	020 7533 5776
Consumers expenditure	020 7533 5999
Family Expenditure Survey	020 7533 5756
Harmonised index of consumer prices	020 7533 5818
Purchasing power parities	020 7533 5819
Retail prices index	020 7533 5855
Retail sales	01633 812609
Bank of England	020 7601 3742
Association for Payment Clearing Services	020 7711 6200
European Commission	00 32 2295 9829

Chapter 7 Health

7.1

Incidence of malignant melanoma of the skin: by gender

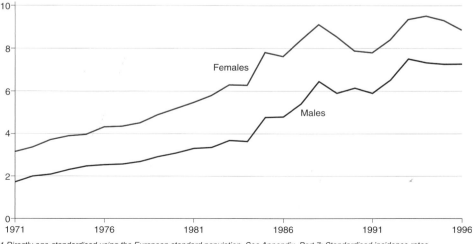

Great Britain
Rates per 100,000 population[1]

1 Directly age-standardised using the European standard population. See Appendix, Part 7: Standardised incidence rates.
Source: Office for National Statistics

7.2

Mortality[1]: by gender and major cause

Great Britain

Rates per million population

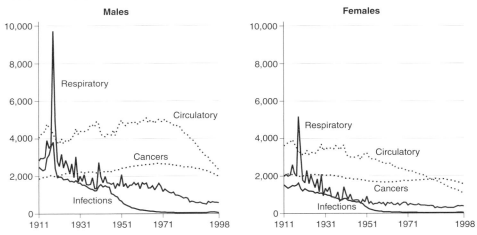

1 People aged 15 to 74. Data have been age-standardised to the European population. See Appendix, Part 7: Standardised death rates and International classification of diseases.

Source: Office for National Statistics

7.3

Infant mortality[1]: by social class[2]

United Kingdom

Rates per 1,000 live births

	1981	1991	1996	1997
Inside marriage				
Professional	7.8	5.0	3.6	4.4
Managerial and technical	8.2	5.3	4.4	4.0
Skilled non-manual	9.0	6.2	5.4	5.4
Skilled manual	10.5	6.3	5.8	5.3
Semi-skilled	12.7	7.2	5.9	6.4
Unskilled	15.7	8.4	7.8	6.8
Other	15.6	11.8	8.3	8.8
All inside marriage	10.4	6.3	5.4	5.2
Outside marriage				
Joint registration	14.1	8.7	6.9	6.8
Sole registration	16.2	10.8	7.2	7.3
All outside marriage	15.0	9.3	7.0	6.9

1 Deaths within one year of birth.
2 Based on occupation of father.

Source: Office for National Statistics; General Register Office for Scotland; Northern Ireland Statistics and Research Agency

The twentieth century has seen very considerable falls in mortality, reflecting major changes in people's health. This reduction in mortality has had a large impact on life expectancy at birth which increased by over 24 years for both males and females between 1911 and 1997. In addition, there has been a marked shift in the distribution of age at death from younger to older age groups. In 1901, deaths in the first year of life accounted for a quarter of all deaths, and those aged 75 and over accounted for only 12 per cent. By 1991 deaths to those aged under one accounted for less than 1 per cent of deaths while those aged 75 and over accounted for 59 per cent.

Causes of death

Changes in the main causes of death have also accompanied this improvement in mortality. Sharp peaks in mortality in the United Kingdom occurred around the First World War, when deaths were mainly due to respiratory and infectious diseases. Such diseases now account for a relatively small proportion of all deaths. They have been replaced by causes such as cancer and circulatory diseases which are much less responsive to modern preventative and curative medicine and the burden of whose mortality is concentrated at older ages.

In the early part of the twentieth century, respiratory diseases were a major cause of death for both males and females. In 1911 there were nearly 3 thousand male deaths per million population from respiratory diseases in Great Britain and just under 2 thousand female deaths per million population (Chart 7.2). Deaths from respiratory diseases and infections together made up nearly a third of all deaths for males and about a quarter of those for females. Under the age of 65, the reduction of infectious diseases was the most important cause of the decline in overall mortality over the century. The reduction in respiratory disease mortality was the second most important reason. It declined for those aged under 15 over the period and substantially for those aged 15 to 64 after the Second World War. By 1998 respiratory disease and infections were the cause of only around 10 per cent of all deaths.

Mortality from several causes did, however, rise over the period. For example, circulatory disease for men aged 45 and over increased after the Second World War but has since decreased. In 1998 circulatory diseases caused 39 per cent of male deaths and 29 per cent of female deaths. There has also been a rise in the total number of deaths from cancer. In 1911, cancers were responsible for 11 per cent of male deaths and 16 per cent of female deaths whereas by 1998 these proportions had increased to 33 and 43 per cent of male and female deaths respectively.

The advent of the National Health Service in 1948 appears to have accelerated the decline in overall mortality. The fall is generally regarded as a consequence of a number of major social and economic trends, including an increase in real incomes, nutrition and housing, higher levels of education, improved health services and developments in medicines and their wider availability to the population. As mentioned earlier, infectious diseases have contributed to much of the reduction in mortality over the last century. The declines in infectious diseases were particularly evident among children aged under one and the downward trend in infant mortality is projected to continue into the early part of the twenty-first century. Indeed, infant mortality fell by 67 per cent between 1971 and 1997 and is projected to fall by a further 56 per cent by the year 2021, based on infant mortality rates up to 1997.

Despite these improvements, there are large variations in infant mortality rates in the United Kingdom by social class (Table 7.3). For babies born inside marriage in 1997, the infant mortality rate for those whose fathers were unskilled was

Expectation of life[1] at selected ages: by gender

United Kingdom								Years
	1911	1931	1951	1971	1991	1997	2011	2021
Males								
At birth	50.4	58.0	66.1	68.8	73.2	74.6	77.4	78.6
At age								
20	44.0	46.5	49.4	50.9	54.2	55.5	58.0	59.1
40	27.5	29.5	30.8	31.8	35.2	36.4	39.0	40.0
60	13.7	14.5	14.8	15.3	17.7	18.8	21.0	22.0
80	4.9	4.8	5.0	5.5	6.4	6.7	7.7	8.3
Females								
At birth	53.9	62.0	70.9	75.0	78.8	79.6	81.6	82.7
At age								
20	46.4	49.4	53.6	56.7	59.6	60.3	62.0	63.1
40	29.8	32.2	34.9	37.3	40.0	40.8	42.5	43.5
60	15.3	16.4	17.8	19.8	21.9	22.6	24.1	25.1
80	5.6	5.6	5.9	6.9	8.4	8.5	9.1	9.9

1 Data are three year averages centred on the year shown. From 2001 the data are from the 1998-based national population projections. See Appendix, Part 7: Expectation of life.
Source: Government Actuary's Department

one and a half times higher than that for those whose fathers were in the professional social class. For babies born outside of marriage, the mortality rate was 6.9 deaths per thousand live births compared with 5.2 deaths per thousand live births for those born inside marriage. There have, however, been large increases in the proportions of babies born outside marriage for all social classes. Many of these births are jointly registered, reflecting the increase in cohabitation. Although infant mortality rates in each class have decreased over the last decade or so, there is no evidence that the class differential has decreased over this period.

Declines in infant mortality have contributed greatly to improvements in overall life expectancy at birth. Large improvements in expectancy of life at birth have been seen over the past century for both males and females (Table 7.4). In 1997, life expectancy at birth in the United Kingdom was approaching 75 years for males and 80 years for females compared with just over 50 years for men and 54 years for women in 1911. Life

7.5

Premature deaths[1] from circulatory diseases: EU comparison, 1995

Rates per 100,000 population

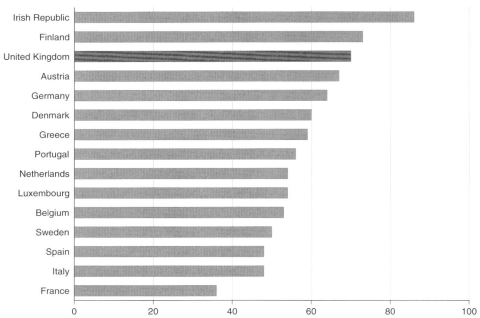

1 Death rates for those aged under 65 standardised to the European population. See Appendix, Part 7: Standardised death rates.
Source: World Health Organisation

7.6

Accidental death rates: by gender and age

England & Wales Rates per million population

	Males					Females				
	Under 15	15-24	25-54	55-74	75 and over	Under 15	15-24	25-54	55-75	75 and over
1901-1910	611	432	652	1,178	2,231	458	62	112	440	2,230
1911-1920	529	548	657	1,066	2,349	359	71	94	398	2,280
1921-1930	437	443	453	875	2,390	256	80	82	379	2,443
1931-1940	407	535	444	827	2,979	233	97	82	453	3,177
1941-1950	440	442	390	711	2,271	250	69	73	332	2,578
1951-1960	241	497	336	591	2,583	133	71	72	339	2,859
1961-1970	236	555	326	542	2,436	130	110	94	362	2,731
1971-1980	162	505	272	425	1,694	88	118	91	289	2,026
1981-1990	106	397	229	314	1,223	58	92	69	204	1,284
1991-1998	59	290	205	254	1,074	32	76	59	152	1,072

Source: Office for National Statistics

expectancies for adults did not, however, start improving until later on in the twentieth century. Over recent years it has been this increase in life expectancy among older adults that has been particularly dramatic. For example, life expectancy for men aged 60 increased by over three years between 1971 and 1997 compared with an increase of only one year between 1921 and 1971. In addition, the 1998-based population projections indicate that in 2021 the expectation of life at age 60 will be a further 22.0 years compared with 18.8 years in 1997. During the first 70 years of the twentieth century the excess of life expectancy at birth for females over males rose in the United Kingdom. However it has since fallen to around five years and is projected to fall to just over four years in 2021. Between 1911 and 1996, expectation of life at age 80 increased by 2.9 years for women and 1.7 years for men.

The Government recently published a White Paper, *Saving Lives: Our Healthier Nation* and similar strategies have been published for Scotland, Wales and Northern Ireland. One of the target areas for improvement is to reduce the death rate from coronary heart disease and stroke. The United Kingdom has one of the highest premature death rates from circulatory disease (which includes heart disease and stroke) in Europe, after the Irish Republic and Finland (Chart 7.5). For those aged under 65, the rate for men in the United Kingdom is two and a half times greater than that in France, the country with the lowest death rates, while for women the rate is over four times higher. A number of risk factors have been identified which are known to increase a person's risk of circulatory disease, including the lack of regular exercise, high blood pressure, obesity and smoking. These are looked at later on in this chapter in Table 7.20, Table 7.14, Table 7.15 and Table 7.18 respectively.

7.7

Another priority area identified in the White Paper is deaths from accidents. Accidents are responsible for around 10,000 deaths a year in England and are the most common cause of death in people under 35. Deaths from this cause are considered avoidable and therefore preventable. Over a long period of time there have been considerable improvements in accident fatality rates. The decline in age-standardised death rates over the century has been slightly larger for men than for women, falling by 63 per cent for men and 52 per cent for women.

Trends in accidental death rates at different ages vary considerably (Table 7.6). There have been dramatic falls in the rates for children. In the 1900s the death rate from accidents among boys aged under 15 in England and Wales was 611 per million population. By the 1980s, this had declined to 106 deaths per million population. However, there has been little change in death rates for young adults of either gender, and the highest rates for 15 to 24 year olds were seen in the 1960s for men and in the 1970s for women. These rates have since declined so that the rate for young men during the 1980s was lower than in the first decade of the century. It is very likely that the peak for young men in the 1960s reflects the rapid growth of motor vehicle travel and accidents during the 1960s and 1970s with the slightly later increase for women reflecting increases in the number of licence-holders. The reductions in road traffic accident deaths that occurred during the 1980s have contributed substantially to the recent downward turn in accidental death rates. This improvement is linked to tighter government legislation on seatbelts and improved car design with crumple zones and airbags fitted as standard on many new models.

Suicide rates[1]: by gender and age

United Kingdom					Rate per 100,000 population	
	1971	1976	1981	1986	1991	1997
Males						
15-24	6.9	9.6	10.6	12.7	15.9	16.4
25-44	13.5	15.0	19.5	20.1	24.3	21.8
45-64	19.8	21.0	23.1	22.6	20.4	17.5
65 and over	25.4	23.8	23.7	26.4	18.4	15.4
Females						
15-24	3.3	4.6	3.4	3.4	4.0	4.0
25-44	7.7	8.9	7.7	6.6	5.9	6.2
45-64	15.9	14.3	15.0	12.0	8.2	6.9
65 and over	16.5	15.0	15.5	13.6	8.6	6.3

1 Includes deaths undetermined whether accidentally or purposely inflicted. Age-standardised to the European population. See Appendix, Part 7: Standardised death rates and International Classification of Diseases.

Source: Office for National Statistics; General Register Office for Scotland; Northern Ireland Statistics and Research Agency

Deaths from suicide have fluctuated widely over time (Table 7.7). The highest rates occurred around 1931 when rates for the older age groups were considerably higher than those of the youngest. There has been a marked increase in suicide death rates in people aged 15 to 24 since the end of the 1950s. Between 1971 and 1997 the suicide death rate for men aged 15 to 24 rose from 6.9 per 100,000 population in to 16.4 per 100,000 population. For women in this age group there was a fall from the mid-1970s to the mid-1980s, and the rate was 4.0 per 100,000 population in 1997. Suicide among men aged 25 to 44 has risen since the 1950s to a level higher than among any other group. Rates among those over the age of 44 have declined. Suicide rates are associated with mental health problems, such as depression. More detail on services for mentally ill people is contained in Table 8.16 in Chapter 8: Social Protection.

7.8

Self-reported limiting longstanding illness[1]: by gender

Great Britain

Percentages

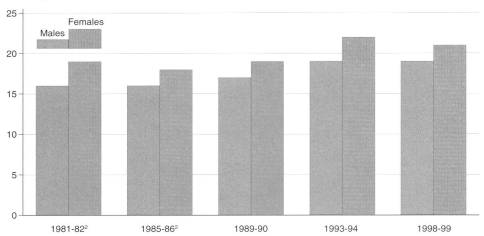

1 Percentage aged 16 and over reporting a longstanding illness or disability that limited their activities.
2 Calendar years up to 1988.
Source: General Household Survey, Office for National Statistics

7.9

Self-reported health problems[1]: by gender and age, 1996-97

United Kingdom   Percentages

	16-44	45-64	65-74	75 and over	All aged 16 and over
Males					
Pain or discomfort	18	39	52	56	32
Mobility	6	22	36	50	18
Anxiety or depression	12	19	20	19	15
Problems performing usual activities	5	16	21	27	12
Problems with self-care	1	6	8	14	5
Females					
Pain or discomfort	20	40	51	65	34
Mobility	6	21	37	60	19
Anxiety or depression	18	24	25	30	22
Problems performing usual activities	7	17	23	40	15
Problems with self-care	2	5	9	21	6

1 Percentages of respondents who reported having problems with their general health and the activities of daily life. See Appendix, Part 7: Self-reported health problems.
Source: General Household Survey, Office for National Statistics; Continuous Household Survey, Northern Ireland Statistics and Research Agency

The nation's health

Despite increases in life expectancy, many people report suffering from an illness or disability that limits their activities. The proportion of people reporting such an illness has increased over the past three decades. In 1975, 15 per cent of adults said they had a longstanding illness that limited their activities compared with 20 per cent in 1998-99 (Chart 7.8). This may be a result of changes in people's perceptions of illness as well as a real increase in morbidity. In contrast, rates of medical consultation have fallen from the levels recorded in the 1950s, reflecting improvements in therapies and in medical management.

In nearly all age groups in 1996-97, women in the United Kingdom were more likely than men to report having problems with their general health and the normal activities of life (Table 7.9). The most common problem was pain or discomfort, reported by around a third of both men and women. The likelihood of having these problems increases with age. For example, 50 per cent of men and 60 per cent of women aged 75 and over experienced mobility problems compared with 6 per cent of 16 to 44 year olds. Problems performing their usual activities were experienced by more than a quarter of men and two-fifths of women aged 75 and over.

The incidence of different types of cancer has altered over the last decade or so, with the reduction in smoking by men resulting in a marked decline in lung cancer, although there has been a slight rise in women. Breast cancer among women has risen over the period (Chart 7.10) and is now the main cause of death among women aged 35 and under. The incidence of breast cancer peaked in 1992 following the introduction of the NHS breast screening programme in the late 1980s but has since almost returned to the pre-screening level. This is a result of the majority of women in the screening age group (50 to 64 years) having been screened at least once. Incidence rates have also increased for some other cancers, most notably for malignant melanoma of the skin, testicular cancer and prostate cancer.

Skin cancer is largely a preventable cancer if people take care in the sun and avoid getting burnt. Certain people are particularly at risk, especially those who live in very sunny climates and have fair skin. The incidence of malignant melanoma of the skin has been rising rapidly in the white populations around the world for several decades. Incidence rates in Great Britain increased from around 2 per 100,000 population for males and 3 per 100,000 population for females in 1971 to 7 and 9 per 100,000 population for men and women respectively in 1996, a threefold increase (see Chart 7.1 at the beginning of this chapter). The likely reason, as with other countries, is an increase in intermittent sun exposure of untanned skin, on holidays and other outside pursuits. (See Table 7.26 for information on the use of suncream.) Incidence of skin cancer has increased to a greater extent than mortality, partly as a result of improved treatment and of earlier presentations of melanomas at a stage when they can be treated more successfully.

Asthma is another disease that has become more widespread over recent years, especially among young adults and children. It is now the most common chronic childhood disease in Britain. Its prevalence is rising, as in other countries, and, although there is some debate about causes, possible explanations for this rise include exposure to outdoor and indoor pollution and allergens. A climate conducive to house dust mites may also contribute to the risk and could explain some of the geographic variations in the prevalence of the disease. In England the prevalence of doctor-diagnosed asthma is higher among young males than young females (Chart 7.11). In the period 1995 to 1997, 23 per cent of males and 18 per cent of females aged 2 to 15 reported a diagnosis of asthma made by a doctor. The variation in the diagnosis of asthma by

Standardised incidence rates[1] of selected cancers: by gender

Great Britain
Rates per 100,000 population

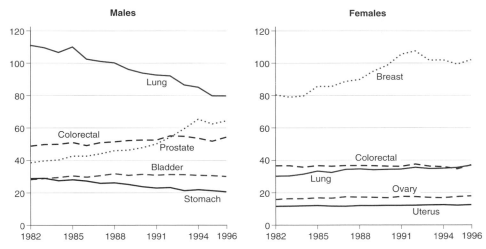

1 Age-standardised to the European population. See Appendix, Part 7: Standardised incidence rates.
Source: Office for National Statistics

Young people with doctor-diagnosed asthma: by age, 1995-1997

England
Percentages

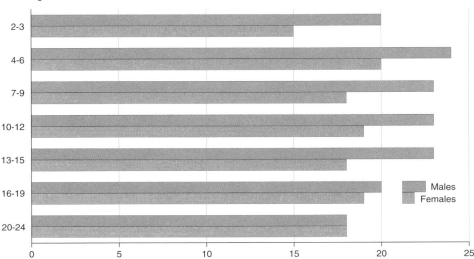

Source: Health Survey for England, Department of Health

7.12

Ten most common symptoms on which advice is sought from NHS Direct, 1999[1]

England

Adults	Children
Abdominal pain	Fever
Headache	Rash
Fever	Vomiting
Chest pain	Diarrhoea
Back pain	Cough
Vomiting	Abdominal pain
Breathing difficulty	Cold/influenza
Diarrhoea	Headache
Urinary symptom	Head injury
Dizziness	Ingestion/overdose/ poisoning

1 Based on information collected monthly from 13 NHS Direct sites between April and September 1999.
Source: Department of Health

gender reduced with age so that 19 per cent of males and 18 per cent of females aged 16 to 24 had asthma and in the 20 to 24 age groups there was no difference between the proportions of males and females with asthma.

Almost everyone will use health services at some point in their lives. More information on these services is contained in Chapter 8: Social Protection. The first point of contact with the NHS for most people is their GP and since the 1970s there has been an increase in the proportion of GP consultations taking place at a surgery or health centre. This has been accompanied by a decrease in consultations at home – they fell from 22 per cent in 1971 to 8 per cent in 1996-97. In addition to GPs, specialist services are being developed to improve people's access to professional heath advice and information. NHS

Direct is a new nurse-led helpline which by December 1999 had been introduced in 17 pilot sites throughout England covering around 65 per cent of the population. The nurse, prompted by a clinical computer decision support system, asks the caller about their symptoms. The most common symptoms on which calls were made included abdominal pain, headache and fever for adults and fever, rash and vomiting for children (Table 7.12).

Morbidity studies in general practice have shown that the consultation rate for back pain has risen in the past 10 years. Estimates of the extent of back pain among the British population suggest that the lifetime occurrence is consistently higher in men than in women and approaches 70 per cent by the age of 60. For some people back pain may last for a short period of time whereas for others it may be more persistent. Forty per cent of adults responding to the ONS Omnibus Survey in Great Britain in 1998 said they had suffered from back pain lasting for more than one day in the previous 12 months. The prevalence of persistent back pain increased with age: around one in three men and one in four of women aged 65 and over suffered for the whole year with back pain compared with around one in 12 men and women aged between 25 and 44 (Table 7.13).

Over the last 10 years there has been a sharp increase in sickness and invalidity benefit due to back pain. Whether this is a result of a real increase in the prevalence of back pain or from less willingness to tolerate it is not clear. Of back pain sufferers aged 16 to 64 in 1998 who were not in employment in the four weeks before interview, 13 per cent mentioned back pain as a reason why they were not in work. In addition, of those who had been employed in the four weeks before interview, 5 per cent had taken time off during that period due to back pain.

7.13

Adults experiencing back pain: by age and total time suffered in previous 12 months, 1998

Great Britain   Percentages

	1-6 days	7-28 days	29-364 days	Whole year	All experiencing back pain
Males					
16-24	49	35	17	0	100
25-44	22	34	36	7	100
45-54	19	35	29	17	100
55-64	20	38	25	18	100
65 and over	22	21	25	32	100
All aged 16 and over	23	32	29	16	100
Females					
16-24	23	27	42	8	100
25-44	21	31	41	8	100
45-54	20	21	50	8	100
55-64	19	24	37	20	100
65 and over	8	21	47	25	100
All aged 16 and over	17	25	44	15	100

Source: Omnibus Survey, Office for National Statistics

7.14

Diet and lifestyle

Changes in people's diet and lifestyles in the past have influenced morbidity and mortality patterns today. Increasingly, dietary concerns in Britain have shifted from the early twentieth century problems of under-nutrition towards the problems of over-nutrition, and hence obesity, and the health-related properties of particular foods. A number of risk factors for cardiovascular disease have been identified, many of which are influenced by people's lifestyles today.

High blood pressure is a risk factor for a number of conditions including cardiovascular disease. A reduction in premature deaths from circulatory diseases is one of the areas targeted by the Government in its White Paper. Many people with high blood pressure go unrecognised or are treated ineffectively and so remain at increased risk. High blood pressure can, however, be treated very effectively both by drugs and changes to diet, alcohol intake and levels of exercise.

The prevalence of high blood pressure increases with age. In 1997, four in ten men and five in ten women aged 75 and over in England had high blood pressure (either treated or untreated) compared with around one in ten men and women aged 45 to 54 (Table 7.14). High blood pressure can be treated using medication: a fifth of men aged 75 and over had normal blood pressure as a result of treatment although a quarter had untreated high blood pressure. Among women of the same age, over a quarter were being successfully treated whereas just over a fifth were untreated.

Another risk factor for cardiovascular disease is being overweight. The proportion of men and women in England who are obese rose to one in six men and one in five women in 1997 (Table 7.15). The likelihood of being overweight or obese

Blood pressure level[1]: by gender and age, 1997

England — Percentages

	16-24	25-34	35-44	45-54	55-64	65-74	75 and over	All aged 16 and over
Males								
Normal (untreated)	98	97	93	83	58	47	38	79
Normal (treated)	0	0	1	8	17	24	23	8
High (treated)	-	0	0	2	8	13	15	4
High (untreated)	2	3	6	8	17	17	24	9
All males	100	100	100	100	100	100	100	100
Females								
Normal (untreated)	100	98	93	84	62	42	26	77
Normal (treated)	1	1	3	9	21	22	28	10
High (treated)	-	0	0	2	6	15	24	5
High (untreated)	-	0	3	6	11	21	22	8
All females	100	100	100	100	100	100	100	100

1 See Appendix, Part 7: Blood pressure level.

Source: Health Survey for England, Department of Health

7.15

Body mass[1]: by gender and age, 1997

England — Percentages

	Underweight	Desirable	Overweight	Obese	Total
Males					
16-24	17	56	22	5	100
25-34	4	40	43	13	100
35-44	2	32	48	18	100
45-54	1	25	52	22	100
55-64	1	25	47	27	100
65-74	1	25	56	18	100
75 and over	4	34	50	12	100
All aged 16 and over	4	34	45	17	100
Females					
16-24	17	56	19	9	100
25-34	8	51	27	15	100
35-44	7	44	32	18	100
45-54	4	38	37	23	100
55-64	4	29	37	30	100
65-74	4	27	44	25	100
75 and over	8	30	41	22	100
All aged 16 and over	7	40	33	20	100

1 Using the body mass index. See Appendix, Part 7: Body mass index.

Source: Health Survey for England, Department of Health

7.16

Changing patterns in the consumption of foods at home

Great Britain
Grams per person per week

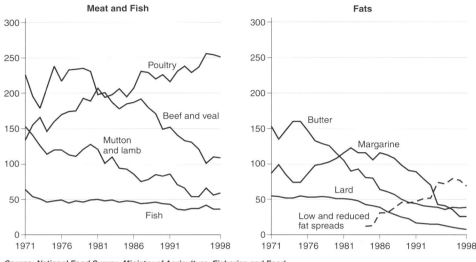

Meat and Fish

Poultry

Beef and veal

Mutton and lamb

Fish

Fats

Butter

Margarine

Lard

Low and reduced fat spreads

Source: National Food Survey, Ministry of Agriculture, Fisheries and Food

7.17

Changes to diet[1] in last year, 1997

England   Percentages[2]

	Males	Females
Eats less fatty/fried food	8	10
Eats more fruit and vegetables	7	9
Eats more pasta, rice, bread	4	4
Eats fewer sweets/cakes	3	6
Eats more fatty foods, snacks, fast foods	2	3
Stopped eating meat	1	1
Cut down on alcohol	1	1
Other changes	5	7

1 Adults aged 16 to 74 in 1996.
2 Respondents could give more than one answer.
Source: Health Education Monitoring Follow-up Survey, Office for National Statistics

increases up to the age of 65 and then declines as people get older. In 1997, around a quarter of both men and women aged 16 to 24 were overweight or obese compared with three-quarters of men aged 55 to 64 and two-thirds of women of the same age. Among those aged 75 and over, however, this proportion drops to around three-fifths of both men and women.

There have been substantial changes in the pattern of food consumption in the United Kingdom over the course of the twentieth century. At the beginning, the problem for many was having an adequate diet, not an excessive one or obesity. Over the war period individual food choice was largely imposed by availability. After this period more plentiful supplies allowed households to return to what would then have been regarded as normal diets. By the mid-1950s the post-war rise in living standards was underway and the effect for many households was to lift the income constraint. This increased consumption of foods such as cheese, shellfish, chicken and chocolate biscuits. During the 1970s prices became much more important as an influence on patterns of food consumption. A watershed appears to have occurred for a number of food groups around 1975 to 1980. Stable or rising consumption was

replaced by decline, as is the case with red meat and fish; fruit decline and stability was replaced by growth.

Year to year fluctuations reflect both economic and social effects but, despite this, distinct long-term trends are discernable. The consumption of beef, veal and sheep meat in Great Britain have all declined since the 1970s, while there have been dramatic rises in the consumption of poultry (Chart 7.16). Consumption of certain fats has also shown a decline. Butter consumption plummeted over the period and margarine and lard has also joined the decline. In 1998 consumption of butter per person was only half that in 1984 and a quarter of that in 1971. Butter and margarine have been replaced in our diets to some extent by low and reduced fat spreads which have increased by more than fivefold since 1984.

In 1975 each person in Great Britain ate an average of nearly 500 grams of fresh fruit each week at home; by 1998 this had risen to over 700 grams. In contrast, fresh vegetable consumption is now only slightly higher than in 1975 at just over 730 grams in 1998. However, the type of vegetables consumed changed during the period, with consumption of fresh green vegetables declining and that of other fresh vegetables, such as carrots, increasing.

Some people deliberately change their diet to become healthier. In 1996 the Health Education Monitoring Survey asked people whether they wanted to change their diet and followed up the same people in 1997. The majority of respondents said they had not changed their diet in the previous year, with only 22 per cent of women and 17 per cent of men saying that what they ate and drank was different from a year ago. Older people were less likely than younger people to have altered their diet with 10 per cent of men and 13 per cent of women aged 65 to 74 having changed compared with 26 per cent of men and 34 per cent of women aged 16 to 24.

Social Trends 30, © Crown copyright 2000

7.18

When asked how their diet had changed most respondents mentioned changes towards a healthier diet. The two most frequently cited differences were eating less fatty or fried food and snacks and increased intake of fruit and vegetables (Table 7.17). Women were also more likely than men to have cut down on eating sweets and cakes: 6 per cent of women compared with 3 per cent of men mentioned this as a change. Five per cent of men and 7 per cent of women mentioned changes which were grouped into 'other changes'. Examples of this included eating less red meat, eating a sensible or more balanced diet and eating more fibre or wholemeal bread. All of the above changes are ones that reflect dietary guidelines. However, 2 per cent of men and 3 per cent of women said that the change to their diet involved increasing their intake of fatty foods, snacks or fast foods.

In the United Kingdom more cancer deaths can be attributed to smoking tobacco than to any other single risk factor. Smoking is also an important component of differences in mortality between social classes. The proportion of smokers is higher among those in the manual socio-economic groups for both men and women than among those in the non-manual groups. The proportion of people who smoke has fallen in Great Britain since the 1970s, although this decline has been greater for some groups than others (Table 7.18). In 1972, a third of both men and women in the professional social class were smokers but by 1998-99 this had reduced by more than a half. The largest fall in percentage points for men was in the skilled manual group where the proportion who smoked fell from 57 per cent in 1972 to 33 per cent in 1998-99. For women the largest falls were among those from the professional, employers and managerial groups. Changes in smoking pattern by gender meant that in 1998-99, similar proportions of men and women were smokers across the majority of the socio-economic groups, with the exception of the semi and unskilled manual groups where a higher proportion of men were smokers than women.

Current smokers[1]: by gender and socio-economic group[2]

Great Britain				Percentages
	1972	1982	1996-97	1998-99
Males				
Professional	33	20	12	15
Employers and managers	44	29	20	21
Intermediate and junior non-manual	45	30	24	23
Skilled manual	57	42	32	33
Semi-skilled manual	57	47	41	38
Unskilled manual	64	49	41	45
All aged 16 and over[1]	52	38	29	28
Females				
Professional	33	21	11	14
Employers and managers	38	29	18	20
Intermediate and junior non-manual	38	30	28	24
Skilled manual	47	39	30	30
Semi-skilled manual	42	36	36	33
Unskilled manual	42	41	36	33
All aged 16 and over[1]	42	33	28	26

1 Adults aged 16 and over, except for 1972 which relates to those aged 15 and over.
2 Classified according to respondents' own job, or for those not currently working, their last job. Married or cohabiting women whose husbands are in the household are classified according to the husband's present, or last, job.
Source: General Household Survey, Office for National Statistics

7.19

The consumption of alcohol in excessive amounts can lead to ill health, and an increased likelihood of problems such as high blood pressure, heart disease, cancer and cirrhosis of the liver. The current Department of Health advice on alcohol is that consumption of between three and four units a day for men and two to three units a day for women will not accrue significant health risks, but consistently drinking four or more units a day for men (three or more units for women) is not advised because of the progressive health risks. While the proportion of men drinking over 21 units a week has remained broadly similar since 1988 at around 27 per cent, the proportions for women (drinking over 14 units) has increased from 10 per cent to 15 per cent between 1988 and 1998-99 (Table 7.19). In 1998-99, a quarter of women aged between 16 and 24 drank over this amount compared with just under a sixth of those of the same age in 1988.

Percentage of adults consuming over selected weekly limits[1] of alcohol: by gender and age

Great Britain			Percentages
	1988	1994-95	1998-99
Males			
16-24	31	29	36
25-44	34	30	27
45-64	24	27	30
65 and over	13	17	16
All aged 16 and over	26	27	27
Females			
16-24	15	19	25
25-44	14	15	16
45-64	9	12	16
65 and over	4	7	6
All aged 16 and over	10	13	15

1 21 units for men and 14 units for women. See Appendix, Part 7: Alcohol consumption.
Source: General Household Survey, Office for National Statistics

7.20

Physical activity[1]: by gender and age[2], 1998

England   Percentages

	16-24	25-34	35-44	45-54	55-64	65-74	75 and over	All aged 16 and over
Males								
Less than one day a week	15	16	21	28	33	45	64	27
1-2 days a week	20	24	23	26	28	29	22	24
3-4 days a week	13	14	16	12	10	10	7	12
5 or more days a week	53	46	40	33	29	15	7	36
All males	100	100	100	100	100	100	100	100
Females								
Less than one day a week	34	21	22	30	36	51	72	35
1-2 days a week	33	30	31	27	31	30	20	29
3-4 days a week	12	16	14	12	13	8	4	12
5 or more days a week	21	33	33	32	21	11	4	24
All females	100	100	100	100	100	100	100	100
All								
Less than one day a week	24	18	22	29	35	48	69	31
1-2 days a week	26	27	27	26	29	30	21	27
3-4 days a week	13	15	15	12	11	9	5	12
5 or more days a week	37	40	37	32	25	13	5	30
All adults	100	100	100	100	100	100	100	100

1 Frequency of at least moderate intensity activity for 30 minutes or more.
2 Adults aged 16 and over.
Source: Health Education Monitoring Survey, Office for National Statistics

7.21

Percentage of 16 to 24 year olds who have used drugs in the past year, 1998

England & Wales   Percentages

	Males	Females	All
Cannabis	32	22	27
Amphetamines	12	8	10
Ecstasy	6	4	5
Magic mushrooms	5	2	4
LSD	5	2	3
Cocaine	4	3	3
Any drug	36	24	29

Source: British Crime Survey, Home Office

Keeping physically active provides strong protection against coronary heart disease and stroke. It also has beneficial effects on weight control, blood pressure and diabetes, all of which are cardiovascular disease risk factors in their own right. Regular exercise also protects against brittle bones, maintains muscle power and increases people's general sense of well-being. There is evidence to suggest that physical activity has been decreasing over recent years. As a result of this, the Health Education Authority developed a national promotional programme in 1998 aimed at encouraging people to be more physically active. Part of the programme recommended participation in physical activity on five or more occasions a week of at least moderate intensity lasting 30 minutes per occasion. Moderate intensity activity includes brisk or fast walking, heavy housework, heavy gardening or DIY and swimming or cycling. Men, particularly those in the younger age groups, were more active than women: 53 per cent of men aged 16 to 24 in England had participated in moderate activity on at least five days a week compared with only 21 per cent of women of the same age (Table 7.20). In 1998, over a quarter of men and a third of women were sedentary using this classification. This proportion increased with age: a fifth of women aged between 25 and 34 were sedentary compared with over a half of those aged between 65 and 74 and nearly three-quarters of those aged 75 and over.

Drug misuse is associated with a range of illnesses such as life-threatening infections, physical injury and psychiatric complications including suicide. The Government's drug strategy emphasises the importance of reducing the proportion of young people under 25 reporting use of illegal drugs. In 1998 the British Crime Survey showed that 29 per cent of those aged between 16 and 24 in England and Wales had used an illegal drug in the past year (Table 7.21) and 19 per cent had used an illegal drug in the past month. The most commonly used illegal drug among both men and women in England and Wales in 1998 was cannabis, which had been used by a third of young men and over a fifth of young women in the previous year. Amphetamines were the next most common drug, used by one in ten young people in the previous year, followed by ecstasy (5 per cent). Although only 3 per cent of young people reported using cocaine in the last year, there had been a significant increase in the proportions using this drug since 1996. Use of cocaine was more apparent in London, the South and Merseyside than elsewhere in England and Wales.

7.22

Prevention

Taking preventative measures such as immunisation and screening can, at least in part, control some aspects of health. Many children are immunised against a variety of diseases before their second birthday. Over the years there have been a number of campaigns to encourage parents to have their children immunised against major infectious diseases.

Diphtheria was a leading cause of death in children until 1941 when immunisation was introduced; by the end of the 1950s the disease had almost disappeared. In the 1980s only 30 cases were reported, many of them imported infections or contacts of imported cases.

Whooping cough immunisation started in the 1950s, which led to a sharp decline in deaths and notifications. In 1974, however, a study suggested that encephalopathy and brain damage might be a rare complication of immunisation. By 1978, only 30 per cent of children under 2 years were immunised and large outbreaks of whooping cough followed in 1978 and 1982. New evidence showed that the association between immunisation and encephalopathy was not causative and vaccine uptake rates increased. By 1997, uptake rates had reached 94 per cent.

Measles immunisation was introduced in 1968 and although immunisation was slow to gain general acceptance, notifications fell by about two-thirds to an average of about 90 thousand per year in the early 1980s. In 1988, the measles/mumps/rubella (MMR) vaccine was introduced and a higher uptake of immunisation was achieved, and notifications fell to their lowest recorded annual total of 9.6 thousand in 1993. Recent scares about the MMR combined vaccine have led to a reduction in uptake, although between 1991 and 1998 between around 90 to 91 per cent of children had been vaccinated by their second birthday (Table 7.22).

Immunisation of children[1] by their second birthday

United Kingdom				Percentages
	1981[2]	1991-92	1994-95[3]	1997-98
Diphtheria	82	94	95	96
Tetanus	82	94	93	96
Poliomyelitis	82	94	95	96
Whooping cough	45	88	95	94
Measles, mumps, rubella[4]	52	90	91	91

1 See Appendix, Part 7: Immunisation.
2 Data exclude Scotland.
3 Data for Scotland are for calendar years.
4 Includes measles only vaccine for 1981. Combined vaccine was not available prior to 1988.

Source: Department of Health; National Assembly for Wales; National Health Service in Scotland; Department of Health and Social Services, Northern Ireland

7.23

Average number and condition of teeth among adults with natural teeth: by age, 1998

United Kingdom					Numbers
			Average number of teeth that were[1]:		
	Present	Missing	Decayed or unsound	Had sound restoration	Sound and untreated
16-24	27.9	4.1	1.6	2.8	23.4
25-34	28.1	3.9	1.8	7.1	19.1
35-44	26.7	5.3	1.4	9.8	15.4
45-54	24.0	8.0	1.4	10.8	11.7
55-64	19.9	12.1	1.3	8.9	9.6
65-74	18.3	13.7	1.2	8.1	9.0
75 and over	15.4	16.6	1.3	6.4	7.6
All aged 16 and over	24.8	7.2	1.5	7.9	15.3

1 Number of sound and untreated teeth, decayed or unsound teeth and teeth with sound restorations may not add to number of teeth present due to the rounding of values and that the dental examiners could not assess the condition of some teeth.

Source: Adult Dental Health Survey, Office for National Statistics

7.24

**Percentage of target population[1]
screened for cervical cancer in the
previous five years: by age[2] and country,
31 March 1998**

		Percentages
	England	Wales	Scotland
25-34	82.9	78.8	81.7
35-44	86.9	87.8	91.7
45-54	86.2	87.3	92.7
55-64	79.3	83.7	85.5
All aged 25 to 64	84.2	83.6	87.0

1 Target population in England excludes those no longer
eligible because of clinical reasons.
2 For Wales, the age groups are 20-34, 35-44,45-54, 55-64
and 20-64 respectively. For Scotland they are 20-34, 35-44,
45-54, 55-59 and 20-59 respectively.

*Source: Department of Health; National Assembly for
Wales; National Health Service in Scotland*

In 1994 the Department of Health published *An
oral health strategy for England*. This document
set a number of targets to be met by 1998. Two of
the targets related to the retention of teeth among
older adults: 33 per cent of adults aged over 75
should have some natural teeth and 10 per cent
should have more than 20 natural teeth. Data from
the Adult Dental Health Survey showed that in
1998 among adults aged 75 and over living in
England, 44 per cent had retained some of their
teeth and 10 per cent had more than 20 teeth.

Among adults in the United Kingdom with natural
teeth (dentate adults) those aged 25 to 34 had the
highest average number of teeth; and the average
number of teeth decreased with age. Older
dentate adults tended to have, on average, fewer
sound and untreated teeth, which varied from 23.4
among 16 to 24 year olds to 7.6 among those
aged 75 and over (see Table 7.23 on the previous
page). The condition of teeth also varied between
countries. Dentate adults living in Scotland and

Northern Ireland had lower average numbers of
decayed and unsound teeth compared with
dentate adults from England and Wales.

The NHS provides screening programmes for
breast and cervical cancer with the aims of early
treatment and improved survival. National policy
for cervical screening is that women should be
screened every three to five years. The
programme invites women aged 20 to 64 for
screening but since many women are not invited
immediately when they reach their 20th birthday,
the age group 25 to 64 gives a more accurate
estimate of coverage of the target population. In
1997-98 around 84 per cent of women of this age
in England had been screened at least once in the
previous five years (Table 7.24). This is a
considerable improvement since 1988 when
44 per cent of the target population had
undergone a smear test in the previous five years.
Cervical cancer is most commonly preceded by a
long pre-cancerous stage that can be treated. The
cervical screening programme is estimated to
have prevented 800 deaths from cervical cancer
in 1997.

7.25

Breast cancer screening[1]: by region

United Kingdom

				Percentages
	1991-92	1993-94	1995-96	1997-98
United Kingdom	71	72	76	..
Trent	78	78	81	81
Anglia & Oxford	79	76	82	79
South West	77	75	79	79
Northern & Yorkshire	74	73	77	79
West Midlands	72	72	78	76
North West	71	74	77	75
South Thames	69	69	74	73
North Thames	59	60	66	66
England	72	72	76	75
Wales	77	77	77	..
Scotland	72	69	72	..
Northern Ireland	63	69	74	74

1 As a percentage of women aged 50 to 64 invited for screening.

*Source: Department of Health; National Assembly for Wales; National Health Service in Scotland; Department of Health and
Social Services, Northern Ireland*

Nearly a third of cancer cases and a fifth of cancer
deaths in women are due to breast cancer (see
incidence rates in Chart 7.10). Around two-thirds
of women with breast cancer survive for at least
five years after diagnosis. It is estimated that
regular screening of women aged 50 to 64 years
will eventually save up to an estimated 1,250 lives
each year in the United Kingdom. Around
75 per cent of the women invited from the target
population aged 50 to 64 had undergone
screening for breast cancer (Table 7.25). The
highest breast cancer screening rate in 1997-98
was in the Trent region where uptake reached just
over 80 per cent; in the Anglia and Oxford, the
South West and the Northern and Yorkshire
regions the uptake was only slightly lower.

7.26

Skin cancers are some of the most common forms of cancer in this country and sunburn is known to be associated with certain forms of skin cancer (see Chart 7.1 at the beginning of this chapter for incidence rates of skin cancer.) Four out of every five cases of skin cancer are preventable and protection from excessive exposure to the sun is an important preventative measure. Men were found to be less likely than women to use suncream. In 1998, one in three men reported not using suncream, compared with only one in five women (Table 7.26). Between 1996 and 1998 there has been an increase in the proportions of both men and women using suncream, particularly when abroad. In 1996, 27 per cent of men used suncream when outdoors abroad compared with 37 per cent in 1998. For women the proportion increased from 35 per cent to 46 per cent over the same period.

Occasions on which people[1] use suncream: by gender, 1996 and 1998

England				Percentages
	Males		Females	
	1996	1998	1996	1998
Uses suncream				
Sunbathing abroad	41	48	47	53
Outdoors abroad, but not sunbathing	27	37	35	46
Sunbathing in this country	32	38	49	55
Outdoors in this country, doing something else	26	36	38	52
All using suncream	61	66	74	79
Does not use suncream	38	33	23	18
Never goes out in the sun	1	1	2	3

1 Adults aged 16-74.
Source: Health Education Monitoring Survey, Office for National Statistics

References and further reading

The following list contains selected publications relevant to **Chapter 7: Health**. Those published by The Stationery Office are available from the addresses shown on the inside back cover of *Social Trends*.

Annual Report of the Registrar General for Northern Ireland, The Stationery Office

Annual Report of the Registrar General for Scotland, General Register Office for Scotland

Asthma, an Epidemiological Overview, Department of Health

Better Health Better Wales, The Stationery Office

Cancer Statistics Registrations (Series MB1), The Stationery Office

Communicable Disease Statistics (Series MB2), The Stationery Office

Designed to Care: Renewing the National Health Service in Scotland, The Stationery Office

European Community Household Panel (ECHP): methods, vol.1, Eurostat

Health in England 1996 – What people know, what people think, what people do, The Stationery Office

Health Inequalities (Series DS no 15), The Stationery Office

Health and Personal Social Services Statistics for England, The Stationery Office

Health and Personal Social Services Statistics for Northern Ireland, DHSS Northern Ireland

Health and Personal Social Services Statistics for Wales, Welsh Office

Health Survey for England, The Stationery Office

Hospital Episode Statistics, Department of Health

Key Health Statistics from General Practice (Series MB6), The Stationery Office

Living in Britain: Results from the General Household Survey, The Stationery Office

Mortality Statistics for England and Wales (Series DH1, 2, 3, 4), The Stationery Office

National Food Survey, The Stationery Office

National Food Survey – Northern Ireland, Department of Agriculture for Northern Ireland

References and further reading

On the State of Public Health, The Stationery Office

Population Trends, The Stationery Office

Saving Lives: Our Healthier Nation, The Stationery Office

Social Focus on Women and Men, The Stationery Office

Statistical Publications on Aspects of Health and Personal Social Services Activity in England (various), Department of Health

The Health of Adult Britain 1841-1994 (Series DS12 and DS13), The Stationery Office

World Health Statistics, World Health Organisation

Working Together for a Healthier Scotland, The Stationery Office

Contacts

Telephone contact points for further information relating to

Chapter 7: Health

Office for National Statistics	
Chapter author	020 7533 6117
Adult Dental Health Survey	020 7533 5510
Cancer statistics	020 7533 5230
Child health and mortality statistics	020 7533 5641
General Household Survey	020 7533 5444
Health Education Monitoring Survey	020 7533 5329
Mortality Statistics	020 7533 5251
Department of Health	
Health Survey for England	020 7972 5675
Smoking, misuse of alcohol and drugs	020 7972 5551
Department of Agriculture for Northern Ireland	028 9052 4594
Department of Health and Social Services, Northern Ireland	028 9052 2800
General Register Office for Scotland	0131 314 4243
General Register Office for Northern Ireland	028 9025 2031
Government Actuary's Department	020 7211 2667
Health and Safety Executive	0151 951 3819/3431
Home Office	020 7273 2084
Ministry of Agriculture, Fisheries and Food	020 7270 8563
National Assembly for Wales	029 2082 5080
National Health Service in Scotland	0131 551 8899
Northern Ireland Statistics and Research Agency	028 9025 2521
Eurostat	00 352 4231 13727

Social Trends 30, © Crown copyright 2000

Chapter 8 Social Protection

Overview　Spending on social security benefits in Great Britain increased by almost two-thirds in real terms between 1981-82 and 1998-99, to £96 billion. (Page 134)

At the end of March 1999, 1.1 million patients in England were waiting for NHS treatment as an in-patient or daycase and around three-quarters of these patients had been waiting under six months. (Table 8.10)

There are an estimated 22 million people in Great Britain regularly taking part in voluntary activity. (Page 138)

Sick and disabled people　The average duration of stay in NHS hospitals in the acute sector has reduced from just over eight days in 1981 to around five days in 1997-98. (Table 8.14)

In England and Wales there were over 300 thousand new outpatient attendances for psychiatric specialities in 1997-98, an increase of over 40 per cent since 1987-88. (Table 8.16)

Families　In 1960, one in three births in England and Wales was at home compared with only around one in 50 in 1997. (Chart 8.21)

The proportion of all antenatal contacts in England that took place in the community has increased from 51 per cent in 1997-98 to 69 per cent in 1998-99. (Page 144)

In 1998 there were over 300 thousand places in day nurseries in England and Wales compared with around 60 thousand in 1987. (Table 8.24)

8.1

Places in residential care homes for elderly people[1]: by type of care home

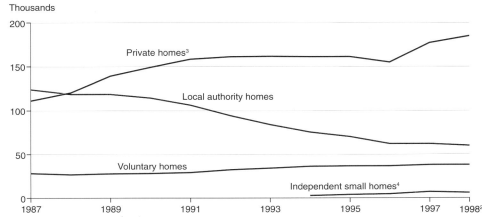

England, Wales & Northern Ireland

Thousands

1 In England places for elderly mentally ill people in all years. Includes places for people aged 65 or over in small homes for the mentally ill in 1994 to 1996. Data are not available for Wales in 1996.
2 From 1 April 1988 data for Northern Ireland are for financial years therefore there is no information for 1998.
3 Independent homes in Wales.
4 Data are for England only.

Source: Department of Health; National Assembly for Wales; Department of Health and Social Services, Northern Ireland

Social protection encompasses the various ways in which central government, local authorities, the private and voluntary sectors and individuals provide help for people in need or potentially at risk. Risk or need may arise through a variety of circumstances, such as ill health, infirmity or inadequate income. Generally people who are in need of help are identified in other chapters of *Social Trends*. This chapter focuses on the support provided for groups such as elderly people, those who are sick or disabled, and families.

Overview

The provision by the state of social care and welfare services to people in need has developed over the century. In the early 1900s these services hardly existed with the exception of the Poor Law which provided some assistance to those with very low incomes. The major development in social security came in 1942 with the Beveridge report which introduced the concept of the welfare state. This included the establishment of family allowances and a universal health service. A large proportion of expenditure on social protection today is funded by the government on similar programmes including social security benefits, training programmes and the National Health Service. These are designed specifically to protect people against common sources of financial hardship such as problems associated with old age, sickness, unemployment and disability. Non-government social protection expenditure is aimed principally at elderly people or survivors (for example, widows) in the form of occupational pensions, but also at sick and disabled people in the form of sick pay and compensation for occupational accidents or diseases, and at expectant mothers in the form of maternity pay.

In order for spending on social protection to be compared across the member countries of the European Union (EU), Eurostat has designed a framework for the presentation of information on such expenditure and this has been adopted by member states as the European System of Integrated Social Protection Statistics (ESSPROS). For this purpose, programmes specifically designed to protect people against common sources of hardship are collectively described as expenditure on social protection

8.2

Expenditure on social protection benefits in real terms[1]: by function, 1993-94 and 1997-98

United Kingdom

£ billion at 1997-98 prices[1]

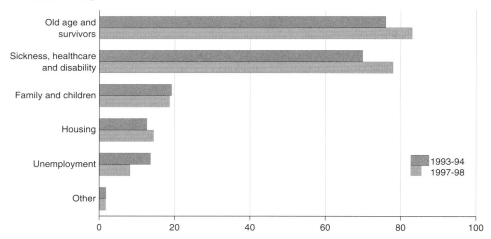

1 Adjusted to 1997-98 prices using the GDP market prices deflator.
Source: Office for National Statistics

Social Trends 30, © Crown copyright 2000

benefits, and are those from which households can readily perceive a direct benefit, whether in cash or kind.

In the United Kingdom, a total of £204 billion was spent in 1997-98 on social protection benefits, an increase of 6 per cent in real terms since 1993-94. Around two-fifths of all such expenditure is spent on programmes aimed at helping people in old age and a similar proportion is spent on sickness, healthcare and people with disabilities (Chart 8.2). It is this latter function where expenditure has increased the most over the period, by 11 per cent in real terms between 1993-94 and 1997-98. The amount spent on families and children has decreased slightly or remained fairly stable over the same period.

Chart 8.3 compares the expenditure on social protection benefits per head for the 15 EU countries and shows wide disparities between member states. To compare expenditure between countries, the expenditure must be expressed in the same currency. However, this takes no account of differences in the general level of prices of goods and services within each country. Thus in order to make direct real terms comparisons between countries, expenditure is expressed in purchasing power standards. The differences shown in the chart between countries reflect differences in the social protection systems, demographic structures, unemployment rates and other social, institutional and economic factors. In general, spending is much higher in the more northerly countries than in those in the south. Luxembourg spent the most per head in 1996; at just under £6 thousand this was over three times the amount spent by Portugal, the country that spent the least. The United Kingdom spent around £3 thousand per head of population, just below the average for the EU.

Expenditure[1] on social protection benefits per head: EU comparison, 1996

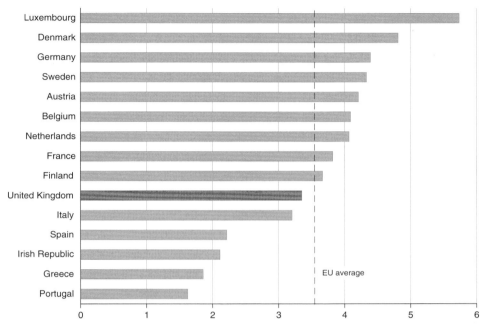

£ thousand

1 Before deduction of tax, where applicable. Figures are Purchasing Power Parities per inhabitant.
Source: Eurostat

In Great Britain, spending on social security benefits constitutes a major part of social protection expenditure today. This was not always the case. In the early part of the century, Poor Law relief, set at such a low level only to avert starvation, was the only statutory benefit providing almost all cash payments in 1900. Its contribution then fell dramatically with assistance grants accounting for an increasing proportion of the total. By the 1940s the social security system had grown into an amalgamation of voluntary and state provision which had no overall cohesion. The *National Insurance Act* in 1946, the core of the Beveridge report, aimed to overhaul the existing arrangements and replace them with a state-run insurance system paid for by employers, employees and the general taxpayer – similar to the one in place today.

8.4

Social security benefit expenditure: by recipient group[1], 1998-99

Great Britain

Percentages

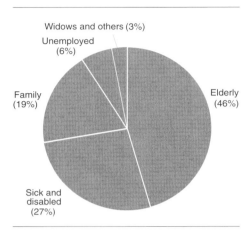

1 See Appendix, Part 8: Benefits to groups of recipients.
Source: Department of Social Security

Approximately £96 billion was spent in 1998-99 in Great Britain on a wide range of social security benefits for a large number of recipients. In Chart 8.4, benefit expenditure is classified according to the main reasons a benefit is paid so that, for example, a disability benefit paid to an elderly person is allocated to the sick and disabled group rather than to the elderly. Nevertheless, benefits for the elderly make up the largest group accounting for nearly half of all expenditure. Sick and disabled people are the second largest recipient group, receiving over a quarter of all benefit expenditure; this includes benefits such as incapacity benefit, war pensions and statutory sick pay.

The amount spent on social security benefits has increased by almost two-thirds in real terms between 1981-82 and 1998-99. The largest increases have been on benefits for sick and disabled people, which rose in real terms from £8 billion in 1981-82 to £25 billion in 1998-99. The unemployed are the only recipient group on which expenditure was lower in real terms in 1998-99 than in 1981-82, reflecting changing levels of unemployment and changes to the benefit system relating to unemployed people.

Benefits of one type or another are received by most people at some point in their lives. Information from the Family Resources Survey shows that around three in five families in Great Britain received some type of benefit in 1997-98 (Table 8.5). Some benefits, such as child benefit, are universally available whereas others, such as the state retirement pension, require contributions. The vast majority of pensioners receive a retirement pension from the government although the proportion of pensioner families receiving other benefits, such as income support, housing benefit and council tax benefit, varies according to whether or not they are single or in a couple. Single pensioners are more likely than pensioner couples to receive an income-related benefit and, in addition, single female pensioners are more likely to receive these benefits than single male pensioners. In 1997-98, nearly one in four single female pensioners received income support compared with one in seven single male pensioners and one in 20 pensioner couples. In 1996-97 around one in eight single people with no dependent children were receiving income support whereas in 1997-98 this proportion had decreased to only one in 15.

8.5

Receipt of selected social security benefits: by family type[1], 1997-98

Great Britain   Percentages

	Housing benefit	Council tax benefit	Income support	Retire-ment pension	Job-seeker's allowance	Child benefit	Any benefit
Pensioners[2]							
Couple	12	20	5	97	-	1	100
Single							
Male	31	39	14	95	0	-	99
Female	31	44	23	96	0	-	99
Couples							
Dependent children	8	11	5	-	3	98	99
No dependent children	5	8	4	8	2	-	27
Single person							
Dependent children	57	63	57	-	1	98	99
No dependent children							
Male	10	12	6	-	10	-	25
Female	10	12	8	-	5	-	25
All family types[3]	14	19	11	23	4	23	59

1 See Appendix 8: Benefit units.
2 People aged 60 and over for females and 65 and over for males.
3 Components do not add to the total as each benefit unit may receive more than one benefit.

Source: Family Resources Survey, Department of Social Security

People's attitudes towards spending on benefits varies depending on the type of recipient (Table 8.6). In 1998 the British Social Attitudes Survey asked respondents whether they would like to see more or less government spending on each of the following groups: carers of the sick and disabled, disabled people, retired people, parents who work on very low incomes, single parents and the unemployed. It found that over four-fifths of respondents aged 18 and over in Great Britain thought that more money should be spent on benefits for people who care for those who are sick or disabled. In addition, around seven in ten respondents thought that more money should be spent on benefits for disabled people who cannot work, benefits for retired people and benefits for parents who work on very low incomes.

Attitudes tend to vary by the age of the respondent. As one might expect, the proportion thinking that more money should be spent on benefits for retired people was greater for older people than young people: 74 per cent of those age 65 and over thought retirement benefits should be more compared with 64 per cent of those aged 18 to 34. Conversely, 45 per cent of people aged 18 to 34 thought that more money should be spent on benefits for single parents compared with only 17 per cent of those aged 65 and over.

Attitudes towards extra spending on social benefits: by age, 1998

Great Britain Percentages

	18-34	35-54	55-64	65 and over	All aged 18 and over
Benefits for people who care for those who are sick or disabled					
Spend more	79	84	83	80	82
Spend the same as now	18	14	14	14	15
Spend less	-	1	1	1	1
Benefits for disabled people who cannot work					
Spend more	68	73	79	72	72
Spend the same as now	27	23	18	22	23
Spend less	2	1	1	2	2
Benefits for retired people					
Spend more	64	75	72	74	71
Spend the same as now	30	21	24	23	24
Spend less	4	1	2	1	2
Benefits for parents who work on very low incomes					
Spend more	74	71	68	54	68
Spend the same as now	23	24	23	36	26
Spend less	1	4	4	4	3
Benefits for single parents					
Spend more	45	35	29	17	34
Spend the same as now	40	44	39	39	41
Spend less	12	18	26	37	21
Benefits for the unemployed					
Spend more	18	23	27	22	22
Spend the same as now	41	39	35	44	40
Spend less	39	35	35	29	35

Source: British Social Attitudes, National Centre for Social Research

8.7

Real[1] growth in social security benefits and National Health Service expenditure

United Kingdom
£ billion at 1998-99 prices[1]

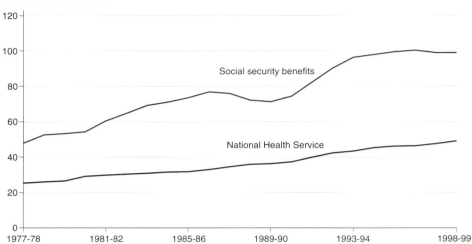

1 Adjusted to 1998-99 prices using the GDP market prices deflator.

Source: Department of Health; Department of Social Security; Department of Health and Social Services, Northern Ireland

8.8

Outcomes of calls to NHS Direct, April to June 1999

England   Percentages

	April to June 1999
Nurse advice given	
Gave self-care advice	35
Advised an urgent GP visit (within 24 hours)	24
Advised a routine GP visit	15
Advised a visit to accident and emergency	12
Advised patient to contact other professionals	8
Arranged for an emergency ambulance	3
Other/call aborted	2
All calls receiving nurse advice (=100%)(thousands)	165
Other calls (thousands)	37
All calls (thousands)	202

Source: Department of Health

Around a third of the government's total managed expenditure in the United Kingdom is spent on the social security programme (see Table 5.32 in the Income and Wealth chapter). In 1998-99 expenditure on social security benefits amounted to £99 billion, more than double in real terms the amount in 1977-78 (Chart 8.7). Spending on social security tends to follow a cyclical pattern whereas spending on the NHS increases year on year. Expenditure on the NHS in the United Kingdom grew to £49 billion in 1998-99. The NHS is financed mainly through general taxation (75 per cent in 1998-99) with an element of national insurance contributions paid by employed people, their employers and self-employed people (13 per cent). The remainder is financed through charges, such as drugs prescribed by family doctors, receipts from land sales and the proceeds of income generation schemes. Nearly three-quarters of NHS expenditure is spent on hospitals and community health services and a quarter is spent on family health services.

In July 1999 the government published a White paper *Saving Lives: Our Healthier Nation* setting out its health strategy for England. Similar strategies have been published for Wales, Scotland and Northern Ireland. As part of the Healthy Citizens programme introduced with the White Paper a telephone helpline, called NHS Direct, was set up. This major new initiative aims to give people rapid access to professional health advice and information so that they are better able to care for themselves and their families. In November 1999 there were 17 sites in England covering 60 per cent of the population. In most sites, expert call handlers answer the telephone, take the caller's name and address details, pass the caller to a nurse adviser if they need advice or clinical information, or transfer the caller direct to the 999 emergency service if they need an emergency ambulance. Between April and June 1999, NHS Direct received 202 thousand calls and 82 per cent of these needed nurse advice. The nurse, prompted by a clinical computer system, asks the caller about their symptoms, and based on the answers to those questions advises the patient what to do next. The nurse may call an ambulance for the patient, may advise the patient to contact their GP or go to accident and emergency, or may give advice on how to treat the problem at home. In the sample period, over a third of callers were given self-care advice and around a quarter were advised to arrange a GP visit within the next 24 hours (Table 8.8). For around 3 per cent of calls an emergency ambulance was called. The service has been particularly popular with young parents and around 40 per cent of calls have been about children.

In 1989, free NHS sight tests were restricted to children, full-time students under the age of 19, adults on low incomes and people who had, or were at particular risk of, eye disease. In April 1999, the government restored free sight tests to

Social Trends 30, © Crown copyright 2000

8.9

all people aged 60 and over. In 1997-98, 1,417 eye tests per 10,000 people in Great Britain were carried out under the NHS and 1,241 per 10,000 people privately (Chart 8.9). The age distribution of people who have NHS eye tests has two peaks, in the younger and older age groups. In contrast, the proportion of people who have private eye tests generally increases with age, peaking in the 65 to 74 age group. The number of NHS sight tests paid for by health authorities has increased steadily since 1990-91, the first full year that NHS sight tests were restricted to these groups. In 1998-99, 3.8 million vouchers towards the cost of spectacles were reimbursed, a decrease of 3 per cent on 1997-98 but 55 per cent more than 1990-91. The number of vouchers reimbursed by health authorities increased between the first full year of the scheme (1987-88) and 1996-97.

As part of the Patient's Charter, the government pledged to reduce NHS waiting lists and times and has stated that by the end of the present Parliament, NHS waiting lists in England will be 100,000 shorter than the figure of 1.2 million inherited on 1 May 1997. In 1998-99, £417 million was made available to help achieve this target and a further £320 million in 1999-00. Part of the money has been used to establish a National Booked Admissions Programme that will enable patients to pre-book their appointments for a time convenient to them.

At the end of March 1999, 1.1 million patients in England were waiting for NHS treatment as an in-patient or daycase. Around three-quarters of these patients had been waiting under six months (Table 8.10). The average time spent waiting by those on the list at 31 March 1999 was longest in the North and South Thames regions and shortest in the West Midlands region. The government also pledged that no patient should have to wait longer than 18 months for admission and this was achieved for the first time in March 1998.

Sight tests: by age and provider, 1997-98

Great Britain

Rates per 10,000 people

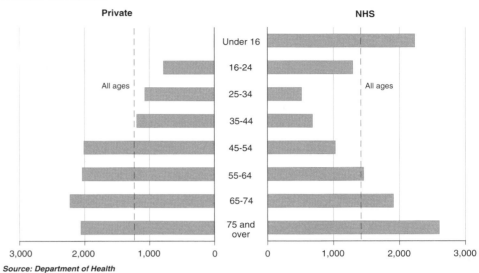

Source: Department of Health

8.10

National Health Service hospital waiting lists[1]: by region, 1999

United Kingdom   Percentages

	Less than 6 months	6 months but less than 12	12 months or longer	Average time spent waiting (months)
Northern and Yorkshire	77	22	-	3.9
North West	76	20	4	4.1
Trent	74	21	5	4.3
West Midlands	79	18	3	3.8
Anglia and Oxford	74	22	5	4.3
North Thames	69	24	7	4.8
South Thames	69	25	6	4.8
South and West	76	20	4	4.1
England	74	22	4	4.3
Wales	..	11	..	..
Scotland[2]	86	12	1	2.4
Northern Ireland	63	19	18	..

1 At 31 March. People waiting for admission as either an in-patient or a day case.
2 Figures are at 31 March 1998. See Appendix, Part 8: Waiting lists.

Source: Department of Health; National Assembly for Wales; National Health Service in Scotland; Department of Health and Social Services, Northern Ireland

8.11

Households covered by private medical insurance: by socio-economic group of the head of household, 1998-99

United Kingdom	Percentages
	1998-99
Professional, employers and managers	18
Intermediate non-manual	8
Junior non-manual	12
Skilled manual	6
Semi-skilled and unskilled manual	6
Self-employed	14
Retired[1]	8
Unoccupied[2]	5
All households	9

1 Males aged 65 and over and females aged 60 and over who are not economically active.
2 Males aged under 65 and females aged under 60 who are not working, nor actively seeking work.

Source: Family Expenditure Survey, Office for National Statistics

Another standard set as part of the Patient's Charter was the time spent waiting for an ambulance to arrive in an emergency. In England, the target times are 14 minutes in urban areas and 19 minutes in rural areas. Following a review of ambulance performance standards in 1995-96 further changes were introduced requiring ambulance services to prioritise their procedures to ensure that immediately life threatening cases get the quickest response. In 1998-99, of the 16 ambulance services that had prioritised their procedures, 10 achieved the Patient's Charter standard of reaching patients where the call had been identified as life threatening. Of the 21 ambulance services yet to prioritise their services, 10 achieved the Patient's Charter standard for call

response times. Between 1997-98 and 1998-99, the number of emergency calls rose by 8 per cent from 3.6 million to 3.8 million and the number of patient journeys rose by 2 per cent.

The NHS is available to all people in the United Kingdom. Some people, however, receive treatment in private hospitals and clinics or NHS hospital pay beds in return for annual subscriptions to private health care schemes. The Family Expenditure Survey collects information on households covered by private health insurance in the United Kingdom. The proportion of all households covered has increased from 6 per cent in 1985 to 9 per cent in 1998-99. Households headed by someone from the professional, employer or manager group are the most likely to be covered: 18 per cent were members of such a scheme in 1998-99 compared with 8 per cent of households with a retired household head (Table 8.11).

8.12

Reasons[1] volunteers gave for volunteering, 1997

Great Britain
Percentages

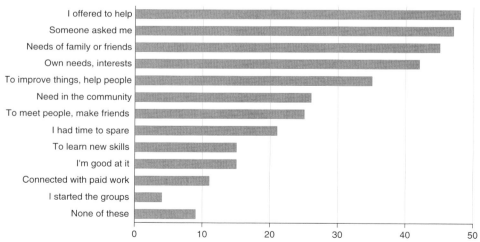

1 Respondents were allowed to give more than one reason.
Source: National Survey of Volunteering, National Centre for Volunteering

While the NHS and the private sector can provide essential health care services, more localised and specialised services are often provided by the voluntary sector. The National Survey of Volunteering, carried out in 1997, found that 48 per cent of respondents were engaged in formal voluntary work and 74 per cent were doing more informal volunteering. This means that 22 million people in Great Britain regularly take part in voluntary activity, and each week volunteers contribute a collective 88 million hours. The survey also looked at the reasons why people choose to volunteer and found that people's motives were a mixture of altruism and self-interest. The largest proportion of people gave the reason as being they 'offered to help' followed by 'someone asked me' (Chart 8.12). Around a quarter were volunteering as a result of a need in the community and to meet people and make friends. Older people were more likely to stress free time as a motivating factor, while younger respondent cited the learning of new skills.

Many people are involved in helping others in less formal ways. In 1995-96 the General Household Survey asked adults in Great Britain whether they were providing care for a dependent person in the community. Women were more likely to be providing this sort of informal care than men: 14 per cent of women compared with 11 per cent of men. Thus an estimated 3.3 million women and 2.4 million men were providing care. The proportion of people providing care varied with age, rising to a peak among those aged 45 to 64 – a fifth of all people in this age group were providing care for a dependent person.

There have been changes in the distribution of certain types of staff employed by the NHS over the past decade or so. The total number of directly employed health service staff declined by 6 per cent between 1981 and 1998 (Table 8.13). The main reasons for this fall were the changes to the training regime and funding for student nurses in the early 1990s which meant that they were no longer directly employed by the NHS, and reductions in the number of ancillary staff directly employed by the NHS as a result of contracting out some support services, such as cleaning and catering. In contrast, the number of medical and dental staff grew by around 46 per cent over the same period while the number of local authority personal social services staff increased by 15 per cent up to 1994 and has declined slightly since then. In addition the number of GPs increased by a third between 1981 and 1998. The

personal social services group includes local authority social work staff, home helps and those working in residential homes, day centres and special locations.

Sick and disabled people

The nature of health and ill health among the population is discussed in Chapter 7: Health; this section focuses on the response provided to support sick and disabled people.

The number of in-patient episodes in all NHS hospitals has increased since 1981, and the fastest rate of increase has been for people with

8.13

Health and personal social services staff

Great Britain					Thousands
	1981	1986	1991	1994	1998
NHS hospital and community health service staff					
Direct care staff					
Medical and dental	48	51	56	60	70
Nursing, midwifery and health visitors	457	472	470	426	407
Other non-medical staff	473	436	429	432	448
All direct care staff	978	959	955	918	927
General medical practitioners	27	29	31	32	35
General dental practitioners[1]	15	17	18	19	20
Personal social services[2]	240	270	289	294	276

1 Headcount of General Dental Service dentists on Family Health/Health Authority lists at 30 September.
2 Includes staff employed only at local authority social work departments (whole time equivalent).
Source: Department of Health; National Assembly for Wales; National Health Service in Scotland

8.14

National Health Service activity for sick and disabled people[1]: in-patients

United Kingdom

	1981	1986	1991-92	1996-97	1997-98
Acute[2]					
Finished consultant episodes[3] (thousands)	5,693	6,239	6,729	7,260	7,425
In-patient episodes per available bed					
(numbers)	31.1	36.9	45.9	52.9	54.6
Mean duration of stay (days)	8.4	7.2	6.0	5.2	5.5
Mentally ill					
Finished consultant episodes[3] (thousands)	244	265	281	300	296
In-patient episodes per available bed					
(numbers)	2.2	2.7	4.0	5.8	5.9
Mean duration of stay (days)	..	..	114.8	59.3	58.5
People with learning disabilities					
Finished consultant episodes[3] (thousands)	34	59	62	63	65
In-patient episodes per available bed					
(numbers)	0.6	1.2	2.2	4.4	5.2
Mean duration of stay (days)	..	..	544.1	200.6	163.6

1 Excludes NHS beds and activity in joint-user and contractual hospitals.
2 Wards for general patients, excluding elderly, maternity and neonate cots in maternity units.
3 All data for Wales, Scotland and data for Northern Ireland except acute after 1986 are for deaths and discharges and transfers between specialities. See Appendix, Part 8: In-patient activity.

Source: Department of Health; National Assembly for Wales; National Health Service in Scotland; Department of Health and Social Services, Northern Ireland

8.15

National Health Service activity for sick and disabled people: accident and emergency, and acute out-patients and day cases

United Kingdom   Thousands

	1981	1986	1991-92	1996-97	1997-98
Accident and emergency services					
New attendances	11,321	12,663	13,397	15,191	15,569
Total attendances	15,957	16,606	16,289	17,308	17,598
Out-patient services					
New attendances	8,619	9,495	9,862	12,431	12,703
Total attendances	36,160	38,822	38,944	43,602	44,535
Day case finished consultant					
episodes[1]	817	1,204	1,894	3,585	3,818

1 Excludes Northern Ireland in 1981 and 1986. Data for Northern Ireland from 1991-92 are for day case admissions.

Source: Department of Health; National Assembly for Wales; National Health Service in Scotland; Department of Health and Social Services, Northern Ireland

learning disabilities (Table 8.14). An overall decline in the mean duration of stay in NHS hospitals has occurred across all specialities. In the acute sector, for example, the mean duration of stay was just over eight days in 1981 compared with around five days in 1997-98 (Table 8.15). As well as an increase in the number of in-patients, the number of people being treated as an accident and emergency patient or an out-patient or a day case has also increased. The number of day case admissions in the acute sector was more than four times higher in 1997-98 than in 1981. The number of acute attendances in the out-patient sector also increased, by over a fifth over the same time period.

One of the key Patient's Charter standards includes cancelled operations which are affected by emergency care pressures. The standard was set to ensure that patients whose operations are cancelled by the hospital, for non-medical reasons, on the day of their operation or after they have arrived in hospital, have their operations rescheduled as soon as possible, and certainly within one month of their operation being cancelled. The number of breaches of the standard increased from 2.3 thousand in the fourth quarter of 1997-98 to 3.2 thousand in the same quarter in 1998-99 – an increase of 39 per cent. The change in performance is most noticeable during the winter months and by the first quarter of 1999-00, performance was returning to normal.

Mental health problems are a major cause of ill health, disability and mortality (see Table 7.9 in the Health chapter). Specialist services exist to help people with a mental illness, including day

8.16

care facilities as well as out-patient services and community nursing services. In England and Wales there were over 300 thousand new out-patient attendances for psychiatric specialities in 1997-98, an increase of over 40 per cent since 1987-88 (Table 8.16). These increases are partly a result of the changes in the way people with mental illnesses are looked after. At present, government policy aims to ensure that people with mental illnesses have access to the full range of services they need as locally as possible and with support from community-based teams. As a result of this, the number of patients who have contact with community psychiatric nursing has increased by over 40 per cent since the early 1990s.

Some help provided by the government for sick and disabled people comes in the form of cash benefits. The number of long-term sick and disabled people receiving benefit has increased rapidly since 1981 whereas the number receiving incapacity benefit (and its predecessors, sickness and invalidity benefits) for being sick for short periods has declined (Table 8.17). Incapacity benefit was introduced in April 1995 and is paid at three rates depending on the duration of the incapacity. In 1997-98, almost 2 million long-term sick and disabled people in Great Britain were in receipt of incapacity benefit or severe disablement benefit which was more than double the number on the equivalent benefits in 1981-82. The rise in the number of those receiving these invalidity benefits is partly due to an increase in the duration of claims rather than an increase in new claims. In addition, in Northern Ireland in 1997-98, 114 thousand people were receiving incapacity benefit or severe disablement benefit.

NHS outpatient, community and day care contacts for people with a mental illness[1]

England & Wales				Thousands
	1987-88	1992-93	1996-97[2]	1997-98[2]
Consultant outpatient				
New attendances[3]	219	238	304	312
Total attendances	1,712	1,928	2,225	2,262
Day case finished consultant episodes	..	1	2	1
First patient contacts with clinical psychology and community nursing services				
Community learning disability nursing	..	43	56	59
Clinical psychology services[4]	..	191	244	257
Community psychiatric nursing	..	430	600	618
First attendances at NHS day care facilities				
Mental illness[3]	..	60	71	68
Old age psychiatry[3]	..	28	41	34
Child and adolescent psychiatry[3]	..	3	2	2

1 In Wales includes mental illness, child and adolescent psychiatry, forensic psychiatry, psychotherapy and old age psychiatry.
2 1996-97 and 1997-98 data for England are provisional and ungrossed.
3 Data for 1992-93 are for England only.
4 Data are for England only.

Source: Department of Health; National Assembly for Wales

8.17

Recipients of benefits for sick and disabled people

Great Britain					Thousands
	1981-82	1986-87	1991-92	1996-97	1997-98
Long-term sick and people with disabilities[1]					
Incapacity benefit[2]/severe disablement allowance	826	1,228	1,741	1,996	1,931
One of the above benefits plus income support[3]	103	136	240	366	391
Income support only[3]	..	..	229	498	530
Short-term sick					
Incapacity benefit only[1,2]	393	110	138	117	109
Incapacity benefit[2] and income support[3]	24	16	28	48	36
Income support only[3]	..	..	79	174	172
Disability living allowance[4]	582	1,113	1,758	3,020	3,192

1 Long-term disability cases will include cases which are classified on the basis of a partner's disability.
2 Incapacity benefit was introduced in April 1995 to replace sickness and invalidity benefits.
3 Income-based jobseeker's allowance (JSA) replaced income support for the unemployed from October 1996. Income support includes some income-based JSA claimants.
4 Includes attendance allowance and, before April 1992, mobility allowance.

Source: Department of Social Security

8.18

Home care, day care and meal provision for elderly people: by age

England	Rates per 1,000 population	
	1992	1997
Home care[1]		
65-74	11	9
75-84	29	23
85 and over	18	20
Day care		
65-74	..	6
75-84	..	9
85 and over	..	6
Meals		
65-74	4	6
75-84	9	14
85 and over	5	10

1 For home care the rates are per 1,000 households.
Source: Department of Health

8.19

Recipients of selected benefits[1] for elderly people[2]

Great Britain					Percentages
	1981-82	1986-87	1991-92	1996-97	1997-98
Retirement pension only	78	79	79	77	78
Retirement pension with income support[3]	18	16	12	13	12
UK pensions payable overseas	3	4	6	7	7
Pensioners with income support only[3]	1	1	3	3	3
All recipients (=100%)(millions)	9.2	9.7	10.3	10.9	11.1

1 Retirement pension data are at 31 March except 1981 which is at 30 June. Income support/supplementary benefit data are from annual and quarterly enquiries.
2 Income support cases: all aged 60 and over, retirement pension rates: men aged 65 and over, women aged 60 and over.
3 Income support replaced supplementary benefit in April 1988. Income-based jobseeker's allowance (JSA) replaced income support for the unemployed from October 1996. Income support figures include income-based JSA claims.
Source: Department of Social Security

Elderly people

There were four times as many people aged 65 and over in the United Kingdom in 1998 as in 1901 (see Table 1.6 in the Population chapter). The provision and type of services for elderly people has changed considerably since the early 1900s. Care at the beginning of the century was mainly carried out in institutions with the institutional Poor Law representing almost all of the cost of welfare services. By the time of the *National Insurance Act* in 1946, there had been a general shift from the provision of care in institutions to those provided in the community, such as meals on wheels and other services, and the replacement of workhouses by old people's homes. The number of older people in public residential accommodation has, however, increased dramatically since 1900 reflecting the changing age structure of the population.

Chart 8.1 at the beginning of the chapter shows places in residential care homes for elderly people in England, Wales and Northern Ireland. In 1998 there were a total of 288 thousand places in homes of this type, around three-fifths of which were provided by the private sector. The number of places in local authority homes has fallen over recent years and by 1998 provided around a fifth of all places. The number of voluntary homes has been steadily increasing over the last 10 years, from 27 thousand in 1988 to 38 thousand in 1998.

Major developments in domiciliary care did not come until the Second World War. Since the 1930s the home nursing service has expanded greatly with a rise in both the number of nurses and the cases dealt with. In 1970 over half the cases were people aged over 65. Domestic help services have also only been available since the war but the expansion is marked and again the majority of recipients are old people.

Community care reforms, introduced in April 1993, further encouraged the development of services such as home help and care, meals services and day care as an alternative to residential accommodation. Home care is the most commonly provided social support service. In 1997, 23 per 1,000 households where the oldest client was aged 75 to 84 received home care and 20 per 1,000 households of those aged 85 and over (Table 8.18). Rates for day care and meals on wheels are lower with rates of 9 per 1,000 and 14 per 1,000 respectively for those aged 75 to 84.

The social security benefit system provides financial assistance for elderly people to complement the health and social services provided by the NHS and local authorities. These benefits include retirement pensions and income support. Around 11 million British people were in receipt of one or other of these benefits in 1997-98, 78 per cent of whom were receiving a retirement pension alone (Table 8.19). The proportion of overseas recipients has increased at a faster rate than that for those living in Great

8.20

Britain; in 1997-98 around 7 per cent were receiving their pension overseas compared with 3 per cent in 1981-82.

The age at which men and women receive a state pension is to be equalised to 65 in phases over ten years, starting in April 2010. Women born before 6 April 1950 will be unaffected, while the pensionable age for those born between 6 April 1950 and 5 March 1955 will gradually increase. All women born on or after 6 March 1955 will not become eligible to receive a state retirement pension until they reach the age of 65.

Although some people continue to work and have income from earnings after state pension age, many obtain most of their income from pensions, either from the state or from occupational schemes or from both. Just before the Second World War, 15 per cent of the workforce were members of an occupational pension scheme but during the 1950s and 1960s the number of people with these schemes grew rapidly. Since the 1960s around half of employees have been members of a scheme. For each successive cohort of 65 to 69 year olds, the proportion with an occupational pension increases slightly. Men and couples aged 80 and over are, however, as likely as those in their seventies to be in receipt of an occupational pension (Table 8.20). This is because those with an occupational pension are generally less likely to die than those without, so a more of those still alive have an occupational pension. The lower proportion of single women aged 80 and over with income from an occupational pension is due to a combination of the lower percentage of women who were in employment when they were younger and the lower likelihood that female employees would have been a member of a scheme. The effect of these factors outweighs the different mortality rates of those with and those without an occupational pension.

Percentage of families with income[1] from pensions[2]: by age of head, 1997-98

Great Britain
Percentages

	50-59	60-64	65-69	70-79	80 and over
Couples					
State retirement pension[3]	3	30	98	99	99
Occupational pension	22	52	75	73	74
Single males					
State retirement pension	0	0	93	99	99
Occupational pension	16	42	54	62	62
Single females					
State retirement pension	0	93	96	98	98
Occupational pension	21	49	50	52	38

1 Includes pension income based on the contributions of a late spouse.
2 Figures are based on respondent's own assessment.
3 Retirement pension and any other national insurance benefits for the elderly: widow's benefit and incapacity benefit.
Source: Family Resources Survey, Department of Social Security

Families

Families and children receive help in a number of different ways. Children may be born into families with low incomes and receive benefits; all families are also eligible to receive child benefit. Children may be the victims of abuse and have to be moved into local authority accommodation or they may have parents who are unable to look after them and consequently need to be fostered or adopted.

In 1997 there were 726 thousand live births in the United Kingdom (see Chart 1.1 in the Population chapter), the majority of which took place in hospital. The proportion of births delivered at home has declined over the last 30 or so years. In 1960, one in three births in England and Wales was at home compared with only around one in 50 in 1997 (Chart 8.21). There has, however, been a slight increase in recent years in the popularity of home births following the move to a more flexible

8.21

Births: by place of delivery[1]

England & Wales
Percentages

1 In addition, a small number of births take place elsewhere.
Source: Office for National Statistics

8.22

Maternity services

United Kingdom

	1981-82[1]	1986-87[2]	1991-92	1996-97	1997-98
In-patient services					
Finished consultant episodes[3] (thousands)	986	1,088	1,160	1,333	1,315
In-patient episodes per available bed (numbers)	43	54	66	98	97
Mean duration of stay (days)	5.1	4.0	2.9	1.9	1.6
Out-patient services					
New attendances (thousands)	897	891	828	713	712
Average attendances per new patient (numbers)	5.1	4.7	4.3	3.8	3.6

1 Data for England, Wales and Northern Ireland are for 1981.
2 Data for England and Northern Ireland are for 1986.
3 Data in 1981 are for deaths and discharges. See Appendix, Part 8: In-patient activity.

Source: Department of Health; National Assembly for Wales; National Health Service in Scotland; Department of Health and Social Services, Northern Ireland

8.23

Recipients of benefits for families

Great Britain   Thousands

	1981-82	1986-87	1991-92	1996-97	1997-98
Child benefit					
Children	13,079	12,217	12,401	12,752	12,612
Families	7,174	6,816	6,852	7,009	6,955
Lone parent families					
One parent benefit only[1]	469	607	475	1,011	1,049
One parent benefit and income support[2]	146	253	340	394	386
Income support only[1,2]	222	376	531	639	597
Other benefits					
Maternity allowance[3]	115	109	11	11	13
Statutory maternity pay	.	.	85	90	..
Family credit	139	218	356	734	760

1 From April 1997 the supplement for the eldest or only child where someone brings up children alone, formally known as One Parent Benefit, was incorporated into the main child benefit rates.
2 Income support data includes some income-based jobseeker's allowance (JSA) claimants. Income-based JSA replaced income support for the unemployed from October 1996.
3 Maternity allowance figures are February quarterly figures from 1996-97.

Source: Department of Social Security

service based on the needs of mothers and babies. During the late 1980s only around 1 per cent of births were at home compared with 2.3 per cent in 1997.

In common with other hospital services, the number of maternity in-patient episodes has been increasing along with the number of episodes per available bed. As a consequence, the mean duration of stay in hospitals in the United Kingdom has declined from just over five days in 1981-82 to one and a half days in 1997-98 (Table 8.22). In addition, the average number of out-patient attendances per new patient has declined slightly. This may reflect changes over time in the type of service provided for women. A change in the frequency of contacts by midwives has led to an increase in antenatal contacts and a decline in postnatal contacts. The proportion of all antenatal contacts in England that took place in the community increased from 51 per cent in 1997-98 to 69 per cent in 1998-99. The number of midwife-only clinics rose by 92 per cent over the same period, reflecting the growing trend to midwife-led care.

Families with dependent children are offered support by the social security benefit system in the form of cash benefits. Indeed, almost all couples and single people with dependent children received some sort of benefit in 1997-98 (see Table 8.5 earlier in this chapter). The most significant non-income related benefit for families, in terms of both recipients and expenditure, was child benefit which was received by 7 million families in Great Britain in 1997-98 (Table 8.23). The growth in lone parent families has meant that the number of recipients of one parent benefit has increased over the last decade. In 1981-82 around

600 thousand families received lone parent benefit and this more than doubled to over 1.4 million in 1997-98. The number of lone parent families receiving income support alone almost tripled between 1981-82 and 1996-97 but decreased slightly between 1996-97 and 1997-98.

The Department for Education and Employment launched the National Childcare Strategy Green Paper *Meeting the Childcare Challenge* in May 1998. It proposed that plans for establishing and developing early years and childcare services should be drawn up and implemented at local level by local childcare partnerships. Over 150 partnerships in England are now in operation. In addition, the new working families tax credit, which replaced family credit, came into effect on 5 October 1999. The aim of the tax credit was to integrate tax and benefits to help around 1.5 million families, including 3 million children, by providing a 'top-up' to their pay and help with childcare costs. For people who currently pay for registered childcare and who are eligible for the benefit, the childcare tax credit within working families tax credit will provide up to £70 a week for one child and £105 a week for two or more children up to age 15.

Day care facilities are provided for young children by childminders, voluntary agencies, private nurseries and local authorities as well as nannies and relations. In 1998 there were around 1.1 million places with childminders, in playgroups and day nurseries for children under the age of eight in England and Wales (Table 8.24). In Northern Ireland there were 39 thousand places in registered day nurseries, childminders and playgroups in 1998. The numbers of places in day nurseries and with childminders have shown particularly large increases since the late 1980s whereas those in playgroups have declined. In 1987 there were around 60 thousand places in day nurseries in England and Wales compared with over 300 thousand in 1998. In Northern Ireland the increase has been equally dramatic with the number of places in playgroups increasing from around 300 in 1987 to 4 thousand in 1998. After school clubs (held either before or after school) have been introduced in recent years and in 1998 there were 97 thousand such places in England and Wales.

8.24

Day care places for children[1]

England & Wales				Thousands
	1987	1992	1997	1998
Day nurseries				
Local authority provided[2]	29	24	20	19
Registered	32	96	180	211
Non-registered[2]	1	1	2	1
After school clubs	.	.	.	97
All day nursery places	62	122	202	329
Childminders				
Local authority provided	2	2	4	4
Other registered person	152	262	379	384
All childminder places	153	265	383	388
Playgroups				
Local authority provided	3	2	2	1
Registered	423	434	408	407
Non-registered	7	3	3	1
All playgroup places	433	439	413	410

1 Under the age of eight.
2 England only.

Source: Department for Education and Employment; National Assembly for Wales

Local authorities must provide accommodation for children who have no parent or guardian, who have been abandoned, or whose parents are unable to provide for them. If local authorities consider taking a child into their care would promote the child's welfare, they may apply to a court for a care order. The number of children looked after by local authorities in England, Wales and Northern Ireland increased from 55 thousand in 1994 to 59 thousand in 1998 (Chart 8.25). The number of children placed in foster homes has increased by around 12 per cent over the same period and the number placed in children's homes has declined by 17 per cent. In England, half of the children leaving care at the age of 16 and over

have been looked after continuously for more than two years. Adoption is one way children in care are able to leave – around a third of all children adopted are looked after by a local authority prior to their adoption. Among those who were adopted, the average age fell from 5 years 11 months in 1993-94 to 4 years 11 months in 1997-98.

Scotland has a different definition of children in care which means data are not comparable with the rest of the United Kingdom. In Scotland, children who have committed offences or are in need of care and protection may be brought before a Children's Hearing, which can impose a supervision requirement if it thinks that compulsory measures are appropriate. Under these requirements most children are allowed to remain at home under the supervision of a social worker, but some may live with foster parents or in a residential establishment while under supervision. Those under supervision are considered to be in care while in the rest of the United Kingdom those under a supervision order are not. Supervision requirements are reviewed at least once a year until ended by a Children's Hearing.

In addition, personal social services help children who are considered to be at risk of abuse. All local authority social services departments hold a central register of such children. Registration takes place following a case conference in which decisions are made about the level of risk to the child. Subsequently, the child's name may be placed on the register and a plan set out in order to protect the child. In 1998, 36 thousand children in England, Wales and Northern Ireland were on such a register (Table 8.26). The total number on

8.25

Children looked after by local authorities[1]: by type of accommodation, 1994 and 1998

England, Wales & Northern Ireland

Thousands

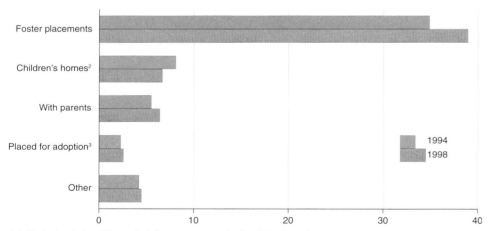

1 In England, excludes children looked after under an agreed series of short-term placements.
2 In England includes local authority, voluntary sector and private children's homes.
3 Not collected for Northern Ireland.

Source: Department of Health; National Assembly for Wales; Department of Health and Social Services, Northern Ireland

8.26

the registers peaked, since the introduction in 1989 of the current definition, in 1991 at 50 thousand and then fell by about a quarter until 1993 before levelling out. This fall followed the implementation in October 1991 of the *Children Act*, the overriding purpose of which was to promote and protect children's welfare by enabling local authorities to work with families to provide help to keep the family together. There has not been much change in the age distribution of children on protection registers in the last 10 years, with the exception of a slight increase in the proportions of children aged under 1 year.

Children on child protection registers: by age

England, Wales & Northern Ireland   Thousands

	Under 1	1-4	5-9	10-15	16 and over	All children[1]
1989[2]	2.9	14.4	13.9	10.5	1.7	43.3
1990[2]	2.9	15.0	14.8	11.5	1.7	45.9
1991	3.1	15.9	15.7	12.6	1.8	49.3
1992	2.7	13.0	13.3	11.3	1.6	42.2
1993	2.5	10.9	11.0	9.9	1.2	35.6
1994	2.9	11.5	11.7	10.6	1.1	38.0
1995	3.2	11.8	11.6	10.5	1.0	38.2
1996	2.9	11.0	10.9	9.6	1.1	35.6
1997	3.1	10.9	11.2	9.5	0.9	35.8
1998	3.1	10.8	11.2	9.4	0.8	35.5

1 Figures for Northern Ireland for 1991 to 1994 include age not known.
2 Data are for England and Wales only.

Source: Department of Health; National Assembly for Wales; Department of Health and Social Services, Northern Ireland

References and further reading

The following list contains selected publications relevant to **Chapter 8: Social Protection**. Those published by The Stationery Office are available from the addresses shown on the inside back cover of *Social Trends*.

Community Statistics for Northern Ireland, Department of Health and Social Services, Northern Ireland

Department of Health Departmental Report, The Stationery Office

Dimensions of the Voluntary Sector, Charities Aid Foundation

ESSPROS manual, Eurostat

Family Resources Survey, Department of Social Security

Health and Personal Social Services Statistics for England, The Stationery Office

Health and Personal Social Services Statistics for Northern Ireland, Department of Health and Social Services, Northern Ireland

Health Statistics Wales, Welsh Health Survey 1995, Welsh Office

Hospital Episode Statistics for England, Department of Health

Hospital Statistics for Northern Ireland, Department of Health and Social Services, Northern Ireland

Scottish Health Statistics, National Health Service in Scotland, Common Services Agency

Social Protection Expenditure and Receipts, Eurostat

Social Security Departmental Report, The Stationery Office

Social Security Statistics, The Stationery Office

Statistical Publications on aspects of Health and Personal Social Services activity in England (various), Department of Health

Contacts

Telephone contact points for further information relating to

Chapter 8: Social Protection

Office for National Statistics	
Chapter author	020 7533 6117
General Household Survey	020 7533 5444
Department of Health	
Adults' services	020 7972 5585
Children's services	020 7972 5581
Community and cross-sector services	020 7972 5524
General dental and community dental services	020 7972 5392
General medical services	0113 254 5911
General ophthalmic services	020 7972 5507
General pharmacy services	020 7972 5504
Hospital activity	0113 254 5522
Mental illness/handicap	020 7972 5546
NHS expenditure	0113 254 5356
NHS medical staff	0113 254 5892
NHS non-medical manpower	0113 254 5744
Non-psychiatric hospital activity	020 7972 5525
Personal social services budget data	020 7210 5699
Prescription analysis	020 7972 5515
Social services staffing and finance data	020 7972 5595
Waiting lists	0113 254 5555
Department of Social Security	020 7962 8000
Family Resources Survey	020 7962 8092
Department of Health and Social Services, Northern Ireland	
Health and personal social services activity	028 9052 2800
Health and personal social services workforce	028 9052 2008
Social security	028 9052 2280
National Assembly for Wales	029 2082 5080
National Health Service in Scotland, Common Services Agency	0131 551 8899
Northern Ireland Statistics and Research Agency	028 9034 8100
Scottish Executive, Social Work Services Group	0131 244 5432
Eurostat	00 352 4231 13727

Social Trends 30, © Crown copyright 2000

Chapter 9 Crime and Justice

Offences

There were seven times more drugs seizures in the United Kingdom in 1997 than in 1981. (Chart 9.8)

The police and parking attendants dealt with 9.8 million motoring offences in England and Wales in 1997 and, in the same year, automatic cameras provided evidence for 390 thousand traffic light and speeding offences. (Page 154 and Table 9.9)

Victims

In 1997, 32 per cent of households in inner-city areas were the victims of a household offence compared with 23 per cent of households located in rural areas. (Table 9.10)

In 1996, 23 per cent of women and 15 per cent of men aged 16 to 59 in England and Wales said that a current or former partner had assaulted them at some time in their lives. Around 4 per cent of both women and men said that they had experienced domestic assault in the previous year. (Table 9.12)

Offenders

In 1998, 674 per 10,000 population of 16 to 24 year old men were found guilty of, or cautioned for, an indictable offence, compared with a rate of 131 per 10,000 women in the same age group. (Table 9.13)

Police and courts action

In 1997-98 the police stopped and searched over one million people and/or vehicles in England and Wales, 20 per cent more than in the previous year. (Table 9.18)

Probation and prisons

In 1998, 95 per cent of the sentenced prison population in England and Wales were male. This amounted to 49.8 thousand male sentenced prisoners compared with just 2.4 thousand females, although the proportion of prisoners who are female has been increasing slowly in recent years. (Page 160)

Civil justice

In England and Wales there were 31.7 thousand complaints against the police dealt with in 1998-99, some 4 thousand fewer than in the previous year. (Table 9.24)

9.1

Offenders[1] as a percentage of the population: by gender and age, 1997-98

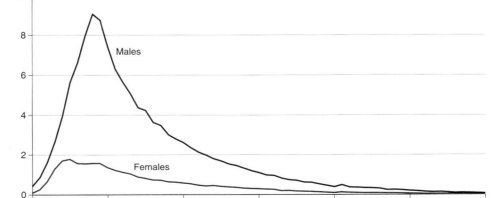

England & Wales
Percentages

1 People found guilty or cautioned for indictable offences in 1997-98.
Source: Home Office

9.2

Crimes committed: by outcome[1]

England & Wales		Percentages
	Reported to the police	Recorded by the police
1981	36	22
1991	49	30
1993	47	26
1995	46	23
1997	44	24

1 As a percentage of offences committed.
Source: British Crime Survey, Home Office

Crime, in some form, affects many people during their lives. Dealing with crime and its impact is a continual problem for both society and government.

England and Wales, Scotland and Northern Ireland are often shown separately in this chapter because of their different legal systems.

Offences

Measuring the true level of crime in the country is fraught with difficulties. There are two main measures of crime which are used in this chapter, each with its own particular strengths and weaknesses. One measure is the amount of crime recorded by the police. This information is a by-product of the administrative procedure of completing a record for crimes investigated by the police. While this provides detailed data on crime,

many crimes are never reported to the police and some that are reported are not recorded. The second main measure of crime comes from surveys of victims, such as the British Crime Survey (BCS) which is carried out every two years in England and Wales. This measure includes not only reported crime but also unrecorded and unreported crimes against individuals and their property, although it covers a narrower range of crimes than police records. Similar surveys are conducted in Scotland and Northern Ireland every four years.

The proportion of crime reported to, and recorded by, the police has changed over time. For those offences that are comparable between police records and BCS offences, the proportion reported to the police increased during the 1980s but fell slowly through the 1990s to 44 per cent in 1997 (Table 9.2). In Scotland, 50 per cent of crimes were reported to the police in 1995.

The rise in reporting during the 1980s might be linked to the increase in telephone ownership which made crimes easier to report. Also, more victims became insured during this period which could have led to higher reporting rates as reporting to the police may be a necessary step in making a claim. The proportion of crimes reported also varies between different offences. More than four in five burglaries with loss were reported to the police in England and Wales in 1997 compared with just under one in four acts of vehicle vandalism.

Not all crimes that are reported to the police will be recorded by them. A little over half of the crimes reported to the police in England and Wales in 1997 were recorded. The police may

9.3

Notifiable offences[1] recorded by the police

Rates per 1,000 population

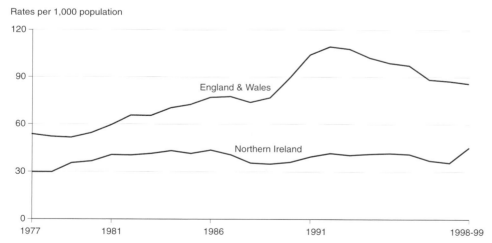

1 Indictable offences up to and including 1978. Includes all offences of criminal damage in England and Wales. Includes possession of controlled drugs in Northern Ireland. For England and Wales the data are based on the old counting rules and include an estimate for 1998-99; they are for financial years from 1997-98. For Northern Ireland the data are based on the old counting rules and exclude criminal damage valued at less that £200. See also Appendix, Part 9: Types of offences in England and Wales, and Types of offences in Northern Ireland.
Source: Home Office; Royal Ulster Constabulary

Social Trends 30, © Crown copyright 2000

9.4

choose not to record a reported crime for a number of reasons. They may consider that the report of a crime is mistaken, too trivial or that there is insufficient evidence. Alternatively, the victim may not want the police to proceed.

While the police figures for the number of notifiable offences recorded do not cover the complete picture, these data do allow quite detailed analyses to be carried out. Due to differences in the legal systems, recording practices and classifications, comparisons between England and Wales, Scotland and Northern Ireland should only be made with care. In Scotland the term 'crimes' is used for the more serious criminal acts (roughly equivalent to indictable and triable-either-way offences in England and Wales) while less serious crimes are termed 'offences'. Scottish figures are given for crimes only, unless otherwise stated. In Northern Ireland the definitions used are broadly comparable with those in England and Wales.

The number of notifiable offences recorded by the police in England and Wales increased steadily from the early 1950s, when there were less than half a million per year, to peak at 5.6 million in 1992. Since then the numbers have decreased to 4.5 million in 1998-99, when measured under the old counting rules. New counting rules were introduced in April 1998 to include all indictable and triable-either-way offences (together with a few closely linked summary offences). The new rules have increased the coverage of offences and have also increased the emphasis on measuring one crime per victim. A detailed explanation of these changes is contained in Appendix, Part 9: Types of offences in England and Wales. Under the new rules a total of

5.1 million notifiable offences were recorded by the police in England and Wales in 1998-99. For this chapter, where an item shows a trend it will be based on the 'old' counting rules, whereas a snapshot item will be based on the 'new' rules.

As the number of recorded crimes can be affected by the size of the population, the rate of crime per 1,000 population gives a clearer picture of the trend. The rate of notifiable offences per 1,000 population in England and Wales tripled between 1971 and 1992, when it reached 109 (Chart 9.3). It then decreased steadily to 86 in 1998-99, as measured under the 'old' counting rules. In Northern Ireland the rate has fluctuated and was 45 per 1,000 population in 1998-99. The number of recorded crimes per 1,000 population in Scotland decreased each year from the peak rate of 112 in 1991 to 82 in 1997. However, the numbers rose again slightly in 1998 to 84 per 1,000 population

In general, those police force areas that include large urban conurbations have higher rates of recorded crime than those in more rural locations. In 1998-99, all the metropolitan police areas apart from Merseyside had rates of over 100 crimes per 1,000 population. Humberside had the highest rate of all the police force areas in England and Wales, at 148 crimes per 1,000 population, while Dyfed-Powys had the lowest rate at 51 (Chart 9.4). In addition, the BCS also found that for the types of crimes that it covers, the risk of victimisation was lower for households in rural areas than elsewhere. In 1995, 3.9 per cent of households in rural areas were burgled compared with 10.3 per cent of those in inner-city areas and 6.3 per cent of those in other urban areas.

Crime rates[1]: by police force area, 1998-99

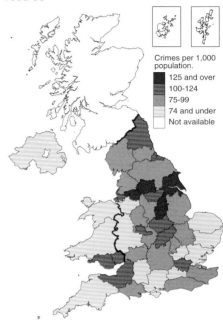

Crimes per 1,000 population.
- 125 and over
- 100-124
- 75-99
- 74 and under
- Not available

1 Recorded crime.
Source: Home Office; Royal Ulster Constabulary

9.5

Notifiable offences[1] recorded by the police: by type of offence

Thousands

	England & Wales			Scotland			Northern Ireland		
	1981	1991	1998-99[2]	1981	1991	1998	1981	1991	1998-99[2]
Theft and handling stolen goods,	1,603	2,761	2,127	201	284	192	25	32	35
of which: theft of vehicles	333	582	391	33	44	28	5	8	10
theft from vehicles	380	913	681	..	..	50	7	7	6
Burglary	718	1,220	952	96	116	57	20	17	15
Criminal damage[3]	387	821	834	62	90	79	5	2	10
Violence against the person	100	190	231	8	16	16	3	4	7
Fraud and forgery	107	175	174	21	26	24	3	5	5
Robbery	20	45	66	4	6	5	3	2	1
Sexual offences,	19	29	35	2	3	5	-	1	1
of which: rape	1	4	8	-	1	1	-	-	-
Drug offences[4]	..	11	21	2	12	31	-	-	-
Other notifiable offences[5]	9	23	42	12	20	22	3	1	2
All notifiable offences	2,964	5,276	4,482	408	573	432	62	63	77

1 See Appendix, Part 9: Types of offences in England and Wales, Types of offences in Northern Ireland and Offences and crimes.
2 Estimates of the number of offences under the old counting rules.
3 In Northern Ireland excludes criminal damage valued at £200 or less.
4 In England and Wales trafficking was the only notifiable drugs offence counted under the old counting rules to 1 April 1998. In Scotland, trafficking was the only recorded drugs crime in 1981.
5 In Northern Ireland includes 'possession of controlled drugs' and 'offences against the state'. In Scotland excludes 'offending while on bail' from 1991 onwards.

Source: Home Office; Scottish Executive; Royal Ulster Constabulary

9.6

Burglaries of domestic dwellings: by time of day, 1997

England & Wales
Percentages

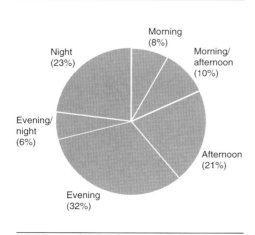

Night (23%)
Morning (8%)
Morning/ afternoon (10%)
Evening/ night (6%)
Afternoon (21%)
Evening (32%)

Source: British Crime Survey, Home Office

Although the total number of notifiable offences recorded by the police has fallen in the 1990s, this has varied for different categories of offence. For example, for the largest category, theft and handling stolen goods, the number of notifiable offences recorded by the police in England and Wales decreased by 23 per cent between 1991 and 1998-99 (Table 9.5). The number of notifiable offences of burglary also fell, by 22 per cent, over the same period. In contrast, the number of notifiable offences of violence against the person, robbery and drugs offences have all risen.

In 1998-99, 952 thousand crimes of burglary were notified to the police in England and Wales, making it the second largest category of crime. In 1998 the BCS asked people who had been victims of domestic burglary in the previous 14 months about when the incident happened. Around 30 per cent of burglaries were said to have occurred during a weekend (6pm Friday to 6am Monday) which suggests that the risk of burglary is no higher at weekends than during the week.

Burglaries were more likely to have occurred during the evening or night than during the day – three-fifths of burglaries took place between 6pm and 6am (Chart 9.6).

There are a number of factors that can influence the risk of being a victim of burglary. The presence of occupants may act as a deterrent to burglary. The BCS found that those households who left their homes unoccupied for more than a month during a year had a 43 per cent higher risk of being a victim than households identical in all other aspects, but who never left their dwelling unoccupied overnight. The survey also found that household security was strongly related to the risk of burglary. As levels of household security devices increase, the risk of victimisation decreases. As well as with crime overall (as mentioned in Chart 9.4) the type of area also affects risk of burglary, as does the type of accommodation. For example, detached houses are at higher risk of burglary than other types of housing; flats are the least at risk. This may be

Social Trends 30, © Crown copyright 2000

9.7

due to a detached house being more accessible to offenders, with more entry points and less likelihood of being overlooked. The 1998 BCS also found that households that had been burgled in the previous four years were more likely to be burgled again than those who had not.

Although offences involving firearms are still relatively rare in this country, these offences are potentially more serious than other sorts of offence. In 1997, firearms were used in just 0.3 per cent of offences in both England and Wales. However, some offences are more likely to involve the use of firearms. In England and Wales, 8.0 per cent of homicides and 4.8 per cent of robberies involved firearms in 1997; this compares with 6.3 per cent and 3.1 per cent respectively in Scotland (Table 9.7). The number of firearms covered by certificates in England and Wales declined dramatically between the end of 1996 and the end of 1997, from 418 thousand to 305 thousand. This is a direct result of the *Firearms (Amendment) Act 1997* which banned handguns of more than .22 calibre with effect from 1 October 1997, with a hand-in exercise taking place between 1 July and 30 September 1997. Some smaller calibre guns were also voluntarily surrendered before the end of 1997 in anticipation of further legislation. All handguns were subsequently prohibited from 1 February 1998. In contrast, over the same period, the number of shotguns held on certificate in England and Wales increased slightly to 1.3 million.

There has been a dramatic increase in the number of drug offences in recent years. Over four times as many people were found guilty, cautioned or dealt with by compounding for drug offences in 1997 than ten years previously. Drug offenders are predominantly male and tend to be slightly older than the average offender. Males accounted for about nine in ten of all drug offenders in 1997, when the average age for all drug offenders was a little over 25 years old. The type of action taken against drug offenders has changed over time. In 1987 the most common

Percentages of selected offences in which firearms were reported to have been used

Percentages

	England & Wales				Scotland			
	1971	1981	1991	1997	1971	1981	1991	1997
Homicide	8.3	6.1	7.6	8.0	..	7.9	8.0	6.3
Robbery	7.7	9.3	11.7	4.8	..	2.2	7.1	3.1
Attempted murder/acts endangering life	5.7	5.0	5.9	2.7	..	6.3	7.7	3.5
Other violence against the person[1]	2.0	2.9	1.0	0.9	..	1.0	0.8	0.5
Criminal damage[2]	0.3	1.4	0.6	0.8	..	0.9	0.7	0.5

1 In Scotland relates to assaults.
2 Includes damage valued at £100 or more in 1971, £20 or more in subsequent years. In Scotland relates to vandalism offences.
Source: Home Office; Scottish Executive

9.8

Seizures[1] of drugs

United Kingdom
Thousands

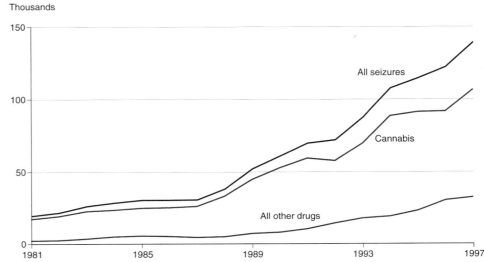

1 Seizures by the police and HM Customs. A seizure can include more than one type of drug. See Appendix, Part 9: Drugs seizures.
Source: Home Office

9.9

Motoring offences detected by automatic cameras: by type of action taken

England & Wales   Thousands

	Fixed penalty[1]	All prosecutions	All offences
Speeding			
1992	-	-	-
1993	25.8	6.4	32.2
1994	95.5	20.6	116.1
1995	170.0	36.9	206.9
1996	212.6	49.6	262.2
1997	288.6	48.1	336.7
Traffic lights			
1992	6.0	12.0	18.0
1993	19.2	20.3	39.5
1994	25.9	14.0	40.0
1995	33.3	14.8	48.1
1996	33.4	19.4	52.8
1997	34.6	18.8	53.3

1 Fixed penalty paid and no further action taken.
Source: Home Office

9.10

Proportion of households which were victims of crime[1]: by type of crime and type of area[2], 1997

England & Wales   Percentages

	Inner city	Urban	Rural
Vehicle crime (owners)			
All thefts	23.7	16.2	12.0
Vandalism	9.2	7.2	4.9
Bicycle thefts (owners)	8.9	5.2	2.4
Burglary	8.5	5.9	3.4
Home vandalism	4.3	3.7	2.6
Other household	8.4	6.8	5.4
Any household offence	32.2	28.6	22.8

1 Percentage victimised once or more.
2 Area type classification based on CACI ACORN codes, copyright CACI Ltd 1994.
Source: British Crime Survey, Home Office

form of action was a fine, with two-fifths of offenders receiving this punishment. However, in 1997 just over a fifth were fined while half were cautioned.

Between 1981 and 1997 there has been a seven-fold increase in the number of drugs seizures in the United Kingdom (see Chart 9.8 on the previous page). Seizures rose by 14 per cent in 1997 over the previous year, to reach 139 thousand, the highest recorded figure. Cannabis accounted for over three-quarters of seizures. However, while seizures involving cannabis increased by 16 per cent between 1996 and 1997, seizures involving heroin increased by 27 per cent and those involving cocaine by 33 per cent.

Motoring offences make up a large proportion of summary offences – the less serious category of offence. The police and parking attendants dealt with 9.8 million motoring offences in England and Wales in 1997. Legislation to facilitate the use of automatic cameras to provide evidence for motoring offences was first introduced in England and Wales on 1 July 1992 and, since then, the number in use has been increasing. During 1997 automatic cameras provided evidence for 390 thousand motoring offences in England and Wales, about a quarter more than in the previous year (Table 9.9). The proportion of breath test producing positive results in England and Wales fell by around 9 per cent between 1997 and 1998, suggesting that there continues to be a change in driver behaviour with regard to drinking and driving.

Victims

As mentioned earlier in the chapter, the area in which people live can affect their likelihood of being a victim of crime. Generally, people living in inner city areas are more likely to be victims than those living elsewhere. In 1997, 32 per cent of households in inner-city areas were the victims of a household offence compared with 23 per cent of households located in rural areas (Table 9.10). This is particularly true for certain types of crime. For example, information for England and Wales from the BCS indicates that in 1997, a household located in an inner city area was 44 per cent more likely to be the victim of a burglary than an identical household in a non-inner city area. Other factors that can increase the risk of burglary victimisation have been mentioned in the commentary relating to Chart 9.6 on page 152. Factors associated with an increased risk of a household being the victim of a vehicle-related theft include households where the head of household is aged between 16 and 44, single parent families, unemployed heads, households with an annual income above £30 thousand, and homes that are rented or are flats or terraced properties.

In addition to people in inner cities generally being more likely to be a victim of crime, those living in such areas also worry more about all types of crime (Table 9.11). Regionally, those in the north of the country tend to be more concerned than those in the south and east, although those living in London are an exception. Apart from vehicle crime, women worry more than men about most types of crime and are particularly worried about violent crime. Concern about crime is linked to people's beliefs about their chance of being a victim and how vulnerable they feel. Fear of crime can have implications on the quality of people's lives. Eight per cent of BCS respondents indicated that the fear of crime had a substantial effect on the quality of their lives; half said it had little or no effect.

One area of crime and justice where it is particularly difficult to obtain data is domestic violence. Such crimes often go unreported, possibly because of the relationship between the victims and offenders. In Table 9.12 domestic

assault relates to physical violence by current and former partners of the victim; the terms 'chronic' and 'intermittent' refer to the frequency of domestic assault rather than severity. Twenty-three per cent of women and 15 per cent of men aged 16 to 59 in England and Wales said that a current or former partner had assaulted them at some time in their lives. Around 4 per cent of both women and men said that they had experienced domestic assault in the previous year. Women were twice as likely as men to say they had been injured by such an assault and were more likely to have experienced repeated assaults during the year. There were an estimated 6.6 million incidents of domestic assault in 1995. Although, on average, women were more likely to have experienced repeated assault, the total number of assaults in the year was evenly split between women and men as there are more men than women aged 16 to 59 in the population. Among women, it was the 20 to 24 year olds who were the most likely to say they had experienced domestic assault while for men it was those aged 30 to 34.

9.11

Concern about crime[1]: by type of area[2], 1998

England & Wales		Percentages
	Inner city	Non-inner city
Burglary	30	18
Mugging	27	16
Rape[3]	39	30
Physical attack	27	17
Theft of car[4]	36	20
Theft from car[4]	27	16

1 Percentage victimised once or more.
2 Area type classification based on CACI ACORN codes, copyright CACI Ltd.
3 Females only.
4 Percentage of car owners.
Source: British Crime Survey, Home Office

9.12

Incidence of domestic assault[1]: by gender

England & Wales			Percentages
	Males	Females	All
In lifetime			
No domestic assault	85	77	81
Chronic levels of assault[2]	5	12	9
Intermittent levels of assault[3]	10	11	10
All	100	100	100
In last year			
No domestic assault	96	96	96
Chronic levels of assault[2]	2	2	2
Intermittent levels of assault[3]	3	2	3
All	100	100	100

1 The survey was carried out in 1996. Respondents were aged 16 to 59.
2 Victims who reported three or more assaults.
3 Victims who reported one or two assaults.
Source: British Crime Survey, Home Office

By its nature, domestic assault is often hidden from public view and opportunities for intervention depend largely on victims telling others about their experiences. Over half of the victims of domestic assault had not told anyone about the last attack; but of those who had told someone, nearly all had told a friend or relative, even if they had also told someone else.

Offenders

In 1998, 532 thousand people were found guilty, or cautioned, for an indictable offence in England and Wales (Table 9.13). The vast majority of these, 82 per cent, were male. In order to provide a straightforward comparison of offending rates by age of offender, the information shown in the table is expressed as offenders per 10,000 population in each age group. For both males and females it is young adults who offend the most. In 1998, 674 per 10,000 population of men aged 16 to 24 were found guilty of, or cautioned for, an indictable offence, compared with a rate of 131 per 10,000 women in the same age group. For each offence group, men aged 16 to 24 were the most likely to have committed an offence.

According to police and court figures, the peak age for offending for males in England and Wales was 18 in 1997-98 – 9 per cent of 18 year old males were found guilty of, or cautioned for, an indictable offence in that year. (See Chart 9.1 at the beginning of this chapter.) For females, rates of offending were lower and the peak age was younger at 15 – 2 per cent of 15 year old females offended in 1997-98. These peak ages have changed over time. Before 1972 the peak age of offending for both males and females was 14; this rose to 15 for males following the raising of the school leaving age from 15 to 16 in 1972. By 1988 the peak age for males had risen to 18 while that for females fluctuated between 14 and 15. In 1997-98, the peak age for male offending in Northern Ireland was 19, and 14 per cent of this group were found guilty of an offence at the Crown Court or magistrate's court. The equivalent peak for females was age 18, and 2 per cent of this group were found guilty of an offence.

Action taken by the police and courts against an offender will be, at least partly, intended as a deterrent against reoffending. The likelihood of reoffending varies according to a number of factors including age, gender and number of previous convictions. Despite the deterrent of one or more previous sentences, of those commencing probation or community service in England and Wales in 1995, 57 per cent of males and 42 per cent of females were reconvicted within two years. Of those discharged from prison in England and Wales in 1995, 58 per cent of males and 47 per cent of females were

9.13

Offenders found guilty of, or cautioned for, indictable offences[1]: by gender, type of offence and age, 1998

England & Wales — Rates per 10,000 population

	10-15	16-24	25-34	35 and over	All aged 10 and over (thousands)
Males					
Theft and handling stolen goods	133	221	88	18	152.6
Drug offences	15	177	70	9	96.0
Violence against the person	31	74	33	8	51.7
Burglary	40	66	18	2	37.2
Criminal damage	11	18	8	1	12.4
Robbery	6	11	2	-	5.6
Sexual offences	3	4	3	2	5.5
Other indictable offences	11	104	61	12	74.3
All indictable offences	250	674	282	53	435.9
Females					
Theft and handling stolen goods	73	75	30	7	56.8
Drug offences	2	18	10	1	11.5
Violence against the person	11	12	5	1	8.9
Burglary	4	3	1	-	2.0
Criminal damage	1	2	1	-	1.3
Robbery	1	1	-	-	0.6
Sexual offences	-	-	-	-	0.1
Other indictable offences	3	21	13	2	15.0
All indictable offences	95	131	61	12	96.1

1 See Appendix, Part 9: Types of offences in England and Wales and Types of offences in Northern Ireland.
Source: Home Office

reconvicted within two years. The length of time to reconviction for a standard list offence of offenders who had been released from prison service establishments in 1995 is shown in Chart 9.14. Among young male offenders, 77 per cent were reconvicted within two years while 16 per cent were reconvicted within three months. Overall there was little difference in the reconviction rates for those released from prison and those who had served community sentences.

Police and courts action

In England, Wales and Northern Ireland, following an arrest the police may release the suspect without further action; issue a caution, either formally or informally; or make a charge. Offences are said to be cleared-up by primary means (for example, those where someone is cautioned, charged or summoned to appear in court) or by secondary means (for example, when a prisoner admits to further offences). The new counting rules introduced on 1 April 1998 had an effect on the clear-up rates, although its precise extent cannot be quantified. A number of the newly notifiable offences, such as drug possession, common assault and dangerous driving have relatively high clear-up rates, which have increased the overall clear-up rate. However, all offences of criminal damage are now included in the clear-up rate, whereas previously only those where the damage was valued at over £20 were included – this will have reduced the overall clear-up rate.

Clear-up rates vary according to the type of offence. Of the main categories of offences, drug offences were the most likely to be cleared up in 1998-99 and theft from vehicles the least (Table 9.15). In England and Wales, combined primary and secondary clear-up rates were 38 per cent in 1981 and 29 per cent in 1998-99, under the new counting rules. Twenty-six per cent were cleared up by primary means and 3 per cent by secondary means. Secondary means of clear-up

9.14

Time to reconviction[1]: by gender

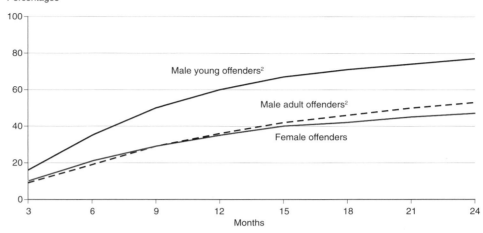

England & Wales
Percentages

1 Time to first reconviction for offenders who had been released from Prison Service establishments in 1995 and subsequently were reconvicted for a standard list offence. See Appendix, Part 9: Types of offences in England and Wales.
2 Young offenders are aged under 21 on the sentencing date; adults are aged 21 and over on the sentencing date.
Source: Home Office

9.15

Clear-up rates for notifiable offences[1]: by type of offence, 1998-99

Percentages

	England & Wales	Scotland[2]	Northern Ireland
Drug offences	97	100	90
Violence against the person	71	80	57
Sexual offences,	68	77	76
of which: rape	64	77	76
Fraud and forgery	36	76	44
Robbery	23	33	19
Theft and handling stolen goods	22	31	23
of which: theft of vehicles	18	28	13
theft from vehicles	10	15	6
Burglary	19	21	17
Criminal damage[3]	17	23	14
Other notifiable offences[4]	78	95	71
All notifiable offences	29	41	29

1 See Appendix, Part 9: Types of offences in England and Wales, Types of offences in Northern Ireland, and Offences and crimes. Combined primary and secondary clear-up rates for England and Wales; primary only in Scotland and Northern Ireland as secondary means of clear-up are not used.
2 Scottish figures refer to 1998 crimes.
3 In Northern Ireland, under new counting rules all criminal damage is recorded.
4 In Northern Ireland includes 'offences against the state'.
Source: Home Office; Scottish Executive; Royal Ulster Constabulary

9.16

Offenders cautioned for indictable offences[1]: by type of offence

England & Wales   Thousands

	1971[2]	1981	1991	1992	1996	1997	1998
Theft and handling stolen goods	53.5	79.2	108.5	130.3	93.6	82.8	83.6
Drug offences[2]	..	0.3	21.2	27.6	47.5	56.0	58.7
Violence against the person	2.3	5.6	19.4	23.5	21.8	23.6	23.5
Burglary[3]	12.4	11.2	13.3	14.4	10.2	9.4	8.4
Fraud and forgery	1.0	1.4	5.6	7.5	7.5	7.2	7.4
Criminal damage	3.6	2.1	3.8	4.0	3.1	2.8	2.7
Sexual offences	3.9	2.8	3.3	3.4	2.0	1.9	1.7
Robbery	0.2	0.1	0.6	0.6	0.6	0.7	0.6
Other	0.3	1.3	4.1	4.8	4.4	5.0	5.0
All offenders cautioned	77.3	103.9	179.9	216.2	190.8	189.4	191.7

1 Excludes motoring offences.
2 Adjusted to take account of the Criminal Damage Act 1971. Drug offences data for 1971 are included in 'Other'.
3 See Appendix, Part 9: Offenders cautioned for burglary.
Source: Home Office

are not used in either Scotland or Northern Ireland, and both had primary clear-up rates of 41 per cent and 29 per cent respectively in 1998-99.

In England and Wales, when an offender has admitted their guilt, there is sufficient evidence for a conviction and it does not seem in the public interest to institute criminal proceedings, a formal caution may be given by a senior police officer. In 1998, 192 thousand people were given such a caution for an indictable offence in England and Wales – a fall from the peak of 216 thousand in 1992 (Table 9.16). Prior to this, the number had risen steadily since 1979 when only 97 thousand cautions were given. The number of cautions for drug offences rose sharply in the 1980s and continued to rise in the 1990s. There were only a few hundred cautions for drug offences in England and Wales in 1981 but the number had grown to

9.17

Offenders sentenced for indictable offences[1]: by type of offence and type of sentence[2], 1997-98

England & Wales   Percentages

	Discharge	Fine	Community sentence	Fully suspended sentence	Immediate custody	Other	All sentenced (=100%) (thousands)
Theft and handling stolen goods	25	25	31	-	17	2	125.2
Drug offences	15	48	18	1	17	1	48.8
Violence against the person	15	13	37	2	30	3	37.1
Burglary	8	4	39	1	47	1	31.1
Fraud and forgery	19	18	39	2	21	1	19.6
Criminal damage	28	18	36	1	11	6	10.7
Motoring	6	56	20	1	17	1	9.0
Robbery	3	-	24	-	71	1	5.6
Sexual offences	5	6	26	2	59	2	4.6
Other offences	12	47	16	1	16	8	49.3
All indictable offences	18	28	28	1	23	3	341.1

1 See Appendix, Part 9: Types of offences in England and Wales.
2 See Appendix, Part 9: Sentences and orders.
Source: Home Office

more than 20 thousand in 1991. By 1998 cautions for drug offences had increased to 59 thousand, almost a third of all cautions for indictable offences.

When an offender has been charged or summoned and then found guilty, the court will impose a sentence. Sentences in England, Wales and Northern Ireland can include immediate custody, a community sentence, a fine or, if the court considers that no punishment is necessary, a discharge. In 1997-98, 341 thousand people were sentenced for indictable offences in England and Wales (Table 9.17). The form of sentence varied according to the type of offence committed. Those sentenced for motoring offences were the most likely to be fined, with 56 per cent receiving this form of sentence. Offenders sentenced for robbery were the most likely to get immediate custody while those sentenced for burglary or fraud and forgery were the most likely to receive a community sentence.

The proportion of offenders given different types of sentence has changed over time. In 1981, 45 per cent of offenders sentenced for indictable offences in England and Wales received fines, since when the proportion has been decreasing. In 1998, 28 per cent of offenders sentenced for indictable offences in England and Wales received a fine.

In Scotland there were a total of 150 thousand court proceedings for those with charges proved in 1997, a third of which were for crimes (the more serious type of transgression). For those sentenced for crimes, a fine was the most common form of sentence, with 47 per cent receiving this sentence; 22 per cent were sentenced to custody while 12 per cent were admonished, a form of formal warning. Males, who accounted for 85 per cent of convictions for crimes in 1997, were sentenced to custody on 24 per cent of occasions compared with 7 per cent for convicted females.

Certain powers under the *Police and Criminal Evidence Act 1984* were implemented in January 1986, covering stops and searches of people or vehicles, road checks, detention of people and intimate searches of people. During 1997-98 the police stopped and searched over one million people and/or vehicles in England and Wales, which was 20 per cent more than in the previous year (Table 9.18) and over nine times that in 1986, the first year of the legislation. During 1997-98, around 10 per cent of stops and searches led to an arrest, the lowest proportion since 1986. These arrest rates varied by reason: stops and searches for offensive weapons had an arrest rate of 13 per cent, while going equipped had a low rate at 5 per cent. A third of all stops and searches made in 1997-98 took place in the Metropolitan police area. This compares with the Metropolitan police area having just under a fifth of notifiable offences recorded by the police in England and Wales in the same period.

9.18

Stops and searches made by the police: by reason

England & Wales				Thousands
	1987	1991	1995	1997-98
Stolen property	49	114	253	398
Drugs	38	110	232	343
Going equipped	14	51	126	169
Offensive weapons	9	16	40	60
Firearms	1	3	6	7
Other	8	11	34	73
All	118	304	690	1,051

Source: Home Office

9.19

Prison population[1] and accommodation[2]

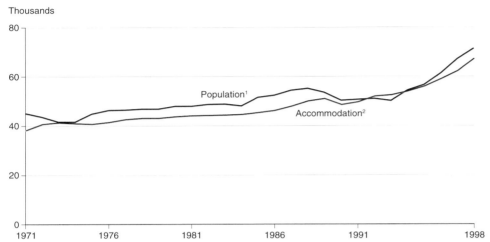

Great Britain

Thousands

1 Includes those held in police cells in England and Wales up to June 1995. Includes non-criminal prisoners.
2 In use Certified Normal Accommodation at 30 June each year in England and Wales; design capacity in Scotland. From 1993 accommodation which is not yet operational is excluded in England and Wales.

Source: Home Office; Scottish Executive

9.20

Average sentence length at Crown Court: by gender[1]

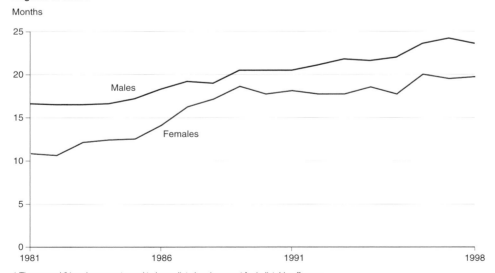

England & Wales

Months

1 Those aged 21 and over sentenced to immediate imprisonment for indictable offences.
Source: Home Office

Probation and prisons

The prison population in Great Britain fell from the late 1980s, but has been growing again since 1994. In 1998 there were over 71 thousand people in Prison Service establishments, around 6 per cent more than in the previous year (Chart 9.19). Throughout most of the 1970s and 1980s the prison population exceeded the certified normal population of prisons. The reverse was true in 1992 and 1993, but since 1994 increases in the prison population have meant that the number in prisons have exceeded the certified normal accommodation once again. In Northern Ireland the prison population fell throughout most of the 1980s before rising in the early 1990s. However, since 1994 the prison population of Northern Ireland has been decreasing, to 1.5 thousand in 1998.

The vast majority of the prison population are men. In 1998, 95 per cent of the sentenced prison population in England and Wales were male. This amounted to 49.8 thousand male sentenced prisoners and just 2.4 thousand females. The overall proportion of prisoners who are female has been slowly increasing in recent years.

Custodial sentences will normally be imposed on the most serious, dangerous and persistent offenders. In 1998 the average sentence length imposed on men aged 21 and over in the Crown Court in England and Wales was 23.6 months, a rise from a little under 17 months in the early 1980s (Chart 9.20). Men sentenced for robbery tended to get the longest sentences at an average of 92 months in 1998. For women the longest sentences were given to those convicted of drug offences at an average of 30.4 months. Life sentences are mandatory for convictions of murder and can also be passed as a result of other serious offences. The proportion of prisoners serving life sentences in England and Wales has fluctuated gently over time. In 1981, 4 per cent of

Social Trends 30, © Crown copyright 2000

9.21

prisoners were serving a life sentence. This proportion rose steadily to 7 per cent in 1992 to 1994, but then fell slightly to 6 per cent in 1995 to 1997.

Sentence lengths imposed by magistrates' courts are generally much shorter, mainly due to the nature of the cases that are heard in each type of court. Sentences imposed by magistrates' courts must be between five days and six months for one offence and not more than 12 months in total for two or more offences. Average sentence lengths imposed by magistrates' courts on men have remained at around three months since the early 1980s.

In 1998 there were over 91 thousand sentenced receptions into Prison Service establishments in England and Wales (Chart 9.21). This was 4 per cent higher than in the previous year, and almost double the number in 1961. Much of the sharp rise in receptions between 1993 and 1994 can be attributed to the implementation of the *Criminal Justice Act 1993*. This allowed the court to take into account any previous convictions or failure to respond to earlier sentences, which was previously only allowed in certain circumstances. Offending while on bail also became a mandatory factor to be taken into account when sentencing. The fall in the number of receptions of fine defaulters in the late 1990s was a Court of Appeal judgement in November 1995 which clarified the requirement for courts to try or consider all other methods of enforcement before committing a fine defaulter to prison.

In Scotland there were a total of 21 thousand receptions under sentence in 1998 (excluding non-criminal prisoners), a decrease of about 12 per cent over the previous year. Around 13 per cent of these were directly sentenced young offenders (ie excluding fine defaulters). In Northern Ireland there were 3.2 thousand receptions under sentence in 1998, a slight

Receptions under sentence[1] into prison service establishments

England & Wales

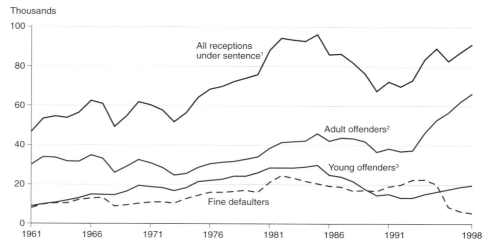

1 Excludes non-criminal prisoners.
2 Includes approved places; excludes fine defaulters.
3 Excludes fine defaulters. See also Appendix, Part 9: Young offenders institutions.
Source: Home Office

9.22

People commencing criminal supervision orders[1]

England & Wales   Thousands

	1981	1986	1991	1996	1997	1998
Probation	36	40	45	49	52	55
Community service	28	35	42	47	48	50
Combination	.	.	.	17	19	21
Under the *Children and Young Persons Act 1969*	12	6	2	3	3	2
Other	8	7	8	9	8	7
All[2]	79	83	91	115	120	125

1 Supervised by the probation service. See Appendix, Part 9: Sentences and orders.
2 Individual figures do not sum to the total because each person may have more than one type of order.
Source: Home Office

9.23

Claims issued[1] at the county courts and High Court

England & Wales
Millions

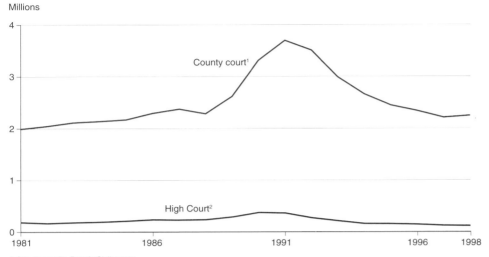

1 See Appendix, Part 9: Civil courts.
2 Queen's Bench Division.
Source: Court Service

9.24

Complaints against the police[1]: by outcome

England & Wales   Thousands

	Substantiated	Unsub-stantiated	Informally resolved[2]	Withdrawn/not proceeded with	All complaints
1981	1.5	14.7	.	16.2	32.4
1986	1.1	12.7	4.0	11.3	29.2
1991	0.8	11.3	9.0	14.2	35.3
1995-96	0.7	7.9	11.7	15.5	35.8
1996-97	0.8	10.0	11.6	14.3	36.7
1997-98	0.8	9.0	12.3	13.7	35.8
1998-99	0.7	8.5	11.0	11.4	31.7

1 Complaints are counted in the year in which they are completed.
2 Informal resolution of complaints was introduced on 29 April 1985.
Source: Home Office

decrease on the previous year. Almost 60 per cent of these receptions were fine defaulters, with just under 30 per cent of the total being adult offenders.

While custody is the sentence given for some of the more serious offences, other crimes are more likely to result in the offender receiving a criminal supervision order. In 1998, some 125 thousand people started a criminal supervision order in England and Wales, about 5 per cent more than in 1997 (see Table 9.22 on the previous page). As the same people may receive more than one order, the number of orders exceeds the number of persons receiving orders. In 1998, 40 per cent of the orders issued were community service orders, while a slightly higher proportion (44 per cent) were probation orders.

Civil justice

While this chapter has so far looked at cases where a charge has been made as part of the official legal system, for example by the Crown Prosecution Service in England and Wales, a case may also be brought under civil law by others, including an individual or a company. The majority of these cases are handled by the county courts and High Court in England, Wales and Northern Ireland and by the Sheriff Court and Court of Session in Scotland. The High Court and Court of Session deal with the more substantial and complex cases. Civil cases may include consumer problems, claims for debt, negligence and recovery of land.

Following the issuing of a claim, many cases are settled without the need for a court hearing. The total number of claims issued in England and Wales rose sharply from 2.2 million in 1981 to peak at 4.1 million in 1991 (Chart 9.23). This rise may be explained, in part, by the increase in lending as a consequence of financial deregulation that led to more cases concerned with the recovery and collection of debt. In 1998 the number of claims issued was 2.4 million, a slight increase on the previous year, due to an increase in the number of claims issued in the county courts. In 1997 there were 134 thousand cases heard in the Sheriff Court and 4.5 thousand in the Court of Session in Scotland.

Individuals and organisations may also make a complaint against the police. In England and Wales there were 31.7 thousand complaints dealt with in 1998-99 (Table 9.24); this was some 4 thousand fewer than in the previous year. The proportion of complaints which are substantiated is small – only 2 per cent of complaints were substantiated in 1998-99.

The number of complaints varies by police force area. The area with the lowest rate of complaints in England and Wales in 1997-98 was Durham, with 11 complaints for every one hundred officers. This compares with Merseyside, the force with the highest rate, at 54 complaints per one hundred police officers.

Resources

Labour costs form the largest component of police force expenditure. At 31 March 1999, 179 thousand people were employed by the police service in England and Wales including 53 thousand civilians (Table 9.25). Overall, this represents around 34 police service employees per 10,000 population, an increase of 35 per cent over 1971. In Scotland, 20 thousand people were employed in the police service in 1998 of which 5 thousand were civilians.

The 43 police forces in England and Wales also employed around 3.3 thousand traffic wardens on 31 March 1999. In addition to paid police service employees, there were 16.5 thousand special constables in post, around a third of which were female. This was almost 10 per cent fewer special constables in post than 12 months previously.

There was the equivalent of 124 thousand police officers in England and Wales in the 43 police force areas at 31 March 1999 (ie, excluding those on secondment); 16 per cent of these were female (Table 9.26). In the 43 forces, constables formed the majority of officers, representing 78 per cent of police officer strength. While 75 per cent of male police officers were constables, the proportion was 90 per cent for female officers.

9.25

Employment in the criminal justice system

England & Wales

	Thousands					Rates per 10,000 population		
	1971	1981	1991	1997-98	1998-99	1971	1997-98	1998-99
Police service[1]								
Police	97	120	127	127	126	19.7	24.4	24.2
Civilian staff[2]	28	38	46	53	53	5.7	10.2	10.2
All police service	125	157	174	180	179	25.4	34.6	34.3
Prison service[3]	17	24	33	41	43	3.5	7.9	8.2
Probation service[4]	..	13	18	17	17	..	3.3	3.3

1 1971 and 1981 as at December each year; 1991, 1997-98, and 1998-99 as at 31 March each year.
2 Excludes traffic wardens and cadets.
3 For 1991 and earlier years excludes headquarters staff and prison officer class trainees.
4 Full-time plus part-time workers and includes some temporary officers and also some trainees from 1981 onwards. Excludes non-probation officer grade hostel staff. Data for 1997-98 and 1998-99 are for calendar years.
Source: Home Office

9.26

Police officer strength[1]: by rank and gender, at 31 March 1999

England & Wales		Numbers
	Males	Females
Chief Constable	47	2
Assistant Chief Constable	142	9
Superintendent	1,156	57
Chief Inspector	1,511	93
Inspector	5,602	334
Sergeant	17,196	1,542
Constable	78,302	17,848
All ranks	103,956	19,885

1 Full-time equivalents employed in the 43 police force areas in England and Wales. With officers on secondment, the total police force strength was 126,096.
Source: Home Office

References and further reading

The following list contains selected publications relevant to **Chapter 9: Crime and Justice**. Those published by The Stationery Office are available from the addresses shown on the inside back cover of *Social Trends*.

A Commentary on Northern Ireland Crime Statistics, The Stationery Office

British Crime Survey, Home Office

Chief Constable's Annual Report, Royal Ulster Constabulary

Civil Judicial Statistics, Scotland, The Stationery Office

Costs, Sentencing Profiles and the Scottish Criminal Justice System, Scottish Executive

Crime and the quality of life: public perceptions and experiences of crime in Scotland, Scottish Executive

Criminal Statistics, England and Wales, The Stationery Office

Crown Prosecution Service, Annual Report, The Stationery Office

Digest 4: Information on the Criminal Justice System in England and Wales, Home Office

Digest of Information on the Northern Ireland Criminal Justice System 3, The Stationery Office

Home Office Annual Report and Accounts, The Stationery Office

Home Office Research Findings, Home Office

Home Office Statistical Bulletins, Home Office

Judicial Statistics, England and Wales, The Stationery Office

Local Authority Performance Indicators, Volume 3, Audit Commission

Northern Ireland Judicial Statistics, Northern Ireland Court Service

Police Statistics, England and Wales, CIPFA

Prison Service Annual Report and Accounts, The Stationery Office

Prison Statistics, England and Wales, The Stationery Office

Prisons in Scotland Report, The Stationery Office

Probation Statistics, England and Wales, Home Office

Race and the Criminal Justice System, Home Office

Regional Trends, The Stationery Office

Report of the Parole Board for England and Wales, The Stationery Office

Report on the work of the Northern Ireland Prison Service, The Stationery Office

Scottish Crime Survey, Scottish Executive

Statistics on the Race and Criminal Justice System, Home Office

The Criminal Justice System in England and Wales, Home Office

Scottish Executive Statistical Bulletins: Criminal Justice Series, Scottish Executive

The Work of the Prison Service, The Stationery Office

Young People and Crime, Home Office

Contacts

Telephone contact points for further information relating to
Chapter 9: Crime and Justice

Office for National Statistics

Chapter author	020 7533 5778
Home Office	020 7273 2084
Court Service	020 7210 1773
Northern Ireland Office	028 9052 7534/8
Royal Ulster Constabulary	028 9065 0222 ext. 24135
Scottish Executive	0131 244 2227

Chapter 10 Housing

Housebuilding and dwelling stock

In the early post-Second World War years, councils in Great Britain undertook around 85 per cent of the construction of new dwellings compared with virtually none in 1998. (Chart 10.1)

Tenure

Between 1961 and 1998 the number of owner-occupied dwellings in the United Kingdom more than doubled, to 16.9 million, while the number of rented dwellings fell by a sixth. (Chart 10.4)

Housing mobility

In 1998-99 the most mobile households in the United Kingdom were those who rented furnished accommodation, half of whom had been at their current address for less than a year and nine in ten had lived there for less than five years. (Table 10.11)

Housing standards

In 1996, just under 90 per cent of homes in England had central heating, a tenth more than in 1991. (Page 174)

Almost three in ten privately renting households in England lived in poor housing in 1996 compared with fewer than one in ten owner-occupiers who had lived in their home for 19 years or less. (Chart 10.18)

Housing costs and expenditure

In 1998 the average dwelling price in the United Kingdom was nearly £82,000, although the price of a dwelling bought by a first-time buyer was around 60 per cent that of a dwelling bought by a former owner-occupier. (Table 10.23)

Between 1983 and 1998 the proportion of new mortgages taken out by women on their own doubled. (Chart 10.25)

There were 130 thousand warrants issued for repossession of properties in England and Wales in 1998, the highest number since 1991. (Chart 10.28)

10.1

Housebuilding completions: by sector

Great Britain

Thousands

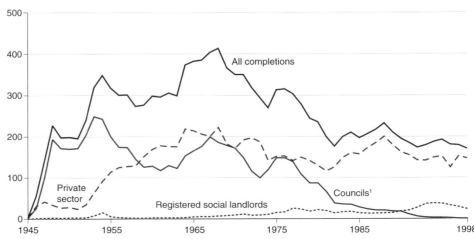

1 Includes local authorities, new towns, government departments and Scottish Homes.

Source: Department of the Environment, Transport and the Regions; National Assembly for Wales; Scottish Executive

Housing, whether rented or owner-occupied, is an essential part of everyone's life. The condition of our accommodation and the area in which we live can have a substantial impact on the quality of our physical and mental well-being. The condition of dwellings has improved since the early 1900s; problems of over-crowding and housing lacking basic amenities have largely been eradicated.

Housebuilding and dwelling stock

The English House Condition Survey estimated that since 1850, 25 million homes have been built or provided through conversion in England, while only 4 million have been lost from the residential stock through demolition and conversion to other uses. Much of the present housing stock therefore reflects some 150 years of residential building.

The inter-war and post-war period saw a trend away from building terraced houses in favour of detached and semi-detached houses and purpose-built flats or maisonettes. These differences are reflected in the age of the current occupied dwelling stock. Half of detached homes in Great Britain were built since 1970 while about a sixth were built before 1919 (Table 10.2). Around three in five purpose-built flats or maisonettes were also built since 1971 and only one in ten were built before 1919.

In the early post-Second World War years councils undertook most of the construction (see Chart 10.1 at the beginning of the chapter). In the 1970s registered social landlords (including housing associations) became active in acquiring and renovating much of the rented stock from private landlords, while in more recent years they have built new homes and some have acquired whole blocks of dwellings from local authorities through Large Scale Voluntary Transfers. Local authorities undertook a massive housebuilding programme between the wars and from the end of the Second World War until 1980, but since then this has become negligible. Registered social landlords now dominate building in the social sector. Private sector building accelerated in the 1950s and there have been more completions by the private sector than by either registered social landlords or the council sector in most years since 1959.

The rate of housebuilding completions varies throughout the United Kingdom (Table 10.3). In 1998 Northern Ireland had the highest rate, with 6.0 completions per thousand population. This was more than three times the rate in London, which at 1.8 was lower than in any other region. In England, the highest rates of completions were in the East and the East Midlands – double the rate of completions in London.

10.2

Type of dwelling: by construction date, 1998-99

Great Britain					Percentages
	Before 1919	1919-1944	1945-1970	1971 or later	All
House or bungalow					
Detached	17	13	18	52	100
Semi-detached	10	28	32	29	100
Terraced	37	19	17	27	100
Flat or maisonette					
Purpose-built	9	10	25	56	100
Other	67	22	7	4	100
All dwellings[1]	21	19	23	37	100

1 Includes other types of accommodation, such as mobile homes.
Source: General Household Survey, Office for National Statistics

10.3

The number of households in England is projected to increase from 20.2 million in 1996 to 24.0 million in 2021. This is partly due to increasing numbers of people living on their own (see Chapter 2: Households and Families). The Government has been considering the implications of increasing numbers of households alongside its commitments to the protection of the countryside and the regeneration of urban areas. In February 1998 it announced the tightening of targets for the proportion of new homes built on previously developed sites from 50 per cent to 60 per cent over the next ten years; the establishment of a new national database of land use to help identify previously developed sites; and a task force to help local authorities make better use of such sites, especially in urban areas. Planning guidance is being reviewed.

Tenure

In the 1920s and 1930s the number of building societies grew and there was a considerable increase in owner-occupiers. In addition, the building of local authority houses resulted in substantial numbers of local authority tenants. Following the Second World War, building of council housing as 'general needs housing' grew dramatically to reach a peak of almost 250 thousand in 1953. During this time there was a positive discouragement of private sector initiatives through various development controls. The 1950s saw a period of growth in prosperity alongside initiatives to improve house building; this was accompanied by deregulation in both planning and the building industry. Thus, owner-occupation increased from 29 per cent in 1951 to 45 per cent in 1964.

Between 1961 and 1998 the number of owner-occupied dwellings in the United Kingdom more than doubled while the number of rented dwellings

Housebuilding completions: by region

				Rates per 1,000 population
	1981	1991	1994	1998
United Kingdom	3.6	3.3	3.3	2.8
North East	..	2.5	2.6	2.7
North West	3.3	2.7	3.0	2.8
Yorkshire and the Humber	3.1	2.7	2.9	2.7
East Midlands	3.9	3.9	4.1	3.6
West Midlands	3.6	3.1	3.1	2.5
East	5.1	4.2	4.3	3.7
London	2.9	2.4	2.2	1.8
South East	4.3	3.6	3.3	3.0
South West	4.1	4.1	3.4	3.4
England	3.7	3.2	3.2	2.9
Wales	3.3	3.5	3.3	2.7
Scotland	3.9	3.7	3.9	4.3
Northern Ireland[1]	4.5	4.6	4.1	6.0

1 Data relate to financial years.

Source: Department of the Environment, Transport and the Regions; National Assembly for Wales; Scottish Executive; Department of the Environment, Northern Ireland

10.4

Stock of dwellings[1]: by tenure

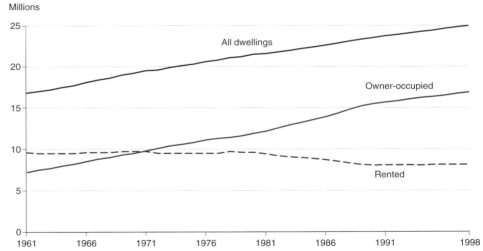

United Kingdom
Millions

1 See Appendix, Part 10: Dwellings. At December each year.

Source: Department of the Environment, Transport and the Regions; National Assembly for Wales; Scottish Executive; Department of the Environment for Northern Ireland

10.5

Owner-occupied dwellings: EU comparison, 1995

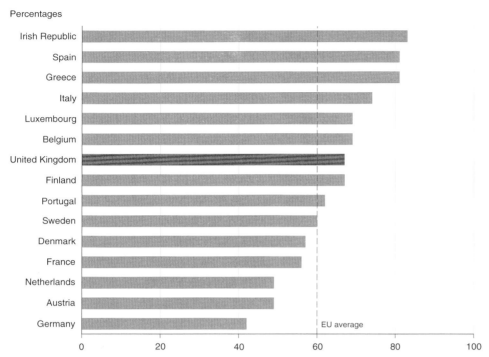

Percentages

Source: European Community Household Panel, Eurostat

10.6

Socio-economic group[1] of head of household: by tenure, 1998-99

United Kingdom   Percentages

	Owned outright	Owned with mortgage	Rented from social sector	Rented privately[2]	All tenures
Economically active					
Professional	16	74	..	10	100
Employers and managers	14	75	4	6	100
Intermediate non-manual	14	66	6	13	100
Junior non-manual	14	59	17	10	100
Skilled manual	15	62	16	8	100
Semi-skilled manual	14	42	32	13	100
Unskilled manual	16	36	41	7	100
All economically active	15	63	13	9	100
Economically inactive					
Retired	62	8	26	4	100
Other	20	17	51	11	100
All economically inactive	50	11	33	6	100
All socio-economic groups	29	42	21	8	100

1 Excludes members of the armed forces, economically active full-time students and those who were unemployed and had never worked.
2 Includes rent-free accommodation.

Source: General Household Survey, Office for National Statistics; Continuous Household Survey, Northern Ireland Statistics and Research Agency

fell by a sixth (see Chart 10.4 on the previous page). In 1998 there were twice as many owner-occupied as rented dwellings. In 1995 almost seven in ten householders were owner-occupiers, which is just above the European Union (EU) average (Chart 10.5). In the Irish Republic, Spain and Greece about eight in ten householders owned their homes, the highest of any EU country, while Germany had about half this proportion.

Another factor contributing to the increase in owner-occupied dwellings and the fall in rented dwellings in the United Kingdom is the sale of social sector housing by local authorities, new towns and registered social landlords to tenants under the right-to-buy legislation introduced in the 1980s. Public tenants across the United Kingdom with secure tenancies of at least two years' standing were entitled to buy their house or flat at a discount, depending upon the length of their tenancy. By the end of 1998, some 2.3 million council, housing association and new town development corporation houses in Great Britain had been sold into owner-occupation.

Traditionally, housing tenure in the United Kingdom has been closely related to social class and economic status. In 1998-99 home ownership was generally more common among those in non-manual groups than those in the manual groups (Table 10.6), even though increases in home ownership over the previous 15 years were most marked among the manual groups. Among the economically active, nine out of ten household heads in the professional, and employer and manager groups were owner-occupiers in 1998-99, compared with half of those in the unskilled manual group.

Tenure patterns also vary markedly with ethnic group (Table 10.7). In 1998-99 households headed by someone from the Indian or Pakistani

10.7

Ethnic groups were more likely than those headed by a White person to own their property with a mortgage, but less likely to own outright. This reflects, to a large extent, the older age structure of the White group. The Black and Bangladeshi groups were by far the most likely to be renting from the social sector while the Pakistani group were among the most likely to be renting privately. For many, these tenure patterns still reflect some of their historical origins. During periods when immigration was high, newly arrived people tended to find accommodation in the private rented sector – the most accessible part of the market. Over the following years, many of these people were joined in this country by other family members and they therefore needed to find larger accommodation. For many, council housing was not available at this stage because in many areas a person had to have been resident for a certain period of time in that area to qualify. The main option for many immigrants was to buy the cheaper properties on the market.

These factors led to the different patterns of tenure and quality of housing which were seen among the different ethnic groups in the 1970s. For example, the South Asian groups had high levels of owner-occupation, even among those with lower paid jobs. For South Asians in particular, the preference to live closer to other members of their ethnic group is thought to have affected these ownership patterns.

The tenure of housing in which people live also varies with the stage of their life cycle. Heads of household under the age of 25 are more likely to rent privately than those from any other age group. This reflects the tendency for private renters in furnished accommodation to be young, single and male. Around a fifth of heads of households in the under 25 age group were owner-occupiers in 1998-99, and very few of

Ethnic group of head of household: by tenure, 1998-99

England   Percentages

	Owned outright	Owned with mortgage	Rented from social sector	Rented privately[1]	All tenures (=100%) (millions)
White	27	43	21	10	19.2
Black	9	31	50	10	0.4
Indian	22	54	11	13	0.3
Pakistani	17	53	12	18	0.2
Bangladeshi	5	31	54	10	0.1
Other groups[2]	11	35	27	27	0.3
All ethnic groups[3]	26	43	21	10	20.4

1 Includes rent-free accommodation.
2 Includes those of mixed origin.
3 Includes those who did not state their ethnic group.
Source: Survey of English Housing, Department of the Environment, Transport and the Regions

10.8

Age of head of household: by tenure, 1998-99

United Kingdom   Percentages

	Under 25	25-34	35-44	45-54	55-64	65-74	75 and over	All ages
Owner-occupied								
Owned outright	..	2	6	19	44	65	57	28
Owned with mortgage	20	58	68	60	32	9	4	41
Rented from social sector								
Council	31	17	12	13	15	18	25	17
Housing association	11	6	5	3	4	4	8	5
Rented privately[1]								
Furnished	17	6	2	1	1	..	-	2
Unfurnished[2]	20	11	7	5	4	4	6	7
All tenures	100	100	100	100	100	100	100	100

1 Includes rent-free accommodation.
2 Includes partly furnished.
Source: General Household Survey, Office for National Statistics; Continuous Household Survey, Northern Ireland Statistics and Research Agency

10.9

Tenure: by type of accommodation, 1998-99

United Kingdom						Percentages
	House or bungalow			Flat or maisonette		
	Detached	Semi-detached	Terraced	Purpose-built	Other	All dwellings[1]
Owner-occupied						
Owned outright	37	36	21	6	1	100
Owned with mortgage	27	36	29	6	2	100
Rented from social sector						
Council	1	28	28	39	3	100
Housing association	..	19	26	46	7	100
Rented privately[2]						
Furnished	9	12	26	23	30	100
Unfurnished[3]	17	22	30	15	14	100
All tenures	23	32	26	14	4	100

1 Includes other types of accommodation, such as mobile homes.
2 Includes rent-free accommodation.
3 Includes partly furnished.

Source: General Household Survey, Office for National Statistics; Continuous Household Survey, Northern Ireland Statistics and Research Agency

10.10

Household type: by type of dwelling, 1998-99

United Kingdom						Percentages
	House or bungalow			Flat or maisonette		
	Detached	Semi-detached	Terraced	Purpose-built	Other	All dwellings[1]
One person	14	25	25	28	8	100
Two or more unrelated adults	7	30	39	18	6	100
One family households[2]						
Couple						
No children	33	33	22	10	3	100
Dependent children[3]	29	37	28	6	1	100
Non-dependent children only	32	39	26	3	0	100
Lone parent						
Dependent children[3]	7	30	38	20	4	100
Non-dependent children only	14	44	30	11	1	100
Multi-family households	13	49	32	5	1	100
All households	24	32	26	14	4	100

1 Includes other types of accommodation, such as mobile homes.
2 Other individuals who were not family members may also be included.
3 May also include non-dependent children.

Source: General Household Survey, Office for National Statistics; Continuous Household Survey, Northern Ireland Statistics and Research Agency

these owned their home outright. However, 58 per cent of 25 to 34 year olds were buying with a mortgage and this rose to 68 per cent in the 35 to 44 age group. About six in ten retired people owned their homes outright compared with only one in 25 who rented privately (see Table 10.8 on the previous page).

In general, homeowners are far more likely than social sector renters to live in detached houses. In 1998-99, 23 per cent of households in the United Kingdom lived in detached houses, and this ranged from 64 per cent among owner-occupiers to only 2 per cent of those who rented from the social sector (Table 10.9).

In 1998-99, one in four households in the United Kingdom lived in a detached house or bungalow while one in three lived in semi-detached accommodation (Table 10.10). The type of home in which people live is often a reflection of the size and type of the household. Two or more unrelated adults were the least likely to live in a detached home and the most likely to live in a terraced home. People living alone and households containing two or more unrelated adults were the most likely to live in a flat or maisonette, followed by lone parents with dependent children.

Housing mobility

Tenure has an impact on the length of time people remain living in the same home. The most mobile group are those who rent furnished accommodation, mainly young people. Almost half of private furnished renters had been at their current address for less than a year in 1998-99 and nine in ten had durations of less than five years (Table 10.11).

Information from the British Household Panel Survey suggests that the average length of time households remain in the same home is between five and ten years, with about one in ten adults moving house every year. Surprisingly, for one in six adults who move with the whole of their household, the move is from owner-occupation to the private-rented sector (Table 10.12). There are a number of reasons for this, such as elderly people moving into sheltered accommodation, moves resulting from evictions and repossessions and moves for job reasons. When part of the household moves there is an even greater shift from owner-occupation into privately rented accommodation. This is due to the characteristics of those moving, who are mainly children leaving home for the first time or separating couples, one of whom in many cases moves into rented accommodation. Private renting is, to a certain degree, a transitory tenure status, so the shifts into owner-occupation are less surprising; for example, a third of private renters who move each year become owner-occupiers.

The length of time people spend in the same property may also be linked to the labour market and the need for mobility in seeking employment. People in higher socio-economic groups tend to move further than those in the lower socio-economic groups. Of those who rented privately just under a third moved more than 20 miles away from their previous home compared with less than a tenth of those who rented from the social sector (see Table 10.13 overleaf). In 1998-99, a fifth of those who rented privately reported a change of job or that they wanted to be nearer to their job as the main reason for moving (Table 10.14). Of those in the professional socio-economic group, just under three in ten, moved more than 20 miles away from their previous home, compared with

10.11

Tenure: by length of time at current address, 1998-99

United Kingdom						Percentages
	Under 1 year	1-4 years	5-10 years	10-19 years	20 years and over	All
Owner-occupied						
Owned outright	3	10	9	22	56	100
Owned with mortgage	9	30	22	27	11	100
Rented unfurnished						
Council/new town	11	29	17	20	22	100
Housing association	17	38	19	19	6	100
Privately	32	36	8	8	15	100
Rented furnished	48	42	..	..	..	100
Rented with job or business	22	38	13	13	14	100
All tenures	10	25	16	22	25	100

Source: General Household Survey, Office for National Statistics; Continuous Household Survey, Northern Ireland Statistics and Research Agency

10.12

Adults moving house each year: by tenure before and after move, 1991-1996[1]

Great Britain				Percentages
	Tenure after move			
	Owner-occupied	Rented from social sector	Rented privately	All movers
Tenure before move				
Whole household moves				
Owner-occupied	82	4	14	100
Rented from social sector	11	78	11	100
Rented privately	34	16	50	100
Part of household moves				
Owner-occupied	50	9	41	100
Rented from social sector	27	51	22	100
Rented privately	37	7	56	100

1 Changes in tenure for the periods 1991 to 1992, 1992 to 1993, 1993 to 1994, 1994 to 1995 and 1995 to 1996 have been analysed separately and then combined in this table.

Source: British Household Panel Survey, Institute for Social and Economic Research

10.13

Tenure: by distance moved[1], 1998-99

England				Percentages
	Owner-occupied	Rented from social sector	Rented privately	All movers
Under 1 mile	21	31	20	23
1 but not 10 miles	50	53	42	48
10 but not 20 miles	9	7	7	8
20 but not 50 miles	6	3	6	5
50 miles or more	12	5	16	12
Abroad	2	1	8	4
All moves	100	100	100	100

1 Distance of head of household's present home from previous home.

Source: Survey of English Housing, Department of Environment, Transport and the Regions

only two in ten of those in the skilled manual and semi-skilled and unskilled manual groups. Private renters had a higher proportion of moves abroad than any other tenure, which further reflects the mobility of private renters.

Homelessness

Homelessness often arises from a change in personal circumstances. In 1998-99, just over a quarter of all households accepted as homeless in England were in their situation because parents, other relatives or friends were no longer able or willing to accommodate them, particularly young homeless people. A further quarter gave the breakdown of a relationship with a partner as their main reason for the loss of their last settled home (Chart 10.15). Research has shown that older homeless people also identified family crises, such as widowhood or marital breakdown, alongside eviction, redundancy and mental illness as reasons for homelessness.

10.14

Tenure: by main reason for moving[1], 1998-99

England						Percentages
	Owned outright	Owned with mortgage	Rented from council	Rented from housing association	Rented privately	All tenures
Wanted larger or better accommodation	9	23	13	10	13	16
Change of job or nearer to job	4	9	0	4	21	11
Other personal reasons	22	6	17	21	9	11
To move to better area	12	11	8	8	7	9
Wanted own home or to live independently	5	9	8	12	8	8
Divorce or separation	10	6	10	7	9	8
Marriage or cohabitation	2	11	9	7	6	8
Wanted to buy	5	15	-	0	-	6
Wanted smaller or cheaper accommodation	17	3	6	6	4	5
Accommodation no longer available	-	-	9	7	7	5
Could not afford mortgage or rent	1	1	4	2	2	2
Other reasons	12	5	16	18	14	12
All households (=100%)(millions)	0.2	0.8	0.4	0.2	0.8	2.4

1 Current tenure of continuing household heads who moved in the year before interview.

Source: Survey of English Housing, Department of the Environment, Transport and the Regions

10.15

When a household in difficulty applies to a local authority for housing it must first be assessed as to whether the case is one of homelessness and, if so, whether the applicants are in priority need. The priority need group includes households with dependent children or containing a pregnant woman; people who are vulnerable as a result of old age, mental or physical illness or disability or other special reason; and people who are homeless in an emergency. If both criteria are satisfied then suitable housing must be found, though not necessarily from the council's own stock. It could be arranged with registered social landlords or private landlords. Local authorities may also, at their discretion, assist homeless households not classified as being in priority need.

In 1998-99 local authorities in England made a total of 245,480 decisions on applications for housing from households eligible under the homelessness provisions of the 1985 and 1996 *Housing Acts*. They accepted more than 105,470 households as meeting the conditions of eligibility for assistance.

Households accepted as homeless[1] by local authorities: by main reason for loss of last settled home, 1998-99

England

Percentages

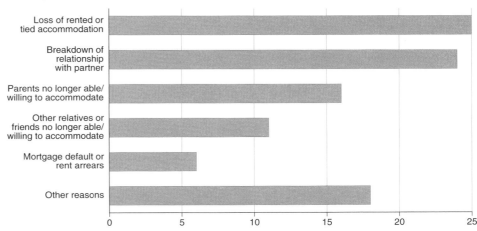

1 See Appendix, Part 10: Homeless households.

Source: Department of the Environment, Transport and the Regions

10.16

Housing standards

We expect a number of basic facilities to be available in our homes. Over the years, our expectations have changed in line with technological developments. For many years the Census has contained questions on the amenities available in each household in England and Wales, but these too have changed over time. Results from the 1951 Census, indicated that nearly two-fifths of households lacked a fixed bath or shower, and one in seven had neither an internal nor external flush toilet (Table 10.16). By the time of the last Census, conducted in 1991, the proportion of households lacking either of these facilities was negligible.

Households lacking basic amenities

England & Wales Percentages

		Flush toilet		
	Bath or shower	Internal or external[1]	Internal	Hot water tap
1951	38	14	..	..
1961	22	7	..	22
1971	9	1	..	6
1981	2	..	3	..

1 In 1961, the data refer to internal WCs and external WCs that were attached to the dwelling.

Source: Census, Office for National Statistics

10.17

Homes with selected amenities: by construction date, 1996

England Percentages

	Central heating	Mains gas supply	Double glazing	Parking[1] Street[2]	Off street[3]
Before 1919	78	84	42	30	37
1919-1944	85	92	66	18	71
1945-1964	87	89	64	20	69
1965 or later	95	82	65	11	85
All	88	86	59	19	67

1 Figures for houses only because of difficulties assessing whether designated parking is available for flats.
2 Excludes houses with 'inadequate' or no street parking and those with off-street parking available. 'Adequate' street parking is where space is generally available outside or adjacent to the house and where such parking allows easy passage of traffic.
3 Includes a small proportion of houses with off-street parking available elswhere than the plot.
Source: English House Condition Survey, Department of the Environment, Transport and the Regions

10.18

Poor housing[1]: by tenure, 1996

England
Percentages

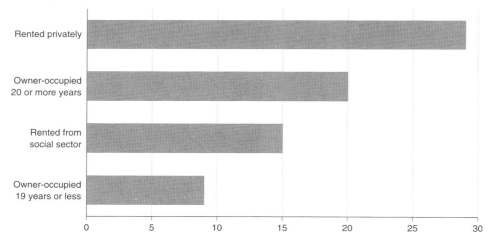

1 Percentage of housing in each tenure group which is deemed 'poor'. Poor housing is an indicator combining unfitness, substantial disrepair and where essential modernisation is needed.
Source: English House Condition Survey, Department of the Environment, Transport and the Regions

Up to 1996-97 the English House Condition Survey (EHCS) identified dwellings in England which lacked the basic amenities of a kitchen sink, a bath or shower in a bathroom, a wash-hand basin, hot and cold water to each of these and an indoor toilet. In 1996, 207 thousand dwellings, less than 1 per cent of the stock, lacked one or more of these basic amenities. Properties that lacked amenities were likely to be lived in by long-term resident elderly people and be in private ownership. Around half of the dwellings lacking amenities were vacant, and may have therefore been in the process of renovation, or have been long-term vacant. A proportion of the occupied stock may also lack an amenity on a purely temporary basis while improvement or repair work is being carried out. The installation of central heating has also increased. In 1996, just under 90 per cent of houses had central heating, almost 10 per cent more than in 1991.

Since virtually all dwellings now possess these five amenities, the EHCS currently defines a modern dwelling as one which has had its kitchen and bathroom installed after 1964, has PVC wiring, modern sockets and modern light fittings and a central or programmable heating system which is 30 years old or less. As would be expected, modern facilities are most commonly found in newer dwellings. The homes most likely to lack modern facilities are those built between 1945 and 1964. This is because older dwellings are more likely to have gone through at least one cycle of modernisation. Flats and pre-1919 terraced and semi-detached houses are less likely to have all these modern facilities. Some 95 per cent of dwellings built after 1964 have central heating installed, primarily as a planned aspect of their initial design (Table 10.17). Although older properties are less likely to have central heating than their more modern counterparts the great majority have been improved with its installation.

As a result of more purpose-built flats being constructed with electric or other forms of heating provision, post-1964 dwellings are less likely to

Social Trends 30, © Crown copyright 2000

10.19

have a supply of mains gas. Old, largely rural dwellings are also less likely to have mains gas. Almost two-thirds of dwellings built from 1919 have double-glazing installed, reflecting the popularity of this form of improvement among owner-occupiers and, in more recent years, social landlords. The private rented sector – with a high concentration of older properties – has the lowest incidence of dwellings with double-glazing (35 per cent).

As the number of cars in use increases (see Chart 12.5 in the Transport chapter) there is concern about whether homes have adequate parking provision. Off street parking facilities are most likely to be available for the most recently built houses and least likely for older properties constructed before 1919. Older houses are also least likely to have adequate street parking available as an alternative, probably because of the relative concentration of these properties in city or urban areas.

Approximately 14 per cent of households in England are living in 'poor housing', which is an indicator combining unfitness, substantial disrepair and a requirement for essential modernisation. On this definition, private tenants are most likely to be in poor housing; three in ten privately rented households in England lived in poor housing in 1996 (Chart 10.18).

A report by the Social Exclusion Unit – *A National Strategy for Neighbourhood Renewal* – found that despite a rise in the standard of living, a greater divide has developed between the poorest neighbourhoods and the rest of Britain. The report noted that poor neighbourhoods were not in the typical stereotyped areas, such as high rise council estates, but many were publicly owned, privately rented or owner-occupied dwellings.

The length of time which a person has owned their home also has an impact on the quality of their housing. Almost two in ten people who have owned their home for 20 years or more lived in

Under-occupation[1] and overcrowding[2]: by type of household, 1998-99

United Kingdom		Percentages
	Under-occupied	Overcrowded
Multi-family households	6	8
Two or more unrelated adults	10	8
Lone parent with dependent children only	4	7
Couple with dependent children	17	4
Couple with non-dependent children	17	2
Lone parent with non-dependent children only	12	1
One person under pensionable age	33	0
One person over pensionable age	37	0
Couple with no children	63	0
All households	34	2

1 Two or more above bedroom standard. See Appendix, Part 10: Bedroom standard.
2 One or more below bedroom standard. See Appendix, Part 10: Bedroom standard.
Source: General Household Survey, Office for National Statistics; Continuous Household Survey, Northern Ireland Statistics and Research Agency

10.20

Satisfaction[1] with accommodation and area: by type of area[2], 1998-99

England		Percentages
	Accommodation	Area
Affluent family areas	94	93
Mature home-owning areas	93	90
Affluent suburban and rural areas	95	95
New home-owning areas	91	85
Council estates and low income areas	85	74
Affluent urban areas	89	86
All types of areas	91	87

1 Heads of household or partners who replied that they were 'very satisfied' or 'fairly satisfied'.
2 Based on the ACORN classification. See Appendix, Part 10: Area type.
Source: Survey of English Housing, Department of the Environment, Transport and the Regions

10.21

Problems[1] with aspects of the area: by type of area[2], 1998-99

England						Percentages
	Affluent family areas	Mature home-owning areas	Affluent suburban and rural areas	New home-owning areas	Council estates and low income areas	Affluent urban areas
Crime	56	58	52	60	68	63
Traffic	35	43	40	42	39	59
Vandalism and hooliganism	40	45	33	50	64	50
Litter and rubbish	29	36	23	44	54	50
Noise	18	23	17	26	35	41
Dogs	26	30	24	33	35	29

1 Head of household or partners who replied that they had 'a serious problem' or 'a problem, but not serious'.
2 Based on the ACORN classification. See Appendix, Part 10: Area type.
Source: Survey of English Housing, Department of the Environment, Transport and the Regions

10.22

New mortgages: average mortgage repayments as a percentage of average household income

United Kingdom
Percentages

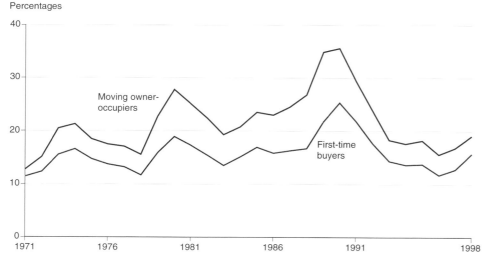

Source: Department of the Environment, Transport and the Regions

poor housing compared with just less than one in ten of those who owned their home for 19 years or less.

Other important indicators of housing standards are overcrowding and under-occupancy. There are records of overcrowding in the 1901 Census, although these are believed to be an unreliable reflection of the true figure. Since 1921 overcrowding in Great Britain has dropped sharply and is now relatively rare.

In 1998-99, 2 per cent of households in the United Kingdom were in accommodation below the bedroom standard (a comparison of the number of bedrooms available to a household with a calculation of its bedroom requirements – see Appendix, Part 10: Bedroom standard). Couples with no children were more likely than other households to live in under-occupied accommodation. Multi-family households and households consisting of two or more unrelated adults were far more likely to be in overoccupied accommodation (see Table 10.19 on the previous page).

It is not surprising that the area in which people live has an impact on their levels of satisfaction with their accommodation. Those living in 'affluent family', 'mature home-owning' and 'affluent suburban and rural' areas are more likely to be satisfied with both their accommodation and area than people in other areas (see Table 10.20 on the previous page). The highest levels of dissatisfaction are found in council estates and low-income areas. Those living in new home-owning areas are more satisfied with their accommodation than their area.

The 1998-99 Survey of English Housing asked further questions about the areas in which people lived. People were asked to say whether various problems occurred in their area and, if so, whether

Social Trends 30, © Crown copyright 2000

or not they were serious (Table 10.21). Overall, nearly six in ten householders said that crime was a problem. Those living in 'council estates and low income areas' were most likely to say that it was a problem (68 per cent) while people living in 'affluent suburban and rural areas' were least likely to do so (52 per cent). Vandalism and hooliganism were also common problems, particularly in 'council estates and low income areas', where nearly two-thirds reported problems. Noise was considered the least problem overall, particularly in 'affluent suburban and rural family areas' with just under a fifth reporting that they had problems with it in their area.

Housing costs and expenditure

Affordability is a concern to both first-time buyers and moving owner-occupiers. In 1990 owner-occupiers who moved and bought a new home spent, on average, over a third of their income on their mortgage repayments, while first-time buyers spent a quarter of their income (Chart 10.22). In four years of housing recession between 1990 and 1993 there were declining mortgage interest rates and an increase in real earnings. House prices began stabilising in 1993 and by 1998 first-time buyers were spending almost 16 per cent and moving owner-occupiers 19 per cent of their income on mortgage repayments.

In 1998 the average dwelling price in the United Kingdom was nearly £82,000 but there was a big difference in the average amount spent by first-time buyers and by those who already owned a home (Table 10.23). Overall, the price of a dwelling bought by first-time buyers was around 60 per cent of that of a dwelling bought by a former owner-occupier. There are also marked regional variations in house prices overall, with buyers in London paying on average more than double the £56,000 paid in the North East.

Housing constitutes a significant proportion of a household's budget regardless of whether their home is owned or rented. Households from different tenure groups face very different levels and types of housing costs. In 1998-99 those who owned their house with a mortgage in the United Kingdom spent on average nearly 40 per cent more than private renters (Table 10.24). Council tenants paid about the same as outright owner-occupiers. Owner-occupiers spent an average of £10 per week on repairs, maintenance and decoration.

Owner-occupiers' housing expenditure can vary considerably, depending on whether a mortgage is being repaid and for how long it has been running. Households who bought their property many years ago are likely to have much smaller payments

10.23

Average dwelling prices[1]: by region, 1998

£ thousand

	First-time buyers	Other	All buyers	Percentage increase 1997-1998
United Kingdom	61.3	101.3	81.8	8
North East	43.7	69.9	56.0	6
North West	50.6	84.5	66.8	5
Yorkshire and the Humber	47.8	77.2	62.2	4
East Midlands	49.6	82.8	66.2	7
West Midlands	52.7	90.3	71.9	6
East	64.9	107.7	88.7	9
London	90.2	146.0	114.8	8
South East	77.3	125.4	106.4	12
South West	61.0	94.7	80.2	10
England	63.5	104.3	84.7	7
Wales	48.0	76.5	60.9	4
Scotland	49.0	80.0	63.6	10
Northern Ireland	48.9	73.9	59.4	11

1 All borrowers' average dwelling price.
Source: Department of the Environment, Transport and the Regions

10.24

Average weekly household expenditure on housing costs[1]: by tenure, 1998-99

United Kingdom	£ per week
	1998-99
Owner-occupied	
Owned outright	29
Owned with mortgage	87
Rented from council	28
Rented from housing association	32
Rented privately	63
All tenures	57

1 Net of housing benefit, rebates and allowances received.
Source: Family Expenditure Survey, Office for National Statistics

10.25

New mortgages[1]: by gender of borrower

United Kingdom
Percentages

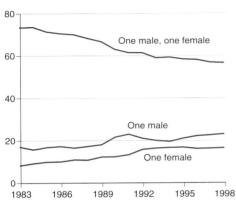

One male, one female

One male

One female

1983 1986 1989 1992 1995 1998

1 Data prior to 1993 are for new mortgages advanced by building societies and Abbey National plc; since 1993 new mortgages advanced by other major lenders have been included. Includes sitting tenants.

Source: Department of the Environment, Transport and the Regions

now than households who have bought more recently, or during a housing boom. It should be noted that the figures in Table 10.24 are net of means-tested benefits – that is housing benefit and income support – which make a large contribution towards housing costs, and that all figures for mortgage interest payments are net of tax relief given at source through the MIRAS scheme.

Most new mortgages are taken out by couples, although the proportion has declined steadily since the early 1980s from 74 per cent in 1984 to 56 per cent in 1998 (Chart 10.25). Over the same period the proportion of new mortgages taken out by one person increased, from around 25 per cent to 39 per cent. The greatest increase was in the

proportion of mortgages taken out by women on their own which doubled over the period. This change reflects several factors, including greater financial independence for women as they have increasingly moved into the labour market and as a result of higher levels of divorce.

As with housing prices and costs, people's attitudes towards value for money of renting privately vary considerably depending on the region of England in which they live. In the 1998-99 Survey of English Housing (SEH) respondents were asked: 'what do you think of the level of the present rent for your accommodation?'. High proportions (15 per cent) of those living in the North East and West Midlands considered that the price of renting their accommodation was 'very high considering what you get' (Table 10.26).

In some cases people receive financial gifts and loans from family and friends in order to buy a property. The SEH found that single people buying with a mortgage were more than twice as likely as couples to have received this form of financial help. People under the age of 30, especially women, were particularly likely to benefit.

In 1998-99, 3 per cent of owner-occupiers were in mortgage arrears while, of those who rented from the social sector, 11 per cent were at least two weeks in arrears (Table 10.27). House prices are now increasing after falling for four years in the early 1990s; interest rates are also more stable. Economic circumstances meant that interest rates began to increase rapidly from the middle of 1988, and mortgage rates followed, increasing from 9.8

10.26

Attitudes towards value for money of renting privately[1]: by region, 1998-99

England Percentages

	Very high for what you get	Slightly high	About right	Slightly low	Very low for what you get	All
North East	15	13	65	3	4	100
North West	7	27	50	7	9	100
Yorkshire and the Humber	10	16	58	9	7	100
East Midlands	5	16	61	14	4	100
West Midlands	15	20	51	9	5	100
East	9	21	51	8	10	100
London	11	27	44	12	7	100
South East	13	19	52	10	7	100
South West	8	16	53	11	13	100
England	10	21	52	10	8	100

1 Respondents were asked: 'what do you think of the level of the present rent for your accommodation?'.

Source: Survey of English Housing, Department of the Environment, Transport and the Regions

10.27

per cent in the second quarter of 1988 to 13.4 per cent a year later and reaching a peak of 15.25 per cent in the third quarter of 1990. The resulting increased payments led to a rise in financial difficulties and arrears and repossessions in the early 1990s, with the number of loans in arrears reaching a peak in 1992. New homebuyers who had borrowed a high proportion of the value of their properties to enter the housing market were particularly exposed to the increased rates. The situation has improved since then, and in 1998 the number of loans in arrears were at around a third of the 1992 level.

The warning given with every mortgage is that 'your home is at risk if you do not keep up repayments on a mortgage or other loan secured on it'. The same is true of rented property. In 1998-99, those who rented from the social sector in England were more likely to be in arrears with their rent compared with those who owned their house or rented privately.

When people fall behind with rent or mortgage repayments and are unable to reach an alternative payment arrangement with their landlord or mortgage lender, a county court possession summons might be issued, with the view to obtaining a court order. Not all orders will result in possession; it is not uncommon for courts to make suspended orders that provide for arrears to be paid off within a reasonable period. If the court decides not to adjourn the proceedings or suspend a possession order, the warrant will be executed and the home repossessed by the landlord or mortgage lender.

The number of warrants issued for properties in England and Wales peaked at 134 thousand in 1991; since then it has fluctuated but overall has declined to around 111 thousand in 1996 (Chart 10.28). By 1998 it had increased again to 130 thousand which is the highest number since 1991. The number of warrants executed remained fairly steady at around 50 thousand between 1993 and 1997, then in 1998 rose by 20 per cent.

Households in arrears with mortgage or rent payments: by tenure, 1998-99

England	Percentages
	1998-99
Owner-occupied	
Less than 3 months in arrears	2
3 to 6 months in arrears	-
Over 6 months in arrears	-
All in arrears	3
Rented from social sector	
Owing by 2 weeks or more	11
Rented privately	
Owing by 2 weeks or more	5

Source: Survey of English Housing, Department of the Environment, Transport and the Regions

10.28

Repossession of properties[1]: warrants issued and executed

England & Wales
Thousands

1 Rented and mortgaged.
Source: Court Service

References and further reading

The following list contains selected publications relevant to **Chapter 10: Housing**. Those published by The Stationery Office are available from the address shown on the inside back cover of *Social Trends*.

Bringing Britain Together: A National Strategy for Neighbourhood Renewal, Social Exclusion Unit

Britain Yearbook, The Stationery Office

British Social Attitudes, Ashgate Publishing

British Social Trends since 1900, Macmillan Press

Changing Households: The British Household Panel Survey, Institute for Social and Economic Research

Department of the Environment Annual Report, The Stationery Office

English House Condition Survey, The Stationery Office

Family Resources Survey, The Stationery Office

Family Spending, The Stationery Office

Housing Finance, Council of Mortgage Lenders

Housing in England, The Stationery Office

Living in Britain, The Stationery Office

Local Housing Statistics, The Stationery Office

Northern Ireland House Condition Survey, Northern Ireland Housing Executive

Northern Ireland Housing Statistics, CSRB, Department of the Environment for Northern Ireland

Private Renting in England, The Stationery Office

Private Renting in Five Localities, The Stationery Office

Projections of Households in England to 2016, The Stationery Office

Regional Trends, The Stationery Office

Social Focus on Ethnic Minorities, The Stationery Office

Social Portrait of Europe, Eurostat

Statistical Bulletins on Housing, Scottish Executive

Statistics on Housing in the European Community, Commission of the European Communities

Welsh House Condition Survey, National Assembly for Wales

Welsh Housing Statistics, National Assembly for Wales

Contacts

Telephone contact points for further information relating to

Chapter 10: Housing

Office for National Statistics	
Chapter author	020 7533 6174
Family Expenditure Survey	020 7533 5756
General Household Survey	020 7533 5444
Department of the Environment, Transport and the Regions	020 7890 3303
Court Service	020 7210 1752
Department of the Environment for Northern Ireland	028 9054 0799
National Assembly for Wales	029 2082 5087
Northern Ireland Statistics and Research Agency	028 9025 2521
Scottish Executive	0131 244 7232
Council of Mortgage Lenders	020 7440 2207
Eurostat	00352 4301 33012
Institute for Social and Economic Research	01206 872957

Chapter 11 Environment

Environmental concern and conservation

In 1996-97, 51 per cent of adults in England and Wales said that they had regularly taken paper to a paper-bank for recycling. (Table 11.2)

Climate and atmosphere

Globally, seven out of the ten hottest years on record have been in the 1990s. (Page 184)

Between 1971 and 1997, carbon dioxide emissions from road vehicles almost doubled in the United Kingdom. (Chart 11.8)

Germany and the United Kingdom collectively contribute nearly half of the EU emissions of carbon dioxide. (Table 11.9)

Water quality

The proportion of bathing waters in the United Kingdom complying with the EU mandatory coliform standards increased from 76 per cent in 1991 to 91 per cent in 1999. (Table 11.12)

Land cover and use

Between 1961 and 1998 the amount of land used for agricultural purposes in the United Kingdom fell by around 6 per cent. (Table 11.16)

The area covered by forest and woodland in the United Kingdom has more than doubled this century. (Page 190)

Natural resources

At the end of 1998, there were an estimated 685 million tonnes of proven oil reserves remaining from discovered oilfields in the United Kingdom continental shelf. (Table 11.21)

11.1

Global and Central England Temperature variations[1]

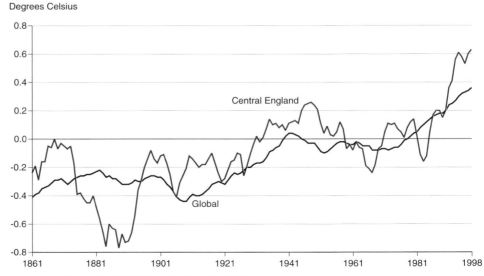

Degrees Celsius

1 Average surface temperature; difference from 1961–1990 average.

Source: Department of the Environment, Transport and the Regions; Hadley Centre for Climate Prediction and Research

11.2

Personal actions taken 'on a regular basis' for environmental reasons[1]: by age, 1996-97

England & Wales   Percentages

	18-24	25-44	45-64	64 and over	All aged 18 and over
Domestic actions					
Made sure that your noise did not disturb others	55	78	81	79	76
Taken paper to a paper-bank or separated paper for recycling	47	46	57	63	51
Taken glass to a bottle bank or separated glass for recycling	44	44	51	57	48
Cut down the use of a car for short journeys	29	36	30	31	33
Buying actions					
Used unleaded petrol in your car	81	71	75	69	73
Used recycled paper at home	29	41	44	35	39
Used diesel in your car	20	32	32	19	29
Reactions					
Reduced sunbathing or taken greater care when in the sun because of increased UV rays	51	61	57	48	57
Avoided bathing in rivers and sea because of pollution	48	42	47	31	43

1 Respondents were asked about actions they had taken for environmental reasons in the last 12 months. Respondents for whom an action was 'not applicable' have been excluded from the total (for example, people without access to a car are excluded from the total of people who might use unleaded petrol).

Source: Attitudes to the Environment Survey, Department of the Environment, Transport and the Regions

11.3

Membership of selected environmental organisations

United Kingdom   Thousands

	1971	1981	1991	1997	1998
National Trust[1]	278	1,046	2,152	2,489	2,557
Royal Society for the Protection of Birds	98	441	852	1,007	1,012
Civic Trust	214	..	222	330	..
Wildlife Trusts[2]	64	142	233	310	320
World Wide Fund for Nature	12	60	227	241	240
The National Trust for Scotland	37	105	234	228	228
Woodland Trust	..	20	150	195	200
Greenpeace	..	30	312	215	194
Ramblers Association	22	37	87	123	126
Friends of the Earth[1]	1	18	111	114	114
Council for the Protection of Rural England	21	29	45	45	47

1 Covers England, Wales and Northern Ireland.
2 Includes The Royal Society for Nature Conservation.

Source: Organisations concerned

Public concern about issues such as poor air quality, noise pollution and urban development have meant that in recent years the profile of environmental issues has been raised locally and nationally; this is reflected in the introduction of the government's new UK-wide strategy for sustainable development. Over the course of a century, conservation has moved from being a fringe activity to one of central social and political importance.

Environmental concern and conservation

In the Attitudes to the Environment Survey, conducted by the Department of the Environment, Transport and the Regions in 1996-97, people were asked which environmental issues they were worried about. Some of the issues of greatest concern were chemicals being discharged into rivers and the sea, sewage on beaches or in bathing waters and traffic exhaust fumes and urban smog. People were also asked what actions they had taken on a 'regular basis' for environmental reasons. Over three-quarters said they had made sure that their noise did not disturb others (Table 11.2). Nearly the same proportion said they had used unleaded petrol in their car and just under a third of adults chose to use diesel. Older people were more willing than younger people to take environmental action that involved recycling. For example, 63 per cent of adults aged over 64 said they had taken paper to a paper-bank for recycling compared with 47 per cent of adults aged 18 to 24.

Although the Attitudes to the Environment Survey has only been running since the mid-1980s and comparisons with the earlier surveys are not always possible, some changes in people's attitudes can still be noted over this relatively short period. The proportion of people who said they had reduced sunbathing or taken greater care in the sun because of increased UV rays rose from just under half of all adults in the 1993 survey to almost three-fifths in 1996-97. Similarly there has been an increase between the two surveys in the numbers avoiding bathing in rivers or the sea because of pollution: from a third in 1993 to just over two-fifths in 1996-97. Again this could reflect publicity about pollution incidents and water quality.

Concern about issues such as pollution and the need to preserve and protect both land and wildlife has meant that the number of people joining environmental organisations has increased. The National Trust has the largest number of members; by 1998 its membership had reached over 2.5 million, more than nine times the number of members in 1971 (Table 11.3). Along with The National Trust for Scotland, the organisation is responsible for protecting areas of natural beauty and historic interest.

Many volunteers belonging to environmental organisations are directly involved with projects to improve or preserve aspects of the countryside. The National Trust for Scotland runs 'Thistle Camps' where volunteers can take part in a wide variety of activities including repairing paths and building fences and footbridges. Members of the Council for the Protection of Rural England are involved locally in many issues, for example responding to planning applications, housing developments and campaigning for safety on country lanes. Civic Trust members are generally active in issues relating to the urban environment, such as encouraging urban regeneration and campaigning for better planning.

Practical conservation is also important to the Royal Society for the Protection of Birds (RSPB), another organisation which has shown a large increase in membership over the last quarter of a century. It works to protect wild birds and their habitats. One of the many successes of the RSPB has been the re-introduction of the red kite to areas of England and Scotland where it had

virtually become extinct. In 1903 there were only four pairs found in Wales, but following a careful breeding programme they increased to an estimated 263 breeding pairs in 1998.

All wild birds in the United Kingdom are protected by the *Countryside Act 1981*. Many of the UK's native birds are monitored through surveys by the British Trust for Ornithology and Rare Breeding Birds Panel. Populations of the more common farmland and woodland birds are in long-term decline (Chart 11.4). For example, numbers of certain farmland birds (like the corn bunting and skylark) fell by more than half between the mid-1970s and 1998. This decline could be due to a number of factors, including changes in farming practice, loss of habitat diversity, urban development and climate change. Populations of other birds, such as many open water birds and rare birds like the osprey and goshawk have been stable or rising. Under the government's new strategy for sustainable development, populations of wild birds will be monitored with an aim to reverse the long-term decline in farmland and woodland birds.

11.4

Populations of wild birds

United Kingdom

Index (1970=100)

Source: British Trust for Ornithology; Royal Society for the Protection of Birds; Department of the Environment, Transport and the Regions

11.5

Protected areas, 1997

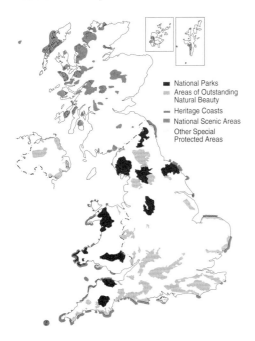

National Parks
Areas of Outstanding
Natural Beauty
Heritage Coasts
National Scenic Areas
Other Special
Protected Areas

Source: Countryside Commission; English Nature; Scottish Natural Heritage; Department of the Environment, Northern Ireland; Countryside Council for Wales

11.6

Complaints about noise received by Environmental Health Officers, 1981 and 1996-97

England & Wales	Number per million population	
	1981	1996-97
Domestic premises	764	5,051
Industrial/commercial premises	478	1,455
Road works, construction and demolition	65	242
Road traffic	32	62
Aircraft	16	58
Other	57	391
All types	1,412	7,259

Source: Chartered Institute of Environmental Health Officers

Since 1949 there has been a framework of statutory measures to safeguard the wildlife habitats and natural features of the environment. Around half of the land area of the United Kingdom is designated or protected by legislation in one way or another in order to preserve the landscape or conservation value of these areas. National Parks and Areas of Outstanding Natural Beauty in England, Wales and Northern Ireland and National Scenic Areas in Scotland comprise the main areas designated because of their value to the landscape (Chart 11.5).

In 1997 National Parks covered over 1,400 thousand hectares of England and Wales, with almost 30 per cent of this area being in Wales. Areas of Outstanding Natural Beauty are most prominent in the South East and South West regions where they cover around 30 per cent of each region's total area. The South West region also has the highest proportion of Heritage Coast in England and Wales – at 41 per cent of the total. Sites of Special Scientific Interest (SSSIs) are afforded additional protection because of their importance to our natural heritage in terms of flora, fauna, or geological or physiographical features. There are around 6,300 SSSIs and 161 Special Protection Areas (SPAs) across the United Kingdom as a whole. Wildlife and habitats, in particular changes in natural/semi natural habitats and populations of selected species, will be monitored under the sustainable development strategy.

Noise pollution is a serious and very common problem. The World Health Organisation (WHO) sets a daytime limit of 50 decibels as the level above which noise causes annoyance. The number of complaints has increased over the past couple of decades. In 1996-97, the highest rate of complaints received by Environmental Health Officers in England and Wales related to domestic premises: at 5 thousand complaints per million

population it was over six times the rate in 1981 (Table 11.6). The second highest rate of complaints was for industrial and commercial premises, which was over three times the rate in 1981. It should be noted that these rises do not necessarily only indicate an increase in noise levels but may also reflect an increasing tendency for people to complain about noise.

Noise abatement is generally enforced by Environmental Health Officers under the *Control of Pollution Act 1974* and the *Environmental Protection Act 1990*. These give local authorities the power to prosecute offenders for most types of noise pollution. The introduction *of The Noise Act 1996* along with other recent legislation has extended the powers of local authorities to confiscate noise-making equipment and deal with excessive domestic noise, in particular from amplified music and parties.

Climate and atmosphere

Concentrations of greenhouse gases such as carbon dioxide and methane in the atmosphere are rising due to human activities. A consequence of this is the rise in global temperature and associated climate change – globally, seven out of the ten hottest years on record have been in the 1990s. The hottest year since global records began in 1860 occurred in 1998, partly due to the El Nino effect – the warming of the eastern tropical Pacific. Climate change has also had an impact on global sea level which has risen between 10 and 25 centimetres since the late nineteenth century. During the twentieth century the annual mean Central England temperature warmed by about 0.6°C (see Chart 11.1 at the beginning of the chapter). Three of the five warmest years since reliable records began in 1772 have been in the 1990s.

11.7

Although there has been no discernible overall change in annual rainfall for the United Kingdom as a whole over the last 100 years, since the mid-1970s there has been a tendency for a greater proportion of annual rainfall to fall in the winter half-year (from October to March) rather than during the summer (Chart 11.7). Over the last decade there have been a number of exceptionally wet winters and intensely dry summers.

Carbon dioxide is the principal greenhouse gas, with concentrations in the atmosphere rising at approximately 0.5 per cent per annum. The United Kingdom alone contributes an estimated 2 per cent to global man-made emissions of carbon dioxide. Emissions of carbon dioxide have fallen in the United Kingdom since the early 1980s. In 1997, 148 million tonnes of carbon dioxide (expressed as weight of carbon using the UNECE classification) were emitted, around half of which came from power stations and road transport (Chart 11.8). Since 1971 total emissions from power stations have fallen, reflecting the replacement of coal by gas and nuclear energy, as well as general improvements in conversion efficiencies at power stations. On the other hand emissions by road vehicles have almost doubled over the period.

Whereas Chart 11.8 measures carbon dioxide in terms of weight of carbon emitted, Table 11.9 (overleaf) measures it in terms of the weight of carbon dioxide. On this basis, the European Union (EU) country that has experienced the greatest absolute fall in emissions of carbon dioxide between 1990 and 1997 was Germany with a reduction of 112 million tonnes, a fall of around 12 per cent. Only in two other countries, including the United Kingdom, did the total level of emissions fall. Portugal experienced the greatest percentage increase with carbon dioxide emissions rising by

Winter and summer rainfall[1]

United Kingdom
Millimetres

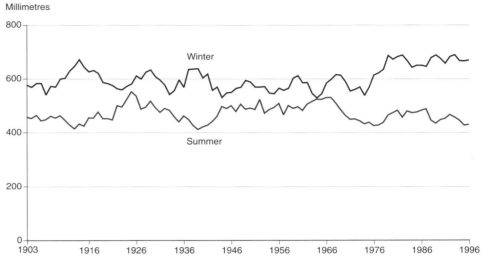

1 Data are five year running means of the summer half-year and winter half-year rainfall figures and are plotted at mid-point.
Source: Institute of Hydrology

11.8

Carbon dioxide emissions[1]: by source

United Kingdom
Million tonnes

1 Expressed in terms of weight of carbon emitted using the UNECE classification.
2 Comprises iron, steel and other industrial combustion.
Source: National Environmental Technology Centre

11.9

Emissions of carbon dioxide[1]: EU comparison, 1990 and 1997

Million tonnes

	1990	1997	Percentage change 1990-1997
Luxembourg	11	9	-20
Germany	943	831	-12
United Kingdom	568	530	-7
France	354	359	1
Sweden	51	52	2
Italy	391	402	3
Austria	55	60	8
Belgium	105	116	10
Netherlands	153	169	11
Finland	52	59	14
Greece	71	83	17
Spain	204	243	19
Denmark	53	64	21
Irish Republic	30	36	22
Portugal	39	48	23
EU total	3,078	3,058	-1

1 From fossil fuel combustion.

Source: Eurostat

23 per cent. Despite showing a reduction in emissions, Germany and the United Kingdom are still the highest producers of carbon dioxide, collectively accounting for nearly half of the EU total.

One of the outcomes of the 'Earth Summit' in Rio in 1992 was the United Nations Framework Convention on Climate Change under which developed countries had to take measures aimed at returning greenhouse gas emissions to their 1990 levels by the year 2000. Under the Protocol agreed at the Kyoto conference in 1997, the United Kingdom has a legally binding target to reduce emissions of the basket of six greenhouse gases by 12.5 per cent relative to the 1990 level over the period 2008 to 2012. It also has a domestic goal to cut carbon dioxide emissions by 20 per cent below 1990 levels by 2010.

Air quality

For many years, there has been concern about air pollution and its effects on people and ecosystems. The impact of air pollution on the environment is far reaching, from acid rain damaging plant life, acidifying water, and damaging buildings to adverse effects on human and animal health. The Department of Health estimated in 1998 that the deaths of between 12 and 24 thousand people in Great Britain may be brought forward by short-term exposure to air pollution each year.

Up to and through the first half of the twentieth century, the main cause of air pollution was the burning of coal, particularly in domestic premises. Past events, such as the London smog in December 1952 which lasted four days and led to an estimated 4 thousand premature deaths, were caused by large amounts of coal-generated black smoke and sulphur dioxide being produced by factories and homes. The *Clean Air Act* in 1956 created a framework for the reduction of emissions from chimneys in the United Kingdom and together with subsequent Acts which included the introduction of smokeless domestic fuels and smokeless zones has virtually eliminated this type of smog. However, since the 1960s, traffic sources of pollution have increased. The rise in motorised traffic has vastly increased the quantity of exhaust gases entering the atmosphere and has led to occasional summertime and wintertime smogs. Part of the problem is that traffic pollution enters the atmosphere at a much lower level than stack emissions from power stations and other industrial sources and therefore has a much more immediate impact. The fact that in urban areas, two daily peaks of many air pollutants coincide with the morning and evening rush hours show that traffic pollution has become a key factor in the overall issue of air quality.

11.10

Air pollutants: emissions of selected gases

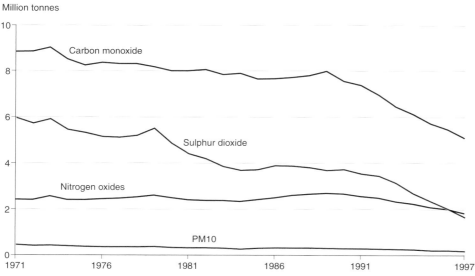

United Kingdom

Million tonnes

Source: National Environmental Technology Centre

The Department of the Environment, Transport and the Regions funds three national automated networks to monitor air pollution: one based in rural areas, one in urban areas and one monitoring levels of hydrocarbons. These give hourly measurements of five main pollutants: ozone, sulphur dioxide, nitrogen oxides, carbon monoxide and particulate matter (PM10) at various locations around the country. Between 1971 and 1997 emissions of PM10 fell by about three-fifths and sulphur dioxide fell by nearly three-quarters (Chart 11.10). The fall in sulphur dioxide emissions was primarily due to the reduction in the use of coal by power stations. The EC Large Combustion Plants Directive requires the United Kingdom to reduce emissions of sulphur dioxide by 60 per cent from large combustion plants by 2003, taking 1980 as the baseline. Emissions of carbon monoxide peaked in 1973 at 9 million tonnes and then fell by two-fifths by 1997. The decline in carbon monoxide, and also nitrogen oxide, emissions is attributed in part to the introduction of catalytic converters on petrol cars and the small increase in the use of diesel cars. In 1997 road transport accounted for three-quarters of all carbon monoxide emissions and almost half of nitrogen oxide emissions in the United Kingdom.

The National Air Quality Strategy, introduced in March 1997, set targets for the reduction of major air pollutants to be achieved by 2005. The government has proposed revised objectives that will be published in the Air Quality Strategy for England, Scotland, Wales and Northern Ireland. Levels of pollutants such as benzene, 1,3-butadiene, carbon monoxide and lead are expected to meet the targets; more concern exists about levels of nitrogen oxides and particulate matter. Further action may be necessary to control emissions of these pollutants in order to achieve the targets.

Water quality

Water quality is dependent on both climatic conditions and human activities. Periods of low rainfall can lead to a reduction in water quality because there is less water to dilute waste effluents. Conversely, high rainfall can also affect quality by causing leaching of pollutants in the soil into the water supply.

Since 1990 the Environment Agency (formerly the National Rivers Authority) has monitored the chemical quality of rivers and canals in England and Wales by a system called the General Quality Assessment Scheme. It is estimated that there has been a net upgrading in overall water quality of 25 per cent of the total length of rivers and canals in England and Wales between 1990 and 1998. In the period 1996 to 1998, 90 per cent of rivers and canals in England and Wales were of 'good' or 'fair' quality. In Wales this proportion rose to 99 per cent (Table 11.11). Many of the poorer-quality waters are in older industrial areas where there are residues of mercury, lead, cadmium and

11.11

River and canal quality[1]: by region, 1996-1998

Percentages

	Very good/ good	Fairly good/ fair	Poor	Bad	All
Welsh	92	7	1	-	100
Scotland[2]	91	7	2	-	100
South West	78	20	3	-	100
North East	61	27	11	1	100
North West	58	29	11	2	100
Southern	54	34	11	1	100
Northern Ireland	51	45	4	1	100
Midlands	48	42	9	1	100
Thames	48	37	15	-	100
Anglian	25	57	18	-	100

1 Chemical water quality based on the General Quality Assessment Scheme.
2 Water quality is based upon the Scottish River Classification Scheme of 20 June 1997. Data excludes islands.

Source: Environment Agency; Department of the Environment for Northern Ireland

11.12

Bathing waters complying with mandatory EU coliform standards[1]: by coastal region, 1991 and 1999

	Identified bathing waters (numbers)		Percentage complying	
	1991	1999	1991	1999
United Kingdom	453	535	76	91
Northern Ireland	16	16	100	100
Thames	3	3	67	100
Welsh	51	70	88	99
Northumbrian	33	33	64	97
Wessex	39	43	92	95
Anglian	33	36	88	94
Southern	67	79	67	94
Yorkshire	22	22	86	91
South West	133	141	79	89
North West	33	34	30	68
Scotland	23	58	65	68

1 See Appendix, Part 11: Quality of bathing water.

Source: Environment Agency; Scottish Environment Protection Agency; Department of the Environment for Northern Ireland

11.13

Waste disposal: by region and method, 1997-98

Percentages

	Landfill	Incineration without energy recovery	Incineration with energy recovery	RDF[1] manufacture	Recycled /composted	Other	All methods
North West	95	0	-	0	5	0	100
Yorkshire & the Humber	94	0	1	0	5	0	100
Wales	92	0	0	0	5	3	100
North East	90	1	2	3	5	0	100
East	89	0	-	0	11	0	100
South West	86	-	0	0	14	0	100
East Midlands	84	0	7	0	9	0	100
South East	83	0	0	3	14	-	100
London	76	0	19	0	6	0	100
West Midlands	71	2	20	0	6	1	100

1 Refuse derived fuel.

Source: Department of the Environment, Transport and the Regions

other heavy metals in the rivers and estuaries, for example in the Mersey Basin which is one of the most polluted waters in the United Kingdom. These pollutants remain in the sediment for many years and are slowly released into the water.

The quality of bathing waters and beaches has been a relatively high profile issue in recent years as these areas are sometimes affected by discharges from sewerage works, storm sewerage overflows and pollutants discharged from ships and boats. The proportion of bathing waters in the United Kingdom complying with the EU mandatory coliform standards has increased from 76 per cent in 1991 to 91 per cent in 1999 (Table 11.12). The North West had the lowest compliance rate in 1999 of all the English regions with around two-thirds of its bathing waters meeting the standard, while in the Thames region and Northern Ireland all the identified bathing waters met the EU standards.

In 1987 the 'Blue Flag' award was set up by the Foundation for Environmental Education in Europe in co-operation with the EU. The award covers resort bathing beaches that meet criteria on beach facilities, safety and cleanliness. In 1998 a record 45 UK beaches were given the Blue Flag award but this fell to 41 in 1999.

Recycling

Effective waste management is integral to any overall environmental strategy. The government's sustainable development strategy includes indicators that will monitor two areas in particular: household waste produced and proportion recycled, and proportion of waste sent to final disposal.

11.14

Households in England and Wales produce an estimated 22 kg of waste per week. Almost 27 million tonnes of municipal waste were produced in England and Wales in 1997-98; just over 90 per cent was derived from household sources. The most common methods for dealing with waste are disposal to landfill sites, incineration and recycling. Most municipal waste (around 85 per cent in 1997-98) is sent to landfill sites with just 8.2 per cent being recycled in the same year. Although landfill is the most commonly used disposal option across England and Wales, there are wide variations by region. In the North West region around 95 per cent of waste was sent directly to landfill compared with only 71 per cent in the West Midlands (Table 11.13).

In 1997-98, approximately 3.5 million tonnes of municipal waste had some value recovered from it through materials recycling, centralised composting or energy from waste schemes. This amounted to 14 per cent of total municipal waste, much lower than the target to recover 40 per cent of municipal waste in England and Wales by 2005.

Many local authorities run schemes to promote recycling, from the provision of 'drop-off' sites such as bottle banks to kerbside collection schemes. An estimated 2 million tonnes of household waste was collected separately for recycling or composting in England and Wales in 1997-98. The majority of materials collected were from 'drop-off' sites although kerbside collection has become an increasingly popular method of recycling. In 1997-98 around 40 per cent of households were covered by separate kerbside schemes, while virtually all had access to some recycling at civic amenity or bring sites operated by their local authority. Paper and card make up the bulk of materials recycled by local authorities through kerbside collection schemes (Table 11.14).

Until recently a large proportion of waste (including industrial, construction and sewage wastes) was disposed of by dumping it at sea. Recent changes in regulations have eliminated this method of disposal for all but limited classes of waste of natural origin which would cause no adverse effect on the marine environment.

Land cover and use

Over the last 50 years, one of the most visible signs of environmental change has been the land itself. Since the late 1940s, there has been an increase in woodland and urban land in England and Wales and a decrease in agricultural land and semi-natural vegetation. A balance has to be sought between increasing demands for social and industrial developments and conservation and agriculture. In 1996, nearly three-quarters of the land in the United Kingdom was used for agriculture (Chart 11.15). The majority of agricultural land in the United Kingdom, around 11 million hectares, is grassland and sole right rough grazing.

Recycling of household material, 1997-98

England & Wales

	Kerbside collection schemes		Civic amenity and bring sites for household waste		All schemes (thousand tonnes per year)
	Thousand tonnes per year	Percentage of households covered	Thousand tonnes per year	Percentage of households covered	
Total paper and card	326	33	410	100	736
Compost	31	4	372	60	403
Glass	33	9	325	100	358
Co-mingled material	72	6	11	.	83
Total cans	7	14	12	94	20
Other	21	16	362	.	383
Total	490	41	1,492	100	1,982

Source: Department of the Environment, Transport and the Regions

11.15

Land use, 1996

United Kingdom

Percentages

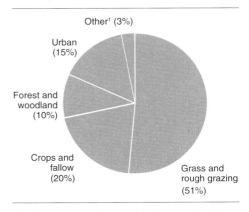

- Other[1] (3%)
- Urban (15%)
- Forest and woodland (10%)
- Crops and fallow (20%)
- Grass and rough grazing (51%)

1 Land on agricultural holdings not elsewhere classified, for example, farm roads, yards, buildings, gardens, ponds, derelict land and land in set-aside schemes, woodland etc.

Source: Ministry of Agriculture, Fisheries and Food; Ordnance Survey; Forestry Commission; Department for Agriculture for Northern Ireland

11.16

Agricultural land use[1]

United Kingdom					Thousand hectares
	1961	1971	1981	1991	1998
Crop areas					
Wheat	739	1,097	1,491	1,981	2,045
Barley	1,549	2,288	2,327	1,395	1,255
Other cereals (excluding maize)	768	424	161	127	120
Rape grown for oil seed[2]	..	5	125	440	506
Sugar beet not for stockfeeding	173	190	210	196	189
Potatoes (early and maincrop)	285	256	191	177	164
Other crops	761	577	490	643	692
All crop areas	4,276	4,838	4,995	4,957	4,972
Bare fallow	123	74	76	67	34
Grasses	7,999	7,240	7,013	6,935	6,653
Sole right rough grazing[3]	7,359	5,550	5,021	4,950	4,624
Common rough grazing	..	1,128	1,214	1,233	1,221
Woodland	..	154	277	372	490
Set-aside[4]	.	.	.	97	314
All other land on agricultural holdings	..	131	211	242	287
All agricultural land[5]	19,757	19,115	18,808	18,854	18,593

1 Includes estimates for minor holdings in England, Wales and Northern Ireland for all years and in Scotland prior to 1991.
2 Data are for England and Wales only in 1971 and 1981.
3 Includes common rough grazing in 1961.
4 Data are for England only in 1991.
5 Excludes woodland and all other land on agricultural holdings in 1961.
Source: Ministry of Agriculture, Fisheries and Food; National Assembly for Wales; Scottish Executive; Department of Agriculture, Northern Ireland

11.17

Forest health[1]

Great Britain				Percentages
	1991	1993	1996	1998
Sitka spruce	51	55	71	60
Beech	41	53	52	60
Norway spruce	52	57	54	53
Scots pine	43	48	53	49
Oak	29	20	28	26

1 Trees within 25 per cent of the 'ideal tree'.
Source: Forestry Commission

Despite the seemingly large area used for these purposes, agricultural land use has been declining. Between 1961 and 1998 the amount of land used for agricultural purposes fell by around 6 per cent (Table 11.16). This has not been attributable purely to urban development pressures but also to the effect of EC schemes and funding. For example, a reduction in the cropped area of over 450 thousand hectares between 1992 and 1993 was mainly due to the EC set aside schemes which were put in place to reduce the amount of agricultural land in arable production. Although the overall agricultural land area has been decreasing, certain crop areas have increased over the last 30 years. A particular success has been rape produced for oil seed which increased from 5 thousand hectares in 1971 to 506 thousand hectares in 1998.

Changes in consumer demand have had an impact on the types of food being grown. Organic produce, while only accounting for 0.5 per cent of agricultural output, is becoming more popular with consumers who are worried about the amount of pesticides that are finding their way into food. The 'Organic Aid Scheme' run by the Agricultural Departments and part-funded by the EU, provides some financial assistance to farms converting to organic production; almost 140 thousand hectares in the United Kingdom were converted by this scheme in 1998. In the past couple of years, the issue of genetically modified (GM) crops has also become an area of concern. Trials of 'GM' crops are taking place at various sites throughout the United Kingdom to research the long-term effects.

The area covered by forest and woodland in the United Kingdom has more than doubled this century. It increased by an average of 24 thousand hectares a year during the 1980s and now covers more than 10 per cent of the land area. Areas of woodland and forest serve an important function not only in providing natural habitats for many species of wildlife, but also in reducing the effects of global warming through absorbing harmful carbon dioxide. While there has been a decline in new conifer plantings in recent years from the peak reached towards the end of the 1980s, there has been a marked increase in the new planting of broadleaved species since 1988 following the introduction of the Woodland Grant Scheme.

The 1998 UK Forestry Standard sets criteria for sustainable forestry and indicators at a national level and also within individual forests. These include monitoring the number of trees felled and planted and regular assessment of the general health of species. The Forestry Commission has monitored changes in forest condition since 1987 and annually reassesses five tree species throughout Great Britain by measuring the density of foliage against an 'ideal tree' and also since 1993 against a local tree with full foliage under

11.18

local conditions. Factors influencing the tree foliage density include air pollution and drought conditions. From 1989 to 1996 there was a gradual improvement in the condition of Sitka spruce, although this showed a fall again in 1998 (Table 11.17). Most other species have fluctuated showing little evidence of a long term trend. In 1998 the Beech and Sitka spruce appeared to be in the best health.

Under the sustainable development strategy the area of woodland and ancient and semi-natural woodland in the United Kingdom will be monitored. Urban areas will also be encouraged to improve the local environment and restore former industrial sites by planting new woodlands.

Natural resources

Conservation of our natural resources, such as water, is essential for our future welfare. The decade to 1998 has been characterised by substantial variations in overall reservoir stocks for England and Wales due to unusual climatic conditions (Chart 11.18). Stress on water resources occurred in 1989, 1990 and again in 1995 when, following the second wettest winter this century, England and Wales experienced the driest five-month period in over 200 years.

Sustained rainfall towards the end of 1997 and the spring of 1998 saw the focus of concern switch from the risk of drought to the threat of flooding. Spate conditions were common in 1998 and unprecedented flooding over the Easter period prompted a wide-ranging review of existing flood warning procedures, flood alleviation and planning constraints on floodplain development. The abundant run-off helped maintain overall reservoir stocks close to capacity throughout most of 1998, and to restore levels in most of the aquifers from which about a third of public water supplies are taken.

Almost all of the population in England and Wales is served by the public water supply. Household water consumption increased in the early 1990s. Unmetered consumption then fell between 1995-96 and 1996-97, from 154 to 149 litres per head per day; metered consumption remained static at 134 litres and then rose to 138 litres per head per day in 1997-98 (Table 11.19). While there are no specific causes that can be attributed to this increase, it may be influenced by the rise in the numbers of new households being given water meters. Only one of the ten major water and sewerage companies in England and Wales, Welsh Water, does not automatically meter new properties. The metering of new households is not compulsory. The *Water Industry Bill 1999* gave all household customers the right to opt for a meter free of installation charges with the option to revert to an unmeasured charge within a year of installation. In 1997-98, 11 per cent of households in England and Wales had a meter.

Reservoir stocks[1]

England & Wales

Percentages

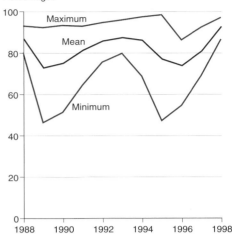

1 For each year, the maximum, mean and minimum percentage of overall net capacity based on network of large reservoirs.
Source: Environment Agency; water services companies

11.19

Household water consumption[1]: by region

Litres per head per day

	Unmetered households			Metered households		
	1995-96	1996-97	1997-98	1995-96	1996-97	1997-98
North West	144	138	141	116	109	134
Northumbrian	149	144	144	130	122	119
Yorkshire	137	132	136	124	118	125
Severn Trent	140	137	137	133	130	130
Anglian	155	153	153	128	128	141
Thames	159	159	161	148	151	155
Southern	164	160	161	134	130	138
Wessex	150	145	141	120	124	124
South West	163	153	155	136	138	123
Welsh	150	146	146	127	136	134
Scotland	153	154	155	..	..	..

1 Excluding underground supply pipe leakage.
Source: Office of Water Services; Scottish Executive Water Services Unit

Not all water put into the public water supply is used effectively; some of the water is lost through leakages in waterpipes owned by consumers and the water companies. Water companies have made progress towards reducing total leakage over the last three years. Nine out of the ten major water and sewerage companies in England and Wales met their 1997-98 targets for reducing total leakage. Anglian was the only company to fail to meet its target.

Drinking water quality is closely monitored by the water companies and independently through various government agencies. In 1997, 99.7 per cent of the 3 million tests carried out on UK drinking water met the relevant standards. However, 95 incidents affected the quality of water to an estimated 3.5 million customers, although most of these did not involve water that was unfit for consumption. Market research published by the Drinking Water Inspectorate in 1998 indicated that 70 per cent of people in England and Wales were satisfied with the quality of their tap water, but 20 per cent were dissatisfied, because of the taste, cloudiness or discoloration.

Another important natural resource is the marine and coastal waters that surround the United Kingdom. These have a diverse ecosystem which can be influenced by natural factors and also by commercial exploitation. This effect is most evident in the levels of fish stocks and the fine balance between fishing activity and the natural ability of fish stocks to regenerate. North Sea herring stocks were seriously affected by over-fishing during the 1970s, but the closure of the North Sea Fishery between 1978 and 1982 allowed them to recover (Chart 11.20). Over the last decade there has again been a decline in stocks of North Sea herring; stocks of haddock, whiting and plaice were also far lower in 1997 than in 1987. In 1996, for nearly half the stocks assessed, the spawning population was estimated to be at a level where there was a risk of stock collapse.

Two other important natural resources are oil and gas, providing energy and essential chemicals for industry, the transport system and the home. For centuries small quantities of oil have been produced in Great Britain. Oil production originally came from shales that were used to produce kerosene, known as 'lamp oil', the production of which peaked in 1913 at more than 3 million tonnes. During the 1930s a concentrated effort was made to find other sources of oil and gas. The first successes came in 1937 when an onshore gas field was found in Yorkshire followed by the discovery of a small oilfield near Nottingham. By the 1940s around 40,000 tonnes of oil were being produced per year.

The manufacture of 'town gas' in the United Kingdom declined at the end of the 1960s so that none is produced nowadays. At the same time there was a surge in natural gas production which, following the first significant discovery of offshore gas in 1965, has continued to the present. With oil remaining the basis of primary fuel for motorised transport, production has also increased since the 1960s: 18 new UK oil fields started production between June 1997 and May 1998. By mid-March

11.20

North Sea fish stocks and stocks of North-East Atlantic Mackerel[1]

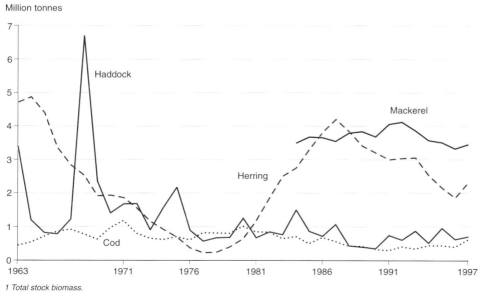

Million tonnes

1 Total stock biomass.

Source: Centre for the Environment, Fisheries and Aquaculture Science; International Council for the Exploration of the Sea

Social Trends 30, © Crown copyright 2000

11.21

There were around 685 million tonnes of proven oil reserves remaining from discovered oilfields in the United Kingdom continental shelf at the end of 1998; these are reserves that have a better than 90 per cent chance of being produced (Table 11.21). By 1999, the total cumulative production from oilfields in the United Kingdom amounted to over 2.3 billion tonnes of oil and 1.3 thousand billion cubic metres of gas.

Oil and gas are used in the generation of electricity. The impact on the environment of using these and other non-renewable fuels is twofold: the direct damage caused to the environment through air pollution and mining of fossil fuels, and the stresses put on finite natural resources. Nuclear power also uses non-renewable resources and is the main fuel used for electricity generation on average in the EU (Table 11.22). It presents quite different environmental problems from those caused by fossil fuels. Treatment and disposal of nuclear waste is difficult and expensive, and carries the additional risk of radioactive contamination from both power-plant operation and from waste disposal. Nuclear power generation in the United Kingdom increased by 84 per cent between 1983 and 1993; by 1997 it constituted over a quarter of our electricity generation. France has over three-quarters of its electricity generated through nuclear power, while in Luxembourg the renewable sources of wind and hydraulic power predominate. Changes in fiscal policies to take account of the environmental cost of using fossil fuels could eventually encourage the development of renewable energy sources. This development of renewable sources is increasingly likely to occur as part of the drive to achieve UK and EC targets for the reduction of greenhouse gas emissions.

1999 there were 204 offshore fields in production comprising 109 oil fields, 79 gas and 16 gas-condensate fields. A total of 132.6 million tonnes of oil and 95.6 billion cubic metres of gas were produced in 1998.

Oil and gas reserves, 1998

United Kingdom continental shelf

	Oil (million tonnes)	Gas (billion cubic metres)
Fields already discovered		
Proven reserves[1]	685	755
Probable reserves	575	585
Possible reserves	535	455
Total remaining reserves in present discoveries	685-1,795	755-1,795
Already recovered	2,306	1,311
Estimates of potential future discoveries	275-2,550	440-1,595
Total recoverable reserves	960-4,345	1,195-3,390
Potential additional reserves	95-335	65-235

1 Excludes volumes of oil and gas already recovered.
Source: Department of Trade and Industry

11.22

Electricity generation: by fuel used, EU comparison, 1997

Percentages

	Nuclear	Coal	Oil	Other fossil fuel[1]	Hydraulic and wind	Other[2]	All fuels (=100%) (000 GWh)
France	78	4	2	1	13	1	504
Belgium	60	17	2	15	2	4	79
Sweden	47	2	2	0	46	3	149
Germany	31	26	1	35	4	3	552
Spain	30	30	7	12	19	1	187
Finland	30	28	2	10	18	12	69
United Kingdom	28	35	2	31	2	2	345
Netherlands	3	27	4	58	1	8	87
Denmark	0	65	12	15	4	3	44
Portugal	0	38	20	0	39	3	34
Irish Republic	0	34	17	43	5	0	20
Italy	0	8	45	24	19	4	251
Austria	0	8	5	17	66	5	57
Greece	0	1	19	71	9	0	44
Luxembourg	0	0	1	14	74	11	1
EU average	35	19	8	21	13	3	2,423

1 Includes gas and brown coal.
2 Includes geothermal, derived gas and biomass and others.
Source: Eurostat

References and further reading

The following list contains selected publications relevant to **Chapter 11: Environment**. Those published by The Stationery Office are available from the addresses shown on the back cover of *Social Trends*.

Bathing Water Quality in England and Wales, The Stationery Office

Biodiversity: The UK Action Plan, The Stationery Office

Contaminants Entering the Sea, The Stationery Office

Development of the Oil and Gas Resources of the United Kingdom, Department of Trade & Industry

Digest of Environmental Statistics, The Stationery Office

Digest of United Kingdom Energy Statistics, The Stationery Office

Environmental Digest for Wales, Welsh Office

Environment Handbook, The Stationery Office

Environment Statistics, (available from The Stationery Office)

General Quality Assessment, The Environment Agency

Hydrological summaries for the United Kingdom, Institute of Hydrology and British Geological Survey

Indicators of Sustainable Development for the United Kingdom, The Stationery Office

Making Waste Work, Department of the Environment, Transport and the Regions

OECD Environmental Data Compendium, OECD

Organic Farming, Ministry of Agriculture, Fisheries and Food

Radon Affected Areas, The Stationery Office

Report of the International Council for the Exploration of the Sea's Advisory Committee on Fisheries Management 1995, ICES

Scottish Environmental Statistics, Scottish Executive

The Energy Report, Volume 2: Oil and Gas Resources of the United Kingdom, The Stationery Office

The Householder's Guide to Radon, Department of the Environment, Transport and the Regions

The UK Environment, The Stationery Office

Water Pollution Incidents in England and Wales, The Stationery Office

Waterfacts, Water Services Association

Contacts

Telephone contact points for further information relating to
Chapter 11: Environment

Office for National Statistics	
Chapter author	020 7533 5795
Department of the Environment, Transport and the Regions	020 7890 6497
Department of Trade and Industry	020 7215 2697
Forestry Commission	0131 334 0303
Institute of Hydrology	01491 838800
OFWAT	0121 625 1300
Scottish Environment Protection Agency	01786 457 700
Scottish Executive	0131 244 0445
The Environment Agency	01733 371811
Eurostat	00 352 4301 37286

Chapter 12 Transport

Overview

Children are travelling by cars more and walking less. Half of all children's journeys in 1996-1998 were as car or van passengers compared with only 35 per cent in 1985-1986. (Table 12.4)

Private transport

Only three out of ten British households had a car in 1961, but by 1998 seven out of ten households had at least one. (Chart 12.5)

Road traffic has increased from 53 billion vehicle kilometres in 1951 to 455 billion in 1998 and is projected to continue rising. (Chart 12.8)

Cycle traffic on public roads fell dramatically from 23 billion passenger kilometres in 1952 to around 4 billion kilometres in 1998. (Page 200)

Public transport

The number of passenger rail journeys has increased since 1981-82, and is now approaching the levels of the late 1950s. Because of the great increase in car travel, however, rail has a much smaller share of total travel than in the 1950s. (Table 12.15)

In 1998 domestic air travellers flew 7 billion passenger kilometres within Great Britain, compared with just under 3 billion in 1981 and 200 thousand in 1952. (Chart 12.17)

International travel

In 1998 the Channel Tunnel accounted for 12 per cent of overseas visits (to or from the United Kingdom). Almost one in five of these visits were for business. (Page 204)

Safety

In 1998 the United Kingdom had one of the lowest road accident death rates in the European Union, at 6 per 100,000 population for adults and 2 per 100,000 for children. (Table 12.20)

12.1

Passenger transport[1]: by mode

Great Britain
Percentages

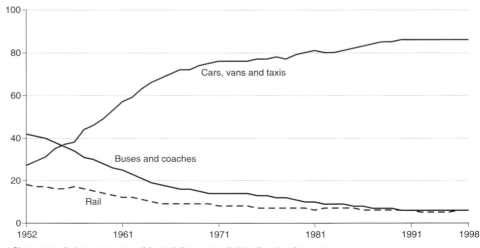

1 Distance travelled as a percentage of the total distance travelled by all modes of transport.

Source: Department of the Environment, Transport and the Regions

12.2

Journeys per person per year: by main mode and journey purpose[1], 1996-1998

Great Britain   Percentages

	Car	Walk	Bus, coach and rail[2]	Other	All modes
Social/entertainment	26	20	18	28	24
Shopping	20	24	27	13	21
Other escort and personal business	21	14	11	10	18
Commuting	18	7	25	26	16
Education	3	11	14	11	7
Escort education	4	8	1	.	5
Business	5	1	2	4	3
Holiday/day trip	3	1	2	8	3
Other, including just walk	-	15	.	.	4
All purposes (=100%) (numbers)	643	288	79	41	1,051

1 See Appendix, Part 12: Journey purpose.
2 Includes London Underground.
Source: National Travel Survey, Department of the Environment, Transport and the Regions

12.3

Distance travelled per person per year: by access to a car and main mode, 1996-1998

Great Britain   Percentages

	People in households with car			People in households without car	All
	Main driver	Other driver	Non-driver		
Car	91	78	76	37	82
Rail[1]	4	10	4	13	5
Local bus	-	3	7	22	4
Walk	1	3	4	11	3
Bicycle	-	1	1	2	1
Other[2]	4	6	8	14	6
All modes (=100%) (thousand km)	16.9	12.0	7.2	4.0	10.8

1 Includes London Underground.
2 Includes motorcycles.
Source: National Travel Survey, Department of the Environment, Transport and the Regions

The twentieth century saw dramatic changes in patterns of travel. At the turn of the century the rail network was largely in place but cars were a rarity. Now the car dominates, with rapid growth since the 1950s. New roads were built and 13 kilometres of the first motorway opened in 1959. The rail network also grew in the first 20 years of the century, then later declined particularly during the 1960s with the closure of many branch lines. Horse drawn trams gave way to motorised buses, but buses then declined. Commercial air flights began. Change slowed in the 1990s, however, while concern grew about issues such as pollution and congestion.

Overview

There has been a general switch from public to private passenger transport in Great Britain, particularly during the 1950s and 1960s (Chart 12.1). This has put great pressure on roads, while noise and pollution affect health and the environment. The pattern stabilised during the 1990s, with cars, vans and taxis accounting for 86 per cent of total distance travelled by passengers since 1991. In absolute terms, however, car, van and taxi distance travelled grew by 6 per cent from 1991 to 1998. This was in line with the 5 per cent growth in distance travelled for all modes, which was much slower than in earlier decades – there was a threefold increase overall from the early 1950s to 1991.

Though growth has slowed, people still travel greater distances than two decades ago (the earliest period for which consistent data are available). People used cars for three-fifths of all journeys in 1996-1998 and made over a quarter of journeys on foot, whereas in 1975-1976 cars accounted for less than half of all journeys and walking for a third. When a household has a car, its members travel more by car and less by bus, by bicycle or on foot. They also travel further.

12.4

Social and entertainment trips accounted for a quarter of journeys in 1996-1998 (Table 12.2). Public transport was used most for shopping and commuting whereas cars were used most for social and entertainment trips. While there is little difference between the average number of trips made by men and women, men tend to travel further and consequently spend more time travelling than women do. Men make more commuting journeys than women, but fewer trips shopping or taking children to school. Women are also more likely to use public transport or to walk. When commuting, taking children to school, or on business, men are more likely than women to use a car.

Different access to a car accounts for some of the difference in the total distances travelled by men and women. Four in five male licence holders were the main driver of a household car in 1996-1998, compared with only about two in three female licence holders. In a household with an adult man and woman, if there is only one car, it tends to be used more by the man. Women's travel changes more when the household gets a second car. However, these differences between men and women are reducing, as more women acquire driving licences (see Chart 12.6) and become main drivers in households.

People with cars tend to travel further than those without access to a car. Main drivers used their cars for 91 per cent of all their distance travelled in 1996-1998 (Table 12.3). Even people who lived in households without cars used cars for 37 per cent of their distance travelled. Those with cars also make more journeys than those without cars – main drivers averaged 1,283 journeys a year in 1996-1998 compared with 800 a year for people in households without a car.

Children are also travelling by car more and walking less. Half of all children's journeys in 1996-1998 were as car or van passengers

Children's journeys per person per year: by age and mode, 1996-1998

Great Britain					Percentages
	Under 3	3-4	5-10	11-16	All aged 16 or under
Car/van passenger	58	61	55	35	50
Walk	37	34	37	39	37
Bus	3	4	5	17	9
Bicycle	-	-	1	5	2
Other	-	-	2	4	2
All modes (=100%)(numbers)	920	970	874	941	917

Source: National Travel Survey, Department of the Environment, Transport and the Regions

(Table 12.4) compared with only 35 per cent in 1985-1986. The proportion of journeys on foot fell from 47 per cent to 37 per cent over the same period. Older children are more likely than younger ones to travel by bicycle or bus; nearly a fifth of journeys made by 11 to 16 year olds were by bus in 1996-1998 compared with one in 20 of those made by 5 to 10 year olds.

12.5

Private transport

At the end of the twentieth century the motor car continues to dominate. Car ownership has increased steadily: only three out of ten households in Great Britain had a car in 1961, but by 1998 seven out of ten households had at least one (Chart 12.5). Over the same period the proportion of households with two or more cars has grown from 2 per cent in 1961 to 28 per cent in 1998. The number of cars licensed in Great Britain has risen steadily since the 1950s; there are now more than ten times as many cars as there were in 1950.

In 1997, 11 per cent of currently registered cars were company cars, below the rate of 13 per cent in 1990. Around half of new registrations each year are company cars.

Households with regular use of a car[1]

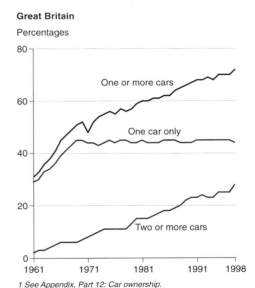

Great Britain

Percentages

1 See Appendix, Part 12: Car ownership.

Source: Department of the Environment, Transport and the Regions

12.6

Percentage of adults with a full car driving licence: by gender and age, 1975-1976 and 1996-1998

Great Britain
Percentages

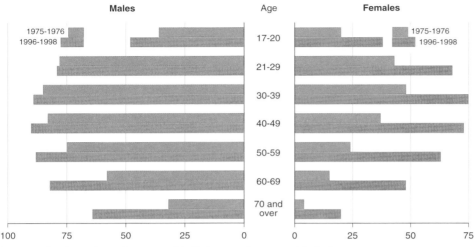

Source: National Travel Survey, Department of the Environment, Transport and the Regions

12.7

Households with one or more cars: by type of area[1], 1996-1998

Great Britain	Percentages
	1996-1998
London borough	61
Metropolitan built-up area	59
Large urban	69
Medium urban	70
Small urban	78
Rural	83
All areas	70

1 See Appendix Part 12: Type of area.

Source: National Travel Survey, Department of the Environment, Transport and the Regions

In 1996-1998, 31 million people aged 17 or over held full driving licences in Great Britain – 81 per cent of men and 58 per cent of women. Among young adults, 43 per cent of 17 to 20 year olds were qualified. Only 38 per cent of those aged 70 or over held full licences. For both genders and all age groups, higher proportions now hold licences than in 1975-1976, but the increases are more marked for women than for men (Chart 12.6).

Nowadays, in order to obtain a full driving licence, people in the United Kingdom have to pass both a theory and practical test. In 1998-99, 61 per cent of candidates passed their theory tests and 46 per cent passed their practical car driving tests. Women have higher pass rates for the theory tests but lower pass rates for the practical tests. Most categories (including motorcycle and goods vehicle tests) saw a slight dip in pass rates during 1998-99. A further drop is forecast for cars and motorcycles for early 1999-00 because of changes in the tests. An IT based theory test will be introduced in January 2000, which can provide results within half an hour with feedback on incorrect answers.

Despite the costs of motoring, there is no evidence of recent switching to smaller cars. The proportion of small cars on the road in Great Britain has fallen. In 1998, 27 per cent of cars had engine capacity up to 1,300 cc compared with 47 per cent in 1989. Diesel cars, which tend to have larger engines, are becoming more common, accounting for 11 per cent of all cars in 1998 compared with 3 per cent in 1989.

Car ownership is related to household income. Three-fifths of households in the bottom quintile of the income distribution in 1996-1998 did not have a car, while almost half of those in the top quintile had two or more cars. For some households, use of a car may be a necessity rather than a reflection of income. Households in rural and small urban areas are more likely to own a car than those in London and built-up areas (Table 12.7). People living in rural and small urban areas also travel further on average than those living in more urban areas. In general they have a poorer public transport service, and need to travel greater distances to shops and services, such as doctors' surgeries and hospitals. The urban/rural pattern has changed little over time, despite the overall increase in car ownership.

One result of the increasing level of car use is road congestion. Traffic levels are rising (Chart 12.8) and are projected to continue doing so, rising from 455 billion vehicle kilometres (excluding two wheeled motor vehicles) in 1998 to 478 billion kilometres in 2001 and 524 billion kilometres by 2006. In particular, the average daily flow on motorways more than doubled from 1981 to 1998 (Table 12.9). Along with increased traffic go reduced average speeds. Motor vehicles averaged 56 miles an hour on motorways in 1998, compared with 63 miles an hour in 1995. For built-

12.8

up roads, the average speed fell from 34 to 30 miles an hour over the same period, and for other roads it fell from 57 to 53 miles an hour.

Nevertheless, 55 per cent of cars on motorways were travelling over the speed limit in 1998, according to the National Traffic Census and 19 per cent exceeded 80 miles an hour. Similarly, 54 per cent were speeding on dual carriageways, though for single carriageways it was 10 per cent. Speeding was also widespread on urban roads – 69 per cent of cars exceeded the 30 miles an hour limit.

Motorbikes offer one way to avoid congestion; for example they are used to get paramedics to emergency calls where ambulances may get held up in traffic. The number of licensed motorcycles peaked in the early 1960s and again, to a lesser degree, in the 1980s. Since then the number of licensed motorcycles on the roads has declined, from nearly 1.4 million licensed at the beginning of the 1980s to around 0.6 million in 1995 (see Chart 12.10 on the next page). However there are signs of an upturn, as the number licensed rose to nearly 0.7 million in 1998 and there has recently been a rise in new registrations. In addition there were around 130 thousand motorcycles in 1998 not included in the motorcycle tax class of licences, for example emergency services or vehicles over 25 years old.

Men are far more likely than women to possess a motorcycle licence. In 1996-1998 less than 1 per cent of women held a licence compared with 11 per cent of men. National Travel Survey data suggest that the age profile of motorbike riders has changed from young to older men. In 1996-1998 fewer than one in ten men under the age of 30 held a motorcycle licence, rising to 15 per cent for men aged 30 to 49, whereas almost a quarter of men in their fifties (who could have been young riders during the 1960s motorcycle peak) held a motorcycle licence.

Road traffic[1]

Great Britain

Billion vehicle kilometres

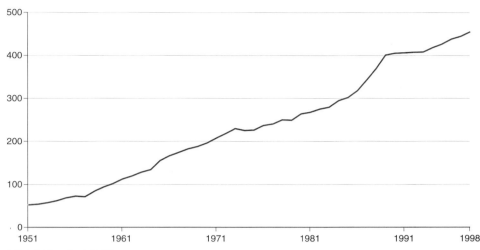

1 Excludes two-wheeled traffic.

Source: Department of the Environment, Transport and the Regions

12.9

Average daily flow[1] of motor vehicles: by class of road

Great Britain				Thousands
	1981	1991	1996	1998
Motorways[2]	30.4	53.8	62.4	67.1
Major roads				
Built-up	12.4	15.5	15.5	15.1
Non built-up	5.9	9.5	10.1	10.7
All major roads	7.9	11.2	11.7	12.0
All minor roads	1.0	1.4	1.4	1.4
All roads	2.2	3.1	3.3	3.4

1 Flow at an average point on each class of road.
2 Includes motorways owned by local authorities.

Source: Department of the Environment, Transport and the Regions

12.10

Motorcycles[1] currently licensed and new registrations

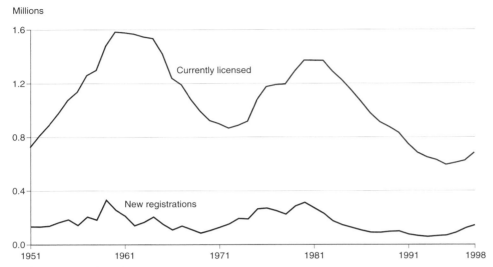

Great Britain

Millions

1 Includes scooters and mopeds.

Source: Department of the Environment, Transport and the Regions

year (Table 12.11). The peak age group was 11 to 17 year olds. There is considerable concern about the increasing trend towards car travel among school children, partly due to the increasing road congestion that this is causing, but also in terms of the loss of independence and the long-term health risks of taking less exercise. At the same time, distances between school and home are increasing, so fewer children can feasibly walk to school. The average length of the journey to school for secondary age children increased from 3.7 to 5.0 kilometres from 1985-1986 to 1996-1998, while for primary pupils it rose from 1.8 to 2.1 kilometres.

The average distance people walk has also declined over the last decade. For males the average distance walked fell from 388 kilometres in 1985-86 to 309 kilometres in 1996-1998 and for females fell from 396 to 312 kilometres. Walking accounts for over a third of journeys for both young people up to the age of 17 and elderly people over the age of 70.

12.11

Distance travelled per person per year by bicycle: by age and gender, 1996-1998

Great Britain			Kilometres
	Males	Females	All
5-10	23	15	19
11-17	191	44	119
18-29	157	21	85
30-49	138	27	81
50 and over	71	18	43
All aged 5 and over	112	23	66

Source: National Travel Survey, Department of the Environment, Transport and the Regions

Alternatives to motorised transport, particularly for local journeys, are cycling and walking. Cycle traffic on public roads fell dramatically from 23 billion passenger kilometres in 1952 to around 4 billion kilometres in the early 1970s. Despite rising to 6 billion passenger kilometres in the early 1980s it was back at 4 billion kilometres in 1998. The National Cycling Strategy, announced in 1996, aims to double cycle use by the year 2002 from the 1996 base of 16 bicycle journeys per person per year, and to double it again by 2012. The transport charity Sustrans is co-ordinating the development of the National Cycle Network, a linked series of traffic-free paths and traffic calmed roads providing safe and attractive routes. Concern about road safety is a major reason for people not cycling (see also Table 12.24).

In 1996-1998, males aged 5 or over cycled 112 kilometres a year on average on the public highway, while females cycled 23 kilometres a

Public transport

There have been a number of measures aimed at reducing people's reliance on cars. The Government's 1998 White Paper *A New Deal for Transport* gives public transport a higher profile and aims to encourage people to use other modes of travel than cars.

Buses are the dominant form of public transport in terms of journeys, if not distance, carrying about twice as many passengers as all rail modes and long distance coaches in Great Britain. The number of bus, trolleybus and tram journeys grew rapidly between the wars, but then declined steadily from the 1950s. However, bus use in

12.12

Great Britain has in recent years been stable at about 4.3 billion journeys a year (Chart 12.12). This relatively stable situation includes a recent increase in the South East (outside London). The distance travelled has risen since the mid-1980s.

The White Paper focuses on partnerships between bus operators and local authorities, to raise vehicle and service quality and to enable appropriate investment in traffic management and bus priority measures (for example bus lanes). The intention is to introduce powers to promote service stability, more flexible ticketing and better passenger information. In 1998-99 about 10 per cent of the bus fleet had 'super low floors', or ramps or other aids for the disabled, improving access for parents with young children and people with heavy shopping as well as the disabled.

In addition most local authorities offer concessionary fares to groups who are least likely to have access to a car. In 1999, 41 per cent of local authorities responding to the Department of the Environment, Transport and the Regions' surveys had a scheme for children and 48 per cent had a scheme for further education students. In 1997, 97 per cent of local authorities in England and Wales had a concessionary fare scheme for the elderly. Most local authorities with a permit scheme for the elderly also had schemes for the disabled. The government has proposed a national minimum standard of half fares for the elderly on buses, while local authorities may also provide concessionary travel on other forms of local transport. Local authorities are increasingly providing half fare schemes; the proportion of local authorities with such a scheme rose from 26 per cent in 1986 to 43 per cent in 1997 (Table 12.13). The take-up among pensioners living in areas with schemes available is higher in London (82 per cent) and metropolitan built-up

Bus travel[1]

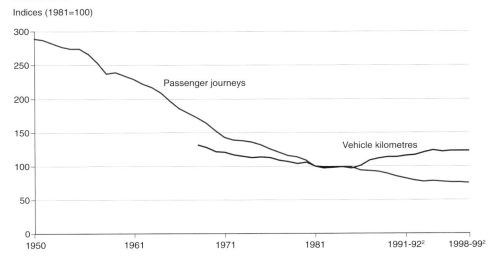

Great Britain
Indices (1981=100)

Passenger journeys

Vehicle kilometres

1 Local services only. Includes trams and trolleybuses.
2 Financial years from 1985-86.

Source: Department of the Environment, Transport and the Regions

areas (76 per cent) than elsewhere, but has fallen overall from 60 per cent in 1989-1991 to 52 per cent in 1996-1998. Take up in rural areas is low, only 31 per cent in 1996-1998, which may be due to car ownership being higher in such areas (see Table 12.7).

The bus and coach industry has undergone consolidation since deregulation in 1986 and three large groups (Arriva, FirstGroup and Stagecoach) provide nearly half of all local bus mileage in Great Britain. The number of local authority bus operators has declined to 17, accounting (together with two traditional tram companies, Blackpool Trams and Great Orme Trams) for 7 per cent of passenger journeys in 1997-98. Apart from these, many hundreds of small businesses continue to run local bus services. Most bus services are run commercially, but about 16 per cent are subsidised, generally following competitive tendering. Use of buses is also influenced by

12.13

Local authorities with a concessionary fare scheme available: by type of scheme

England & Wales		Percentages	
	1986	1992	1997
Half fares	26	26	43
Tokens	15	20	26
Free fares	25	25	13
Flat fares	11	12	11
Other reduced fares	17	16	4
Any scheme	94	98	97
No scheme	6	2	3
All	100	100	100

Source: Department of the Environment, Transport and the Regions

12.14

Time taken to walk to nearest bus stop or rail station: by type of area[1], 1996-1998

Great Britain   Percentages

	Bus stop				Rail station			
	6 minutes or less	7-13 minutes	14-26 minutes	27 minutes or more	6 minutes or less	7-13 minutes	14-26 minutes	27 minutes or more
London borough	89	9	1	1	26	34	31	9
Metropolitan built-up area	92	8	1	-	7	10	24	58
Large urban	90	9	1	-	7	12	25	56
Medium urban	91	7	2	-	6	12	29	53
Small urban	82	11	4	2	4	8	16	71
Rural	77	11	6	6	3	4	5	88
All areas	87	9	2	1	8	13	23	57

1 See Appendix Part 12: Type of area.
Source: National Travel Survey, Department of the Environment, Transport and the Regions

12.15

Rail journeys[1]: by operator

Great Britain   Millions

	1981-82	1991-92	1993-94	1996-97	1997-98	1998-99
Main line/underground						
National Rail	719	792	740	801	846	892
London Underground	541	751	735	772	832	866
Glasgow Underground	11	14	14	14	14	15
All main line/underground	1,271	1,557	1,489	1,587	1,692	1,773
Light railways and trams						
Tyne and Wear PTE	14	41	38	36	35	34
Docklands Light Railway	.	8	8	17	21	28
Greater Manchester Metro	.	.	11	13	14	13
South Yorkshire Supertram	.	.	.	8	9	10
All light railways and trams	14	49	58	74	79	85
All journeys by rail	1,285	1,605	1,547	1,661	1,771	1,858

1 Excludes railways operated principally as tourist attractions.
Source: Department of the Environment, Transport and the Regions

factors such as the frequency of services and the distance to the nearest bus stop. Around nine-tenths of people in urban areas lived within six minutes walk of a bus stop in 1996-1998 (Table 12.14).

The number of passenger rail journeys, both national main line and London Underground, has increased since 1981-82 (Table 12.15), and is now approaching the levels of the late 1950s. Because of the great increase in car travel, however, rail has a much smaller share of total travel than in the 1950s. An important recent development in rail services is investment in the London Underground network, refurbishing the infrastructure and rolling stock, and the opening of the Jubilee Line extension in preparation for the Millennium celebrations at the Dome in Greenwich. Freight traffic on railways has fallen over the last decade, mainly reflecting a reduction in coal traffic. Other freight has been broadly stable in recent years, though at a level well below the peak of the late 1980s.

Social Trends 30, © Crown copyright 2000

12.16

A significant development in recent years has been the increase in the number of rail operators. Following privatisation in 1996, passenger rail services on the national network are provided by 25 franchise holders which lease rolling stock and pay access charges to Railtrack plc for use of the track. The franchise holders are regulated through the Franchising Director of the Shadow Strategic Rail Authority (SSRA), which monitors performance and controls fares. In addition, a non-franchised passenger train operator provides a service between central London and Heathrow Airport, and there are an increasing number of privately owned railways for leisure and tourism.

Over half the complaints reported to the Office of the Rail Regulator in 1998-99 were about poor train service performance (Chart 12.16). Passenger train operators received 1.1 million complaints, equivalent to 122 per 100,000 passenger journeys, an increase of 8 per cent over the previous year. However this increase should be seen against a rise of 5 per cent in the number of journeys in the same year. Overall, train service worsened during this period, as measured by punctuality and reliability (the percentage run, not cancelled) by the SSRA. At the same time, a number of train operators have improved their accessibility, particularly by phone, and this may have affected the numbers of complaints.

Domestic air travel has increased steadily since the 1950s and more rapidly in the last two decades. In 1998 domestic travellers flew 7 billion passenger kilometres within Great Britain, compared with just under 3 billion in 1981 and only 200 thousand in 1952 (Chart 12.17).

Rail complaints: by category, 1998-99

Great Britain
Percentages

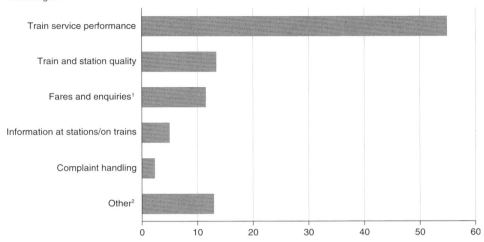

1 Includes retail and refunds and national rail enquiry service.
2 Includes praise, safety and security, special needs, timetable, connection service and staff conduct.
Source: Office of the Rail Regulator

12.17

Domestic air passengers

Great Britain
Billion passenger kilometres

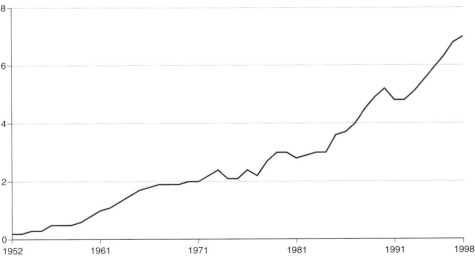

Source: Department of the Environment, Transport and the Regions

12.18

International travel: by mode[1]

United Kingdom						Millions
	1981	1986	1991	1996	1997	1998
Visits to the United Kingdom by overseas residents						
Air	6.9	8.9	11.6	16.3	16.9	17.5
Sea	4.6	5.0	5.5	6.2	5.7	5.1
Channel Tunnel	.	.	.	2.7	2.9	3.2
All visits to the United Kingdom	11.5	13.9	17.1	25.2	25.5	25.7
Visits abroad by UK residents						
Air	11.4	16.4	20.4	27.9	30.3	34.3
Sea	7.7	8.6	10.4	10.7	11.5	10.5
Channel Tunnel	.	.	.	3.5	4.1	6.1
All visits abroad	19.0	24.9	30.8	42.1	46.0	50.9

1 Mode of travel from, and into, the United Kingdom.
Source: International Passenger Survey, Office for National Statistics

12.19

Passenger car arrivals at, and departures from, UK ports: by overseas country

					Thousands
	1981	1986	1991	1996	1998
By sea[1]					
France	1,689	2,162	3,517	4,380	4,453
Irish Republic	378	345	611	710	886
Netherlands	259	325	399	353	351
Belgium	591	478	514	279	87
Spain and Portugal	20	27	47	82	83
Scandinavia and Baltic	62	67	56	54	52
Germany	22	21	34	46	44
Denmark	50	45	44	27	25
All overseas routes	3,071	3,470	5,223	5,933	5,982
By Channel Tunnel					
France	.	.	.	2,077	3,351
All overseas routes	3,071	3,470	5,223	8,010	9,333

1 By ship and hovercraft.
Source: Department of the Environment, Transport and the Regions

International travel

There has been a great increase in both the numbers of visits to the United Kingdom by overseas residents and overseas visits by UK residents over the last few decades. This is primarily due to the increase in holidays taken abroad (see Chart 13.1 in Chapter 13), although business visits are also important. The most popular method of travel to and from the United Kingdom is by air – two-thirds of all visits are by air (Table 12.18). The numbers of air passengers and flights are rising.

More people use London's Heathrow airport than any other airport in the United Kingdom for international air travel. In 1998, 53 million passengers went through Heathrow, out of a total of 125 million nationally. The number of people using regional airports for trips from the United Kingdom is rising. Heathrow and Gatwick accounted for 74 per cent of all international air passengers in 1981, but this fell to 63 per cent in 1998.

The Channel Tunnel has been fully operational since mid-1995. In 1998 the Tunnel accounted for 12 per cent of overseas visits (to or from the United Kingdom). Half of these visits were for holidays, while almost a fifth were for business. It is not easy to gauge the impact of the Channel Tunnel since no one can say what would have happened without it. However, total air traffic has continued to grow since the Channel Tunnel's introduction, while sea traffic has seen less growth than before it opened.

In 1998, 9.3 million cars entered or left through UK ports, compared with 3.1 million in 1981 (Table 12.19). France was the most popular destination. The fall in car traffic with Belgium reflects the withdrawal of Sally Line from Ramsgate in 1998. Coach arrivals and departures show a similar pattern. The Channel Tunnel accounts for much of the increase in the 1990s.

12.20

Safety

The United Kingdom has a good record on road safety compared with the rest of the European Union. In 1998 the United Kingdom had among the lowest death rates per 100,000 population, at 6 per 100,000 for adults and 2 per 100,000 for children (Table 12.20). Other major developed countries also have higher rates than the United Kingdom. In the United States in 1997, the adult death rate was 19 per 100,000 population, while it was 12 per 100,000 in Canada, 11 per 100,000 in Australia and 10 per 100,000 in Japan.

Despite the increase in road traffic, travel is getting safer. Both the number of people killed and accident rates are declining, although the risk of being killed or seriously injured varies according to the mode of transport used (Table 12.21). Motorcycles users have the highest rate of fatalities, whether measured against distance travelled, time travelling or number of journeys. Walking and cycling are the next most dangerous. Measured against the number of trips taken, however, walking becomes comparable with car travel while cycling is about four times as dangerous as either walking or going by car.

The general improvement in road deaths is in part attributable to the many government safety awareness campaigns and improved crash protection, plus features such as anti-lock braking systems in new cars. Awareness of road safety issues is high, particularly during campaign periods. Recent publicity campaigns include the rear seat belt campaign in summer 1999 and the Christmas/New Year drink drive campaign. Regular surveys identify attitudes of drivers, and particularly young drivers, to a variety of safety issues. According to the Central Office of Information's road safety campaign tracking, 'driving without motor insurance' is generally less acceptable than 'using a hand held mobile phone whilst driving' or 'driving after drinking two pints'.

Road deaths[1]: EU comparison, 1971 and 1998

Rates per 100,000 population[2]

	1971		1998	
	Adults	Children	Adults	Children
Portugal[3]	24	10	33	8
Greece[3]	15	4	27	4
Austria	46	13	20	2
France	42	12	17	4
Spain	..	..	17	3
Belgium	..	..	16	3
Irish Republic	24	9	16	3
Germany	..	..	15	2
Italy	23	6	13	2
Finland	29	13	12	4
Denmark	28	14	11	3
Netherlands	28	13	11	2
Luxembourg	..	..	9	1
Sweden	18	5	8	1
United Kingdom	16	8	6	2

1 See Appendix, Part 12: Road deaths.
2 Adults aged 15 and over, children aged under 15.
3 Data in 1971 column are for 1970. Data in 1998 column are for 1997.
Source: Department of the Environment, Transport and the Regions

12.21

Passenger death rates[1]: by mode of transport

Great Britain   Rate per billion passenger kilometres

	1981	1986	1991	1996	1997	Average 1988-1997
Motorcycle	115.8	100.3	94.4	92.7	108.8	89.9
Walk	76.9	75.3	62.5	54.3	54.2	68.2
Pedal cycle	56.9	49.6	46.8	47.2	44.6	46.0
Car	6.1	5.1	3.7	3.1	3.1	3.6
Water[2]	0.4	0.5	0.0	0.8	0.4	2.6
Van	3.8	3.8	2.2	1.1	1.2	1.9
Rail	1.0	0.9	0.8	0.4	0.5	0.7
Bus or coach	0.3	0.5	0.6	0.2	0.3	0.4
Air[2]	0.2	0.5	-	-	-	0.1

1 See Appendix Part 12: Passenger death rates.
2 Data are for United Kingdom.
Source: Department of the Environment, Transport and the Regions

12.22

Casualties from road accidents involving illegal alcohol levels

United Kingdom

Thousands

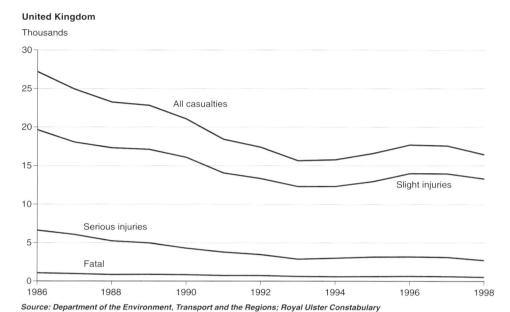

Source: Department of the Environment, Transport and the Regions; Royal Ulster Constabulary

These in turn are less acceptable than 'not wearing a rear seat belt in the back of a car' or 'driving at 40 miles an hour in a 30 miles an hour speed limit area'.

There are a number of factors that increase the risk of a road user having an accident, including speeding, drink driving and the use of illicit drugs. It is estimated that excessive and inappropriate speeds are the major factor in around a third of all road accidents.

In 1998 there were 16 thousand casualties from road accidents involving illegal alcohol levels in the United Kingdom, 3 per cent of which were fatal (Chart 12.22). Deaths have dropped substantially over the last decade, reflecting long-standing drink driving campaigns. In 1998, 13 per cent of people dying in road accidents in Great Britain tested positive for illegal levels of alcohol.

12.23

Costs of transport

Household expenditure[1] per head on transport at constant prices

United Kingdom

£ per week at 1995 prices

	1971	1981	1991	1995	1997	1998
Motoring costs						
Motor vehicles and spares	4.25	4.78	6.18	6.76	7.80	8.16
Petrol and engine oil	2.46	3.26	4.30	3.94	3.97	3.89
Repairs and insurance	1.28	1.92	2.42	2.81	2.83	2.78
Vehicle tax	0.45	0.57	0.86	0.87	0.90	0.94
Other	0.38	0.83	2.28	2.23	2.26	2.36
All motoring costs	8.82	11.22	16.03	16.59	17.76	18.13
Fares and other travel costs						
Air	0.27	0.82	1.28	2.01	2.09	2.26
Rail and tram fares	0.89	0.86	0.94	0.90	1.01	1.01
Bus and coach fares	1.82	1.27	1.04	0.99	1.01	0.97
Other	0.52	0.60	1.01	1.04	1.14	1.20
All fares and other travel costs	2.69	3.31	4.17	4.94	5.24	5.43
All expenditure on transport	11.52	14.55	20.19	21.54	23.00	23.55

1 See Appendix, Part 6: Household expenditure.

Source: Office for National Statistics

Overall household expenditure on transport has been rising in real terms, particularly for motoring costs and air travel, while expenditure on bus and coach fares has fallen (Table 12.23). The cost of travel has roughly kept pace with inflation since 1981, though price increases outstripped inflation for rail, bus and coach fares, and vehicle tax, insurance and maintenance.

Transport also has environmental costs. The White Paper *A Strategy for Sustainable Development for the United Kingdom* aims to encourage a safe, efficient transport system, which provides choice, minimises environmental harm and reduces congestion. New technologies

Social Trends 30, © Crown copyright 2000

12.24

Car users' attitudes towards discouraging car use, 1998

Great Britain   Percentages

	Might use car even more	Might use car a little less	Might use car quite a bit less	Might give up using car	No difference	All respondents[1]
Gradually doubling the cost of petrol over the next ten years	1	31	23	5	38	100
Greatly improving the reliability of local public transport	-	28	27	6	37	100
Greatly improving long distance rail and coach services	-	25	22	4	47	100
Charging all motorists around £2 each time they enter or drive through a city or town centre at peak times	0	23	21	7	45	100
Cutting in half long distance rail and coach fares	0	23	24	7	43	100
Cutting in half local public transport fares	-	21	28	6	42	100
Making parking penalties and restrictions much more severe	-	20	18	4	54	100
Charging £1 for every 50 miles motorists travel on motorways	-	18	15	6	58	100
Special cycle lanes on roads around here	-	10	11	3	73	100

1 All respondents includes 'don't know' and not answered categories.
Source: British Social Attitudes Survey, National Centre for Social Research

and cleaner cars will be part of the solution, but new approaches to travel, living and working will also be needed.

In 1998 the British Social Attitudes Survey explored car users' views about measures to discourage car use (Table 12.24). More people thought they were likely to reduce their car use because of 'gradually doubling the cost of petrol over the next ten years' or 'greatly improving the reliability of local public transport' than for other measures. This survey also found that three in ten agreed that 'many of the short journeys I make by car I could just as easily go by bus', but half disagreed.

References and further reading

The following list contains selected publications relevant to **Chapter 12: Transport.** Those published by The Stationery Office are available from the addresses shown on the inside back cover of *Social Trends.*

A New Deal for Transport: Better for Everyone, The Stationery Office
A Strategy for Sustainable Development for the United Kingdom, The Stationery Office
Annual Report, Central Rail Users Consultative Committee
British Social Attitudes, Ashgate Publishing
Busdata, Department of the Environment, Transport and the Regions
Driving Standards Agency Annual Report and Accounts, The Stationery Office
Focus on Personal Travel: 1998 Edition, The Stationery Office
Focus on Public Transport, The Stationery Office
Focus on Roads, The Stationery Office
International Passenger Transport, The Stationery Office
People's Panel, Cabinet Office
Rail Complaints, Office of the Rail Regulator
Regional Trends, The Stationery Office

Road Accidents Great Britain – The Casualty Report, The Stationery Office
Road Accidents, Scotland, Scottish Executive
Road Accidents Statistics English Regions, The Stationery Office
Road Accidents: Wales, National Assembly for Wales
Road Traffic Accident Statistics Annual Report, The Royal Ulster Constabulary
Road Traffic Statistics Great Britain, The Stationery Office
Scottish Transport Statistics, Scottish Executive
Transport Statistics Bulletins and Reports, Department of the Environment, Transport and the Regions
Transport Statistical Bulletins, Scottish Executive
Transport Statistics Great Britain, The Stationery Office
Transport Trends, The Stationery Office
Travel Trends, The Stationery Office
Vehicle Licensing Statistics, Department of the Environment, Transport and the Regions
Vehicle Speeds in Great Britain, Department of the Environment, Transport and the Regions
Welsh Transport Statistics, National Assembly for Wales

Contacts

Telephone contact points for further information relating to
Chapter 12: Transport

Office for National Statistics	
Chapter author	020 7533 5781
Household expenditure	020 7533 5999
International Passenger Survey	020 7533 5765
Retail prices	020 7533 5874
Department of the Environment, Transport and the Regions	020 7944 4847
Department of the Environment for Northern Ireland	028 9054 0807
Driving Standards Agency	0115 901 2852
Royal Ulster Constabulary	028 9065 0222 ext 24135
Scottish Executive	0131 244 7255/7256
National Centre for Social Research	020 7250 1866 ext 347

Chapter 13 Lifestyles and Social Participation

Overview

The proportion of households in Great Britain with a home computer almost doubled between 1988 and 1998-99, from 18 per cent to 34 per cent. (Page 210)

Home-based activities

Older people watch more television than younger people – people aged 65 and over watched about twice as much television as children aged 4 to 15 on average. (Chart 13.4)

People bought nearly 176 million CDs in the United Kingdom in 1998, representing 84 per cent of all album sales in either CD, cassette or LP format. This is a considerable change from only seven years earlier when CD sales were outnumbered by sales of cassettes. (Chart 13.7)

Activities outside the home

The most common leisure activity away from home continues to be visiting the pub. In 1998-99, around 18 per cent of adults in Great Britain said they had been to a pub the day before they were interviewed. (Page 215)

Men are more likely than women to take part in sports, games and physical activities. In 1996-97, 71 per cent of men and 57 per cent of women in the United Kingdom participated in at least one sporting activity in the four weeks before interview. (Page 215)

In 1998, 56 million holidays of four nights or more were taken by British residents, a third more than in 1971. (Chart 13.1)

Citizenship and social participation

In 1998, about one in five people in Great Britain reported that they had done unpaid charitable work in the previous year. (Table 13.18)

Membership of Trinitarian churches was lower at the end of the twentieth century than at the beginning. (Page 219)

13.1

Holidays[1] taken by Great Britain residents: by destination

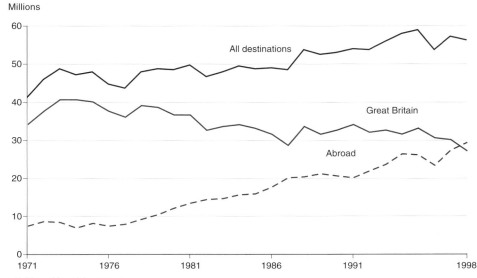

1 Holidays of four nights or more.

Source: British National Travel Survey, British Tourist Authority

13.2

Households with selected consumer durables

Great Britain				Percentages
	1972	1981	1991-92	1998-99
Television	93	97	98	98
Telephone	42	75	88	96
Deep freezer/fridge freezer	..	49	83	93
Washing machine	66	78	87	92
Video recorder	..	..	68	85
Microwave	..	..	55	79
Compact disc player	..	..	27	68
Tumble drier	..	23	48	52
Home computer	..	..	21	34
Dishwasher	..	4	14	24

Source: General Household Survey, Office for National Statistics

13.3

Participation[1] in home-based leisure activities: by gender

Great Britain			Percentages
	1977	1987	1996-97
Males			
Watching TV	97	99	99
Visiting/entertaining friends or relations	89	94	95
Listening to radio	87	89	90
Listening to records/tapes/CDs	64	76	79
Reading books	52	54	58
DIY	51	58	58
Gardening	49	49	52
Dressmaking/needlework/knitting	2	3	3
Females			
Watching TV	97	99	99
Visiting/entertaining friends or relations	93	96	97
Listening to radio	87	86	87
Listening to records/tapes/CDs	60	71	77
Reading books	57	65	71
DIY	22	30	30
Gardening	35	43	45
Dressmaking/needlework/knitting	51	47	37

1 Percentage of those aged 16 and over participating in each activity in the four weeks before interview.
Source: General Household Survey, Office for National Statistics

Leisure is an important part of people's lives. The amount of time people spend working, sleeping and on various household tasks influences the amount of leisure time they have.

Overview

One of the most striking changes during the second half of the twentieth century has been the increasing participation of women in the labour force, while male participation has declined. However, women are more likely than men to be in part-time employment, and therefore women tend to spend fewer hours in paid work than men. In May 1995 the Omnibus Survey found that, on average, women spent more time than men doing domestic chores such as cooking and routine housework. Further information on employment trends is given in Chapter 4: Labour market.

Lifestyles and leisure activities are not just influenced by the amount of time people spend working, but also by the availability of, and access to, consumer durables. Domestic appliances have multiplied in our homes, even over the last quarter of a century. In 1972 only 66 per cent of households in Great Britain had a washing machine, but by 1998-99 this had risen to 92 per cent (Table 13.2). There has been an even more dramatic rise in the proportion of households with dishwashers in the last two decades from 3 per cent in 1978 to 24 per cent in 1998-99.

Technological advances may also provide people with new types of leisure activities. More than four in five households in Great Britain now have a video recorder compared with just under one in five households in 1983, so many people can now watch pre-recorded or self-recorded videos at home. There has also been a dramatic increase in the ownership of home computers. The proportion of households with a home computer almost doubled between 1988 and 1998-99, from 18 per cent to 34 per cent. Of course, certain types of household are more likely than others to have a home computer. In 1998-99, 49 per cent of households with children had a computer, compared with 28 per cent of one person households aged 16 to 59, and just 4 per cent of those aged 60 and over.

Financial resources may also influence people's lifestyles and social participation, and information on people's income and savings can be found in Chapter 5: Income and Wealth. Health and mobility may also influence people's leisure activities, and information on these topics can be found in Chapter 7: Health and Chapter 12: Transport.

Home-based activities

There are some striking differences in the pursuits undertaken by men and women in their own homes. In 1996-97 a higher proportion of men than women in Great Britain had done some DIY in the four weeks before they were interviewed (Table 13.3). The situation was reversed as far as dressmaking, needlework or knitting was concerned, with 37 per cent of women taking part in such activities in the previous four weeks compared with only 3 per cent of men.

Over the last 20 years there have been several changes in participation in home-based leisure activities. For example, a smaller proportion of women participated in dressmaking, sewing or knitting in 1996-97 than in 1977, while the proportions doing DIY and gardening grew. Throughout this period watching television remained the most common activity, closely followed by visiting or entertaining friends or relations.

On average people aged 4 and over in the United Kingdom spent about 25 hours per week watching television in 1998. Generally women watched more television than men did although, among

Television viewing: by gender and age, 1998

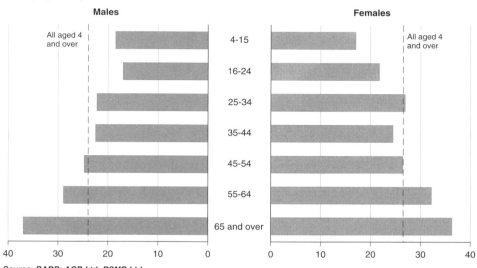

United Kingdom
Hours per person per week

Source: BARB; AGB Ltd; RSMB Ltd

children, boys watched more television than girls (Chart 13.4). Older people watch more television than younger people – people aged 65 and over watched about twice as much television as children aged 4 to 15 on average. The type of television programmes people watch also varies with age. Around 13 to 14 per cent of people aged 65 and over watched news programmes compared with only about 9 per cent of those aged 16 to 44. Overall, drama programmes are the most commonly watched type of television programme.

There have been dramatic changes in the choice of television channels available to people during recent decades. The BBC launched the world's first regular television service in 1936, and the first regular independent television channel in the United Kingdom began broadcasting in 1955. Channel 4 and S4C (in Wales) went on air in 1982 and Channel 5 followed in 1997. More recently there has been an increase in the number of television channels available through satellite and cable technology. Digital television made its commercial debut in the United Kingdom in 1998.

13.5

Subscription to satellite and cable television[1]: by social class[2] of head of household, 1998-99

United Kingdom

Percentages

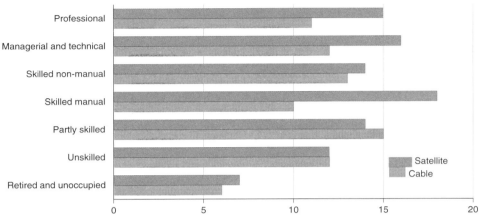

1 Percentage of households paying subscription for satellite or cable television.
2 See Appendix, Part 13: Social class.

Source: Family Expenditure Survey, Office for National Statistics

13.6

Radio listening: by age and gender, 1998

United Kingdom	Hours and minutes per week		
	Males	Females	All
4-14	5:13	6:42	5:57
15-34	18:11	15:14	16:45
35-64	19:56	16:39	18:15
65 and over	16:54	17:34	17:18
All aged 4 and over	16:42	14:59	15:50

Source: RAJAR/RSL Ltd

According to the Family Expenditure Survey, by 1998-99, 13 per cent of households in the United Kingdom were subscribers to satellite television, and 9 per cent subscribed to cable television. These subscription patterns vary by social class. Subscription to satellite is more common than cable among the majority of social groups, especially for households headed by skilled manual people, followed by households headed by managerial, technical and professional people (Chart 13.5). Cable television is most popular among partly skilled households, while households headed by someone from the unskilled group are equally likely to subscribe to cable and satellite. Households where the head is retired or unoccupied are the least likely to be either satellite or cable subscribers.

Despite the increasing number of television channels in recent years, the proportion of people listening to the radio has remained fairly stable, with about nine in ten people in Great Britain reporting listening in the four weeks prior to interview in the General Household Survey in 1996-97. According to a broadcasting industry survey, overall people spent an average of 16 hours per week listening to the radio in the United Kingdom in 1998 (Table 13.6). Women between the ages of 15 and 64 listened to less radio than men, whereas women aged 65 and over listened to 40 minutes more radio per week than men of the same age. Girls between the ages of 4 and 14 listened to one and a half hours more radio than boys of the same age. On average, men aged 35 to 64 listened to the most radio each week at almost 20 hours.

Lord Northcliffe's demonstration of radio as a means for bringing music and speech into the home in the early 1920s signalled the start of the broadcasting era in Britain. The government argued that the scarcity of the airwaves meant all manufacturers should form a single broadcasting company, which by 1927 became the BBC. Following pressure in the 1950s and 1960s from pirate stations such as Radio Caroline, commercial radio was legalised, and in 1973 Capital Radio and LBC became the first legal independent local radio stations in the United Kingdom. The first national commercial licences were issued in 1992. The type of radio programme people listen to varies by age. For example, Radio 1 is popular among young people, while people aged 65 and over spent only a very small proportion of their listening time tuned into this station in 1998.

Listening to music on home music systems is another popular leisure activity. The dramatic rise in sales of CDs in recent years has been accompanied by falls in sales of cassettes and LPs (Chart 13.7). Nearly 176 million CDs were sold in the United Kingdom in 1998, representing 84 per cent of all album sales in either CD, cassette or LP format. This represents a considerable and rapid change from only seven years earlier when the cassette was the leading album format. A similar proportion of men and women buy albums, although men buy them in larger quantities.

13.7

Just over 79 million singles were sold in 1998, lower than in 1997 but higher than in any other year since 1980. Singles buying becomes less popular with age. While young people aged 10 to 19 buy about four in ten of all singles, those in their fifties account for just 3 per cent of overall sales. Cher's *Believe* was the best selling single in 1998, followed by Celine Dion's *My heart will go on*. The United Kingdom's top selling single of all time is Elton John's *Candle in the wind* tribute to Diana, Princess of Wales, released in 1997, while the best selling album of all time is the Beatles' *Sergeant Pepper's Lonely Hearts Club Band* which was released in 1967.

Many people also enjoy reading as a leisure activity. More daily newspapers, national and regional, are sold per person in the United Kingdom than in most other developed countries, although the proportion of people reading a national daily newspaper in Great Britain has fallen since the early 1980s (Table 13.8).

Sales[1] of CDs, LPs, cassettes and singles[2]

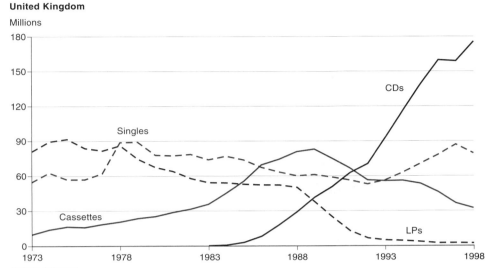

United Kingdom

1 Trade deliveries.
2 All formats combined (7", 12", cassette and CD).
Source: British Phonographic Industry

13.8

Reading of national daily newspapers: by gender[1]

Great Britain   Percentages

	Males				Females			
	1971	1981	1991	1998-99[2]	1971	1981	1991	1998-99[2]
The Sun	26	31	25	24	15	23	19	17
The Mirror	38	27	20	15	29	22	15	12
Daily Mail	13	13	10	12	10	11	9	12
Daily Express	28	16	8	6	20	13	8	5
The Daily Telegraph	10	9	6	6	7	7	5	5
Daily Star	.	13	8	5	.	8	4	2
The Times	3	3	3	5	2	2	2	3
The Guardian	3	4	3	3	2	2	2	2
The Independent	.	.	3	2	.	.	2	1
Financial Times	3	2	2	2	1	1	1	1
Any national daily newspaper[3]	..	76	66	60	..	68	57	51

1 Aged 15 and over.
2 July 1998 to June 1999; earlier years are calendar years.
3 Includes the above newspapers plus the Daily Record, Sporting Life and Racing Post.
Source: National Readership Surveys Ltd

13.9

Reading of popular consumer magazines: by age, 1998-99[1]

Great Britain					Percentages
	15-24	25-44	45-64	65 and over	All aged 15 and over
Sky TV Guide	17	15	12	4	12
M&S Magazine	6	12	14	8	11
Take a Break	11	11	9	7	10
Reader's Digest	4	7	12	11	9
What's on TV	15	11	7	6	9
Radio Times	9	7	9	9	8
AA Magazine	3	8	11	7	8
FHM	28	9	2	..	8
TV Times	10	6	7	6	7
Cable Guide	11	9	5	2	7
Woman's Own	5	6	6	5	6

1 July 1998 to June 1999.
Source: National Readership Surveys Ltd

13.10

Participation[1] in the most popular sports, games and physical activities: by gender and age, 1996-97

United Kingdom								Percentages
	16-19	20-24	25-34	35-44	45-54	55-64	65 and over	All aged 16 and over
Males								
Walking	57	57	50	53	51	50	37	49
Snooker/pool/billiards	54	45	29	19	13	9	5	19
Cycling	36	24	19	18	12	8	5	15
Swimming	18	17	17	20	10	7	5	13
Soccer	47	28	17	10	2	1	-	10
Females								
Walking	45	43	44	45	49	43	25	41
Keep fit/yoga	29	28	24	20	14	12	6	17
Swimming	23	21	26	22	14	12	5	16
Cycling	14	11	10	12	7	4	2	8
Snooker/pool/billiards	24	17	6	3	1	-	-	4

1 Percentage in each age group participating in each activity in the four weeks before interview.
Source: General Household Survey, Office for National Statistics; Continuous Household Survey, Northern Ireland Statistics and Research Agency

The most widely read daily newspaper (by adults aged 15 and over) in Great Britain is *The Sun*, with almost one in four men and just over one in six women reading it, on average, in the year to June 1999. People aged 15 to 24 are the most likely to read *The Sun*, with the proportion falling among older people. In contrast, older people were more likely than younger people to read the *Daily Mail*, *Daily Express* and *The Daily Telegraph*. The oldest surviving national daily newspaper is *The Times*, which was founded in 1785.

The oldest surviving national Sunday newspaper in the world is *The Observer*, which was founded in 1791. In the year to June 1999, 60 per cent of people aged 15 and over said they read a Sunday newspaper, although readership of Sunday newspapers has declined in recent years. The most popular Sunday newspaper in 1998-99 was the *News of the World*, followed by the *Sunday Mirror* and the *Mail on Sunday*.

The most popular magazine in Great Britain in the year to June 1999 was *Sky TV Guide*, which was read by about one in eight people aged 15 and over (Table 13.9). *Reader's Digest* was more popular among older people than younger people, while the reverse was the case for the men's fashion magazine *FHM*. In recent years a wider range of this type of magazine has become available, and they have become increasingly popular. The number of men reading *FHM* increased by 28 per cent between 1997-98 and 1998-99 from 2.2 million to 2.8 million. Similarly, the number of men reading *GQ*, another magazine for men, increased by 7 per cent from 551 thousand to 592 thousand in the same period. The popularity of magazines for women also increased over this period, albeit less dramatically.

Social Trends 30, © Crown copyright 2000

13.11

Activities outside the home

The most common leisure activity away from home continues to be visiting a pub. In 1998-99 around 18 per cent of people aged 16 and over in Great Britain said they had made such a visit the day prior to being interviewed for the Leisure Tracking Survey. Men are more likely than women to visit a public house, with over one in five men saying that they had been to the pub the day before being interviewed, while only one in seven women gave the same response. Driving for pleasure and being a spectator at a sporting event are also more popular among men than women.

Men are also more likely than women to take part in sports, games and physical activities. In 1996-97, 71 per cent of men and 57 per cent of women in the United Kingdom participated in at least one sporting activity in the four weeks before interview in the General Household Survey. While walking was the most common physical activity for both men and women, the second most popular activity for men was snooker, pool or billiards, while for women it was keep-fit or yoga and swimming (Table 13.10). Generally participation in sport decreases with age but older people are more likely to participate in bowls than younger people. Physical exercise is an important component of healthy living. More information may be found in Table 7.20 in the Health chapter.

Attendance at some cultural events also varies by age. Over three-quarters of men and women aged 15 to 34 in Great Britain said they went to the cinema in 1997-98, compared with only about a quarter of those aged 55 and over. Conversely a higher proportion of people aged 35 and over said they attended classical music concerts than those aged 15 to 34.

When asked in 1997-98 whether they attended particular types of cultural events 'these days', fewer than one in ten adults said that they attended ballet or opera, while just under one in four people said they attended plays (Table 13.11). The proportion of adults who attend most cultural events has not changed much over the last decade or so. The exception to this is going to the cinema. Whereas, in 1987-88, about a third of adults said that they went to the cinema, more than half said that they did so in 1997-98.

Recently cinema attendance has seen some resurgence in popularity in Great Britain after nearly 40 years of decline (Chart 13.12). Cinema admissions declined sharply from the 1.4 billion in 1951, to reach a low of 53 million in 1984. This fall was probably influenced by the advent of television, and later of video recorders. Over the next decade, however, cinema admissions rose, and were 123 million in 1998. This revival may be related to the investment and expansion in multiplex cinemas in recent years. *Titanic* was the top box office film of 1998 in the United Kingdom, taking £69 million. This was followed by *Doctor Dolittle* and *Saving Private Ryan*. *Titanic* was also the UK's top box office film of all time as at the end of October 1999, followed by *The Full Monty* and *Star Wars: Episode 1 – The Phantom Menace*.

Attendance[1] at cultural events[2]

Great Britain			Percentages
	1987-88	1991-92	1997-98
Cinema	34	44	54
Plays	24	23	23
Art galleries/ exhibitions	21	21	22
Classical music	12	12	12
Ballet	6	6	6
Opera	5	6	6
Contemporary dance	4	3	4

1 Percentage of resident population aged 15 and over attending 'these days'.
2 See Appendix, Part 13: Cultural events.
Source: Target Group Index, BMRB International

13.12

Cinema admissions

Great Britain
Billions

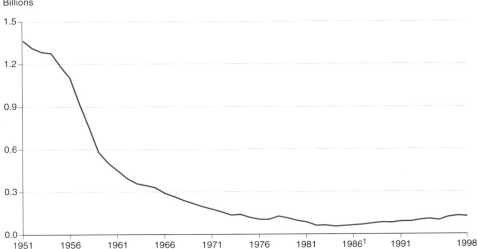

1 Data collection was suspended in 1985 and 1986.
Source: Office for National Statistics

13.13

Day visits from home[1]: by gender and main activity, 1998

Great Britain			Percentages
	Males	Females	All
Eat/drink	21	15	18
Visit friends	14	19	17
Walk/hill-walk/ramble	16	14	15
Shop	9	15	12
Entertainment	5	7	6
Indoor sport	7	4	5
Outdoor sport	8	3	5
Hobby/special interest	4	5	5
Drive/sightsee	3	3	3
Swimming	2	3	3
Leisure attraction	2	2	2
Watching sport	2	1	2
Cycling/mountain biking	3	1	2
Informal sport/games	2	2	2
Other	2	5	3
All visits	100	100	100

1 Visits taken in 1998.

Source: Day Visits Survey, National Centre for Social Research

Day visits are another popular leisure activity. The 1998 UK Day Visits Survey collected information on round trips made for leisure purposes from home to locations anywhere in the United Kingdom. These leisure day visits increased by almost 15 per cent between 1994 and 1998 to over 5.9 billion. Overall the two most popular reasons for taking day visits away from home in 1998 were going out for a meal or drink in a café, restaurant or pub and visiting friends or relatives. However, while men were more likely than women to go out for a meal or drink, the reverse was the case for visiting friends or relatives (Table 13.13). Women were also more likely than men to take a day trip to go shopping.

Blackpool Pleasure Beach has been Britain's most popular tourist attraction for many years, and 7.1 million people visited it in 1998 (Table 13.14). The second most popular free attraction, and the most popular museum, was the British Museum. This attracted 5.6 million people in the same year, which was more than twice as many as in 1981. The most popular museums and galleries are in London, some of which introduced admission charges in the late 1980s. This affected the number of visits made to some of these attractions. For example, the number of visits made to the Natural History Museum and the Science Museum in 1998 were about half the number made in 1981. However, funds have been made available to permit free access for children from April 1999, and free access for pensioners from April 2000, to the currently charging national museums.

While some people may visit tourist attractions on day trips, others may do so while on holiday. The proportion of British adults taking at least one holiday a year of four nights or more has fluctuated around 60 per cent for the last 25 years. The proportion of adults taking two or more holidays a year increased steadily up to 1995 when 27 per cent of adults did so. Since then the proportion has levelled out, and in 1998, 25 per cent of adults had two or more holiday breaks.

In 1998, 56 million holidays of four nights or more were taken by British residents, 36 per cent more than in 1971 (see Chart 13.1 at the beginning of

13.14

Visits to the most popular tourist attractions

Great Britain							Millions
	1981	1991	1998		1981	1991	1998
Museums and galleries				**Historic houses and monuments**			
British Museum	2.6	5.1	5.6	Tower of London	2.1	1.9	2.6
National Gallery	2.7	4.3	4.8	Windsor Castle	0.7	0.6	1.5
Tate Gallery	0.9	1.8	2.2	Edinburgh Castle	0.8	1.0	1.2
Natural History Museum	3.7	1.6	1.9	Roman Baths, Bath	0.6	0.8	0.9
Science Museum	3.8	1.3	1.6	Stonehenge	0.5	0.6	0.8
Theme parks				**Wildlife parks and zoos**			
Blackpool Pleasure Beach	7.5	6.5	7.1	London Zoo	1.1	1.1	1.1
Alton Towers	1.6	2.0	2.8	Chester Zoo	..	0.9	0.9
Pleasureland, Southport	..	1.8	2.1	London Aquarium	.	.	0.7
Chessington World of Adventure	0.5	1.4	1.7	Edinburgh Zoo	..	0.5	0.5
Legoland, Windsor	.	.	1.5	Knowsley Safari Park	..	0.3	0.5

Source: National Tourist Boards

13.15

the chapter). The number of holidays taken in Great Britain has been broadly stable over the last decade while the number taken abroad has grown. In 1998 the number of holidays taken abroad outnumbered those taken in Great Britain for the first time: 29 million holidays were taken abroad by residents of Great Britain compared with 27 million domestic holidays.

Spain was the most popular holiday destination abroad for UK residents in 1998 (Table 13.15). The number of visits to France and the United States were higher in 1998 than in 1971. Europe remains more popular with British holidaymakers than other parts of the world, while the United States is the most popular non-European holiday destination.

People aged 65 and over were the least likely to take a holiday abroad in 1998. Five per cent of men and 4 per cent of women going on holiday abroad were in this age group, although men aged 65 and over made up 13 per cent of the total male population, and women of this age made up 18 per cent of the female population. Those aged 45 to 54 were the most likely to take a holiday abroad. Men aged 24 to 34 spent, on average, the most money abroad on holiday – just over £464.

Among British adults aged 16 and over who spent their holiday (of four nights or more) in Great Britain in 1998, the West Country was by far the most popular destination, accounting for over a quarter of such breaks (Chart 13.16). Scotland and Southern England were the next most popular destinations while Greater London and Northumbria each accounted for only 2 per cent of domestic holidays.

Many people prefer just to relax when they are on holiday. The UK Tourism Survey found that over two in five British residents taking holidays in the United Kingdom engaged in no activity while away

in 1998. Swimming, either indoor or outdoor, was the most popular holiday activity with 17 per cent of people engaging in such a pastime. Hiking and walking, and visiting heritage sites were also popular activities.

Heritage is one of the six causes that receive funding from the National Lottery, which was launched in 1994. The distribution of income from the National Lottery was set out at the start of the licence and amended by the *National Lottery Act 1998*. Over the course of the licence, for each £1 spent on the Lottery, 50 pence will be returned as prizes and 28 pence will go to good causes. Some £8.3 billion had been raised for good causes by the end of October 1999, and nearly 47 thousand awards amounting to £7.2 billion had been distributed. Over two-thirds of the awards have been for less than £50,000.

Holidays[1] abroad: by destination

				Percentages
	1971	1981	1991	1998
Spain[2]	34.3	21.7	21.3	27.5
France	15.9	27.2	25.8	20.2
United States	1.0	5.5	6.8	7.0
Greece	4.5	6.7	7.6	5.3
Italy	9.2	5.8	3.5	4.0
Portugal	2.6	2.8	4.8	3.6
Irish Republic	..	3.6	3.0	3.5
Turkey	..	0.1	0.7	3.0
Netherlands	3.6	2.4	3.5	2.7
Cyprus	1.0	0.7	2.4	2.6
Belgium	..	2.1	2.1	2.3
Germany	3.4	2.6	2.7	1.8
Malta	..	2.6	1.7	1.3
Austria	5.5	2.5	2.4	1.3
Other countries	19.0	13.7	11.8	13.9
All destinations (=100%) (thousands)	4,201	13,131	20,788	32,306

1 A visit made for holiday purposes. Business trips and visits to friends or relatives are excluded.
2 Excludes the Canary Islands prior to 1981.
Source: International Passenger Survey, Office for National Statistics

13.16

Domestic holidays[1] taken by Great Britain residents: by destination, 1998

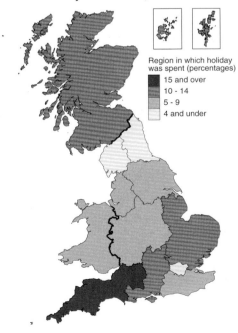

Region in which holiday was spent (percentages)
- 15 and over
- 10 - 14
- 5 - 9
- 4 and under

1 Holidays of four nights or more taken by adults aged 16 and over.
Source: British National Travel Survey, British Tourist Authority

13.17

Percentage of households participating in the National Lottery[1]: by social class[2] of head of household, 1998-99

United Kingdom

Percentages

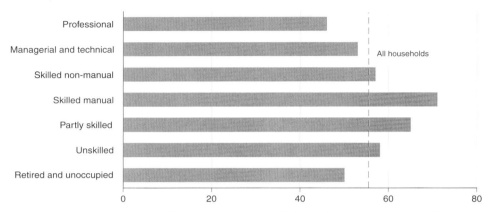

All households

1 Participation in National Lottery (Saturday, Wednesday and joint Saturday/Wednesday draws – excluding scratchcards) in the two week diary keeping period following interview from April 1998 to March 1999.
2 See Appendix, Part 13: Social class.
Source: Family Expenditure Survey, Office for National Statistics

The Family Expenditure Survey (FES) collects data on, among other things, household expenditure on the National Lottery in the United Kingdom. Between April 1998 and March 1999, 56 per cent of households participated in the Saturday or Wednesday night draws during the two-week-diary keeping period following interview (Chart 13.17). Households headed by someone in the skilled manual social class are the most likely to participate in the lottery, while those headed by someone in the professional class are the least likely. According to the FES, participating households in the United Kingdom spent an average of £3.80 a week on the National Lottery draws in 1998-99.

Citizenship and social participation

Serving the community through volunteering is a long-established tradition in the United Kingdom. Voluntary organisations may be staffed by paid workers, but most also rely on the efforts of volunteers at some level. Many volunteers are involved in work that improves the quality of life in their local communities, or give their time to help organise events or groups.

13.18

Participation in voluntary activities[1] in the last year: by gender, 1998

Great Britain
Percentages

	1 to 5 times	6 or more times	Once or more
Males			
Charitable activities	15	5	20
Religious and church-related activities	7	4	11
Political activities[2]	3	1	4
Any other kind of voluntary activities	11	7	19
Females			
Charitable activities	17	6	23
Religious and church-related activities	8	6	14
Political activities[2]	2	-	2
Any other kind of voluntary activities	11	8	19

1 Respondents were asked if they had done any voluntary work in the past 12 months in different areas. Voluntary activity was defined as unpaid work, not just belonging to an organisation or group, of service or benefit to other people or the community and not only to one's family or personal friends.
2 Helping political parties, political movements, election campaigns, etc.
Source: British Social Attitudes Survey, National Centre for Social Research

In 1998 the British Social Attitudes Survey (BSA) asked people in Great Britain if they had done any voluntary work in the past 12 months, that is any unpaid activity of benefit or service to the community or people other than family or friends. About one in five people reported that they had done unpaid charitable work in the last year (Table 13.18). About one in nine men and one in seven women said they had volunteered for religious and church-related activities, while only very small proportions said they had been involved with political activities in a voluntary capacity. When asked about their attitudes to voluntary work and charities, over three-quarters of respondents agreed or strongly agreed with the

13.19

statement that 'doing voluntary work is a good thing for volunteers because it makes them feel they are contributing to society'. However, over half of those interviewed also agreed or strongly agreed with the statement that 'as a society we rely too much on volunteers'. Information on the reasons volunteers give for volunteering may be found in Chart 8.12 in the Social protection chapter, on page 138.

For some people religion is an important part of their lives providing spiritual inspiration, contact with others and a means to participate in the life of the local community. Membership of Trinitarian churches was lower at the end of the twentieth century than at its beginning. In 1970, 9.3 million people in the United Kingdom were active members of a Trinitarian church, but this has declined by almost a third to 6.6 million in 1990 (Table 13.19).

In contrast to the decline in membership of Trinitarian churches, there has been a substantial increase in adult active membership among non-Trinitarian churches and other religions in recent years. This has been particularly the case among the Sikh and Muslim faiths since the 1970s. Nonetheless, membership of these religions is still relatively small, compared with the Trinitarian church.

Despite the decline in church membership in recent years, many people believe in some form of deity. When asked in the 1998 BSA about their religious beliefs, over one in five people agreed with the statement 'I know God really exists and I have no doubts about it' while only one in ten people said they did not believe in God (Table 13.20). In the same survey people were asked about other religious beliefs. One in two people said they definitely or probably believed in life after death while about one in three said that they definitely or probably did not. About half of people professed a lack of belief in religious miracles.

Church Membership[1]

United Kingdom			Thousands
	1970	1980	1990
Trinitarian churches			
Roman Catholic	2,746	2,455	2,198
Anglican	2,987	2,180	1,728
Presbyterian	1,751	1,437	1,214
Other free churches	843	678	776
Methodist	673	540	478
Orthodox	191	203	266
Baptist	272	239	230
All Trinitarian churches	9,272	7,529	6,624
Non-Trinitarian churches			
Mormons	85	114	160
Jehovah's Witnesses	62	85	117
Other non-Trinitarian	138	154	182
All non-Trinitarian churches	285	353	459
Other religions			
Muslim	130	306	495
Sikh	100	150	250
Hindu	80	120	140
Jewish	120	111	101
Others	21	53	87
All other religions	451	740	1,073

1 Active adult members.
Source: Christian Research

13.20

Belief in God[1], 1998

Great Britain	Percentages
	1998
I know God really exists and I have no doubt about it	21
While I have doubts, I feel that I do believe in God	23
I find myself believeing in God some of the time, but not at others	14
I don't believe in a personal God, but I do believe in a Higher Power of some kind	14
I don't know whether there is a God and I don't believe there is any way to find out	15
I don't believe in God	10
Not answered	3
All	100

1 Respondents were asked which statement came closest to their belief about God.
Source: British Social Attitudes Survey, National Centre for Social Research

13.21

Parliamentary seats won at General Elections[1]: by major political party

United Kingdom

Number of seats

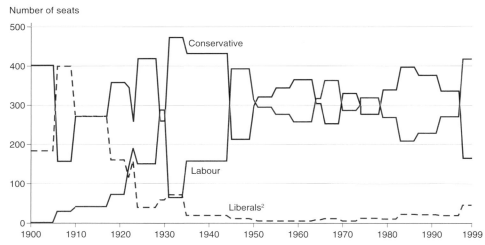

1 The data for 1918 are the party affiliations of coalition and non-coalition MPs combined. The data for 1931 are the party affiliations of 'National Government' and non-coalition MPs combined.
2 Liberals includes National Liberals, Social Democrats, Alliance and Liberal Democrats as the party has evolved.
Source: House of Commons Library

13.22

Participation in EU elections[1]

Percentages

	1979	1984	1989	1994	1999
Belgium[2]	92	92	91	91	90
Luxembourg[2]	89	87	87	89	86
Italy	86	84	82	75	71
Greece	79	77	80	71	70
Spain	.	69	55	59	64
Irish Republic	64	48	68	44	51
Denmark	47	52	46	53	50
Austria	.	.	.	68	49
France	61	57	49	53	47
Germany	66	57	62	60	45
Portugal	.	72	51	36	40
Sweden	.	.	.	42	38
Finland	.	.	.	60	30
Netherlands	58	51	47	36	30
United Kingdom	32	33	36	36	24
EU average	63	61	59	57	49

1 The figure for Greece in 1979 is for the 1981 election, the figures for Portugal and Spain in 1984 are for the 1987 elections and the figures for Austria, Finland and Sweden in 1994 are for the 1996 elections.
2 Voting is mandatory in Belgium and Luxembourg.
Source: European Parliament

Most people exercise their right to vote at general elections. Electoral turnout has fluctuated considerably across the century in the United Kingdom. The highest turnout was in 1910, when 87 per cent of the electorate voted, while the lowest turnouts were in the general elections of 1922, 1923, 1935 and 1997 when only about 71 per cent of people voted, and in 1918 when 59 per cent voted. The Conservative Party has been in government for longer in the twentieth century than any other party (Chart 13.21).

Westminster is not the only level of political authority within the United Kingdom. Elections were held in 1999 for the Scottish Parliament and Welsh Assembly following the votes for devolution in the referenda of September 1997. The turnout for the elections to the Scottish Parliament was 58 per cent for the constituency votes and 57 per cent for the regional list votes, while the corresponding figures for the elections to the Welsh Assembly were 46 per cent for both counts. Elections to the Northern Ireland Assembly were held in June 1998, following the referendum on the Good Friday Agreement earlier that year. The new Northern Ireland Assembly took up its full responsibilities on 2 December 1999.

Since 1979 elections have been held in the United Kingdom for representatives to the European Parliament, with proportional representation being used for the first time in 1999. Nonetheless the turnout in the United Kingdom, at under a quarter of the electorate, was the lowest of all the countries in the EU. It was also the lowest of all the European Parliament elections held in the United Kingdom since their introduction (Table 13.22). In contrast Belgium and Luxembourg had the highest turnouts at 90 and 86 per cent respectively, although voting is mandatory in these countries. Sweden and Finland elected the highest proportions of female Members of the European Parliament (MEPs) at 45 and 44 per cent respectively; 24 per cent of the United Kingdom's MEPs are female, which is below the overall EU average of 30 per cent.

Social Trends 30, © Crown copyright 2000

References and further reading

The following list contains selected publications relevant to **Chapter 13: Lifestyles and Social Participation**.

Those published by The Stationery Office are available from the addresses shown on the inside back cover of *Social Trends*.

Annual Report of Department for Culture, Media and Sport, The Stationery Office

BBC Handbook, BBC

BPI Statistical Handbook, British Phonographic Industry

British Social Attitudes, Ashgate Publishing

BVA Yearbook, British Video Association

Cinema and Video Industry Audience Research, CAA

Consumer and leisure futures, The Henley Centre

Cultural Trends in Scotland, Policy Studies Institute

Cultural Trends, Policy Studies Institute

Digest of Tourist Statistics, British Tourist Authority

Family Spending, The Stationery Office

Film and Television Handbook, British Film Institute

LISU Annual Library Statistics, LISU, Loughborough University

Living in Britain, The Stationery Office

Religious Trends, Christian Research

Social Focus on Families, The Stationery Office

Social Focus on Women and Men, The Stationery Office

The UK Tourist, Tourist Boards of England, Northern Ireland, Scotland and Wales

Travel Trends, The Stationery Office

UK Day Visits Survey, Countryside Recreation Network, University of Wales Cardiff

Young People and Sport in England, The Sports Council

Contacts

Telephone contact points for further information relating to
Chapter 13: Lifestyles and Social Participation

Office for National Statistics	
Chapter author	020 7533 5781
Family Expenditure Survey	020 7533 5756
General Household Survey	020 7533 5444
International Passenger Survey	020 7533 5765
British Broadcasting Corporation	020 8576 4436
British Phonographic Industry	020 7287 4422
British Tourist Authority	020 8846 9000
Christian Research	020 8294 1989
Cinema Advertising Association	020 7439 9531
National Centre for Social Research	020 7250 1866
National Readership Surveys	020 7632 2915
The Henley Centre	020 7353 9961

Geographical areas of the United Kingdom

Government Office Regions

SCOTLAND

NORTHERN IRELAND

NORTH EAST

YORKSHIRE AND THE HUMBER

NORTH WEST

EAST MIDLANDS

WEST MIDLANDS

WALES

EAST OF ENGLAND

LONDON

SOUTH WEST

SOUTH EAST

— GOR boundary

Standard Statistical Regions

SCOTLAND

NORTHERN IRELAND

NORTH

YORKSHIRE AND HUMBERSIDE

NORTH WEST

EAST MIDLANDS

WEST MIDLANDS

WALES

EAST ANGLIA

SOUTH EAST

SOUTH WEST

— SSR boundary

NHS Regional Office areas (from April 1996)

ENGLAND and WALES

— Health Authority boundary

NORTHERN & YORKSHIRE

NORTH WEST

TRENT

WEST MIDLANDS

WALES

ANGLIA & OXFORD

NORTH THAMES

SOUTH & WEST

SOUTH THAMES

Environment Agency regions

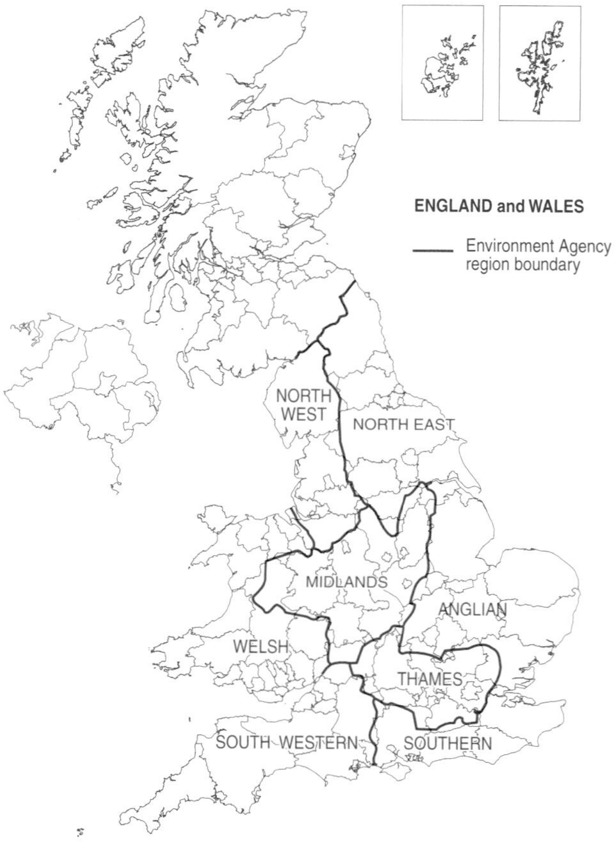

ENGLAND and WALES

— Environment Agency region boundary

NORTH WEST

NORTH EAST

MIDLANDS

ANGLIAN

WELSH

THAMES

SOUTH WESTERN

SOUTHERN

Social Trends 30, © Crown copyright 2000

Geographical areas of the United Kingdom

Police Force areas

Tourist Board regions

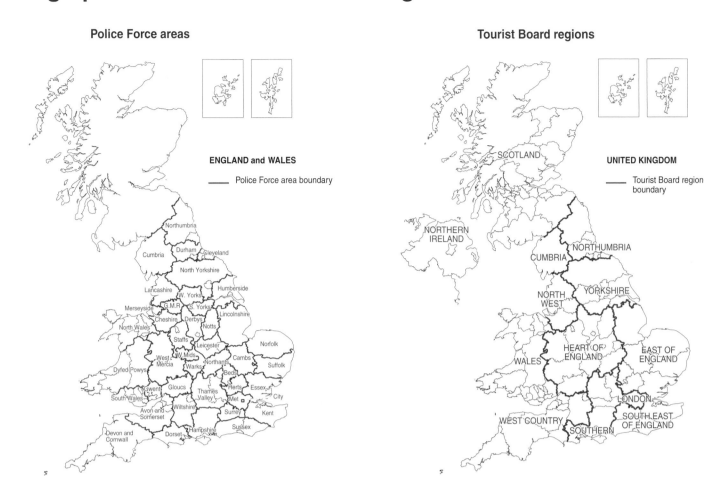

ENGLAND and WALES

——— Police Force area boundary

UNITED KINGDOM

——— Tourist Board region boundary

Appendix: major surveys

	Frequency	Sampling frame	Type of respondent	Coverage	Effective sample size[1] (most recent survey included in *Social Trends*)	Response rate (percentages)
Agricultural and Horticultural Census	Annual	Farms	Farmers	UK	238,000 farms	80
British Crime Survey	Biennial	Postcode Address File	Adult in household	EW	18,983 addresses	79
British Household Panel Survey	Annual	Postal Addresses	All adults in households	GB	5,033 households	95[2]
British Social Attitudes Survey	Annual	Postcode Address File	One adult per household	GB	5,323 addresses	59
Census of Population	Decennial	Detailed local	Adult in household	UK	Full count	98
Continuous Household Survey	Continuous	Valuation and Lands Agency Property	All adults in household	NI	4,147 addresses	70
English House Condition Survey	Quinquennial	Postcode Address File	Any one householder	E	27,200 addresses	49[3]
European Community Household Panel Survey	Annual	Various	All adults in household	EU	60,000 households	70[4]
Family Expenditure Survey	Continuous	Postcode Address File in GB, Rating and Valuation lists in NI	Household	UK	11,424 addresses[5]	59[6]
Family Resources Survey	Continuous	Postcode Address File	All adults in household	GB	34,502 households	68
General Household Survey	Continuous	Postcode Address File	All adults in household	GB	11,831 households	72
Health Education Monitoring Survey	Ad hoc	Postcode Address File	One adult aged 16 and over in household	E	8,168 households	71
Health Survey for England	Continuous	Postcode Address File	Adults and children over 2 years of age	E	12,250 addresses	74[7]
International Passenger Survey	Continuous	International passengers at ports and airports and through the Channel Tunnel	Individual traveller	UK	263,000 individuals	81
Labour Force Survey	Continuous	Postcode Address File	All adults in household	UK	61,000 addresses	78[8]
Longitudinal Study	Continuous	Population	All persons	EW	1 per cent	
National Food Survey	Continuous	Postcode Address File in GB, Valuation and Lands Agency Property in NI	Person responsible for domestic food arrangements	UK	10,321 addresses	65
National Readership Survey	Continuous	Postcode Address File	Adults aged 15 and over	GB	38,000 individuals	60
National Travel Survey	Continuous	Postcode Address File	Household	GB	5,040 households per year	65[9]
New Earnings Survey	Annual records	Inland Revenue PAYE	Employee	GB	[10]	[10]
Omnibus Survey	Continuous	Postcode Address File	One adult per household	GB	2,005 individuals[11]	75[11]
Survey of English Housing	Continuous	Postcode Address File	Household	E	20,802 addresses	80
Youth Cohort Study	Biennial	School records	Young people (Aged 16 to 19)	EW	22,500 individuals	65

1 Effective sample size includes non-respondents but excludes ineligible households.
2 Wave on wave response rate at wave four. This represents 77 per cent of respondents at wave one.
3 The 1996 EHCS response combines successful outcomes from two linked surveys where information is seperately gathered about the household and the dwelling for each address in the sample.
4 Response rate estimated. Response rates vary between EU countries.
5 Basic sample only.
6 Response rate refers to Great Britain.
7 Response rate for fully and partially responding households.
8 Response rate to first wave interviews quoted. Response rate to second to fifth wave interviews 91 per cent of those previously accepting.
9 Response rate for the period January 1996 to January 1998.
10 In the New Earnings Survey employers supply data on a 1 per cent sample of employees who are members of PAYE schemes. For the 1999 sample approximately 223 thousand were selected and there was a 89.9 per cent response but some 43 thousand returned questionnaires did not contain data.
11 The Omnibus Survey changes from month to month. The sample size and response rate are for May 1999.

Appendix: definitions and terms

Symbols and conventions

Reference years. Where, because of space constraints, a choice of years has to be made, the most recent year or a run of recent years is shown together with the past population census years (1991, 1981, 1971, etc) and sometimes the mid-points between census years (1986, etc). Other years may be added if they represent a peak or trough in the series.

Rounding of figures. In tables where figures have been rounded to the nearest final digit, there may be an apparent discrepancy between the sum of the constituent items and the total as shown.

Billion. This term is used to represent a thousand million.

Provisional and estimated data. Some data for the latest year (and occasionally for earlier years) are provisional or estimated. To keep footnotes to a minimum, these have not been indicated; source departments will be able to advise if revised data are available.

Seasonal adjustment. Unless otherwise stated unadjusted data have been used.

Non-calendar years.
Financial year - eg 1 April 1998 to 31 March 1999 would be shown as 1998-99
Academic year - eg September 1997/July 1998 would be shown as 1997/98
Data covering more than one year - eg 1996, 1997 and 1998 would be shown as 1996-1998

Units on tables. Where one unit predominates it is shown at the top of the table. All other units are shown against the relevant row or column. Figures are shown in italics when they represent percentages.

Dependent children. Those aged under 16, or single people aged 16 to 18 and in full-time education.

Germany. Unless otherwise stated data relate to Germany as constituted since 3 October 1990.

Symbols. The following symbols have been used throughout *Social Trends*:
..	*not available*
.	*not applicable*
-	*negligible (less than half the final digit shown)*
0	*nil*

PART 1: POPULATION

Population estimates and projections
The estimated and projected populations are of the resident population of an area, i.e. all those usually resident there, whatever their nationality. Members of HM forces stationed outside the United Kingdom are excluded; members of the United States forces stationed in the United Kingdom are included. Students are taken to be resident at their term-time addresses. Figures for the United Kingdom do not include the population of the Channel Islands or the Isle of Man.

The population estimates for mid-1991 were based on results from the 1991 Census of Population and incorporate an allowance for census under-enumeration. Allowances were also made for definitional and timing differences between Census and estimates. Estimates for later years allow for subsequent births, deaths and migration. The estimates for 1982-90 have been revised to give a smooth series consistent with both 1981 and 1991 Census results. Due to definitional changes, there are minor discontinuities for Scotland and Northern Ireland between the figures for 1971 and earlier years. At the United Kingdom level these discontinuities are negligible.

The most recent set of national population projections published for the United Kingdom are based on the populations of England, Wales, Scotland and Northern Ireland at mid-1998. Further details of these will be found in *1998-based national population projections Series PP2* (The Stationery Office) due for publication later this year. Subnational projections are also made for constituent countries of the United Kingdom. There are no 1996-based sub-national projections for Wales, but the Office for National Statistics have been asked by the National Assembly for Wales to produce 1998-based projections.

International migration estimates
Detailed estimates of migration between the United Kingdom and other countries are derived from the International Passenger Survey (IPS).

The IPS provides information on all migrants into the United Kingdom who have resided abroad for a year or more and stated on arrival the intention to stay in the United Kingdom for a year or more and vice versa. Migrants to and from the Irish Republic, diplomats and military personnel are excluded, as are nearly all persons who apply for asylum on entering the country. It is also highly likely that the IPS migration figures exclude persons who enter the country as short term visitors but remain for 12 months or longer after being granted an extension of stay, for example as students, on the basis of marriage or because they applied for asylum after entering the country. Home Office estimates of asylum seekers and 'visitor switches' are added to the IPS figures. Estimates of migrants between the United Kingdom and the Irish Republic are produced using information from the Irish Labour Force Survey and the National Health Service Central Register. They are agreed between the Irish Central Statistics Office and the Office for National Statistics and are also added to the IPS figures.

PART 2: HOUSEHOLDS AND FAMILIES

Although definitions differ slightly across surveys and the census, they are broadly similar.

Households

A household: is a person living alone or a group of people who have the address as their only or main residence and who either share one meal a day or share the living accommodation.

Students: living in halls of residence are recorded under their parents household and included in the parents family type in the Labour Force Survey, although some surveys/projections include such students in the institutional population.

Families

Children: are never-married people of any age who live with one or both parent(s). They also include stepchildren and adopted children (but not foster children) and also grandchildren (where the parents are absent).

Dependent children: in the 1961 Census, were defined as children under 15 years of age, and persons of any age in full-time education. In the 1971 Census, dependent children were defined as never-married children in families who were either under 15 years of age, or aged 15 to 24 and in full-time education. However, for direct comparison with the General Household Survey (GHS) data, the definition of dependent children used for 1971 in Table 2.3 has been changed to include only never-married children in families who were either under 15 years of age, or aged 15 to 18 and in full-time education. In the 1991 Census and the GHS, dependent children are childless never-married children in families who are aged under 16, or aged 16 to 18 and in full-time education.

A family: is a married or cohabiting couple, either with or without their never-married child or children (of any age), including couples with no children or a lone parent together with his or her never-married child or children. A family could also consist of grandparent or grandparents with grandchild or grandchildren if there are no apparent parents of the grandchild or grandchildren usually resident in the household.

A lone parent family (in the Census) is a father or mother together with his or her never-married child or children.

A lone parent family (in the General Household Survey) consists of a lone parent, living with his or her never-married dependent children, provided these children have no children of their own. Married lone mothers whose husbands are not defined as resident in the household are not classified as lone parents because evidence suggests the majority are separated from their husband either because he usually works away from home or for some other reason that does not imply the breakdown of the marriage (see ONS's *GHS Monitor 82/1*).

A lone parent family (in the Labour Force Survey) consists of a lone parent, living with his or her never-married children, provided these children have no children of their own living with them.

PART 3: EDUCATION AND TRAINING

Main categories of educational establishments

Educational establishments in the United Kingdom are administered and financed in several ways. Most schools are controlled by local education authorities (LEAs), which are part of the structure of local government, but some are 'assisted', receiving grants direct from central government sources and being controlled by governing bodies which have a substantial degree of autonomy. In recent years under the Local Management of Schools initiative all LEA and assisted schools have been given delegated responsibility for managing their own budgets and staff numbers. Since 1988 it has also been possible for LEA schools in England and Wales to apply for grant maintained status, under which they receive direct funding from the Department for Education and Employment or the Welsh Office. The governing bodies of such schools are responsible for all aspects of their management, including use of funds, employment of staff and provision of most educational support services.

Outside the public sector completely are non-maintained schools run by individuals, companies or charitable institutions.

From 1 September 1999, all previous categories of school, including grant-maintained, were replaced by four new categories, all maintained (or funded) by the LEA:

Community - schools formerly known as 'county' plus some former GM schools. The LEA is the legal employer of the school's staff, the land owner and the admissions authority.

Foundation - most former GM schools. The governing body is the legal employer and admissions authority, as well as landowner unless that is a charitable foundation.

Voluntary Aided - schools formerly known as 'aided' and some former GM schools. The governing body is the legal employer and admissions authority, but the landowner is usually a charitable foundation. The governing body contribute towards the capital costs of running the school.

Voluntary Controlled - schools formerly known as 'controlled'. The LEA is the legal employer and admissions authority, but the landowner is usually a charitable foundation.

Further Education (FE) courses in FE sector colleges are largely funded through grants from the Further Education Funding Councils in England and Wales. The FEFC in England is responsible for funding provision for FE and some non-prescribed higher education in FE sector colleges; it also funds some FE provided by LEA maintained and other institutions referred to as 'external institutions'. In Wales, the FEFCW also funds FE provision made by FE institutions via a third party or sponsored arrangements. FE colleges in Scotland are funded by the Scottish FEFC (SFEFC) and FE colleges in Northern Ireland are funded by the Department for Education, Northern Ireland.

Higher education courses in higher education establishments are largely publicly funded through block grants from the HE funding councils in England, the National Assembly for Wales, the Scottish Executive and the Department of Education Northern Ireland. In addition, some designated HE (mainly HND/HNC Diplomas and Certificates of HE) is also funded by the HE funding councils. The remainder is funded by FE funding councils.

Stages of education

Education takes place in several stages: primary, secondary, further and higher, and is compulsory for all children between the ages of 5 (4 in Northern Ireland) and 16. The primary stage covers three age ranges: nursery (under 5), infant (5 to 7 or 8) and junior (up to 11 or 12) but in Scotland and Northern Ireland there is generally no distinction between infant and junior schools. Nursery education can be provided either in separate nursery schools or in nursery classes within primary schools. Most public sector primary schools take both boys and girls in mixed classes. It is usual to transfer straight to secondary school at age 11 (in England, Wales and Northern Ireland) or 12 (in Scotland), but in England some children make the transition via middle schools catering for various age ranges between 8 and 14. Depending on their individual age ranges middle schools are classified as either primary or secondary.

Public provision of secondary education in an area may consist of a combination of different types of school, the pattern reflecting historical circumstance and the policy adopted by the LEA. Comprehensive schools normally admit pupils without reference to ability or aptitude and cater for all the children in a neighbourhood, but in some areas they co-exist with grammar, secondary modern or technical schools. In Northern Ireland, post primary education is provided by secondary and grammar schools.

Special schools (day or boarding) provide education for children who require specialist support to complete their education, for example because they have physical or other difficulties. Many pupils with special educational needs are educated in mainstream schools.

The term further education may be used in a general sense to cover all non-advanced courses taken after the period of compulsory education, but more commonly it excludes those staying on at secondary school and those in higher education, ie courses in universities and colleges leading to qualifications above GCE A Level, SCE H Grade, GNVQ/NVQ level 3, and their equivalents.

Higher education is defined as courses that are of a standard that is higher than GCE A level, the Higher Grade of the Scottish Certificate of Education, GNVQ/NVQ level 3 or the Edexcel (formerly BTEC) or SQA National Certificate/Diploma. There are three main levels of HE course: (i) postgraduate courses are those leading to higher degrees, diplomas and certificates (including postgraduate certificates of education and professional qualifications) which usually require a first degree as entry qualification; (ii) first degrees which includes first degrees, first degrees with qualified teacher status, enhanced first degrees, first degrees obtained concurrently with a diploma, and intercalated first degrees; (iii) other undergraduate courses which includes all other higher education courses, for example HNDs and Diplomas in HE.

Special Educational Needs (SENs)

A child has a SEN if he/she has a learning difficulty which calls for special educational provision to be made for him/her. A child has a learning difficulty if he/she:

has a significantly greater difficulty in learning than the majority of children of the same age.

has a disability which either prevents or hinders the child from making use of educational facilities of a kind provided for children of the same age in schools within the area of the LEA

is under 5 and falls within the definitions above or would do so if special educational provision was not made for the child.

A child must not be regarded as having a learning difficulty solely because the language or form of language of the home is different from the language in which he or she will be taught.

It is part of the legislation that all schools have to 'have regard' to the SEN Code of Practice (DfEE, 1994). As guidance, the Code sets out a five stage model. It stresses that stages are not an automatic progression towards, nor barriers in the way of, statements: they are means of matching provision to need. Moreover, they can and should be firmly embedded in the general work of the school.

Stage 1: the school gathers basic information and there is increased differentiation within the child's normal classroom work.

Stage 2: the school puts an Individual Education Plan in place to plan work and monitor the child's progress more systematically.

Stage 3: the school calls upon the specialist advice from LEA support services.

Stage 4: If the child is still not making progress, the school or the parents/carers can request a statutory assessment from the LEA. The school will need to provide details of the action taken to date and evidence for the lack of progress of the child. The LEA then considers the need for a statutory assessment and, if appropriate, makes a multidisciplinary assessment.

Stage 5: having made an assessment, the LEA considers the need for a statement of special educational needs and, if appropriate, will make a statement and arrange, monitor and review provision, the statutory review process is carried out annually.

Discontinuity in further and higher education statistics

The discontinuity in 1994 in Table 3.10 is due to changes in the data sources. Data prior to 1994 include Further Education Statistical Record data. For 1994 and later years, data include the more recent Individualised Student Record data. This discontinuity also applies in Table 3.13 when comparing 1997/98 (headcounts) with earlier years shown (enrolments).

The National Curriculum: assessments and tests

Under the *Education Reform Act (1988)* a National Curriculum has been progressively introduced into primary and secondary schools in England and Wales. This consists of mathematics, English and science (and Welsh in Welsh speaking schools in Wales) as core subjects with history, geography, information technology and design and technology, music, art, physical education and (in secondary schools) a modern foreign language (and Welsh in non-Welsh speaking schools in Wales) as foundation subjects. For all subjects measurable targets have been defined for four key stages, corresponding to ages 7, 11, 14 and 16.

Pupils are assessed formally at the ages of 7, 11 and 14 by their teachers and by national tests in the core subjects of English, mathematics and science (and in Welsh speaking schools in Wales, Welsh). Sixteen year olds are assessed by means of the GCSE examination. Statutory authorities have been set up for England and for Wales to advise government on the National Curriculum and promote curriculum development generally. Northern Ireland has its own common curriculum which is similar but not identical to the National Curriculum in England and Wales. Assessment arrangements in Northern Ireland became statutory from September 1996. In Scotland, though school curricula are the responsibility of education authorities and individual head teachers, in practice almost all 14 to 16 year olds study mathematics, English, science, a modern foreign language, a social subject, physical education, religious and moral education, technology and a creative and aesthetic subject.

Qualifications

In England, Wales and Northern Ireland the main examination for school pupils at the minimum school leaving age is the General Certificate of Secondary Education (GCSE) which can be taken in a wide range of subjects. This replaced the GCE O Level and CSE examinations in 1987 (1988 in Northern Ireland). In England, Wales and Northern Ireland the GCSE is awarded in eight grades, A* to G, the highest four (A* to C) being regarded as equivalent to O level grades A to C or CSE grade 1.

GCE A Level is usually taken after a further two years of study in a sixth form or equivalent, passes being graded from A (the highest) to E (the lowest).

In Scotland pupils study for the Scottish Certificate of Education (SCE) S (Standard) Grade, approximately equivalent to GCSE, in their third and fourth years of secondary schooling (roughly ages 14 and 15). Each subject has several elements, some of which are internally assessed in school, and an award is only made (on a scale of 1 to 7) if the whole course has been completed and examined. The SCE H (Higher) Grade requires one further year of study and for the more able candidates the range of subjects taken may be as wide as at S Grade with as many as five or six subjects spanning both arts and science. Three or more SCE Highers are regarded as being approximately the equivalent of two or more GCE A levels.

After leaving school, people can study towards higher academic qualifications such as degrees. However, a large number of people choose to study towards qualifications aimed at a particular occupation or group of occupations - these qualifications are called vocational qualifications.

Appendix

Vocational qualifications can be split into three groups, namely National Vocational Qualifications (NVQs), General National Qualifications (GNVQs) and other vocational qualifications.

NVQs are based on an explicit statement of competence derived from an analysis of employment requirements. They are awarded at five levels. Scottish Vocational Qualifications (SVQs) are the Scottish equivalent.

GNVQs are a vocational alternative to GCSEs and GCE A levels . They are awarded at three levels: Foundation, Intermediate and Advanced. General Scottish Vocational Qualifications (GSVQs) are the Scottish equivalent.

There are also a large number of other vocational qualifications which are not NVQs, SVQs, GNVQs or GSVQs , for example, a BTEC Higher National Diploma or a City and Guilds Craft award.

Other qualifications (including academic qualifications) are often expressed as being equivalent to a particular NVQ level so that comparisons can be made more easily.

An NVQ level 5 is equivalent to a Higher Degree.

An NVQ level 4 is equivalent to a First Degree, a HND or HNC, a BTEC Higher Diploma, an RSA Higher Diploma a nursing qualification or other Higher Education.

An NVQ level 3 is equivalent to 2 A levels, an Advanced GNVQ, an RSA advanced diploma, a City & Guilds advanced craft, an OND or ONC or a BTEC National Diploma.

An NVQ level 2 is equivalent to 5 GCSEs at grades A* to C, an Intermediate GNVQ, an RSA diploma, a City and Guilds craft or a BTEC first or general diploma.

Literacy levels

Level	Prose	Document	Quantitative
Level 1	Locate one piece of information in a text that is identical or synonymous to the information in the question. Any plausible incorrect answer present in the text is not near the correct information.	Locate one piece of information in a text that is identical to the information in the question. Distracting information is usually located away from the correct answer. Some tasks may require entering given personal information on a form.	Perform a single simple operation such as addition for which the problem is already clearly stated or the numbers are provided.
Level 2	Locate one or more pieces of information in a text but several plausible distractors may be present or low level inferences may be required. The reader may also be required to integrate two or more pieces of information or to compare and contrast information.	Tasks at this level are more varied. Where a single match is required more distracting information may be present or a low level inference may be required. Some tasks may require information to be entered on a form or to cycle through information in a document.	Single arithmetic operation (addition or subtraction) using numbers that are easily located in the text. The operation to be performed may be easily inferred from the wording of the question or the format of the material.
Level 3	Readers are required to match information that requires low-level inferences or that meet specific conditions. There may be several pieces of information to be identified located in different parts of the text. Readers may also be required to integrate or to compare and contrast information across paragraphs or sections of text.	Literal or synonymous matches in a wide variety of tasks requiring the reader to take conditional information into account or to match on multiple features of information. The reader must integrate information from one or more displays of information or cycle through a document to provide multiple answers.	At this level the operations become more varied - multiplication and division. Sometimes two or more numbers are needed to solve the problem and the numbers are often embedded in more complex texts or documents. Some tasks require higherorder inferences to define the task.
Level 4	Match multiple features or provide several responses where the requested information must be identified through text based inferences. Reader may be required to contrast or integrate pieces of information sometimes from lengthy texts. Texts usually contain more distracting information and the information requested is more abstract.	Match on multiple features of information, cycle through documents and integrate information. Tasks often require higher order inferences to get correct answer. Sometimes, conditional information in the document must be taken into account in arriving at the correct answer.	A single arithmetic operation where the statement of the task is not easily defined. The directive does not provide a semantic relation term to help the reader define the task.
Level 5	Locate information in dense text that contain a number of plausible answers Sometimes high-level inferences are required and some text may use specialised language.	Readers are required to search through complex displays of information that contain multiple distractors, to make high level inferences, process conditional information or use specialised language.	Readers must perform multiple operations sequentially and must state the problem from the material provided or use background knowledge to work out the problem or operations needed.

Social Trends 30, © Crown copyright 2000

National Learning Targets

In October 1998, following consultation, the National Learning Targets were announced. They replaced the former National Targets for Education and Training. The Targets state that by 2002:

80% of 11 year olds will reach at least level 4 in the Key Stage 2 English test;
75% of 11 year olds will reach at least level 4 in the Key Stage 2 Mathematics test;
50% of 16 year olds will achieve 5 GCSEs at grades A*- C, or equivalent;
95% of 16 year olds will achieve at least one GCSE grade A*- G, or equivalent;
85% of 19-year-olds will be qualified to at least NVQ level 2 or equivalent;
60% of 21-year-olds will be qualified to at least NVQ level 3 or equivalent;
28% of economically active adults will be qualified to at least NVQ level 4 or equivalent;
50% of economically active adults will be qualified to at least NVQ level 3 or equivalent;
A learning participation Target is under development;
45% of organisations with 50 or more employees will be recognised as Investors in People; and
10,000 organisations with 10-49 employees will be recognised as Investors in People.

Student support

Students in academic year 1997/98 were funded under the student support arrangements which were introduced in 1990/91 whereby mandatory awards formed only part of the student support package for most students in full-time higher education. Student loans were introduced in 1990/91 to provide extra resources and have partially replaced grants. The main grant rates were frozen at their 1990/91 values until 1995/96 when the shift from grant to loan was accelerated by reducing the level of grant rates and increasing loan rates. Increases in loan rates have compensated for the reducing value of grants. Broad parity between the main rates of grant and loans was achieved in the academic year 1996/97.

New student support arrangements in higher education were announced by the Government on 23 July 1997. From 1998/99, new entrants to full-time higher education courses will, with certain specified exceptions, be expected to contribute up to £1,000 a year (in academic year 1998/99) towards the cost of their tuition. The amount will depend on their own and, if appropriate, their parents' or spouse's income. For 1998/99 only, eligible new entrants will receive support for living costs through both grants and loans. Grants, which will be assessed against family income, will on average form about a quarter of the support available. All students will be entitled to the full loan, which will comprise the remaining three quarters of support available.

New entrants to higher education in 1999/2000, together with most of those who started in 1998/99, will receive support for living costs solely through loans which will be partly income-assessed. The Government intends to retain as allowances those relating to the personal circumstances of students, e.g. the dependant's and lone parent's allowances. Support for course-related costs, e.g. extra weeks, will be in the form of supplementary loans. If students have a disability or a specific learning difficulty (such as dyslexia) they may be able to get extra support from the Disabled Students Allowance, from 1998/99 these allowances are not means-tested. Students starting from 1998/99 will repay their loans for living costs on an income-contingent basis after they graduate.

The financial support arrangements for existing mandatory award holders in 1997/98, and those new students who are to be exceptionally treated as existing award holders in 1998/99 for the purposes of the Mandatory Awards Regulations, will remain largely unchanged. Tuition fees for these students will continue to be paid in full by LEAs as part of their mandatory award. These students will continue to be eligible for a means-tested grant towards their maintenance for the duration of their course. They will also continue to be eligible for loans repayable on the existing mortgage-style basis.

Mandatory awards are made to students who fulfil certain residence conditions and who satisfy the other conditions laid down by the Education (Mandatory Awards) Regulations, attending 'designated' higher education courses in the United Kingdom. 'Designated' courses are principally those leading to a first degree or equivalent qualification, all approved initial teacher training qualifications (including the Postgraduate Certificate in Education), a University Certificate or Diploma, Higher National Diploma and the Diploma of Higher Education. Apart from courses of initial teacher training, only courses of full time study and sandwich courses can be designated. Students not eligible for mandatory awards may qualify for other forms of support including discretionary awards and Career Development Loans.

PART 4: LABOUR MARKET

ILO unemployment

The ILO definition of unemployment refers to people without a job who were available to start work within two weeks and had either looked for work in the previous four weeks or were waiting to start a job they had already obtained. Estimates on this basis are not available before 1984, as the Labour Force Survey did not then collect information on job search over a four week period.

The former GB/UK Labour Force definition of unemployment, the only one available for estimates up to 1984, counted people not in employment and seeking work in a reference week (or prevented from seeking work by a temporary sickness or holiday, or waiting for the results of a job application, or waiting to start a job they had already obtained), whether or not they were available to start (except students not able to start because they had to complete their education).

Labour market analyses

The LFS is now the preferred source for labour market analyses rather than the General Household Survey. However, the General Household Survey (GHS) can provide longer time series. The most recent levels shown in Chart 4.6, which use GHS data, are broadly consistent with comparable estimates from the LFS.

Disabled people

The focus and number of questions in the health and disability module of the LFS questionnaire changed in Spring 1997 to reflect the provisions of the *Disability Discrimination Act 1995*. From Spring 1997, the Labour Force Survey asks all its working age respondents:
'Do you have any health problems or disabilities that you expect will last more that a year?'
If they answer yes to this question, they are also asked to say what kind(s) of health problem or disability(ies) they have, based on a list read to them by the interviewer.
If they then answer yes to the following question:
'Does this (do these) health problem(s) or disability(ies) (when taken singly or together) substantially limit your ability to carry out normal day-to-day activities?'
or they said they had the following health problems:
Progressive illness not included elsewhere (e.g. cancer, multiple sclerosis, symptomatic HIV, Parkinson's disease, muscular dystrophy),
then they are defined as having a current disability covered by the DDA.

People whose health problem(s) or disability(ies) are expected to last more than a year are also asked the following questions:
'Does this health problem affect the *kind* of paid work that you might do?'
or 'the *amount* of paid work that you might do?'
If the respondent fulfils either of these criteria, they are defined as having a work-limiting disability.
Those who meet the criteria for either (or both) DDA or work-limiting definitions of disability are described as having a current long-term disability. For more information, see '*Disabilities data from the LFS*', pp.321-35, *Labour Market Trends*, June 1998, and '*Disability and the labour market: results from the Winter 1998/9 LFS*', pp.455-466, Labour Market Trends, September 1999.

Appendix

Labour disputes

Statistics of stoppages of work caused by labour disputes in the United Kingdom relate to disputes connected with terms and conditions of employment. Small stoppages involving fewer than ten workers or lasting less than one day are excluded from the statistics unless the aggregate number of working days lost in the dispute is 100 or more. Disputes not resulting in a stoppage of work are not included in the statistics.

Workers involved and working days lost relate to persons both directly and indirectly involved (unable to work although not parties to the dispute) at the establishments where the disputes occurred. People laid off and working days lost at establishments not in dispute, due for example to resulting shortages of supplies, are excluded.

There are difficulties in ensuring complete recording of stoppages, in particular near the margins of the definition; for example short disputes lasting only a day or so, or involving only a few workers. Any under-recording would affect the total number of stoppages much more than the number of working days lost.

PART 5: INCOME AND WEALTH

Equivalisation scales

The Department of Social Security (DSS), the Office for National Statistics (ONS), the Institute for Fiscal Studies (IFS) and the Institute for Social and Economic Research (ISER) all use McClements equivalence scales in their analysis of the income distribution, to take into account variations in the size and composition of households. This reflects the common sense notion that a household of five adults will need a higher income than will a single person living alone to enjoy a comparable standard of living. An overall equivalence value is calculated for each household by summing the appropriate scale values for each household member. Equivalised household income is then calculated by dividing household income by the household's equivalence value. The scales conventionally take a married couple as the reference point with an equivalence value of 1; equivalisation therefore tends to increase relatively the incomes of single person households (since their incomes are divided by a value of less than 1) and to reduce incomes of households with three or more persons. For further information see *Households Below Average Income,* Corporate Document Services, Department of Social Security.

The DSS and IFS use both before and after housing costs scales, although only before housing costs scales have been used in this chapter.

McClements equivalence scales:

Household member	Before housing costs	After housing costs
First adult (head)	0.61	0.55
Spouse of head	0.39	0.45
Other second adult	0.46	0.45
Third adult	0.42	0.45
Subsequent adults	0.36	0.40
Each dependent aged:		
0-1	0.09	0.07
2-4	0.18	0.18
5-7	0.21	0.21
8-10	0.23	0.23
11-12	0.25	0.26
13-15	0.27	0.28
16 or over	0.36	0.38

Household sector

Due to fundamental changes introduced in 1998 to the way that the national accounts are compiled, some of the data in Chapter 5 in this year's edition and Social Trends 29 differ from those previously shown in *Social Trends.* These changes, needed to make better international comparisons, have affected the classification of people and institutions as well as transactions and assets.

The household sector is defined here to include non-profit institutions and individuals living in institutions as well as those living in households. The most obvious example of a non-profit institution is a charity: this sector also includes many other organisations of which universities, trade unions and clubs and societies are the most important. The household sector differs from the personal sector, as previously defined in the national accounts, in that it excludes unincorporated private businesses apart from sole traders. More information is given in *United Kingdom National Accounts Concepts, Sources and Methods* published by The Stationery Office.

Individual income

Individual income refers to the gross weekly personal income of women and men as reported in the Family Resources Survey. It includes: earnings, income from self-employment, investments and occupational pensions/annuities, benefit income, and income from miscellaneous other sources. It excludes income which accrues at household level, such as council tax benefit. Income from couples' joint investment accounts is assumed to be received equally. Benefit income paid in respect of dependants such as Child Benefit is included in the individual income of the person nominated for the receipt of payments, except for married pensioner couples, where state

retirement pension payments are separated and assigned to the man and woman according to their entitlements. Full details of the concepts and definitions used may be found in *Women's Individual Income 1996/97,* available from the Analytical Services Division, Department of Social Security.

Combining NES and LFS data

The New Earnings Survey (NES) and the Labour Force Survey (LFS) are two major sources of earnings data for the United Kingdom. The NES provides precise information from employer payroll records and because of its large sample size, it allows very detailed analysis by industry, occupation and for small areas. The LFS, on the other hand, provides information on a more frequent basis and for a wide range of demographic characteristics which are not available from the NES. These two surveys give rise to different estimates for a number of reasons. These include: the limited coverage of employees earning below the weekly Pay-As-You-Earn (PAYE) threshold in the NES; coverage of all jobs in the NES, but only main jobs in the LFS; under-estimation of earnings by proxy responses in the LFS; and differences in reported weekly hours between the surveys.

Work has been undertaken in the Office for National Statistics to produce what it considers to be a best estimate of the proportion of people earning below a given hourly rate. This method gives a range for the proportion from a lower estimate derived from the NES to a higher estimate derived from the LFS after both series have been adjusted for known differences. The best estimate probably lies towards the lower end of the range. The full background to how these estimates are calculated is given in an article in *Labour Market Trends,* May 1998.

Redistribution of income (ROI)

Estimates of the incidence of taxes and benefits on household income, based on the Family Expenditure Survey (FES), are published by the ONS in *Economic Trends.* The article covering 1997-98 appeared in the April 1999 issue, and contains details of the definitions and methods used.

Net wealth of the household sector

Revised balance sheet estimates of the net wealth of the household (and non-profit institutions) sector are published in an article *Economic Trends,* November 1999. These figures are based on the new international system of national accounting and incorporate data from new sources. Quarterly estimates of net financial wealth (excluding tangible and intangible assets) are published in *Financial Statistics.*

Social Trends 30, © Crown copyright 2000

Distribution of personal wealth

The estimates of the distribution of the marketable wealth of individuals relate to all adults in the United Kingdom. They are produced by combining Inland Revenue (IR) estimates of the distribution of wealth identified by the estate multiplier method with independent estimates of total personal wealth derived from the ONS national accounts balance sheets. Estimates have been compiled for 1995 and 1996 on the basis of the new System of National Accounting, but estimates for earlier years are on the old basis. The methods used were described in an article in *Economic Trends* (October 1990) entitled "Estimates of the Distribution of Personal Wealth". Net wealth of the personal sector differs from marketable wealth for the following reasons:

Difference in coverage: the ONS balance sheet of the personal sector includes the wealth of non-profit making bodies and unincorporated businesses, while the IR estimates exclude non-profit making bodies and treat the bank deposits and debts of unincorporated businesses differently from ONS;
Differences in timing: the ONS balance sheet gives values at the end of the year, whereas IR figures are adjusted to mid-year;

IR figures: exclude the wealth of those under 18 and the very wealthy, to avoid producing misleading estimates.

Funded pensions: are included in the ONS figures but not in the IR marketable wealth. Also the ONS balance sheet excludes consumer durables and includes non-marketable tenancy rights, whereas the IR figures include consumer durables and exclude non-marketable tenancy rights.

General government expenditure

There are two different measures of public expenditure used in this report

(a) General government expenditure (GGE), used in Chart 5.31, is the sum of current and capital expenditure including transfer payments, plus two financial transactions; net lending and transactions in company securities (net).

(b) Expenditure of general government (EGG), used in Table 5.32, is specified using a new system of national accounting to allow better international comparisons. It includes current and capital expenditure and transfer payments.

European Union expenditure

The figures in Table 5.33 come from *The Community Budget: The Facts in Figures* and have been converted to sterling at the following exchange rates:

1981 - £1 = 1.8096 ECU
1986 - £1 = 1.4897 ECU
1991 - £1 = 1.4284 ECU
1996 - £1 = 1.2467 ECU
1997 - £1 = 1.4510 ECU

Households Below Average Income (HBAI)

Information on the distribution of income based on the Family Resources Survey is provided in the DSS publication *Households Below Average Income: 1994/95 - 1997/98*. This publication provides estimates of patterns of personal disposable income in Great Britain, and of changes in income over time in the United Kingdom. It attempts to measure people's potential living standards as determined by disposable income. As the title would suggest, HBAI concentrates on the lower part of the income distribution, but provides comparisons with the upper part where appropriate.

Disposable household income includes all flows of income into the household, principally earnings, benefits, occupational and private pensions, investments. It is net of tax, National Insurance contributions, Council Tax, contributions to occupational pension schemes (including additional voluntary contributions), maintenance and child support payments, and parental contributions to students living away from home.

Two different measures of disposable income are used in HBAI: before and after housing costs are deducted. Housing costs consist of rent, water rates, community charges, mortgage interest payments, structural insurance, ground rent and service charges.

Difference between Households Below Average Income and Redistribution of Income series

These are two separate and distinct income series produced by two different government departments. Each series has been developed to serve the specific needs of that department. The DSS series, HBAI, provides estimates of patterns of disposable income and of changes over time and shows disposable income before and after housing costs (where disposable income is as defined in the section on HBAI above). The ONS series, ROI, shows how Government intervention through the tax and benefit system affects the income of households; it covers the whole income distribution and includes the effects of indirect taxes like VAT and duty on beer, as well as estimating the cash value of benefits in kind (e.g. from state spending on education and health care). The ROI results are designed to show the position in a particular year rather than trends in income levels over time, although trends in the distribution of income are given. An important

difference between the two series is that HBAI counts individuals and ROI counts households. Also, whereas ROI provides estimates for the United Kingdom, from 1994/95 onwards HBAI provides estimates for Great Britain only.

PART 6: EXPENDITURE

Household expenditure

The national accounts definition of household expenditure, within consumers' expenditure, consists of: personal expenditure on goods (durable and non-durable) and services, including the value of income in kind; imputed rent for owner-occupied dwellings; and the purchase of second-hand goods less the proceeds of sales of used goods. Excluded are: interest and other transfer payments; all business expenditure; and the purchase of land and buildings (and associated costs). This national accounts definition is also used for regional analysis of household income.

In principle, expenditure is measured at the time of acquisition rather than actual disbursement of cash. The categories of expenditure include that of non-resident as well as resident households and individuals in the United Kingdom.

The methods used for estimating expenditure at constant prices often depend on the methods used for the current price estimates. Where the current price estimate is in value terms only, it is deflated by an appropriate price index. The indices most widely used for this purpose are components of the retail prices index. The index does not, however, cover the whole range of consumers' expenditure, and other indices have to be used or estimated where necessary. If no other appropriate price index is available the general consumer price index implied by the estimates of consumers' expenditure at current and constant prices on all other goods and services is used. Where the estimate at current prices is one of quantity multiplied by current average value, the estimate at constant prices is in most cases the same quantity multiplied by the average value in the base year. All these revaluations are carried out in as great detail as practicable.

For further details see the article entitled 'Consumers' expenditure' in *Economic Trends*, September 1983.

The Family Expenditure Survey definition of household expenditure represents current expenditure on goods and services. This excludes those recorded payments which are partly savings or investments (for example life assurance premiums). Similarly, income tax payments,

Appendix

national insurance contributions, mortgage capital repayments and other payments for major additions to dwellings are excluded. For purchases financed by hire purchase or loans, the amounts paid under the finance agreement are recorded as expenditure as they occur; the full cost of the item is not recorded at the time of the initial transaction. For further details see *Family Spending*.

Retail prices index
The general index of retail prices (RPI) measures the changes month by month in the price levels of the commodities and services purchased by all types of households in the United Kingdom, with the exception of certain higher income households and households of retired people mainly dependent on state benefits. These households are:

(a) the 4 per cent (approximately) where the total household recorded gross income exceeds a certain amount (£1,167 a week in 1997/98).

(b) 'pensioner' households consisting of retired people who derive at least three quarters of their income from state benefits.

The weights which are used to calculate the index are based on the pattern of household expenditure derived from the continuing Family Expenditure Survey. Since 1962 the weights have been revised in February of each year.

Expenditure patterns of one-person and two-person pensioner households differ from those of the households upon which the general index is based. Separate indices have been compiled for such pensioner households since 1969, and quarterly averages are published in the ONS *Business Monitor MM23 (Consumer Price Indices)*. They are chain indices constructed in the same way as the general index of retail prices. It should, however, be noted that the pensioner indices exclude housing costs.

A brief introduction to the RPI is given in the July 1999 issue of ONS *Business Monitor MM23 (Consumer Price Indices)*. Each month's edition of the RPI *Business Monitor* contains further articles of interest, covering topics such as reweighting and indicator items.

Harmonised index of consumer prices (Also published in Consumer Price Indices (MM23))
Under the protocol to Article 109j of the Maastricht Treaty, harmonised indices of consumer prices are needed for assessment of price stability. The harmonisation process was formally initiated by Council Regulation (EC) No 2494/95 of 23 October 1995.

The methodology of the HICP is similar to that of the retail prices index (RPI) but differs in the following ways:

(a) the geometric mean rather than the arithmetic mean is used to aggregate the prices at the most basic level.

(b) the coverage of the indices is based on the international classification system, COICOP (classification of individual consumption by purpose).

(c) a number of RPI series are excluded from the HICP; most particularly, housing costs (ie mortgage interest payments, council tax, house depreciation and buildings insurance)

(d) the HICP includes a series for air fares which is not currently covered in the RPI.

(e) the index for new cars in RPI is imputed from movements in second hand car prices, whereas the HICP uses a quality adjusted index based on published prices of new cars.

(f) in the construction of the RPI weights, expenditure on insurance is assigned to the relevant insurance heading. For the HICP weights, the amount paid out in insurance claims is distributed amongst the COICOP headings according to the nature of the claims expenditure with the residual (ie the service charge) being allocated to the relevant insurance heading.

(g) the average household expenditure pattern on which the HICP is based is that of the all private households. In the RPI, the expenditure of highest income households, and of pensioner households mainly dependent on state benefits, are excluded.

From December 1999, the coverage of goods and services in the HICP will be broadened, in particular to include health and education goods and services which are partly reimbursed by Government and social protection services. From the same date, the population covered by the HICP is being harmonised so that it covers expenditure by institutional households and foreign visitors as well as private households.

An article giving the background to the HICP and describing how it has been harmonised and how it compares with the RPI is available in the February 1998 edition of Economic Trends. Historical estimates of the HICP are given in an article in the November 1998 edition of Economic Trends.

Consumer credit
The figures in Table 6.16 relating to bank loans cover banks and all other institutions authorised to take deposits under the *Banking Act 1987*.

Figures relating to other specialist lenders cover finance houses and credit companies excluding institutions authorised to take deposits under the *Banking Act 1987*.

PART 7: HEALTH

Standardised incidence rates
Directly standardised cancer incidence rates enable comparisons to be made over time, which are independent of changes in the age structure of the population. In each year, the crude incidence rates in each five-year age group are multiplied by the European standard population for that age group. These are then summed and divided by the total standard population to give an overall standardised rate.

Standardised death rates
To enable comparisons to be made over time which are independent of changes in the age structure of the population, directly standardised death rates have been calculated in Chart 7.2.

For each year, the age-specific death rates are multiplied by the European standard population for each age group. These are then summed and divided by the total standard population to give an overall standardised rate. Since the European population is the same for both males and females it is possible to directly compare male and female standardised death rates.

International Classification of Diseases
The International Classification of Diseases (ICD) is a coding scheme for diseases and causes of death. The United Kingdom is currently using the Ninth Revision of the ICD (ICD9), which it has used since 1979 for coding cause of death.

The causes of death included in Chart 7.2 correspond to the following ICD9 codes: circulatory diseases 390-459; cancer 140-208: respiratory diseases 460-519 and infectious diseases 001-139.

Expectation of life
The expectation of life, shown in Table 7.4, is the average total number of years which a person of that age could be expected to live, if the rates of mortality at each age were those experienced in that year. The mortality rates that underlie the expectation of life figures are based, up to 1996, on total deaths occurring in each year.

Self reported health problems
In 1996, a standard set of questions known as EuroQol (European Quality of Life) which have been asked on other European countries and on several other surveys in this country were included on the General Household Survey. For the EuroQol questions, respondents had to choose which of three statements best described

their state of health. The first statement was chosen if people had no problems, the second if there were some (or moderate) problems and the third if there were severe problems. The percentages in Table 7.9 are the percentages of people recording either the second or third statement.

Blood pressure level
On the basis of their blood pressure readings and whether they reported currently taking any drugs prescribed for high blood pressure, Health Survey informants were categorised into one of four categories:
Normal untreated: systolic less than 160mmHg, not currently taking any drug(s) prescribed for high blood pressure
Normal treated: systolic less than 160 mmHg and diastolic less than 95 mmHg, currently taking drug(s) prescribed for high blood pressure
High treated: systolic greater than 159 mmHg and/ or diastolic greater than 94 mmHg, currently taking drug(s) prescribed for high blood pressure
High untreated: systolic greater than 159 mmHg and/or diastolic greater than 94 mmHg, not currently taking drug(s) prescribed for high blood pressure

Blood pressure in the Health Survey was measured using an automatic machine, the Dinamap 8100 monitor. It should be noted that the results may not be directly comparable to readings using a standard mercury sphygmomanometer. Comparison of blood pressure levels from the Health Survey for England with other epidemiological studies which have used different measuring devices is problematic, and should only be done with caution.

Body mass index
The body mass index (BMI) shown in Table 7.15, is the most widely used index of obesity which standardises weight for height and is calculated as weight (kg)/height (m)2. Underweight is defined as a BMI of 20 or less, desirable over 20 to 25, overweight over 25 to 30 and obese over 30.

Alcohol consumption
A unit of alcohol is 8 grams by weight or 10cl/10ml by volume of pure alcohol. This is the amount contained in half a pint of ordinary strength beer or lager, a single measure of pub spirits (1/6 gill or 25 ml), one glass of ordinary wine and a small pub measure of sherry or other fortified wine.

Immunisation
Data shown in Table 7.22 for 1991-92 and 1996-97 for England, Wales and Northern Ireland relate to children reaching their second birthday during the year and immunised by their second birthday. Data for 1981 in England, Wales and Northern Ireland relate to children born two years earlier and immunised by the end of the second year. For Scotland, rates prior to 1995-96 have been

calculated by dividing the cumulative number of immunisations for children born in year X and vaccinated by year X+2, by the number of live births (less neonatal deaths) during year X; rates for 1995-96 have been calculated by dividing the number of 2 year old children completing a primary immunisation course before their second birthday by the total number of two year old children.

PART 8: SOCIAL PROTECTION

Benefits to groups of recipients
Elderly people
Retirement pension
Non-contributory retirement pension
Christmas bonus paid with retirement pension and other non-disability benefits
Principal income-related benefits and social fund payments to people over 60[1]

Sick and disabled people
Incapacity benefit
Attendance allowance
Disability living allowance
Disability working allowance
Industrial disablement benefit
Other industrial injuries benefits
Severe disablement allowance
Invalid care allowance
War pensions
Independent living fund
Motability
Christmas bonus paid with disability benefits
Principal income-related benefits and social fund payments to disabled people[1]
Statutory sick pay

Unemployed people
Jobseekers Allowance
Principal income-related benefits and payments from the social fund to unemployed and their families[1]

Families, widows and others
Child benefit
One parent benefit
Family credit
Income support
Statutory maternity pay
Maternity allowance
Social fund maternity payments
Principal income-related benefits and social fund payments to lone-parent families[1]
Widow's benefits
War widow's pensions
Guardian's allowance and child's special allowance
Industrial death benefit
Social fund funeral payments
Income support paid to people who do not fall within the other client groups

[1] Principal income-related benefits are income-support, housing benefit and council tax benefits.

Benefit units
A benefit unit is a single or married couple living as married together with any dependent children. A pensioner benefit unit is where the head is over state pension age.

Waiting lists
Figures for Scotland exclude all patients awaiting deferred or planned repeat admission. In Scotland, once a person is classed as deferred they remain as deferred and these patients are excluded from the waiting list figures. In England and Wales patients who have been classed as deferred but who are now available for treatment will be included in the waiting list figures. This means that figures for Scotland are not directly comparable with those for other areas of the United Kingdom.

In-patient activity
In-patient data for England and later years for Northern Ireland are based on Finished Consultant Episodes (FCEs). Data for Wales and Scotland and earlier Northern Ireland data are based on Deaths and Discharges and transfers. An FCE is a completed period of care of a patient using a bed, under one consultant, in a particular NHS Trust or directly managed unit. If a patient is transferred from one consultant to another within the same hospital, this counts as an FCE but not a hospital discharge. Conversely if a patient is transferred from one hospital to another provider, this counts as a hospital discharge and as a finished consultant episode.

PART 9: CRIME AND JUSTICE

Types of offences in England and Wales
Notifiable offences recorded by the police provide a measure of the amount of crime committed. The statistics are based on counting rules, which are standard for all the police forces in England and Wales. From 1 April 1998, these counting rules were revised to include all indictable and triable-either-way offences together with a few closely linked summary offences. The new rules have increased the coverage of offences, and have changed the emphasis of measurement to one crime per victim. Between them, these factors have particularly impacted on the offence categories of violence against the person, fraud and forgery, drugs offences, and other offences. Before 1 April 1998, notifiable offences broadly covered the most serious offences, but did not include all indictable and triable-either-way offences.

Indictable only offences: are those for which an adult must be tried at the Crown Court, for example robbery, arson and rape. Figures for indictable offences given in this chapter include those for offences which are triable either way (see below).

Triable either way offences: are offences triable either on indictment or summarily. They may be tried in a magistrates' court unless either the defendant or the magistrate requests a Crown Court hearing. Most thefts, drug offences and less serious violence against the person offences fall into this category.

Summary offences: are those offences which are normally tried at a magistrates' court.

Standard list offences: are offences for which the name of the offender and details of each sentence have been collected by the Home Office since 1963. These are linked by name/criminal record number to enable research into criminal histories. The offences include all indictable offences, triable either way offences and some summary offences. The full list is given in Appendices 4 and 5 of Criminal statistics, England and Wales 1997.

Types of offences in Northern Ireland
Notifiable offences: are broadly the more serious offences. They include most indictable offences and triable either way offences and certain summary offences (for example, unauthorised taking of a motor vehicle). Excludes criminal damage valued at less than £200. As from 1 April 1998, notifiable offences recorded in Northern Ireland are on the same basis as those in England and Wales.

Indictable only offences: are those for which an adult must be tried at the Crown Court, for example robbery, arson and rape. Figures for indictable offences given in this chapter include those for offences which are triable either way (see below).

Triable either way offences: are offences triable either on indictment or summarily. They may be tried in a magistrates' court unless either the defendant or the magistrate requests a Crown Court hearing. Most thefts, drug offences and less serious violence against the person offences fall into this category.

Summary offences: are those offences which are normally tried at a magistrates' court.

Offences and crimes
There are a number of reasons why recorded crime statistics in England and Wales, Northern Ireland and Scotland cannot be directly compared:

Different legal systems: The legal system operating in Scotland differs from that in England and Wales and Northern Ireland. For example, in Scotland children aged under 16 are normally dealt with for offending by the Children's Hearings system rather than the courts.

Differences in classification: There are significant differences in the offences included within the recorded crime categories used in Scotland and the categories of notifiable offences used in England, Wales and Northern Ireland. Scottish figures of 'crime' have therefore been grouped in an attempt to approximate to the classification of notifiable offences in England, Wales and Northern Ireland.

Counting rules: In Scotland each individual offence occurring within an incident is recorded whereas in England, Wales and Northern Ireland only the main offence is counted.

Burglary: This term is not applicable to Scotland where the term used is 'housebreaking'.

Theft from vehicles: In Scotland data have only been separately identified from January 1992. The figures include theft by opening lockfast places from a motor vehicle and other theft from a motor vehicle.

Drugs seizures
Seizures can involve more than one drug and so figures for individual drugs cannot be added together to produce totals. Seizures of unspecified quantities are not included.

Offenders cautioned for burglary
In England and Wales offenders cautioned for going equipped for stealing, etc were counted against Burglary offences until 1986 and against Other offences from 1987. Historical data provided in Table 9.16 have been amended to take account of this change. Drug offences were included under Other offences for 1971.

Sentences and orders
The following are the main sentences and orders which can be imposed upon those persons found guilty. Some types of sentence or order can only be given to offenders in England and Wales in certain age groups. Under the framework for sentencing contained in the Criminal Justice Acts 1991 and 1993, the sentence must reflect the seriousness of the offence. The following sentences are available for adults (a similar range of sentences is available to juveniles aged 10 to 17):

Absolute and conditional discharge: A court may make an order discharging a person absolutely or (except in Scotland) conditionally where it is

inexpedient to inflict punishment and, before 1 October 1992, where a probation order was not appropriate. An order for conditional discharge runs for such period of not more than three years as the court specifies, the condition being that the offender does not commit another offence within the period so specified. In Scotland a court may also discharge a person with an admonition.

Attendance centre order: Available in England, Wales and Northern Ireland for offenders under the age of 21 and involves deprivation of free time.

Probation/supervision: An offender sentenced to a probation order is under the supervision of a probation officer (social worker in Scotland), whose duty it is (in England and Wales and Northern Ireland) to advise, assist and befriend him but the court has the power to include any other requirement it considers appropriate. A cardinal feature of the order is that it relies on the co-operation of the offender. Probation orders may be given for any period between six months and three years inclusive.

Community service: An offender who is convicted of an offence punishable with imprisonment may be sentenced to perform unpaid work for not more than 240 hours (300 hours in Scotland), and not less than 40 hours. In Scotland the Law Reform (Miscellaneous Provisions) (Scotland) Act 1990 requires that community service can only be ordered where the court would otherwise have imposed imprisonment or detention. Probation and community service may be combined in a single order in Scotland.

Combination order: The Criminal Justice Act 1991 introduced the combination order in England and Wales only, which combines elements of both probation supervision and community service.

Imprisonment: is the custodial sentence for adult offenders. In the case of mentally disordered offenders, hospital orders, which may include a restriction order may be considered appropriate. Home Office or Scottish Executive consent is needed for release or transfer. A new disposal, the 'hospital direction', was introduced in 1997. The court, when imposing a period of imprisonment, can direct that the offender be sent directly to hospital. On recovering from the mental disorder, the offender is returned to prison to serve the balance of their sentence. The Criminal Justice Act 1991 abolished remission and substantially changed the parole scheme in England and Wales. Those serving sentences of under four years, imposed on or after 1 October 1992, are subject to Automatic Conditional Release and are released, subject to certain criteria, halfway through their sentence. Those serving sentences of four years or longer are considered for Discretionary Conditional Release after having served half their sentence, but are automatically released at the two-thirds point of sentence. The Crime (Sentences) Act 1997, implemented on 1 October 1997, included, for persons aged 18 or over, an automatic life sentence for a second serious violent or sexual offence unless there are exceptional circumstances. All offenders serving a sentence of 12 months or more are supervised in the community until the three quarter point of sentence. A life sentence prisoner may be released on licence subject to supervision and is always liable to recall. In Scotland the Prisoners and Criminal Proceedings (Scotland) Act 1993 changed the system of remission and parole for prisoners sentenced on or after 1 October 1993. Those serving sentences of less than four years are released unconditionally after having served half of their sentence, unless the court specifically imposes a Supervised Release Order which subjects them to social work supervision after release. Those serving sentences of four years or more are eligible for parole at half sentence. If parole is not granted then they will automatically be released on licence at two thirds of sentence subject to days added for breaches of prison rules. All such prisoners are liable to be 'recalled on conviction' or for breach of conditions of licence ie if between the date of release and the date on which the full sentence ends, a person commits another offence which is punishable by imprisonment or breaches his/her licence conditions, then the offender may be returned to prison for the remainder of that sentence whether or not a sentence of imprisonment is also imposed for the new offence.

Fully suspended sentences: may only be passed in exceptional circumstances. In England, Wales and Northern Ireland, sentences of imprisonment of two years or less may be fully suspended. A court should not pass a suspended sentence unless a sentence of imprisonment would be appropriate in the absence of a power to suspend. The result of suspending a sentence is that it will not take effect unless during the period specified the offender is convicted of another offence punishable with imprisonment. Suspended sentences are not available in Scotland.

Fines: The Criminal Justice Act 1993 introduced new arrangements on 20 September 1993 whereby courts are now required to fit an amount for the fine which reflects the seriousness of the offence, but which also takes account of an offender's means. This system replaced the more formal unit fines scheme included in the Criminal justice Act 1991. The Act also introduced the power for courts to arrange deduction of fines from income benefit for those offenders receiving such benefits. The Law Reform (Miscellaneous Provision) (Scotland) Act 1990 as amended by the Criminal Procedure (Scotland) Act 1995 provides

for the use of supervised attendance orders by selected courts in Scotland. The Criminal Procedure (Scotland) Act 1995 also makes it easier for courts to impose a supervised attendance order in the event of a default and enables the court to impose a supervised attendance order in the first instance for 16 and 17 year olds.

Young offender institutions
The Criminal Justice Act 1991 made a number of changes to the custodial sentencing arrangements for young offenders in England and Wales. A common minimum age of 15 for boys and girls was set for the imposition of a sentence of detention in a young offender institution thus removing boys aged 14 from the scope of this sentence.

Civil courts
England and Wales: The main civil courts are the High Court and the county courts. Magistrates' courts also have some civil jurisdiction, mainly in family proceedings. Most appeals in civil cases go to the Court of Appeal (Civil Division) and may go from there to the House of Lords. Since July 1991, county courts have been able to deal with all contract and tort cases and actions for recovery of land, regardless of value. Cases are presided over by a judge who almost always sits without a jury. Jury trials are limited to specified cases, for example, actions for libel.

Scotland: The Court of Session is the supreme civil court. Any cause, apart from causes excluded by statute, may be initiated in, and any judgement of an inferior court may be appealed to, the Court of Session. The Sheriff Court is the principal local court of civil jurisdiction in Scotland. It also has jurisdiction in criminal proceedings. Apart from certain actions the civil jurisdiction of the Sheriff Court is generally similar to that of the Court of Session.

PART 10: HOUSING

Dwellings
Estimates of the stock of dwellings are based on data from the Censuses of Population (Great Britain) and Rate Collection Agency listings (Northern Ireland), with adjustments for enumeration errors and for definitional changes. The figures include vacant dwellings and temporary dwellings occupied as a normal place of residence. Privately rented dwellings include dwellings rented with farm or business premises and those occupied by virtue of employment.

Homeless households
England and Wales: Households for whom local authorities accepted responsibility to secure accommodation under the *Housing Act 1985*. Data for Wales include some households given advice

and assistance only. Figures for the period 1986-1996 are not strictly comparable with information provided for 1997 due to a change in legislation.

Northern Ireland: Households for whom the Northern Ireland Housing Executive has accepted responsibility to secure permanent accommodation, not necessarily those for whom permanent accommodation has been found.

Area type
ACORN CLASSIFICATION
The ACORN classification is a means of classifying areas according to various Census characteristics devised by CACI limited. An ACORN code is assigned to each Census Enumeration District (ED) which is then copied to all postcodes within the ED.

The list below shows the 6 ACORN major categories and the 17 groups. Each ACORN group is further divided in a number of area types (not shown here). The descriptions are CACI's

Category A: Affluent suburban and rural areas
1. Wealthy achiever, Suburban Areas
2. Affluent Greys, Rural Communities
3. Prosperous Pensioners, Retirement Areas
Category B: Affluent family areas
4. Affluent Executives, Family Areas
5. Well-Off Workers, Family Areas
Category C: Affluent urban areas
6. Affluent Urbanites, Town and City Areas
7. Prosperous Professionals, Metropolitan Areas
8. Better-Off Executives, Inner City Areas
Category D: Mature home owning areas
9. Comfortable Middle Agers, Mature Home Owning Areas
10. Skilled Workers, Home Owning Areas
Category E: New home owning areas
11. New Home Owners, Mature Communities
12. White Collar Workers, Better-Off Multi-Ethnic Areas
Category F: Council estates and low income areas
13. Older People, Less Prosperous Areas
14. Council Estate Residents, Better-Off Homes
15. Council Estate Residents, High Unemployment
16. Council Estate Residents, Greatest Hardship
17. People in Multi-Ethnic, Low-Income Areas

Urban/rural areas
This classification is based on the population size of the area which contains the postal sector (or the largest part of it). Urban areas are those areas with a resident population of at least 10,000.

Bedroom standard
The concept is used to estimate occupation density by allocating a standard number of bedrooms to each household in accordance with its age/sex/marital status composition and the relationship of the members to one another. A separate bedroom is allocated to each married

couple, any other person aged 21 or over, each pair of children under 10. Any unpaired person aged 10-20 is paired if possible with a child under 10 of the same sex, or, if that is not possible, is given a separate bedroom, as is any unpaired child under 10. This standard is then compared with the actual number of bedrooms (including bedsitters) available for the sole use of the household, and deficiencies or excesses are tabulated. Bedrooms converted to other uses are not counted as available unless they have been denoted as bedrooms by the informants; bedrooms not actually in use are counted unless uninhabitable.

PART 11: ENVIRONMENT

Quality of bathing water

Directive 76/160/EEC concerning the quality of bathing water sets the following mandatory values for the coliform parameters:

for total coliform 10,000 per 100 ml; and
for faecal coliforms 2,000 per 100 ml.

The Directive requires that at least 95 per cent of samples taken for each of these parameters over the bathing season must meet the mandatory values. In practice this has been interpreted in the following manner: where 20 samples are taken a maximum of only one sample for each parameter may exceed the mandatory values for the water to pass the coliform standards; where less than 20 samples are taken none may exceed the mandatory values for the water to pass the coliform standards.

PART 12: TRANSPORT

Journey purpose

The purpose of a journey is normally taken to be the activity at the destination, unless that destination is 'home' in which case the purpose is defined by the origin of the journey. The classification of journeys to 'work' are also dependent on the origin of the journey. The following purposes are distinguished:

Commuting: journeys to a usual place of work from home, or from work to home.

Business: personal journeys in course of work, including a journey in the course of work back to work. This includes all work journeys by people with no usual place of work (eg site workers) and those who work at or from home.

Education: journeys to school or college, etc by full time students, students on day-release and part-time students following vocational courses.

Escort: used when the traveller has no purpose of his or her own, other than to escort or accompany another person; for example, taking a child to school. Escort commuting is escorting or accompanying someone from home to work or from work to home.

Shopping: all journeys to shops or from shops to home, even if there was no intention to buy.

Personal business: visits to services eg hairdressers, launderettes, dry-cleaners, betting shops, solicitors, banks, estate agents, libraries, churches; or for medical consultations or treatment, or for eating and drinking unless the main purpose was entertainment or social.

Social or entertainment: visits to meet friends, relatives, or acquaintances, both at someone's home or at a pub, restaurant, etc; all types of entertainment or sport, clubs, and voluntary work, non-vocational evening classes, political meetings, etc.

Holidays or day trips: journeys (within Great Britain) to or from any holiday (including stays of four nights or more with friends or relatives) or journeys for pleasure (not otherwise classified as social or entertainment) within a single day.

Just walk: walking pleasure trips along public highways including taking the dog for a walk and jogging.

Car ownership

Car: the figures for household ownership include four wheeled and three wheeled cars, off-road vehicles, minibuses, motorcaravans dormobiles, and light vans. Company cars normally available for household use are also included.

Type of area

London borough - the 33 London boroughs; Metropolitan built-up area - the built-up area within the administrative areas of the former metropolitan counties of Greater Manchester, Merseyside, the West Midlands, West Yorkshire, Tyne & Wear and Strathclyde;
Large urban - self-contained urban areas of more than 250,000 population in 1991;
Medium urban – self-contained urban areas of not more than 250,000 population in 1991, but more than 25,000;
Small urban – self-contained urban areas of not more than 25,000 population in 1991 but more than 3,000;
Rural - other areas are designated 'rural', including 'urban areas' under 3,000 population in 1991.

Road deaths

The internationally agreed definition of a road accident death is one where death occurs as a result of the accident within 30 days. Most EU countries, including the United Kingdom, collect data to this definition. For those which do not, the national figures have been adjusted to covert them to the 30-day standard.

Passenger death rates

Table 12.21 provides passenger death rates for passenger travel by air, road, rail and water. Wherever possible, travel by drivers and other crew in the course of their work has been excluded from the calculated rates for public transport modes. A casualty rate can be interpreted as the risk a traveller runs of being injured, per kilometre travelled. The coverage varies for each mode of travel and the definitions of deaths and accidents are different. Thus, care should be exercised in drawing comparisons between the rates for different modes.

The air travel data refer to passenger carrying services of United Kingdom airlines for fixed and rotary wing aircraft of over 2,300kg. The accidents therefore cover flights throughout the world, not just within the United Kingdom. The average number of fatal accidents is less than 1 per year, and may not necessarily occur within the United Kingdom.

The rail casualty data refer to passengers in train accidents and train movement accidents. They exclude non-movement accidents such as falling over packages on platforms, confirmed suicides and trespassers. The figures for air and water, similarly, exclude accidents on the land side of air terminals and seaports.

The data for travel by water cover both domestic and international passenger carrying services of United Kingdom registered vessels. Data are not available for non-fatal accidents to passengers prior to 1983. Casualties exclude deaths from disease and confirmed suicides. Injuries are those which incapacitate the person for more than 3 days.

The road data which refer to Great Britain, are for drivers/riders and passengers of vans, cars, two wheeled motor vehicles and pedal cycles. The data for buses and coaches refer to passengers only. They illustrate the risk to passengers of travel on the road system using both public and private transport. The casualty rates per billion kilometres for those on foot are based on estimates of distance walked obtained from National Travel Surveys.

The article Comparative Accident Rates for Passengers by Modes of Transport , which provides additional information on the coverage and definitions used by the various modes was published in *Transport Statistics Great Britain 1994 edition.* These statistics of accidents and casualties are compiled from the reports submitted by the police to the Department of Environment, Transport and the Regions. More detailed information and analyses about road accidents and casualties is available in *Road Accidents Great Britain - the Casualty Report 1998,* published by the Stationery Office.

PART 13: LIFESTYLES AND SOCIAL PARTICIPATION

Social class
The social class definition used in Chart 13.5 and Chart 13.17 is based on occupation and is a classification system that has grown out of the original Registrar-General's social class classification. The five categories are:

I. Professional, etc. occupations
II. Managerial and technical occupations
III. Skilled occupations
      Non-manual
      Manual
IV. Partly skilled occupations
V. Unskilled occupations

For the Family Expenditure Survey, social class of a household refers to the social class based on the occupation of the head of household where the head is economically active. Where the head is economically inactive, the household is allocated to a separate category of retired and unoccupied.

Cultural Events
Data from the Target Group Index 1987-1988 and 1991-1992, BMRB International, and the Target Group Index 1997-1998 Doublebase, BMRB International were used in Table 13.11.

Parliamentary elections and political parties
A general election must be held at least every five years or sooner, if the Prime Minister of the day so decides. The United Kingdom is currently divided into 659 constituencies, each of which returns one member to the House of Commons. To ensure equitable representation, four permanent Boundary Commissions (for England, Wales, Scotland, and Northern Ireland) make periodic reviews of constituencies and recommend any change in the number or redistribution of seats that may seem necessary in the light of population movements or for some other reason.

The Social Democratic Party (SDP) was launched on 26 March 1981. In the 1983 and 1987 general elections the Liberals and SDP contested seats as the Liberal-SDP alliance. In 1988 the Social and Liberal Democrats were formed, after which this party (shortly afterwards renamed the Liberal Democrats) and the SDP contested elections separately. In June 1990 the SDP disbanded and the two remaining SDP MPs both lost their seats at the 1992 general election.

Articles published in previous editions

No. 1 1970
Some general developments in social statistics Professor C A Moser, CSO

Public expenditure on the social services
Professor B Abel-Smith, London School of Economics and Political Science

The growth of the population to the end of the century Jean Thompson, OPCS

A forecast of effective demand for housing in Great Britain in the 1970s A E Holmans, MHLG

No. 2 1971
Social services manpower Dr S Rosenbaum, CSO

Trends in certificated sickness absence
F E Whitehead, DHSS

Some aspects of model building in the social and environmental fields B Benjamin, CSC

Social indicators - health A J Culyer, R J Lavers and A Williams, University of York

No. 3 1972
Social commentary: change in social conditions CSO

Statistics about immigrants: objectives, methods, sources and problems Professor C A Moser, CSO

Central manpower planning in Scottish secondary education A W Brodie, SED

Social malaise research: a study in Liverpool
M Flynn, P Flynn and N Mellor, Liverpool City Planning Department

Crimes of violence against the person in England and Wales S Klein, HO

No. 4 1973
Social commentary: certain aspects of the life cycle CSO

The elderly D C L Wroe, CSO

Subjective social indicators M Abrams, SSRC

Mental illness and the psychiatric services
E R Bransby, DHSS

Cultural accounting A Peacock and C Godfrey, University of York

Road accidents and casualties in Great Britain
J A Rushbrook, DOE

No. 5 1974
Social commentary: men and women CSO

Social security: the European experiment
E James and A Laurent, EC Commission

Time budgets B M Hedges, SCPR

Time budgets and models of urban activity patterns N Bullock, P Dickens, M Shapcott and P Steadman, Cambridge University of Architecture

Road traffic and the environment F D Sando and V Batty, DOE

No. 6 1975
Social commentary: social class CSO

Areas of urban deprivation in Great Britain: an analysis of 1971 Census data
S Holtermann, DOE

Note: Subjective social indicators Mark Abrams, SSRC

No. 7 1976
Social commentary: social change in Britain 1970-1975 CSO

Crime in England and Wales Dr C Glennie, HO

Crime in Scotland Dr Bruce, SHHD

Subjective measures of quality of life in Britain: 1971 to 1975 J Hall, SSRC

No. 8 1977
Social commentary: fifteen to twenty-five: a decade of transition CSO

The characteristics of low income households
R Van Slooten and A G Coverdale, DHSS

No. 9 1979
Housing tenure in England and Wales: the present situation and recent trends
A E Holmans, DOE

Social forecasting in Lucas B R Jones, Lucas Industries

No. 10 1980
Social commentary: changes in living standards since the 1950s CSO

Inner cities in England D Allnutt and A Gelardi, DOE

Scotland's schools D Wishart, SED
No. 14 1984
Changes in the Life-styles of the Elderly 1959-1982 M Abrams

No. 15 1985
British Social Attitudes R Jowell and C Airey, SCPR

No. 16 1986
Income after retirement G C Fiegehen, DHSS

No. 17 1987
Social Trends since World War II Professor A H Halsey, University of Oxford

Household Formation and Dissolution and Housing Tenure: a Longitudinal Perspective A E Holmans and S Nandy, DOE; A C Brown, OPCS

No. 18 1988
Major Epidemics of the 20th Century: from Coronary Thrombosis to AIDS Sir Richard Doll, University of Oxford

No. 19 1989
Recent Trends in Social Attitudes L Brook, R Jowell and S Witherspoon, SCPR

No. 20 1990
Social Trends, the next 20 years T Griffin, CSO

No. 21 1991
The 1991 Census of Great Britain: Plans for Content and Output B Mahon and D Pearce, OPCS

No. 22 1992
Crime statistics: their use and misuse C Lewis, HO

No. 24 1994
Characteristics of the bottom 20 per cent of the income distribution N Adkin, DSS

No. 26 1996
The OPCS Longitudinal Study J Smith, OPCS

British Household Panel Survey J Gershuny, N Buck, O Coker, S Dex, J Ermish, S Jenkins and A McCulloch, ESRC Research Centre on Micro-social Change

No. 27 1997
Projections: a look into the future T Harris, ONS

No. 28 1998
French and British Societies: a comparison
P Lee and P Midy, INSEE and A Smith and C Summerfield, ONS

No. 29 1999
Drugs in the United Kingdom - a jigsaw with missing pieces A Bradley and O Baker, Institute for the Study of Drug Dependence

Index

The references in this index refer to table and chart numbers, or entries in the Appendix.

Index

Printed in the United Kingdom for The Stationery Office
TJ31 C60 1/00 13110

Social Trends 30, © Crown copyright 2000